WEBSTER'S THESAURUS

Dictionary Format

Staff

Kim Nichols

Kathleen Flickinger

Cindy Carter

a *(SYN.)* any, one.

abandon *(SYN.)* relinquish, resign, surrender, leave.
(ANT.) support, keep, fulfill, engage, unite, retain.

abandoned *(SYN.)* depraved, deserted, desolate, forsaken, rejected, cast off.
(ANT.) befriended, cherished, chaste, moral, respectable.

abash *(SYN.)* disconcert, bewilder, confuse, put off.
(ANT.) comfort, relax, hearten, nerve.

abashed *(SYN.)* confused, ashamed, embarrassed.

abate *(SYN.)* lessen, curtail, reduce, decrease, restrain.
(ANT.) grow, prolong, increase, extend, intensify, enhance, accelerate.

abbey *(SYN.)* nunnery, convent, cloisters, monastery.

abbot *(SYN.)* friar, monk.

abbreviate *(SYN.)* shorten, condense, lessen, curtail, reduce, cut.
(ANT.) lengthen, increase, expand, extend, prolong.

abbreviation *(SYN.)* abridgment, reduction, shortening, condensation.
(ANT.) expansion, extension, amplification, lengthening.

abdicate *(SYN.)* relinquish, renounce, vacate, waive.
(ANT.) maintain, defend, stay, retain, uphold.

aberrant *(SYN.)* capricious, devious, irregular, unnatural, abnormal, unusual.
(ANT.) methodical, regular, usual, fixed, ordinary.

aberration *(SYN.)* oddity, abnormality, irregularity, deviation, monster, abortion.
(ANT.) norm, conformity, standard, normality.

abet *(SYN.)* support, connive, encourage, conspire, help.
(ANT.) deter, check, hinder, frustrate, oppose, discourage.

abettor *SYN.)* accomplice, ally, confederate, accessory.
(ANT.) opponent, rival.

abeyance *(SYN.)* inaction, cessation, inactivity, rest.
(ANT.) ceaselessness, con-

tinuation, continuity.

abhor *(SYN.)* dislike, hate, loathe, execrate, avoid, scorn, detest, despise.

abhorrent *(SYN.)* loathsome, horrible, detestable, nauseating, terrible, revolting.

abide *(SYN.)* obey, accept, tolerate, endure, dwell, reside.

ability *(SYN.)* aptness, skill, dexterity, faculty, talent, aptitude, efficiency, capacity.
(ANT.) incapacity, incompetency, weakness, ineptitude, inability, disability.

abject *(SYN.)* sordid, infamous, mean, miserable.

abjure *(SYN.)* relinquish, renounce, waive, desert, forsake, resign, surrender.
(ANT.) cling to, maintain, uphold, stay.

able *(SYN.)* qualified, competent, fit, capable, skilled, efficient, clever, talented.
(ANT.) inadequate, trained, efficient, incapable, weak.

abnegation *(SYN.)* rejection, renunciation, self-denial, refusal, relinquishment.

abnormal *(SYN.)* unnatural, odd, irregular, monstrous, eccentric, weird, strange.
(ANT.) standard, natural, usual, normal, average.

abode *(SYN.)* dwelling, habitat, residence, quarters, lodging.

abolish *(SYN.)* end, eradicate, annul, cancel, revoke, invalidate, abrogate, erase.
(ANT.) promote, restore, continue, establish, sustain.

abominable *(SYN.)* foul, dreadful, hateful, vile, loathsome, detestable.
(ANT.) delightful, pleasant, agreeable, commendable, admirable, noble, fine.

abominate *(SYN.)* despise, detest, hate, dislike, abhor.
(ANT.) love, like, cherish, approve, admire.

abomination *(SYN.)* detestation, hatred, disgust, loathing, revulsion, antipathy.

abort *(SYN.)* flop, fizzle, miscarry, abandon, cancel.

abortion *(SYN.)* fiasco, disaster, failure, defeat.

abortive (SYN.) unproductive, vain, unsuccessful, useless, failed, futile.
(ANT.) rewarding, effective, profitable, successful.

about (SYN.) relating to, involving, concerning, near, around, upon, almost.

above (SYN.) higher than, overhead, on, upon, over.
(ANT.) under, beneath, below.

abrasion (SYN.) rubbing, roughness, chafe, scratching, scraping, friction, chap.

abrasive (SYN.) hurtful, sharp, galling, annoying, grating, irritating, caustic.
(ANT.) pleasant, soothing, comforting, agreeable.

abridge (SYN.) condense, cut, abbreviate, shorten, reduce, summarize, curtail.
(ANT.) increase, lengthen, expand, extend.

abridgment (SYN.) digest, condensation, summary.
(ANT.) lengthening, expansion, enlargement.

abrogate (SYN.) rescind, withdraw, revoke, annul, cancel.

abrupt (SYN.) sudden, unexpected, blunt, curt, craggy, precipitous, sharp, hasty.
(ANT.) foreseen, smooth, courteous, gradual, smooth.

absence (SYN.) nonexistence, deficiency, lack.
(ANT.) attendance, completeness, existence, presence.

absent (SYN.) away, truant, departed, inattentive, lacking, not present, out, off.
(ANT.) attending, attentive, watchful, present.

absent-minded (SYN.) inattentive, daydreaming.
(ANT.) observant, attentive.

absolute (SYN.) unconditional, entire, actual, complete, thorough, total, perfect.
(ANT.) partial, conditional, dependent accountable.

absolution (SYN.) pardon, forgiveness, acquittal, mercy.

absolve (SYN.) exonerate, discharge, acquit, pardon, forgive, clear, excuse.

absorb (SYN.) consume, swallow up, engulf, assimilate, imbibe, engage, engross.
(ANT.) discharge, dispense, emit, exude, weary, drain.

absorbent (SYN.) permeable, spongy, pervious, porous.
(ANT.) moisture-proof, waterproof, impervious.

abstain (SYN.) forbear, forego, decline, resist.
(ANT.) pursue.

abstemious (SYN.) abstinent, sparing, cautious, temperate, ascetic, self-disciplined.
(ANT.) uncontrolled, indulgent, abandoned, excessive.

abstinence (SYN.) fasting, self-denial, continence, sobriety, refrain, abstention.
(ANT.) gluttony, greed, excess, self-indulgence, pursue.

abstract (SYN.) part, appropriate, steal, remove, draw from, separate, purloin.
(ANT.) return, concrete, unite, add, replace, specific, clear.

abstruse (SYN.) arcane, obscure, complicated, abstract, refined, mandarin.
(ANT.) uncomplicated, direct, obvious, simple.

absurd (SYN.) ridiculous, silly, unreasonable, foolish, irrational, nonsensical.
(ANT.) rational, sensible, sound, meaningful.

abundance (SYN.) ampleness, profusion, large amount, copiousness, plenty.
(ANT.) insufficiency, want, absence, dearth, scarcity.

abundant (SYN.) ample, overflowing, plentiful, teeming, profuse, abounding.
(ANT.) insufficient, scant, not enough, scarce, deficient, rare, uncommon, absent.

abuse (SYN.) maltreatment, misuse, mistreat, damage, ill-use, reviling, aspersion.
(ANT.) plaudit, respect, appreciate, commendation.

academic (SYN.) learned, scholarly, theoretical, erudite, formal, pedantic.

(ANT.) ignorant, practical, simple, uneducated.

accede (SYN.) grant, agree, comply, consent, yield.
(ANT.) dissent, disagree, differ, oppose.

accelerate (SYN.) quicken, dispatch, facilitate, hurry, rush, forward, hasten, expedite.
(ANT.) hinder, retard, slow, delay, quicken.

accent (SYN.) tone, emphasis, inflection, stress, consent.

accept (SYN.) take, approve, receive, allow, consent to, believe, adopt, admit.
(ANT.) ignore, reject, refuse.

accessory (SYN.) extra, addition, assistant, supplement.

accident (SYN.) casualty, disaster, misfortune, mishap.
(ANT.) purpose, intention, calculation.

accidental (SYN.) unintended, fortuitous, unplanned, unexpected, unforeseen.
(ANT.) calculated, planned, willed, intended, intentional, on purpose, deliberate.

acclaim (SYN.) eminence, fame, glory, honor.
(ANT.) infamy, obscurity, disapprove, reject, disrepute.

accommodation (SYN.) alteration change, adaptation, acclimatization, aid, help.
(ANT.) inflexibility, rigidity, disservice, stubbornness.

accompany (SYN.) chaperon, consort with, escort, go with, associate with, attend.
(ANT.) abandon, quit, leave, desert, avoid, forsake.

accomplice (SYN. accessory, ally, associate, assistant, sidekick, confederate.
(ANT.) opponent, rival, enemy, adversary.

accomplish (SYN.) attain, consummate, achieve, do, execute, fulfill, complete.
(ANT.) fail, frustrate, spoil, neglect, defeat.

accomplished (SYN.) proficient, skilled, finished, well-trained, gifted, masterly.
(ANT.) unskilled, amateurish, crude.

accomplishment (SYN.) deed, feat, statute, operation, performance, action.
(ANT.) cessation, inhibition, intention, deliberation.

accord (SYN.) concur, agree, award, harmony, conformity, agreement, give, tale.
(ANT.) difference, quarrel, disagreement.

accost (SYN.) approach, greet, speak to, address.
(ANT.) avoid, shun.

account (SYN.) description, chronicle, history, narration, reckoning, rate.
(ANT.) confusion, misrepresentation, distortion.

accredited (SYN.) qualified, licensed, certified, commissioned, empowered.
(ANT.) illicit, unofficial, unauthorized.

accrue (SYN.) amass, collect, heap, increase, accumulate.
(ANT.) disperse, dissipate, waste, diminish.

accumulate (SYN.) gather, collect, increase, accrue.
(ANT.) spend, give away, diminish, dissipate.

accurate (SYN.) perfect, just, truthful, unerring, meticulous, correct, all right.
(ANT.) incorrect, mistaken, false, wrong.

accursed (SYN.) ill-fated, cursed, doomed, condemned, bedeviled, ruined.
(ANT.) fortunate, hopeful.

accusation (SYN.) charge, incrimination, indictment.
(ANT.) pardon, exoneration, absolve.

accuse (SYN.) incriminate, indict, censure, denounce, charge, arraign, blame.
(ANT.) release, vindicate, exonerate, acquit, absolve.

accustomed (SYN.) familiar with, comfortable with.
(ANT.) strange, unusual, rare, unfamiliar.

ace (SYN.) champion, star, king, queen, winner, head.

acerbity (SYN.) bitterness, harshness, acidity unkindness, sourness.

ache *(SYN.)* hurt, pain, throb.

achieve *(SYN.)* do, execute, gain, obtain, acquire, accomplish, perform.
(ANT.) fail, lose, fall short.

achievement *(SYN.)* feat, accomplishment, attainment.
(ANT.) botch, dud, mess, omission, defeat, failure.

acid *(SYN.)* tart, sour, bitter, mordant, biting, biting.
(ANT.) pleasant, friendly, bland, mild, sweet.

acknowledge *(SYN.)* allow, admit, concede, recognize, answer, accept, receive.
(ANT.) reject, refuse, disavow, refute, deny.

acquaint *(SYN.)* inform, teach, enlighten, notify, tell.

acquire *(SYN.)* attain, earn, get, procure, assimilate, obtain, secure, gain.
(ANT.) miss, surrender, lose, forego, forfeit.

aquirement *(SYN.)* training, skill, learning, achievement, attainment, education.

aquisition *(SYN.)* procurement, gain, gift, purchase, proceeds, possession, grant.

aquisitive *(SYN.)* greedy, avid, hoarding, covetous.

acquit *(SYN.)* forgive, exonerate, absolve, cleanse, pardon, found not guilty.
(ANT.) doom, saddle, sentence, condemn.

acrid *(SYN.)* bitter, sharp, nasty, stinging, harsh.
(ANT.) pleasant, sweet.

acrimonious *(SYN.)* sharp, sarcastic, acerb, waspish, cutting, stinging, testy.
(ANT.) soft, kind, sweet, pleasant, soothing.

act *(SYN.)* deed, doing, feat, execution, accomplishment, performance, action, operation, transaction, decree, exploit, pretense.
(ANT.) inactivity, deliberation, intention, cessation.

action *(SYN.)* deed, achievement, feat, activity, exploit, behavior, battle, performance, exercise.
(ANT.) idleness, inertia, repose, inactivity, rest.

activate *(SYN.)* mobilize, energize, start, propel.
(ANT.) paralyze, immobilize, stop, deaden.

active *(SYN.)* working, operative, alert, agile, nimble, sprightly, busy, brisk, lively
(ANT.) passive, inactive, idle, dormant, lazy, lethargic.

activist *(SYN.)* militant, doer, enthusiast.

activity *(SYN.)* action, liveliness, motion, vigor, agility, movement, briskness.
(ANT.) idleness, inactivity, dullness, sloth.

actor *(SYN.)* performer, trouper, entertainer.

actual *(SYN.)* true, genuine, certain, factual, authentic, concrete, real.
(ANT.) unreal, fake, bogus, nonexistent, false.

actuality *(SYN.)* reality, truth, occurrence, fact, certainty.
(ANT.) theory, fiction, falsehood, supposition.

acute *(SYN.)* piercing, severe, sudden, keen, sharp, perceptive, discerning, shrewd, astute, smart, intelligent.
(ANT.) bland, mild, dull, obtuse, insensitive.

adamant *(SYN.)* unyielding, firm, obstinate.
(ANT.) yielding.

adapt *(SYN.)* adjust, conform, accommodate, change, fit, alter, vary, modify.
(ANT.) misapply, disturb.

add *(SYN.)* attach, increase, total, append, sum, affix, unite, supplement.
(ANT.) remove, reduce, deduct, subtract, detach.

address *(SYN.)* greet, hail, accost, speak to, location, oration, presentation.
(ANT.) avoid, pass by.

adept *(SYN.)* expert, skillful, proficient.
(ANT.) unskillful.

adequate *(SYN.)* capable, commensurate, fitting, satisfactory, sufficient, enough,

ample, suitable, plenty, fit.
(ANT.) lacking, scant, insufficient, inadequate.

adhere (SYN.) stick fast, grasp, hold, keep, retain, cling, stick to, keep, cleave.
(ANT.) surrender, abandon, release, separate, loosen.

adjacent (SYN.) next to, near, bordering, touching adjoining, neighboring.
(ANT.) separate, distant, apart.

adjoin (SYN.) connect, be close to, affix, attach.
(ANT.) detach, remove.

adjourn (SYN.) postpone, defer, delay, suspend, discontinue, put off.
(ANT.) begin, convene, assemble.

adjust (SYN.) repair, fix, change, set, regulate, settle, arrange, adapt, suit, accommodate, modify, alter.

administration (SYN.) conduct, direction, management, supervision.

admirable (SYN.) worthy, fine, praise, deserving, commendable, excellent.

admire (SYN.) approve, venerate, appreciate, respect, revere, esteem, like.
(ANT.) abhor, dislike, despise, loathe, detest, hate.

admissible (SYN.) fair, justifiable, tolerable, allowable.
(ANT.) unsuitable, unfair, inadmissible.

admission (SYN.) access, entrance, pass, ticket.

admit (SYN.) allow, assent, permit, acknowledge, welcome, concede, agree.
(ANT.) deny, reject, dismiss, shun, obstruct.

admittance (SYN.) access, entry, entrance.

admonish (SYN.) caution, advise against, warn, rebuke, reprove, censure.
(ANT.) glorify, praise.

admonition (SYN.) advice, warning, caution, reminder.

ado (SYN.) trouble, other, fuss, bustle, activity, excitement, commotion, hubbub.

(ANT.) tranquillity, quietude.

adolescent (SYN.) young, immature, teen-age.
(ANT.) grown, mature, adult.

adoration (SYN.) veneration reverence, glorification.

adore (SYN.) revere, venerate, idolize, respect, love, cherish, esteem, honor.
(ANT.) loathe, hate, despise.

adorn (SYN.) trim, bedeck, decorate, ornament, beautify, embellish, glamorize.
(ANT.) mar, spoil, deform, deface, strip, bare.

adrift (SYN.) floating, afloat, drifting, aimless, purposeless, unsettled.
(ANT.) purposeful, stable, secure, well-organized.

adroit (SYN.) adept, apt, dexterous, skillful, clever, ingenious, expert.
(ANT.) awkward, clumsy, graceless, unskillful, oafish.

advance (SYN.) further, promote, bring forward, adduce, progress, advancement, allege, improvement, promotion, up-grade.
(ANT.) retard, retreat, oppose, hinder, revert, withdraw, flee.

advantage (SYN.) edge, profit, superiority, benefit, mastery, leverage, favor.
(ANT.) handicap, impediment, obstruction, disadvantage, detriment, hindrance.

adventure (SYN.) undertaking, occurrence, enterprise, happening, event, project.

adventurous (SYN.) daring, enterprising, rash, bold.
(ANT.) cautious, timid, hesitating.

adversary (SYN.) foe, enemy, contestant, opponent.
(ANT.) ally, friend.

adverse (SYN.) hostile, counteractive, unfavorable, opposed, disastrous, contrary.
(ANT.) favorable, propitious, fortunate, friendly, beneficial.

adversity (SYN.) misfortune, trouble, calamity, distress, hardship, disaster.
(ANT.) benefit, happiness.

advertise (SYN.) promote,

publicize, make known, announce, promulgate.

advertisement *(SYN.)* commercial, billboard, want ad, handbill, flyer, poster.

advice *(SYN.)* counsel, instruction, suggestion, warning, information, caution, exhortation, admonition.

advise *(SYN.)* recommend, suggest, counsel, caution, warn, admonish.

adviser *(SYN.)* coach, guide, mentor, counselor.

aesthetic *(SYN.)* literary, artistic, sensitive, tasteful.
(ANT.) tasteless.

affable *(SYN.)* pleasant, courteous, sociable, friendly, amiable, gracious.
(ANT.) unfriendly, unsociable.

affair *(SYN.)* event, occasion, happening, party, occurrence, matter, festivity, business, concern.

affect *(SYN.)* alter, modify, concern, regard, touch, feign, pretend, influence, sway, transform, change.

affected *(SYN.)* pretended, fake, sham, false.

affection *(SYN.)* fondness, kindness, emotion, love, feeling, tenderness, attachment, disposition, endearment, liking, friendly, friendliness, warmth.
(ANT.) aversion, indifference, repulsion, hatred, repugnance, dislike, antipathy.

affectionate *(SYN.)* warm, loving, tender, fond, attached.
(ANT.) distant, unfeeling, cold.

affirm *(SYN.)* aver, declare, swear, maintain, endorse, certify, state, assert, ratify, say, confirm, establish.
(ANT.) deny, dispute, oppose, contradict, demur, disclaim.

afflict *(SYN.)* trouble, disturb, bother, agitate, perturb.
(ANT.) soothe.

affliction *(SYN.)* distress, grief, misfortune, trouble.
(ANT.) relief, benefit, easement.

affluent *(SYN.)* wealthy, prosperous, rich, abundant, ample, plentiful, well-off, bountiful, well-to-do.
(ANT.) poor.

afford *(SYN.)* supply, yield, furnish.

affront *(SYN.)* offense, slur, slight, provocation, insult.

afraid *(SYN.)* faint-hearted, frightened, scared, timid, fearful, apprehensive, cowardly, terrified.
(ANT.) assured, composed, courageous, bold, confident.

after *(SYN.)* following, subsequently, behind, next.
(ANT.) before.

again *(SYN.)* anew, repeatedly, afresh.

against *(SYN.)* versus, hostile to, opposed to, in disagreement.
(ANT.) with, for, in favor of.

age *(SYN.)* antiquity, date, period, generation, time, senility, grow old, senescence, mature, era, dotage, ripen, mature, epoch.
(ANT.) youth, childhood.

aged *(SYN.)* ancient, elderly, old.
(ANT.) youthful, young.

agency *(SYN.)* office, operation.

agent *(SYN.)* performer, doer, worker, actor, operator.

aggravate *(SYN.)* intensify, magnify, annoy, irritate, increase, heighten, nettle, make worse, irk, vex, provoke, embitter, worsen.
(ANT.) soften, soothe, appease, pacify, mitigate, ease, relieve.

aggregate *(SYN.)* collection, entirety, accumulate, total, compile, conglomeration.
(ANT.) part, unit, ingredient, element.

aggression *(SYN.)* assault, attack, invasion, offense.
(ANT.) defense.

aggressive *(SYN.)* offensive, belligerent, hostile, attacking, militant, pugnacious.
(ANT.) timid, withdrawn, passive, peaceful, shy.

aghast *(SYN.)* surprised, astonished, astounded, awed, thunderstruck, flabbergasted, bewildered.

agile *(SYN.)* nimble, graceful, lively, active, alert, fast, quick, athletic, spry.
(ANT.) inept, awkward, clumsy.

agility *(ANT.)* quickness, vigor, energy, activity, motion.
(ANT.) dullness, inertia, idleness, inactivity.

agitate *(SYN.)* disturb, excite, perturb, rouse, shake, arouse, disconcert, instigate, inflame, provoke, jar, incite, stir up, toss.
(ANT.) calm, placate, quiet, ease, soothe.

agitated *(SYN.)* jumpy, jittery, nervous, restless, restive, upset, disturbed, ruffled.

agony *(SYN.)* anguish, misery, pain, suffering, torture, ache, distress, throe, woe, torment, grief.
(ANT.) relief, ease, comfort.

agree *(SYN.)* comply, coincide, conform, oncur, assent, accede, tally, settle, harmonize, unite, consent.
(ANT.) differ, disagree, protest, contradict, argue, refuse.

agreeable *(SYN.)* amiable, charming, able, gratifying, pleasant, suitable, pleasure, welcome, pleasing, acceptable, friendly, cooperative.
(ANT.) obnoxious, offensive, unpleasant, disagreeable, quarrelsome, contentious, touchy.

agreement *(SYN.)* harmony, understanding, unison, contract, pact, stipulation, alliance, deal, bargain, treaty, contract, arrangement, settlement, accord, concord.
(ANT.) variance, dissension, discord, disagreement, difference, misunderstanding.

agriculture *(SYN.)* farming, gardening, tillage, husbandry, agronomy, cultivation.

ahead *(SYN.)* before, leading, forward, winning, inadvance.

(ANT.) behind.

aid *(SYN.)* remedy, assist, helper, service, support, assistant, relief, help.
(ANT.) obstruct, hinder, obstacle, impede, hindrance.

ail *(SYN.)* bother, trouble, perturb, suffer, feel sick.

ailing *(SYN.)* sick, ill.
(ANT.) hearty, hale, well.

ailment *(SYN.)* illness, disease, affliction, sickness.

aim *(SYN.)* direction, point, goal, object, target, direct, try, intend, intention, end, objective.

aimless *(SYN.)* directionless, adrift, purposeless.

air *(SYN.)* atmosphere, display, reveal, expose, publicize.
(ANT.) conceal, hide.

airy *(SYN.)* breezy, gay, lighthearted, graceful, fanciful.

aisle *(SYN.)* corridor, passageway, lane, alley, opening, artery.

ajar *(SYN.)* gaping, open.

akin *(SYN.)* alike, related, connected, similar, affiliated, allied.

alarm *(SYN.)* dismay, fright, signal, warning, terror, apprehension, affright, consternation, fear, siren, arouse, startle, bell.
(ANT.) tranquillity, composure, security, quiet, calm, soothe, comfort.

alarming *(SYN.)* appalling, daunting, shocking.
(ANT.) comforting, calming, soothing.

alcoholic *(SYN.)* sot, drunkard, tippler, inebriate.

alert *(SYN.)* attentive, keen, ready, nimble, vigilant, watchful, observant.
(ANT.) logy, sluggish, dulled, list-less.

alias *(SYN.)* anonym, assumed name.

alibi *(SYN.)* story, excuse.

alien *(SYN.)* adverse, foreigner, strange, remote, stranger, different, extraneous.
(ANT.) germane, kindred,

relevant, akin, familiar, accustomed.

alight *(SYN.)* debark, deplane, detrain, disembark.
(ANT.) embark, board.

alive *(SYN.)* existing, breathing, living, live, lively, vivacious, animated.
(ANT.) inactive, dead, moribund.

allay *(SYN.)* soothe, check, lessen, calm, lighten, relieve, soften, moderate, quite.
(ANT.) excite, intensify, worsen, arouse.

allege *(SYN.)* affirm, cite, claim, declare, maintain, state, assert.
(ANT.) deny, disprove, refute, contradict, gainsay.

allegiance *(SYN.)* faithfulness, duty, devotion, loyalty, fidelity, obligation.
(ANT.) treachery, disloyalty.

allegory *(SYN.)* fable, fiction, myth, saga, parable, legend.
(ANT.) history, fact.

alleviate *(SYN.)* diminish, soothe, solace, abate, assuage, allay, soften, mitigate, extenuate, relieve, ease, slacken, relax, weaken.
(ANT.) increase, aggravate, augment, irritate.

alley *(SYN.)* footway, byway, path, passageway, aisle, corridor, opening, lane.

alliance *(SYN.)* combination, partner-ship, union, treaty, coalition, association, confederacy, marriage, pact, agreement, relation, inter-relation, understanding.
(ANT.) separation, divorce, schism.

allot *(SYN.)* divide, mete, assign, give, measure, distribute, allocate, share, dispense, deal, apportion.
(ANT.) withhold, retain, keep, confiscate, refuse.

allow *(SYN.)* authorize, grant, acknowledge, admit, let, permit, sanction, consent, concede, mete, allocate.
(ANT.) protest, resist, refuse, forbid, object, prohibit.

allowance *(SYN.)* grant, fee, portion, ration, allotment.

allude *(SYN.)* intimate, refer, insinuate, hint, advert, suggest, imply, mention.
(ANT.) demonstrate, specify, state, declare.

allure *(SYN.)* attract, fascinate, tempt, charm, infatuate, captivate.

ally *(SYN.)* accomplice, associate, confederate, assistant, friend, partner.
(ANT.) rival, enemy, opponent, foe, adversary.

almighty *(SYN.)* omnipotent, powerful.

almost *(SYN.)* somewhat, nearly.
(ANT.) completely, absolutely.

alms *(SYN.)* dole, charity, donation, contribution.

aloft *(SYN.)* overhead.

alone *(SYN.)* desolate, unaided, only, isolated, unaided, lone, secluded, lonely, deserted, solitary, single, apart, solo, separate.
(ANT.) surrounded, attended, accompanied, together.

aloof *(SYN.)* uninterested, uninvolved, apart, remote, unsociable, standoffish, separate, disdainful, distant.
(ANT.) warm, outgoing, friendly, cordial.

also *(SYN.)* in addition, likewise, too, besides, furthermore, moreover, further.

alter *(SYN.)* adjust, vary, deviate, modify, reserved, change.
(ANT.) maintain, preserve, keep.

alteration *(SYN.)* difference, adjustment, change, modification.
(ANT.) maintenance, preservation.

altercation *(SYN.)* controversy, dispute, argument, quarrel.

alternate *(SYN.)* rotate, switch, spell, interchange.
(ANT.) fix.

alternative *(SYN.)* substitute, selection, option, choice, replacement, possibility.

although *(SYN.)* though, even

if, even though, despite, notwithstanding.

altitude (SYN.) elevation, height.
(ANT.) depth.

altogether (SYN.) totally, wholly, quite, entirely, thoroughly, completely.
(ANT.) partly.

altruism (SYN.) kindness, generosity, charity, benevolence, liberality.
(ANT.) selfishness, unkindness, cruelty, inhumanity.

always (SYN.) evermore, forever, perpetually, ever, unceasingly, continually, constantly, eternally.
(ANT.) never, rarely, sometimes, occasionally.

amalgamate (SYN.) fuse, unify, commingle, merge, combine, consolidate.
(ANT.) decompose, disintegrate, separate.

amass (SYN.) collect, accumulate, heap up, gather, increase, compile, assemble, store up.
(ANT.) disperse, dissipate, spend.

amateur (SYN.) beginner, dilettante, learner, dabbler, neophyte, apprentice, novice, nonprofessional, tyro.
(ANT.) expert, master, adept, professional, authority.

amaze (SYN.) surprise, flabbergast, stun, dumb-found, astound, bewilder, aghast, thunderstruck, astonish.
(ANT.) bore, disinterest, tire.

ambiguous (SYN.) uncertain, vague, obscure, dubious, equivocal, deceptive.
(ANT.) plain, clear, explicit, obvious, unequivocal, unmistakable, certain.

ambition (SYN.) eagerness, goal, incentive, aspiration, yearning, longing, desire.
(ANT.) indifference, satisfaction, indolence, resignation.

ambitious (SYN.) aspiring, intent upon.
(ANT.) indifferent.

amble (SYN.) saunter, stroll.

ambush (SYN.) trap, hiding place.

amend (SYN.) change, mend, better, correct, improve.
(ANT.) worsen.

amends (SYN.) compensation, restitution, payment, reparation, remedy, redress.

amiable (SYN.) friendly, good-natured, gracious, pleasing, agreeable, outgoing, kindhearted, kind, pleasant.
(ANT.) surly, hateful, churlish, disagreeable, ill-natured, ill-tempered, cross, captious, touchy.

amid (SYN.) among, amidst, surrounded by.

amiss (SYN.) wrongly, improperly, astray, awry.
(ANT.) properly, rightly, right, correctly, correct.

ammunition (SYN.) shot, powder, shells, bullets.

among (SYN.) amid, between, mingled, mixed, amidst, betwixt, surrounded by.
(ANT.) separate, apart.

amorous (SYN.) amatory, affectionate, loving.

amount (SYN.) sum, total, quantity, number, price, value, measure.

ample (SYN.) broad, large, profuse, spacious, copious, liberal, plentiful, full, bountiful, abundant, great, extensive, generous, enough, sufficient, roomy.
(ANT.) limited, insufficient, meager, lacking, cramped, small, confined, inadequate.

amplification (SYN.) magnification, growth, waxing, accrual, enhancement, enlargement, increase.
(ANT.) decrease, diminishing, reduction, contraction.

amplify (SYN.) broaden, expand, enlarge, extend.
(ANT.) confine, restrict, abridge, narrow.

amuse (SYN.) divert, please, delight, entertain, charm.
(ANT.) tire, bore.

amusement (SYN.) diversion, entertainment, enjoyment, pleasure, recreation.
(ANT.) tedium, boredom.

amusing *(SYN.)* pleasant, funny, pleasing, entertaining, comical.
(ANT.) tiring, tedious, boring.

analogous *(SYN.)* comparable, like, similar, correspondent, alike, correlative, parallel, allied, akin.
(ANT.) different, opposed, incongruous, divergent.

analysis *(SYN.)* separation, investigation, examination.

analyze *(SYN.)* explain, investigate, examine, separate.

ancestral *(SYN.)* hereditary, inherited.

ancestry *(SYN.)* family, line, descent, lineage.
(ANT.) posterity.

anchor *(SYN.)* fix, attach, secure, fasten.
(ANT.) detach, free, loosen.

ancient *(SYN.)* aged, old-fashioned, archaic, elderly, antique, old, primitive.
(ANT.) new, recent, current, fresh.

anecdote *(SYN.)* account, narrative, story, tale.

anesthetic *(SYN.)* opiate, narcotic, sedative, painkiller, analgesic.

angel *(SYN.)* cherub, archangel, seraph.
(ANT.) demon, devil.

angelic *(SYN.)* pure, lovely, heavenly, good, virtuous, innocent, godly, saintly.
(ANT.) devilish.

anger *(SYN.)* exasperation, fury, ire, passion, rage, resentment, temper, indignation, animosity, irritation, wrath, displeasure, infuriate, arouse, nettle, annoyance, exasperate.
(ANT.) forbearance, patience, peace, self-control.

angry *(SYN.)* provoked, wrathful, furious, enraged, incensed, exasperated, maddened, indignant, irate, mad, inflamed.
(ANT.) happy, pleased, calm, satisfied, content, tranquil.

anguish *(SYN.)* suffering, torment, torture, distress, pain, heartache, agony, misery.

(ANT.) solace, relief, joy, comfort, peace, ecstasy, pleasure.

animal *(SYN.)* beast, creature.

animate *(SYN.)* vitalize, invigorate, stimulate, enliven, alive, vital, vigorous.
(ANT.) dead, inanimate.

animated *(SYN.)* gay, lively, spry, vivacious, active, vigorous, chipper, snappy.
(ANT.) inactive.

animosity *(SYN.)* grudge, hatred, rancor, spite, bitterness, enmity, opposition, dislike, hostility, antipathy.
(ANT.) good will, love, friendliness, kindliness.

annex *(SYN.)* join, attach, add, addition, wing, append.

annihilate *(SYN.)* destroy, demolish, wreck, abolish.

announce *(SYN.)* proclaim, give out, make known, notify, publish, report, herald, promulgate, tell, advertise, broadcast, state, publicize.
(ANT.) conceal, withhold, suppress, bury, stifle.

announcement *(SYN.)* notification, report, declaration, bulletin, advertisement, broadcast, promulgation, notice, message.
(ANT.) silence, hush, muteness, speechlessness.

annoy *(SYN.)* bother, irk, pester, tease, trouble, vex, disturb, molest, inconvenience, irritate, harass.
(ANT.) console, gratify, soothe, accommodate, please, calm, comfort.

annually *(SYN.)* once a year.

anoint *(SYN.)* grease, oil.

answer *(SYN.)* reply, rejoinder, response, retort, rebuttal, respond.
(ANT.) summoning, argument, questioning, inquiry, query, ask, inquire.

antagonism *(SYN.)* opposition, conflict, enmity, hostility, animosity.
(ANT.) geniality, cordiality, friendliness.

antagonize *(SYN.)* against, provoke, oppose, embitter.
(ANT.) soothe.

anticipate *(SYN.)* await, foresee, forecast, hope for.

anticipated *(SYN.)* expected, foresight, preconceived.
(ANT.) dreaded, reared, worried, doubted.

antiquated *(SYN.)* old, out-of-date, outdated, old-fashion.

antique *(SYN.)* rarity, curio, old, ancient, old-fashioned, archaic, out-of-date.
(ANT.) new, recent, fresh.

anxiety *(SYN.)* care, disquiet, fear, concern, solicitude, trouble, worry.
(ANT.) nonchalance, assurance, confidence, contentment, placidity.

anxious *(SYN.)* troubled, uneasy, perturbed, apprehensive, worried, concerned, desirous, bothered.
(ANT.) tranquil, peaceful.

apathy *(SYN.)* unconcern, indifference, lethargy.
(ANT.) interest, feeling.

aperture *(SYN.)* gap, pore, opening, cavity, chasm, abyss, hole, void.
(ANT.) connection, bridge, link.

apex *(SYN.)* acme, tip, summit, crown, top.

apology *(SYN.)* defense, excuse, confession, justification, alibi, explanation, plea.
(ANT.) denial, complaint, dissimulation, accusation.

apostate *(SYN.)* nonconformist, unbeliever, dissenter, heretic, schismatic.
(ANT.) saint, conformist, believer.

appall *(SYN.)* shock, stun, dismay, frighten, terrify.
(ANT.) edify, please.

appalling *(SYN.)* fearful, frightful, ghastly, horrid, repulsive, terrible, awful.
(ANT.) fascinating, beautiful, enchanting, enjoyable.

apparatus *(SYN.)* rig, equipment, furnishings, gear.

apparel *(SYN.)* clothes, attire, garb, clothing, garments.

apparent *(SYN.)* obvious, plain, self-evident, clear, manifest, transparent, unmistakable, palpable.
(ANT.) uncertain, indistinct, dubious, hidden, mysterious.

apparition *(SYN.)* illusion, ghost, phantom, vision.

appeal *(SYN.)* plea, petition, request, entreaty, request, plead, petition, beseech.
(ANT.) repulse, repel.

appear *(SYN.)* look, arrive, emanate, emerge, arise, seem, turn up.
(ANT.) vanish, withdraw, exist, disappear, evaporate.

appearance *(SYN.)* advent, arrival, aspect, demeanor, fashion, guise, apparition, mien, look, presence.
(ANT.) disappearance, reality, departure, vanishing.

appease *(SYN.)* calm, compose, lull, quiet, relieve, assuage, pacify, satisfy, restraint, lesson, soothe.
(ANT.) excite, arouse, incense, irritate, inflame.

appendage *(SYN.)* addition, tail, supplement.

appetite *(SYN.)* zest, craving, desire, liking, longing, stomach, inclination, hunger, thirst, relish, passion.
(ANT.) satiety, disgust, distaste, repugnance.

applaud *(SYN.)* cheer, clap, hail, approve, praise.
(ANT.) disapprove, denounce, reject, criticize, condemn.

appliance *(SYN.)* machine, tool, instrument, device, utensil, implement.

applicable *(SYN.)* fitting, suitable, proper, fit, usable, appropriate, suited.
(ANT.) inappropriate, inapplicable.

apply *(SYN.)* affix, allot, appropriate, use, employ, petition, request, devote, avail, pertain, attach, ask.
(ANT.) give away, demand, detach, neglect, ignore.

appoint *(SYN.)* name, choose, nominate, designate, elect, establish, assign, place.
(ANT.) discharge, fire.

appointment *(SYN.)* rendezvous, meeting, designation,

position, engagement.
(ANT.) *discharge, dismissal.*
appreciate (SYN.) enjoy, regard, value, prize, cherish, admire, improve, rise, respect, esteem, appraise.
(ANT.) *belittle, misunderstand, apprehend, scorn, depreciate, undervalue.*
apprehend (SYN.) seize, capture, arrest, understand, dread, fear, grasp, perceive.
(ANT.) *release, lose.*
apprehension (SYN.) fear, misgiving, dread, uneasiness, worry, fearfulness.
(ANT.) *confidence, composure, self-assuredness.*
apprehensive (SYN.) worried, afraid, uneasy, bothered, anxious, concerned.
(ANT.) *relaxed.*
approach (SYN.) greet, inlet, come near, advance, access.
(ANT.) *avoid, pass by, retreat.*
appropriate (SYN.) apt, particular, proper, fitting, pillage, purloin, rob, steal, apportion, authorize.
(ANT.) *improper, contrary, inappropriate, buy, repay, restore, return, unfit, inapt.*
approval (SYN.) commendation, consent, praise, approbation, sanction, assent.
(ANT.) *reproach, censure, reprimand, disapprove.*
approve (SYN.) like, praise, authorize, confirm, endorse, commend, sanction.
(ANT.) *criticize, nullify, disparage, disapprove, deny.*
approximate (SYN.) near, approach, roughly, close.
(ANT.) *correct.*
apt (SYN.) suitable, proper, appropriate, fit, suited, disposed, liable, inclined, prone, intelligent, receptive.
(ANT.) *ill-becoming, unsuitable, unlikely, slow, retarded, dense.*
aptness (SYN.) capability, dexterity, power, qualification, skill, ability, aptitude.
(ANT.) *incompetency, unreadiness, incapacity.*
arbitrary (SYN.) unrestricted,

absolute, despotic, willful, unconditional.
(ANT.) *contingent, qualified, fair, reasonable, dependent.*
arbitrate (SYN.) referee, settle, mediate, umpire.
ardent (SYN.) fervent, fiery, glowing, intense, keen, impassioned, enthusiastic.
(ANT.) *cool, indifferent, nonchalant, apathetic.*
ardor (SYN.) enthusiasm, rapture, glowing, eagerness.
(ANT.) *unconcern, apathy, disinterest, indifference.*
arduous (SYN.) laborious, hard, difficult, burdensome, strenuous, strained.
(ANT.) *easy.*
area (SYN.) space, extent, region, zone, section, expanse, district, size.
argue (SYN.) plead, reason, wrangle, indicate, prove, show, dispute, denote.
(ANT.) *reject, spurn, ignore, overlook, agree, concur.*
arid (SYN.) waterless, dry, flat, dull, unimaginative, stuffy.
(ANT.) *fertile, wet, colorful.*
arise (SYN.) enter, institute, originate, start, open, commence, emerge, appear.
(ANT.) *terminate, end, finish, complete, close.*
arm (SYN.) weapon, defend, equip, empower, fortify.
armistice (SYN.) truce, pact, deal, peace, treaty, contract, alliance, agreement.
army (SYN.) troops, legion, military, forces, militia.
arouse (SYN.) stir, animate, move, pique, provoke, disturb, excite, foment.
(ANT.) *settle, soothe, calm.*
arraign (SYN.) charge, censure, incriminate, indict.
(ANT.) *acquit, release, vindicate, exonerate, absolve.*
arraignment (SYN.) imputation, charge, accusation.
(ANT.) *pardon, exoneration, exculpation.*
arrange (SYN.) classify, assort, organize, place, plan, prepare, devise, adjust, dispose, regulate, order, group.

(ANT.) jumble, scatter, disorder, confuse, disarrange.

array (SYN.) dress, adorn, attire, clothe, arrange, order, display, exhibit.
(ANT.) disorder, disorganization, disarray.

arrest (SYN.) detain, hinder, restrain, seize, withhold, stop, check, apprehend.
(ANT.) free, release, discharge, liberate.

arrive (SYN.) come, emerge, reach, visit, land, appear.
(ANT.) exit, leave, depart, go.

arrogant (SYN.) insolent, prideful, scornful, haughty, cavalier, proud.
(ANT.) modest, humble.

art (SYN.) cunning, tact, artifice, skill, aptitude, adroitness, painting, drawing, design, composition.
(ANT.) clumsiness, innocence, unskillfulness, honesty.

artful (SYN.) clever, sly, skillful, knowing, deceitful, tricky, crafty, cunning.
(ANT.) artless.

article (SYN.) story, composition, treatise, essay, thing, report, object.

artificial (SYN.) bogus, fake, affected, feigned, phony, sham, unreal, synthetic, assumed, counterfeit.
(ANT.) genuine, natural true, real, authentic.

artist (SYN.) actor, actress, painter, sculptor, singer.

artless (SYN.) innocent, open, frank, simple, honest, candid, natural, unskilled.
(ANT.) artful.

ascend (SYN.) rise, scale, tower, mount, go up, climb.
(ANT.) fall, sink, descend, go down.

ascertain (SYN.) solve, learn, clear up, answer.

ashamed (SYN.) shamefaced, humiliated, abashed, mortified, embarrassed.
(ANT.) proud.

ask (SYN.) invite, request, inquire, query, question, beg, claim, interrogate, expect.
(ANT.) order, reply, insist, answer.

askew (SYN.) disorderly, crooked, awry, twisted.
(ANT.) straight.

asleep (SYN.) inactive, sleeping, dormant.
(ANT.) alert, awake.

aspect (SYN.) appearance, look, view, outlook, attitude, viewpoint, phase.

asphyxiate (SYN.) suffocate, stifle, smother, choke, strangle, throttle.

aspiration (SYN.) craving, desire, hope, longing, objective, passion, ambition.

aspire (SYN.) seek, aim, wish for, strive, desire, yearn for.

ass (SYN.) mule, donkey, burro, silly, dunce.

assault (SYN.) invade, strike, attack, assail, charge, bombard, onslaught.
(ANT.) protect, defend.

assemble (SYN.) collect, gather, meet, congregate, connect, manufacture.
(ANT.) disperse, disassemble, scatter.

assembly (SYN.) legislature, congress, council.

assent (SYN.) consent to, concede, agree, approval, accept, comply, permission.
(ANT.) deny, dissent, refusal, denial, refuse.

assert (SYN.) declare, maintain, state, claim, express, defend, support, aver.
(ANT.) deny, refute, contradict, decline.

assertion (SYN.) statement, affirmation, declaration.
(ANT.) contradiction, denial.

assess (SYN.) calculate, compute, estimate, levy, reckon.

asset (SYN.) property, wealth, capitol, resourses, goods.

assign (SYN.) apportion, ascribe, attribute, cast.
(ANT.) release, relieve, unburden, discharge.

assist (SYN.) help, promote, serve, support, sustain, abet.
(ANT.) prevent, impede, hinder, hamper.

assistant (SYN.) accomplice, ally, associate, confederate.

(ANT.) rival, enemy.

associate (SYN.) affiliate, ally, join, connect, unite, combine, mingle, partner, mix.
(ANT.) separate, disconnect, divide, disrupt, estrange.

association (SYN.) organization, club, union, society, fraternity, sorority.

assorted (SYN.) varied, miscellaneous, classified, different, several, grouped.
(ANT.) alike, same.

assuage (SYN.) calm, quiet, lessen, relieve, ease, allay, moderate, alleviate.

assume (SYN.) arrogate, affect, suspect, believe, appropriate, pretend, usurp.
(ANT.) doff, demonstrate, prove, grant, concede.

assumption (SYN.) presumption, guess, theory, supposition, conjecture, postulate.

assure (SYN.) promise, convince, warrant, guarantee.
(ANT.) equivocate, deny.

astonish (SYN.) astound, amaze, surprise, shock.
(ANT.) tire, bore.

astound (SYN.) shock, amaze, astonish, stun, surprise.

athletic (SYN.) strong, active, ablebodied, gymnastic.

attach (SYN.) connect, adjoin, annex, join, append, stick.
(ANT.) unfasten, untie, detach, separate, disengage.

attachment (SYN.) friendship, liking, regard, adherence.
(ANT.) estrangement, opposition, alienation, aversion.

attack (SYN.) raid, assault, besiege, abuse, censure, offense, seige, denunciation.
(ANT.) surrender, defense, opposition, aid, defend, protect.

attain (SYN.) achieve, acquire, accomplish, gain, get, reach, win, complete, finish.
(ANT.) relinquish, discard, abandon, desert.

attempt (SYN.) essay, experiment, trial, try, undertaking, endeavor, effort.
(ANT.) laziness, neglect.

attend (SYN.) accompany, escort, watch, be serve, care

for, follow, lackey, present.
(ANT.) desert, abandon.

attention (SYN.) consideration, heed, circumspection, notice, watchfulness.
(ANT.) negligence, indifference, omission, oversight.

attentive (SYN.) careful, awake, alive, considerate, mindful, wary, assiduous.
(ANT.) indifferent, unaware, oblivious, apathetic.

attitude (SYN.) standpoint, viewpoint, stand, pose, disposition, opinion.

attract (SYN.) enchant, interest, pull, fascinate, draw, lure, captivate, allure.
(ANT.) deter, repel, repulse, alienate.

attractive (SYN.) enchanting, winning, engaging, pleasant, seductive, magnetic.
(ANT.) unatractive, obnoxious, repellent.

attribute (SYN.) give, apply, feature, nature, credit, quality, assign, ascribe.

audacity (SYN.) effrontery, fearlessness, temerity.
(ANT.) humility, meekness, circumspection, fearfulness.

audible (SYN.) distinct, bearable, plain, clear.
(ANT.) inaudible.

augment (SYN.) enlarge, increase, raise, expand.

auspicious (SYN.) lucky, timely, favorable, promising, fortunate.
(ANT.) untimely, unfortunate.

authentic (SYN.) real, true, correct, verifiable, authoritative, trustworthy.
(ANT.) false, spurious, artificial, counterfeit, erroneous.

authenticate (SYN.) validate, warrant, guarantee, verify.

author (SYN.) father, inventor, originator, writer, composer

authoritative (SYN.) certain, secure, commanding, sure, tried, trustworthy, safe.
(ANT.) uncertain, unreliable, dubious, fallible.

authority (SYN.) dominion, justification, power, permission, authorization.

authorize *(SYN.)* permit, sanction, legalize, assign, enable.
(ANT.) forbid, prohibit.

automatic *(SYN.)* self-acting, mechanical, spontaneous, self-working, self-moving.
(ANT.) hand-operated, intentional, deliberate, manual.

auxiliary *(SYN.)* assisting, helping, aiding.

avail *(SYN.)* help, profit, use, value, benefit, advantage.

available *(SYN.)* obtainable, accessible, prepared.
(ANT.) unavailable, out of reach, inaccessible.

average *(SYN.)* moderate, ordinary, usual, passable, fair, middling, intermediate.
(ANT.) outstanding, exceptional, extraordinary.

averse *(SYN.)* unwilling, opposed, forced, against.
(ANT.) willing.

aversion *(SYN.)* disgust, dislike, distaste, hatred, loathing, abhorrence, antipathy.
(ANT.) devotion, enthusiasm, affection, love.

avoid *(SYN.)* elude, forestall, evade, escape, dodge, avert, forbear, eschew, free, shun.
(ANT.) oppose, meet, confront, encounter, seek.

award *(SYN.)* reward, prize, medal, gift, trophy.

aware *(SYN.)* mindful, perceptive, informed, apprised, realizing, conscious.
(ANT.) unaware, insensible, ignorant, oblivious.

away *(SYN.)* absent, departed, distracted, gone.
(ANT.) present, attentive, at home, attending.

awful *(SYN.)* frightful, horrible, aweinspiring, dire, terrible, unpleasant, imposing, appalling, cruel.
(ANT.) humble, lowly, pleasant, commonplace.

awkward *(SYN.)* inept, unpolished, clumsy, gauche, rough, ungraceful, ungainly.
(ANT.) adroit, graceful, polished, skillful.

babble *(SYN.)* twaddle, nonsense, gibberish, prattle, balderdash, rubbish.

baby *(SYN.)* newborn, infant, wee, little, undersized, midget, papoose, pamper.

back *(SYN.)* help, assist, endorse, support, second, ratify, approve, stand by.
(ANT.) anterior, front, face, undercut, veto, undermine, accessible, near.

backbone *(SYN.)* vertebrae, spine, pillar, support, staff, mainstay, character.
(ANT.) timidity, weakness, cowardice, spinelessness.

backbreaking *(SYN.)* exhausting, fatiguing, tough, tiring.
(ANT.) light, relaxing, undemanding, slight.

backward *(SYN.)* dull, sluggish, stupid, loath, regressive, rearward, underdeveloped, slow, retarded.
(ANT.) progressive, precocious, civilized, advanced, forward.

bad *(SYN.)* unfavorable, wrong, evil, immoral, sinful, faulty, improper, unwholesome, wicked, corrupt, tainted, defective, poor, imperfect, inferior, substandard, contaminated, inappropriate, unsuited, rotten, unsuitable, sorry, upset, sick, suffering, unpleasant.
(ANT.) good, honorable, reputable, moral, excellent.

badger *(SYN.)* tease, question, annoy, pester, bother, taunt, bait, provoke.

baffle *(SYN.)* confound bewilder, perplex, puzzle, mystify, confuse, frustrate.
(ANT.) inform, enlighten.

bait *(SYN.)* enticement, captivate, ensnare, tease, torment, pester, worry, entrap, question, entice, lure, trap, harass, tempt, badger.

balance *(SYN.)* poise, stability, composure, remains, residue, equilibrium, compare.
(ANT.) unsteadiness, instability.

baleful *(SYN.)* evil, immoral

sinful, destructive.

(ANT.) good, moral, reputable, excellent, harmless.

balk (SYN.) unwilling, obstinate, stubborn, stop.

(ANT.) willing.

ball (SYN.) cotillion, dance, globe, sphere, spheroid.

ballad (SYN.) song, ditty.

balloon (SYN.) puff up, enlarge, swell.

(ANT.) shrivel, shrink.

ballot (SYN.) vote, poll.

balmy (SYN.) soft, gentle, soothing, fragrant, mild.

(ANT.) tempestuous, stormy.

ban (SYN.) prohibit, outlaw, disallow, block, bar, exclude, obstruct, forbid.

(ANT.) allow, permit.

banal (SYN.) hackneyed, corny, vapid.

(ANT.) striking, original, fresh, stimulating, novel.

band (SYN.) company, association, crew, unite, gang.

bang (SYN.) hit, strike, slam.

banish (SYN.) drive away, eject, exile, oust, deport.

(ANT.) receive, accept, shelter, admit, harbor, welcome.

bank (SYN.) barrier, slope, storage, treasury, row.

banner (SYN.) colors, standard, pennant, flag.

banquet (SYN.) feast, celebration, festival, dinner, regalement, affair.

banter (SYN.) joke, tease, jest.

bar (SYN.) counter, impediment, saloon, exclude, obstacle, barricade, obstruct, shut out, hindrance, forbid, block, barrier, obstruction.

(ANT.) allow, permit, aid, encouragement.

barbarian (SYN.) brute, savage, boor, ruffian, rude, uncivilized, primitive, uncultured, barbaric, crude.

(ANT.) permit, allow, encouragement.

barber (SYN.) coiffeur, hairdresser.

bare (SYN.) naked, nude, uncovered, undressed, unclothed, barren, empty, disclose, reveal, publicize, bald,

expose, scarce, mere.

(ANT.) dressed, garbed, conceal, hide, disguise, clothed.

barely (SYN.) hardly, scarcely.

bargain (SYN.) agreement, arrangement, deal, contract, arrange, sale.

baroque (SYN.) ornamented, elaborate, ornate.

barren (SYN.) unproductive, bare, unfruitful, infertile, sterile, childless.

(ANT.) productive, fruitful, fertile.

barricade (SYN.) fence, obstruction, shut in, fortification, barrier.

(ANT.) free, open, release.

barrier (SYN.) fence, wall, bar, railing, obstacle, hindrance, fortification, restraint.

(ANT.) assistance, aid, encouragement.

barter (SYN.) exchange, deal.

base (SYN.) bottom, rest, foundation, establish, found, immoral, evil, bad, poor, support, stand, low.

(ANT.) exalted, righteous, lofty, esteemed, noble, honored, refined, valuable.

bashful (SYN.) timorous, abashed, shy, coy, timid, diffident, modest, sheepish.

(ANT.) fearless, out-going, adventurous, gregarious, aggressive, daring.

basic (SYN.) underlying, chief, essential, fundamental.

(ANT.) subsidiary, subordinate.

basis (SYN.) presumption, support, base, principle, groundwork, presupposition, foundation, postulate.

(ANT.) implication, trimming, derivative.

basket (SYN.) hamper, creel, dossier, bassinet.

bastion (SYN.) mainstay, support, staff, tower.

bat (SYN.) strike, hit, clout, stick, club, knock, crack.

batch (SYN.) group, set, collection, lot, cluster, bunch, mass, combination.

bath (SYN.) washing, shower, tub, wash, dip, soaping.

bathe *(SYN.)* launder, drench, swim, cover, medicate, immerse, wet, dip, soak.

bathos *(SYN.)* mawkishness, soppiness, sentimentality.

baton *(SYN.)* mace, rod, staff, billy, crook, stick, fasces.

battalion *(SYN.)* mass, army, swarm, mob, drove, horde, gang, legion, regiment.

batten *(SYN.)* thrive, flourish, fatten, wax, expand, bloom.
(ANT.) decrease, weaken, fail.

batter *(SYN.)* pound, beat, hit, pommel, wallop, bash, smash, mixture, strike.

battle *(SYN.)* strife, fray, combat, struggle, contest, skirmish, conflict, fight, war, flight, warfare, action.
(ANT.) truce, concord, agreement, settlement, harmony, accept, concur, peace.

bauble *(SYN.)* plaything, toy, trinket.

bawl *(SYN.)* sob, shout, wail, cry loudly, bellow, weep, cry.

bay *(SYN.)* inlet, bayou, harbor, lagoon, sound, gulf.

bazaar *(SYN.)* fair, market, marketplace.

beacon *(SYN.)* light, signal, watchtower, guide, flare, warning, alarm.

bead *(SYN.)* globule, drop, pill, blob.

beak *(SYN.)* nose, bill.

beam *(SYN.)* gleam, ray, girder, cross-member, pencil, shine, glisten, glitter, gleam.

beaming *(SYN.)* joyful, bright, happy, radiant, grinning.
(ANT.) sullen, gloomy, threatening, scowling.

bear *(SYN.)* carry, support, take, uphold, suffer, convey, brook, transport, undergo, permit, abide, tolerate.
(ANT.) evade, shun, avoid, refuse, dodge.

bearable *(SYN.)* sufferable, supportable, manageable.
(ANT.) terrible, painful, unbearable, awful, intolerable.

beast *(SYN.)* monster, savage, brute, creature, animal.

beastly *(SYN.)* detestable, mean, low, hateful, loath.

(ANT.) considerate, sympathetic, refined, humane, fine.

beat *(SYN.)* pulse, buffet, pound, defeat, palpitate, hit, rout, smite, throb, punch, conquer, batter, conquer.
(ANT.) stroke, fail, defend, surrender, shield.

beaten *(SYN.)* disheartened, dejected, licked, discouraged, hopeless.
(ANT.) eager, hopeful.

beatific *(SYN.)* uplifted, blissful, elated, happy, wonderful, joyful, divine.
(ANT.) awful, hellish, ill-fated, accursed.

beating *(SYN.)* whipping, drubbing, flogging, lashing, scourging, walloping.

beau *(SYN.)* lover, suitor, swain, admirer.

beautiful *(SYN.)* pretty, fair, lovely, charming, comely, handsome, attractive.
(ANT.) repulsive, hideous, unsightly, foul, homely, plainness, ugly, ugliness.

beauty *(SYN.)* handsomeness, fairness, charm, pulchritude, comeliness, grace.
(ANT.) ugliness, disfigurement, homeliness, plainness, deformity, eyesore.

becalm *(SYN.)* calm, quiet, smooth, still, hush, repose.

because *(SYN.)* inasmuch as, as, since, for.

because of *(SYN.)* as a result of, as a consequence of.

beckon *(SYN.)* call, signal, summon, motion, gesture.

becloud *(SYN.)* obfuscate, confuse, befog, confound.
(ANT.) illuminate, clarify.

become *(SYN.)* change, grow, suit, be appropriate, befit.

becoming *(SYN.)* suitable, meet, befitting, appropriate, attractive, pleasing, flatter.
(ANT.) unsuitable, inappropriate, incongruent, ugly, unattractive, improper.

bed *(SYN.)* layer, cot, vein, berth, stratum, couch, accumulation, bunk, deposit.

bedazzle *(SYN.)* glare, blind, dumbfound, flabbergast, bewilder, furbish, festoon.

bedeck *(SYN.)* deck, adorn, beautify, smarten, festoon.

bedlam *(SYN.)* tumult, uproar, madhouse.
(ANT.) calm, peace.

bedrock *(SYN.)* basis, foundation, roots.
(ANT.) top, dome, apex, nonessentials.

beef *(SYN.)* brawn, strength, heft, gripe, sinew, fitness.

befall *(SYN.)* occur, come about, happen.

before *(SYN.)* prior, earlier, in advance, formerly.
(ANT.) behind, following, afterward, latterly, after.

befriend *(SYN.)* welcome, encourage, aid, stand by.
(ANT.) dislike, shun, desert.

befuddle *(SYN.)* stupefy, addle, confuse, rattle.

beg *(SYN.)* solicit, ask, implore, supplicate, entreat, request, importune, entreat.
(ANT.) grant, cede, give, bestow, favor.

beget *(SYN.)* sire, engender, produce, create, propagate, originate, procreate, father.
(ANT.) murder, destroy, kill, abort, prevent, extinguish.

beggar *(SYN.)* scrub, tatterdemalion, pauper, wretch.

begin *(SYN.)* open, enter, arise, initiate, commence, start, institute, create.
(ANT.) terminate, complete, finish, close, end, stop.

beginner *(SYN.)* nonprofessional, amateur, apprentice.
(ANT.) veteran, professional.

beginning *(SYN.)* outset, inception, origin, source, commencement.
(ANT.) termination, completion, end, close, consummation, closing, ending, finish.

begrime *(SYN.)* soil, dirty, smear, muddy, splotch.
(ANT.) wash, clean, freshen, launder.

begrudge *(SYN.)* resent, envy, stint, withhold, grudge.

begrudging *(SYN.)* hesitant, reluctant, resentful.
(ANT.) willing, eager, quick,

spontaneous.

beguiling *(SYN.)* enchanting, interesting, delightful, intriguing, engaging, bewitching, enthralling, captivating.
(ANT.) boring, dull, unattractive, tedious.

behalf *(SYN.)* benefit, welfare, support, aid, part, interest.

behave *(SYN.)* deport, comport, manage, act, interact.
(ANT.) rebel, misbehave.

behavior *(SYN.)* manners, carriage, disposition, action, deed, conduct, demeanor.
(ANT.) rebelliousness, misbehavior.

behead *(SYN.)* decapitate, guillotine, decollate.

behest *(SYN.)* order, command, decree, mandate.

behind *(SYN.)* after, backward, at the back, in back of.
(ANT.) frontward, ahead, before.

behold *(SYN.)* look, see, view, notice, observe, perceive.
(ANT.) overlook, ignore.

being *(SYN.)* life, existing, existence, living, actuality, organism, individual.
(ANT.) death, nonexistence, expiration.

belabor *(SYN.)* repeat, reiterate, pound, explain.

belated *(SYN.)* late, delayed, overdue, tardy.
(ANT.) well-timed, early.

belch *(SYN.)* emit, erupt, gush, disgorge, bubble.

beleaguered *(SYN.)* bothered, beset, annoyed, beset, harassed, badgered, vexed.

belie *(SYN.)* distort, misrepresent, twist, disappoint.

belief *(SYN.)* trust, feeling, certitude, opinion, conviction, view, creed, assurance.
(ANT.) heresy, denial, incredulity, distrust, skepticism.

believe *(SYN.)* hold, apprehend, fancy, support.
(ANT.) doubt, reject, distrust, disbelieve, question.

believer *(SYN.)* adherent, follower, devotee, convert.
(ANT.) doubter, critic, scoffer.

belittle *(SYN.)* underrate, de-

preciate, minimize, decry, disparage, depreciate.
(ANT.) esteem, admire, flatter, overrate, commend.

bell (SYN.) pealing, ringing, signal, tolling, buzzer.

belligerent (SYN.) aggressive, warlike, hostile, offensive.
(ANT.) easygoing, compromising, peaceful.

bellow (SYN.) thunder, roar, scream, shout, yell, howl.

bellwether (SYN.) leader, pilot, guide, ringleader.

belly (SYN.) stomach, abdomen, paunch.

belonging (SYN.) loyalty, relationship, kinship, acceptance, rapport.

belongings (SYN.) property, effects, possessions.

beloved (SYN.) adored, sweet, loved, cherished, prized.

below (SYN.) under, less, beneath, underneath, lower.
(ANT.) aloft, overhead, above, over.

belt (SYN.) girdle, sash, strap, cummerbund, band, waistband, punch.

bemoan (SYN.) mourn, lament, grieve, sorrow, regret.

bend (SYN.) turn, curve, incline, submit, bow, lean, crook, twist, yield, stoop.
(ANT.) resist, straighten, break, stiffen.

beneath (SYN.) under, below.
(ANT.) above, over.

benediction (SYN.) thanks, blessing, prayer.

beneficial (SYN.) salutary, good, wholesome, advantageous, useful, helpful.
(ANT.) harmful, destructive, injurious, disadvantageous, unwholesome, deleterious.

benefit (SYN.) support, help, gain, avail, profit, account, favor, aid, good, advantage, serve, interest, behalf.
(ANT.) handicap, calamity, trouble, disadvantage.

benevolence (SYN.) magnanimity, charity, tenderness, altruism, humanity, philanthropy, generosity, liberality, good will.

(ANT.) malevolence, unkindness, cruelty, selfishness.

benevolent (SYN.) kindhearted, tender, merciful, generous, altruistic, obliging, kind, good, wellwishing, philanthropy.
(ANT.) malevolent, greedy, wicked, harsh.

bent (SYN.) curved, crooked, resolved, determined, set, inclined, firm, decided.
(ANT.) straight.

berate (SYN.) scold.

beseech (SYN.) appeal, entreat, plead, ask, beg.

beset (SYN.) surround, attack.

besides (SYN.) moreover, further, except for, also, as well, furthermore.

besiege (SYN.) assault, attack, siege, bombard, raid.

bespeak (SYN.) engage, reserve, indicate, show.

best (SYN.) choice, prime, select.
(ANT.) worst.

bestial (SYN.) brutal, beastly, savage, cruel.

bestow (SYN.) confer, place, put, award, give, present.
(ANT.) withdraw, withhold.

bet (SYN.) gamble, give, stake, wager, pledge, ante.

betray (SYN.) reveal, deliver, expose, mislead, trick, deceive, exhibit, show.
(ANT.) shelter, protect, safeguard.

betrothal (SYN.) marriage, engagement, contract.

better (SYN.) superior, preferable, improve.
(ANT.) worsen.

beware (SYN.) take care, watch out, look sharp.

bewilder (SYN.) perplex, confuse, mystify, baffle, puzzle.
(ANT.) clarify, enlighten.

bewitch (SYN.) captivate, charm, delight, enchant.

beyond (SYN.) past, farther, exceeding.

bias (SYN.) slant, inclination, proneness, turn, bent, penchant, tendency, proclivity, prejudice, influence, warp.
(ANT.) fairness, justice, even-

handedness, equity.

bible *(SYN.)* guide, handbook, gospel, manual.

bibulous *(SYN.)* guzzling, intemperate, winebibbing, sottish, alcoholic.
(ANT.) sober, moderate.

bicker *(SYN.)* dispute, argue, wrangle, quarrel.
(ANT.) go along with, agree.

bid *(SYN.)* order, command, direct, wish, greet, say, offer, instruct, invite, purpose.

bidding *(SYN.)* behest, request, decree, call, charge, beck, summons, solicitation, invitation, instruction.

bide *(SYN.)* stay, tarry, delay, wait, remain.

big *(SYN.)* large, huge, bulky, immense, colossal, majestic, august, monstrous, hulking, enormous, tremendous.
(ANT.) small, little, tiny, immature, petite.

big-hearted *(SYN.)* good-natured, liberal, generous, unselfish, open-handed, unstinting, charitable.
(ANT.) cold, selfish, mean, uncharitable.

bigoted *(SYN.)* intolerant, partial, prejudiced, biased.

bigotry *(SYN.)* bias, blindness, intolerance, unfairness, prejudice, ignorance, passion.
(ANT.) acceptance, open-mindedness.

bilk *(SYN.)* defraud, trick, cheat, hoodwink, deceive.

bill *(SYN.)* charge, invoice, account, statement.

billet *(SYN.)* housing, quarters, berth, shelter, barrack.

billow *(SYN.)* surge, swell, rise, rush, peaking.
(ANT.) lowering, decrease.

bin *(SYN.)* cubbyhole, box, container, chest, cubicle.

bind *(SYN.)* connect, restrain, band, fasten, oblige, obligate, engage, wrap, restrict.
(ANT.) unlace, loose, unfasten, untie, free.

binding *(SYN.)* compulsory, obligatory, mandatory, compelling, unalterable, imperative, indissoluble.

(ANT.) adjustable, flexible, elastic, changeable.

birth *(SYN.)* origin, beginning, infancy, inception.
(ANT.) finish, decline, death, disappearance, end.

bit *(SYN.)* fraction, portion, scrap, fragment, particle.

bite *(SYN.)* gnaw, chew, nip, sting, pierce, mouthful.

biting *(SYN.)* cutting, sharp, acid, sneering, sarcastic.
(ANT.) soothing, kind, gentle, agreeable.

bitter *(SYN.)* distasteful, sour, acrid, pungent, piercing, vicious, severe, biting, distressful, stinging.
(ANT.) sweet, mellow, pleasant, delicious.

bizarre *(SYN.)* peculiar, strange, odd, uncommon.
(ANT.) usual, everyday, ordinary, inconspicuous.

black *(SYN.)* sooty, dark, ebony, inky, swarthy, soiled, filthy, dirty, stained, somber, depressing, gloomy.
(ANT.) white, pure, cheerful, light-skinned, sunny, bright.

blackmail *(SYN.)* bribe, payment, bribery, extortion, shakedown, coercion.

blackout *(SYN.)* faint, coma, unconsciousness, oblivion.

bladder *(SYN.)* saccule, sac, vesicle, pouch, pod, cell.

blade *(SYN.)* cutter, lancet, knife, sword.

blame *(SYN.)* upbraid, criticize, fault, guilt, accuse, rebuke, charge, implicate, indict, responsibility.
(ANT.) exonerate, credit, honor, absolve.

blameless *(SYN.)* moral, innocent, worthy, faultless.
(ANT.) blameworthy, culpable, guilty.

blanch *(SYN.)* whiten, bleach, decolorize, peroxide, fade.

bland *(SYN.)* soft, smooth, gentle, agreeable, vapid.
(ANT.) harsh, outspoken, disagreeable.

blandish *(SYN.)* praise, compliment, overpraise, cajole, puff, adulate, salve, fawn,

court, toady, please, jolly.
(ANT.) insult, deride, criticize, belittle.

blandisher *(SYN.)* adulator, booster, sycophant, eulogist, apple polisher, flunkey.
(ANT.) knocker, faultfinder, belittler.

blandishment *(SYN.)* applause, honey, adulation, fawning, compliments.
(ANT.) carping, belittling, criticism, deprecation.

blank *(SYN.)* unmarked, expressionless, uninterested, form, area, void, vacant.
(ANT.) marked, filled, alert, animated.

blanket *(SYN.)* quilt, coverlet, cover, comforter, robe, padding, carpet, wrapper, mantle, comprehensive, universal, panoramic, omnibus.
(ANT.) limited, detailed, restricted, precise.

blare *(SYN.)* roar, blast, resound, jar, scream, swell, clang, peal, trumpet, toot.

blasphemous *(SYN.)* profane, irreverent, impious, godless, sacrilegious, irreligious.
(ANT.) reverent, reverential, religious, pious.

blasphemy *(SYN.)* profanation, impiousness, cursing, irreverence, contempt.
(ANT.) respect, piety, reverence, devotion.

blast *(SYN.)* burst, explosion, discharge, blow-out.

blatant *(SYN.)* shameless, notorious, brazen, flagrant, glaring, bold, obvious.
(ANT.) deft, subtle, insidious.

blaze *(SYN.)* inferno, shine, flare, marking, fire, outburst, holocaust, flame.
(ANT.) die, dwindle.

bleach *(SYN.)* pale, whiten, blanch, whitener.
(ANT.) darken, blacken.

bleak *(SYN.)* dreary, barren, cheerless, depressing, gloomy, bare, cold, dismal, desolate, raw, chilly.
(ANT.) lush, hopeful, promising, cheerful.

bleary *(SYN.)* hazy, groggy,

blurry, fuzzy, misty, clouded, overcast, dim, blear.
(ANT.) clear, vivid, precise.

bleed *(syn.)* pity, lose blood, grieve, sorrow.

blemish *(SYN.)* injury, speck, flaw, scar, disgrace, imperfection, stain, fault, blot.
(ANT.) purity, embellishment, adornment, perfection.

blend *(SYN.)* beat, intermingle, combine, fuse, unify, consolidate, amalgamate, conjoin, mix, coalesce, pound, combination, stir, mixture, commingle.
(ANT.) separate, decompose, analyze, disintegrate.

bless *(SYN.)* thank, celebrate, extol, glorify, adore, delight, praise, gladden, exalt.
(ANT.) denounce, blaspheme, slander, curse.

blessed *(SYN.)* sacred, holy, consecrated, dedicated, hallowed, sacrosanct, beatified.
(ANT.) miserable, sad, dispirited, cheerless.

blight *(SYN.)* decay, disease, spoil, sickness, wither, ruin, damage, harm, decaying, epidemic, destroy.

blind *(SYN.)* sightless, unmindful, rash, visionless, ignorant, oblivious, purblind, unknowing, screen, unaware, thoughtless, shade, without thought, headlong.
(ANT.) discerning, sensible, calculated, perceiving, perceptive, aware.

blink *(SYN.)* bat, glance, flicker, wink, twinkle.

bliss *(SYN.)* ecstasy, rapture, glee, elation, joy, blessedness, gladness, happiness, delight, felicity, blissfulness.
(ANT.) woe, sadness, sorrow, grief, unhappiness, torment, wretchedness, misery.

blissful *(SYN.)* happy, elated, rapturous, ecstatic, paradisiacal, joyous, enraptured.

blister *(SYN.)* bleb, swelling, welt, sore, blob, bubble, inflammation, boil, canker.

blithe *(SYN.)* breezy, merry, airy, lighthearted, light, gay, fanciful, graceful.

(ANT.) morose, grouchy, low-spirited, gloomy.

blitz (SYN.) strike, onslaught, thrust, raid, lunge, drive, incursion, assault, sally.

blizzard (SYN.) storm, snow-storm, snowfall, gale, tempest, blast, blow, swirl.

bloat (SYN.) distend, puff up, inflate, swell.

(ANT.) deflate.

blob (SYN.) bubble, blister, pellet, globule.

block (SYN.) clog, hinder, bar, impede, close, obstruct, barricade, blockade, check.

(ANT.) forward, promote, aid, clear, advance, advantage, assist, further, open.

blockade (SYN.) barrier, fortification, obstruction.

blood (SYN.) murder, gore, slaughter, bloodshed, ancestry, lineage, heritage.

bloom (SYN.) thrive, glow, flourish, blossom, flower.

(ANT.) wane, decay, dwindle, shrivel, wither.

blooming (SYN.) flush, green, vigorous, thriving, vital, abloom, healthy, fresh.

(ANT.) flagging, declining, whithering.

blooper (SYN.) muff, fluff, error, bungle, botch, blunder, fumble, howler.

blossom (SYN.) bloom, flower, flourish.

(ANT.) shrink, wither, dwindle, fade.

blot (SYN.) stain, inkblot, spot, inkstain, blemish, dishonor, obliterate, soil, dry.

blow (SYN.) hit, thump, slap, cuff, box, shock, move, drive, inflate, enlarge.

blue (SYN.) sapphire, azure, gloomy, sad, unhappy, depressed, dejected.

(ANT.) cheerful, optimistic, happy.

blues (SYN.) dumps, melancholy, depression, doldrums, moroseness.

blunder (SYN.) error, flounder, mistake, stumble.

blunt (SYN.) solid, abrupt,

rough, dull, pointless, plain, bluff, edgeless.

(ANT.) tactful, polite, subtle, polished, suave, sharp, keen, pointed, diplomatic.

blur (SYN.) sully, dim, obscure, stain, dull, confuse.

(ANT.) clear, clarify.

blush (SYN.) redden.

board (SYN.) embark, committee, wood, mount, cabinet, food, get on, lumber.

boast (SYN.) vaunt, flaunt, brag, glory, crow.

(ANT.) humble, apologize, minimize, deprecate.

body (SYN.) remains, bulk, mass, carcass, form, company, cadaver, trunk.

(ANT.) spirit, intellect, soul.

bogus (SYN.) counterfeit, false, pretend, fake, phony.

(ANT.) genuine.

boil (SYN.) seethe, bubble, fume, pimple, cook.

boisterous (SYN.) rough, violent, noisy, tumultuous.

(ANT.) serene.

bold (SYN.) daring, forward, adventurous, fearless, insolent, conspicuous, gallant.

(ANT.) modest, bashful, cowardly, timid, retiring.

bolt (SYN.) break away, fastener, flee, take flight, lock.

bombard (SYN.) shell, open fire, bomb, rake, assail.

bond (SYN.) fastener, rope, tie, cord, connection, attachment, link, promise.

(ANT.) sever, separate, untie, disconnect.

bondage (SYN.) slavery, thralldom, captivity, imprisonment, servitude.

(ANT.) liberation, emancipation, free, independence.

bonds (SYN.) chains, cuffs, fetters, shackles, irons.

bonus (SYN.) more, extra, premium, gift, reward, bounty.

book (SYN.) manual, textbook, work, booklet, mon, volume, paperback, text.

boom (SYN.) advance, grow, flourish, progress, gain, increase, roar, beam, rumble.

(ANT.) decline, fail, recession.

boon *(SYN.)* gift, jolly, blessing, pleasant, godsend.

boondocks *(SYN.)* sticks.

boor *(SYN.)* lout, clown, oaf, yokel, rustic, vulgarian.

boorish *(SYN.)* coarse, churlish, uncivil, ill-mannered, ill-bred, uncivilized, crude.
(ANT.) polite, cultivated, cultivated, well-mannered.

boost *(SYN.)* push, lift, help, hoist, shove.
(ANT.) depress, lower, belittle, submerge, disparage, decrease, decline, reduction.

booster *(SYN.)* supporter, fan, rooter, plugger, follower.

boot *(SYN)* shoe, kick.

booth *(SYN.)* enclosure, cubicle, stand, compartment.

booty *(SYN.)* prize, plunder, loot.

booze *(SYN.)* spirits, drink, liquor, alcohol.

border *(SYN.)* fringe, rim, verge, boundary, edge, termination, brink, limit, brim, outskirts, frontier, margin.
(ANT.) interior, center, mainland, core, middle.

bore *(SYN.)* tire, weary, hole, perforate, pierce, drill.
(ANT.) arouse, captivate, excite, interest.

boredom *(SYN.)* ennui, doldrums, weariness, dullness.
(ANT.) stimulation, motive, activity, stimulus, excitement.

borrow *(SYN.)* copy, adopt, simulate, mirror, assume.
(ANT.) allow, advance, invent, originate, credit, lend.

bosom *(SYN.)* chest, breast, feelings, thoughts, mind.

boss *(SYN.)* director, employer, oversee, direct, foreman, supervisor, manager.
(ANT.) worker, employee, underling.

botch *(SYN.)* blunder, bungle, fumble, goof, muff.
(ANT.) perform, realize.

bother *(SYN.)* haunt, molest, trouble, annoy, upset, fleeting, transient, harass.
(ANT.) prolonged, extended, long, protracted, lengthy.

bottle *(SYN.)* container, flask, vessel, decanter, vial, ewer.

bottom *(SYN.)* basis, fundament, base, groundwork.
(ANT.) top, peak, apex, summit, topside.

bound *(SYN.)* spring, vault, bounce, skip, tied, shackled.
(ANT.) unfettered, free.

boundary *(SYN.)* bound, limit, border, margin, outline, division, frontier, edge.

boundless *(SYN.)* limitless, endless, inexhaustible, unlimited, eternal, infinite.
(ANT.) restricted, narrow, limited.

bounty *(SYN.)* generosity, gift, award, bonus, reward.

bourgeois *(SYN.)* common, ordinary, commonplace.
(ANT.) upper-class, unconventional, loose, aristocratic.

bout *(SYN.)* round, contest, conflict, struggle, match.

bow *(SYN.)* bend, yield, kneel, submit, stoop.

bowl *(SYN.)* container, dish, pot, pottery, crock, jug, vase.

bow out *(SYN.)* give up, withdraw, retire, resign.

box *(SYN.)* hit, fight, crate, case, container.

boy *(SYN.)* male, youngster, lad, kid, fellow, buddy.
(ANT.) girl, man.

brace *(SYN.)* strengthen, tie, prop, support, tighten, stay, strut, bind, truss, crutch.

bracing *(SYN.)* stimulating, refreshing, restorative.

bracket *(SYN.)* join, couple, enclose, relate, brace.

brag *(SYN.)* boast, flaunt, vaunt, bluster, swagger.
(ANT.) demean, debase, denigrate, deprecate.

braid *(SYN.)* weave, twine, wreath, plait.

brain *(SYN.)* sense, intelligence, intellect, common sense, understanding.
(ANT.) stupid, stupidity.

brake *(SYN.)* decelerate, stop.
(ANT.) accelerate.

branch *(SYN.)* shoot, limb, bough, tributary, offshoot.

brand *(SYN.)* make, trademark, label, kind, burn.

brave *(SYN.)* bold, daring, gallant, valorous, adventurous, heroic, magnanimous.
(ANT.) weak, cringing, timid, cowardly, fearful, craven.

brawl *(SYN.)* racket, quarrel, fracas, riot, fight, melee.

brazen *(SYN.)* immodest, forward, shameless, bold.
(ANT.) retiring, self-effacing, modest, shy.

breach *(SYN.)* rupture, fracture, rift, break, crack, gap, opening, breaking, quarrel.
(ANT.) observation.

break *(SYN.)* demolish, pound, rack, smash, burst, rupture, opening, rupture.
(ANT.) restore, heal, join, renovate, mend, repair.

breed *(SYN.)* engender, bear, propagate, father, beget.
(ANT.) murder, abort, kill.

breeze *(SYN.)* air, wind, zephyr, breath.
(ANT.) calm.

breezy *(SYN.)* jolly, spry, active, brisk, energetic, lively.

brevity *(SYN.)* briefness, conciseness.
(ANT.) length.

brew *(SYN.)* plot, plan, cook, ferment, prepare, scheme.

bribe *(SYN.)* buy off.

bridle *(SYN.)* control, hold, restrain, harness, curb.
(ANT.) release, free, loose.

brief *(SYN.)* curt, short, fleeting, passing, compendious, terse, laconic, succinct.
(ANT.) long, extended, prolonged, lengthy, protracted, comprehensive, extensive.

brigand *(SYN.)* bandit, robber, thief.

brilliant *(SYN.)* bright, clear, smart, intelligent, sparkling, shining, alert, vivid.
(ANT.) mediocre, dull, lusterless, second-rate.

brim *(SYN.)* border, margin, lip, rim, edge.
(ANT.) middle, center.

bring *(SYN.)* fetch, take, carry, raise, introduce, propose.
(ANT.) remove, withdraw.

brisk *(SYN.)* fresh, breezy, cool, lively, spry, refreshing, quick, active, animated.
(ANT.) musty, faded, stagnant, decayed, hackneyed, slow, lethargic, sluggish, still, dull, oppressive.

briskness *(SYN.)* energy, exercise, motion, rapidity.
(ANT.) inertia, idleness, sloth, inactivity.

brittle *(SYN.)* crumbling, frail, breakable, delicate, splintery, fragile, weak.
(ANT.) tough, enduring, unbreakable, thick, strong.

broach *(SYN.)* set afoot, introduce, inaugurate, start.

broad *(SYN.)* large, wide, tolerant, expanded, vast, liberal, sweeping, roomy.
(ANT.) restricted, slim, tight, limited, negligible.

broadcast *(SYN.)* distribute, announce, transmit, relay.

broaden *(SYN.)* spread, widen, amplify, enlarge, extend, increase, add to.
(ANT.) tighted, narrow, constrict, straiten.

brochure *(SYN.)* booklet, pamphlet, leaflet, mailing.

broken *(SYN.)* flattened, rent, shattered, wrecked, destroyed, reduced, smashed.
(ANT.) whole, integral, united, repaired.

bromide *(SYN.)* banality, platitude, stereotype, commonplace, slogan, proverb.

brook *(SYN.)* rivulet, run, branch, stream, creek.

brother *(SYN.)* comrade, man, kinsman, sibling.
(ANT.) sister.

bruise *(SYN.)* hurt, injure, wound, damage, abrasion, damage, harm, wound.

brunt *(SYN.)* force, impact, shock, strain, oppression.

brush *(SYN.)* rub, wipe, clean, bushes, remove, shrubs, hairbrush, underbrush.

brush-off *(SYN.)* dismissal, snub, slight, rebuff.

brusque *(SYN.)* sudden, curt, hasty, blunt, rough, steep, precipitate, rugged, craggy, gruff, surly, abrupt, short.
(ANT.) smooth, anticipated,

courteous, expected, gradual, personable.

brutal (SYN.) brute, cruel, gross, sensual, ferocious, brutish, coarse, remorseless, ruthless, mean, savage. (ANT.) kind, courteous, humane, civilized, gentle, kindhearted, mild.

brute (SYN.) monster, barbarian, beast, animal, wild.

bubble (SYN.) boil, foam, seethe, froth.

buccaneer (SYN.) sea robber, privateer, pirate.

buck (SYN.) spring, jump, vault, leap.

bucket (SYN.) pot, pail, canister, can.

buckle (SYN.) hook, fastening, fastener, bend, wrinkle, clip, fasten, collapse, yield, warp.

bud (SYN.) develop, sprout.

buddy (SYN.) companion, comrade, friend, partner.

budge (SYN.) stir, move.

budget (SYN.) schedule, ration.

buff (SYN.) shine, polish, burnish, rub, wax.

buffet (SYN.) bat, strike, clout, blow, knock, beat, crack, hit, slap, cabinet, counter.

buffoon (SYN.) jester, fool, clown, jokester, zany, comedian, chump, boor, dolt.

bug (SYN.) fault, hitch, defect, catch, snag, failing, rub, flaw, snarl, weakness, annoy, pester, hector, vex, nag.

build (SYN.) found, rear, establish, constructed, raise, set up, erect, assemble. (ANT.) raze, destroy, overthrow, demolish, undermine.

building (SYN.) residence, structure, house, edifice.

bulge (SYN.) lump, protuberance, bump, swelling, protrusion, extend. (ANT.) hollow, shrink, contract, depression.

bulk (SYN.) lump, magnitude, volume, size, mass, most.

bulky (SYN.) great, big, huge, large, enormous, massive, immense, monstrous, clumsy, cumbersome, unwieldy.

(ANT.) tiny, little, small, petite, handy, delicate.

bull (SYN.) push, force, press, drive, thrust, bump.

bulldoze (SYN.) cow, bully, coerce, thrust, push.

bulletin (SYN.) news, flash, message, statement, newsletter, circular.

bully (SYN.) pester, tease, intimidate, harass, domineer.

bulwark (SYN.) wall, bastion, abutment, bank, dam, rampart, shoulder, parapet, backing, maintainer, embankment, safe-guard.

bum (SYN.) idler, loafer, drifter, hobo, wretch, dwadler, beggar, vagrant.

bumbling (SYN.) bungling, inept, blundering, clumsy, incompetent, awkward, maladroit, lumbering, ungainly. (ANT.) facile, handy, dexterous, proficient.

bump (SYN.) shake, push, hit, shove, prod, collide.

bumpkin (SYN.) hick, yokel, rustic, yahoo.

bumpy (SYN.) uneven, jolting, rough, jarring, rocky, coarse, craggy, irregular. (ANT.) flat, smooth, flush, polished, level.

bunch (SYN.) batch, bundle, cluster, company, collection, flock, group.

bundle (SYN.) package, mass, collection, batch, parcel, packet, box, carton, bunch.

bungalow (SYN.) ranch house, cabana, cabin, cottage, lodge, summer house, villa.

bungle (SYN.) tumble, botch, foul up, boggle, mess up.

bunk (SYN.) berth, rubbish, nonsense, couch, bed, cot.

buoyant (SYN.) light, jolly, spirited, effervescent, blithe, sprightly, lively, resilient, vivacious, afloat, floating. (ANT.) hopeless, dejected, sullen, depressed, heavy, despondent, sinking, low.

bureau (SYN.) office, division, department, unit, commission, board, chest, dresser.

bureaucrat (SYN.) clerk, offi-

cial, functionary, servant.
burglar (SYN.) thief, robber.
burial (SYN.) interment.
burly (SYN.) husky, beefy, heavyset, brawny, strapping. (ANT.) skinny, scrawny.
burnish (SYN.) polish, shine, buff, wax, rub.
burrow (SYN.) tunnel, search, seek, dig, excavate, hunt.
burst (SYN.) exploded, broken, erupt.
business (SYN.) employment, profession, trade, work, art, engagement, vocation, occupation, company, concern, firm, partnership. (ANT.) hobby, avocation.
bustle (SYN.) noise, flurry, action, trouble, fuss, ado, stir. (ANT.) calmness, composure, serenity, peacefulness.
busy (SYN.) careful, industrious, active, patient, assiduous, diligent, perseverant, hardworking. (ANT.) unconcerned, indifferent, apathetic, lethargic, careless, inactive, unemployed, lazy, indolent.
but (SYN.) nevertheless, yet, however, though, although.
butcher (SYN.) kill, murder, slaughter, assassinate, slay. (ANT.) save, protect, vivify, animate, resuscitate.
butt (SYN.) bump, ram, bunt, shove, jam, drive, punch, blow, push, thrust.
buttocks (SYN.) hind end, rump, posterior, backside, behind, bottom, rear, butt.
button (SYN.) clasp, close, fasten, hook.
buy (SYN.) procure, get, purchase, acquire, obtain. (ANT.) vend, sell.
buzz (SYN.) whir, hum, thrum, drone, burr.
by (SYN.) near, through, beside, with, from, at, close to.
bygone (SYN.) bypast, former, earlier, past, older. (ANT.) immediate, present, current, modern.
byway (SYN.) passage, detour.
byword (SYN.) adage, proverb, axiom.

cab (SYN.) coach, taxi, car, hack, taxicab, carriage.
cad (SYN.) knave, rascal, scoundrel, rogue.
cagey (SYN.) cunning, wary, clever, tricky, cautious. (ANT.) innocent, straightfoward, guileless, naive.
calamity (SYN.) ruin, disaster, casualty, distress, hardship, trouble, misfortune. (ANT.) blessing, fortune.
calculate (SYN.) count, compute, figure, estimate, multiply, judge, reckon. (ANT.) guess, miscalculate, assume, conjecture.
call (SYN.) designate, name, yell, cry, ask, shout, speak, phone, ring up, collect, waken, awaken, ring, wake.
callous (SYN.) insensitive, impenitent, obdurate, unfeeling, insensible, heartless. (ANT.) compassionate, tender.
calm (SYN.) appease, lull, quiet, soothe, composed, tranquilize, dispassionate. (ANT.) tempestuous, disturbed, turmoil, inflame.
canal (SYN.) gully, tube, duct.
cancel (SYN.) eliminate, obliterate, erase, delete, nullify, repeal, revoke, cross out, set aside, abolish. (ANT.) perpetuate, confirm, ratify, enforce, enact.
candid (SYN.) free, blunt, frank, plain, open, sincere, honest, outspoken. (ANT.) sly, contrived, wily.
canine (SYN.) pooch, dog.
canny (SYN.) artful, skillful, shrewd, clever, cautious.
cant (SYN.) dissimulation, patois, jargon, shoptalk, deceit, argot, pretense. (ANT.) honesty, condor, frankness, truth.
canyon (SYN.) gulch, gully, arroyo, ravine, gorge.
capability (SYN.) aptness, ability, capacity, aptitude, dexterity, power, efficiency. (ANT.) incapacity, disability.
capable (SYN.) clever, qualified, able, efficient, competent, accomplished.

(ANT.) unfitted, incapable, incompetent, unskilled, inept.

capacity *(SYN.)* capability, power, ability, talent, content, skill, volume, size.
(ANT.) inability, stupidity, incapacity, impotence.

cape *(SYN.)* pelisse, cloak, mantle, neck, point, headland, peninsula.

caper *(SYN.)* romp, frisk, cavort, frolic, gambol.

capricious *(SYN.)* undependable, erratic, inconstant, fickle, changeable, irregular.

captivate *(SYN.)* fascinate, charm, delight.

capture *(SYN.)* catch, grip, apprehend, clutch, arrest, snare, seize, nab, seizure.
(ANT.) set free, lose, liberate, throw, free, release.

carcass *(SYN.)* remains, frame, corpse, form, bulk, mass, corpus, association.
(ANT.) spirit, intellect, soul.

care *(SYN.)* concern, anxiety, worry, caution, solicitude, charge, ward, attention, regard, supervision, consider.
(ANT.) neglect, disregard, indifference, unconcern.

career *(SYN.)* occupation, profession, job, calling, vocation, trade.

caress *(SYN.)* hug, fondle, embrace, pet, pat, stroke, kiss.
(ANT.) spurn, vex, buffet, annoy, tease.

caricature *(SYN.)* exaggeration, parody, spoof, takeoff.

carnage *(SYN.)* massacre, liquidation, slaughter.

carnal *(SYN.)* base, corporeal, animal, lustful, worldly.
(ANT.) intellectual, spiritual, exalted, temperate.

carol *(SYN.)* hymn, song.

carp *(SYN.)* pick, praise.

carry *(SYN.)* convey, transport, support, bring, sustain.
(ANT.) drop, abandon.

carve *(SYN.)* hew, shape, cut, whittle, chisel, sculpt.

case *(SYN.)* state, covering, receptacle, condition, instance, example, occurrence, happening, illustra-

tion, claim, lawsuit, crate.

cash *(SYN.)* currency, money.

casket *(SYN.)* coffin, box.

cast *(SYN.)* fling, toss, throw, pitch, form, company, shape, turn, actors, players.

caste *(SYN.)* class, grade, order, category, status, elegance, set, rank, station, social standing.

casual *(SYN.)* chance, unexpected, informal, accidental, incidental, offhand, unplanned, relaxed.
(ANT.) planned, expected, calculated, formal, deliberate, dressy.

casualty *(SYN.)* calamity, fortuity, mishap, loss, injured, dead, wounded, accident, contingency, victim.
(ANT.) design, purpose, intention, calculation.

catalog *(SYN.)* classify, roll, group, list, inventory, directory, index, record, file.

catastrophe *(SYN.)* mishap, calamity, disaster, adversity, accident, ruin.
(ANT.) fortune, boon, triumph, blessing, advantage.

catch *(SYN.)* hook, snare, entrap, ensnare, capture, grip, apprehend, grasp, take, grab, nab, arrest, contract, snare, seize, apprehension, latch, bolt, pin.
(ANT.) lose, free, liberate, throw, release.

category *(SYN.)* class, caste, kind, order, genre, rank, classification, sort, elegance.

cater *(SYN.)* coddle, oblige, serve, humor, baby, mollycoddle, pamper, spoil.

cause *(SYN.)* effect, incite, create, induce, inducement, occasion, incentive, prompt, principle, determinant.

caustic *(SYN.)* bitter, disagreeable, distasteful, acrid, sour, spiteful, pungent, tart, painful, cruel, insulting.
(ANT.) mellow, sweet, delicious, pleasant.

caution *(SYN.)* heed, vigilance, care, prudence, counsel, warning, wariness, ad-

vice, warn, injunction.
(ANT.) carelessness, heedlessness, incaution, abandon.
cavalcade *(SYN.)* column, procession, parade.
cavalier *(SYN.)* contemptuous, insolent, haughty.
cave *(SYN.)* grotto, hole, shelter, lair, den, cavern.
cavity *(SYN.)* pit, hole, crater.
cavort *(SYN.)* caper, leap, frolic, hop, prance.
cease *(SYN.)* desist, stop, abandon, discontinue, relinquish, end, terminate, leave.
(ANT.) occupy, continue, persist, begin, endure, stay.
cede *(SYN.)* surrender, relinquish, yield.
celebrate *(SYN.)* honor, glorify, commemorate, keep.
(ANT.) decry, overlook, profane, disregard, disgrace.
celestial *(SYN.)* godlike, holy, supernatural, divine, paradisiacal, utopian.
(ANT.) diabolical, profane, mundane, wicked.
cement *(SYN.)* solidify, weld, fasten, secure.
cemetery *(SYN.)* graveyard.
censure *(SYN.)* denounce, reproach, upbraid, blame, disapproval, reprehend.
(ANT.) commend, approval, forgive, approve, praise, applaud, condone.
center *(SYN.)* heart, core, midpoint, middle, nucleus, inside, hub, focus.
(ANT.) rim, boundary, edge, border, periphery, outskirts.
central *(SYN.)* chief, necessary, main, halfway, dominant, mid, middle, inner.
(ANT.) side, secondary, incidental, auxiliary.
ceremony *(SYN.)* observance, rite, parade, formality.
(ANT.) informality.
certain *(SYN.)* definite, assured, fixed, inevitable, sure, undeniable, positive.
(ANT.) probable, uncertain, doubtful, questionable.
certainly *(SYN.)* absolutely, surely, definitely.
(ANT.) dubiously, doubtfully,

questionably.
certainty *(SYN.)* confidence, courage, security, assuredness, firmness, assertion.
(ANT.) humility, bashfulness, modest, shyness.
certify *(SYN.)* validate, affirm, verify, confirm, authenticate, substantiate.
certitude *(SYN.)* confidence, belief, conviction, feeling, faith, persuasion, trust.
(ANT.) doubt, incredulity, denial, heresy.
cessation *(SYN.)* ending, finish, stoppage, termination, conclusion, end.
challenge *(SYN.)* question, dare, call, summon, threat, invite, threaten, demand.
chamber *(SYN.)* cell, salon.
champion *(SYN.)* victor, winner, choice, best, conqueror, hero, support, select.
chance *(SYN.)* befall, accident, betide, disaster, opportunity, calamity, occur, possibility, prospect, happen.
(ANT.) design, purpose, inevitability, calculation, certainty, intention.
change *(SYN.)* modification, alternation, alteration, mutation, variety, exchange, shift, alter, transfigure, veer.
(ANT.) uniformity, monotony, settle, remain, endure, retain, preserve, immutability.
channel *(SYN.)* strait, corridor, waterway, artery, duct, canal, way, trough.
chant *(SYN.)* singing, incantation, hymn, intone, sing, carol, psalm, song, ballad.
chaos *(SYN.)* confusion, jumble, turmoil, anarchy, disorder, muddle.
(ANT.) organization, order, tranquillity, tidiness, system.
chaotic *(SYN.)* confused, disorganized, disordered.
(ANT.) neat, ordered, systematic, organized.
chapter *(SYN.)* part, section.
char *(SYN.)* scorch, singe, burn, sear.
character *(SYN.)* description, class, kind, repute, mark,

individuality, disposition, traits, personality.

charge (SYN.) arraignment, indictment, accusation, sell for, attack, assail, assault.
(ANT.) *pardon, flee, exculpation, excuse, absolve, retreat, exoneration.*

charity (SYN.) benevolence, kindness, magnanimity.
(ANT.) *malevolence, cruelty, selfishness.*

charm (SYN.) allure, spell.

charter (SYN.) lease, hire, rent, alliance.

chase (SYN.) hunt, run after, pursue, trail, follow, persist.
(ANT.) *escape, flee, abandon, elude, evade.*

chasm (SYN.) ravine, abyss, canyon, gorge.

chaste (SYN.) clear, immaculate, innocent, sincere, bare.
(ANT.) *polluted, tainted, foul, impure, sinful, worldly.*

chat (SYN.) argue, jabber, blab, plead, consult, converse, lecture, discuss, talk.

cheap (SYN.) poor, common, inexpensive, shabby, low-priced, beggary, low-cost.
(ANT.) *honorable, dear, noble, expensive, costly.*

cheat (SYN.) deceive, fool, bilk, outwit, victimize, dupe.

check (SYN.) dissect, interrogate, analyze, contemplate, inquire, question.
(ANT.) *overlook, disregard, advance, foster, continue.*

cheek (SYN.) nerve, effrontery, impudence, gall.

cheer (SYN.) console, gladden, comfort, encourage, applause, encouragement, joy, glee, gaiety, mirth.
(ANT.) *depress, sadden, discourage, derision, dishearten.*

cherish (SYN.) prize, treasure, appreciate, nurse, value.
(ANT.) *disregard, neglect, deprecate, scorn, reject.*

chest (SYN.) bosom, breast, coffer, box, case, trunk, casket, dresser, commode.

chew (SYN.) gnaw, munch, bite, nibble.

chill (SYN.) coolness, cold,

cool, coldness, brisk, frosty.
(ANT.) *hot, warm, heat, heated, warmth.*

chirp (SYN.) peep, cheep, twitter, tweet, chirrup.

chivalrous (SYN.) noble, brave, polite, valorous, gallant, gentlemanly.
(ANT.) *crude, rude, impolite.*

chivalry (SYN.) courtesy, nobility, gallantry.

choice (SYN.) delicate, elegant, fine, dainty, exquisite, pure, refined, subtle, splendid, handsome, option.
(ANT.) *coarse, rough, thick, blunt, large.*

choose (SYN.) elect, decide between, pick, select, cull.
(ANT.) *reject, refuse.*

chop (SYN.) hew, cut, fell.

chore (SYN.) routine, task, job, duty, work.

chronic (SYN.) persistent, constant, lingering, continuing, perennial, unending, sustained, permanent.
(ANT.) *fleeting, acute.*

chronicle (SYN.) detail, history, narrative, account, description, narration, recital.
(ANT.) *misrepresentation, confusion, distortion.*

circle (SYN.) disk, ring, set, group, class, club, surround.

circuit (SYN.) circle, course, journey, orbit, revolution.

circumference (SYN.) border, perimeter, periphery, edge.

circumspection (SYN.) care, worry, solicitude, anxiety.
(ANT.) *neglect, negligence.*

circumstance (SYN.) fact, event, incident, condition, happening, position, occurrence, situation.

cite (SYN.) affirm, assign, allege, advance, quote, mention, declare, claim.
(ANT.) *refute, gainsay, deny.*

citizen (SYN.) native, inhabitant, national, denizen, subject, dweller, resident.

civil (SYN.) courteous, cultivated, accomplished, public, municipal, respectful.
(ANT.) *uncouth, uncivil, impertinent, impolite, boorish.*

civilize *(SYN.)* refine, tame, polish, cultivate, instruct.

claim *(SYN.)* aver, declare, allege, assert, affirm, express, state, demand, maintain. *(ANT.)* refute, deny, contradict.

clamor *(SYN.)* cry, din, babel, noise, racket, outcry, row, sound tumult, shouting. *(ANT.)* hush, serenity, silence, tranquillity, stillness, quiet.

clan *(SYN.)* fellowship, kindness, solidarity, family. *(ANT.)* discord, strife, opposition, acrimony.

clandestine *(SYN.)* covert, hidden, latent, private, concealed, secret, unknown. *(ANT.)* exposed, known, conspicuous, obvious.

clarify *(SYN.)* educate, explain, expound, decipher, illustrate, clear, resolve, define, interpret, unfold. *(ANT.)* darken, obscure, baffle, confuse.

clash *(SYN.)* clank, crash, clang, conflict, disagreement, opposition, collision, struggle, mismatch. *(ANT.)* accord, agreement, harmony, blend, harmonize, match, agree.

clasp *(SYN.)* grip, hold, grasp, adhere, clutch, keep, have, maintain, possess, occupy. *(ANT.)* relinquish, vacate, surrender, abandon.

class *(SYN.)* category, denomination, caste, kind, genre, grade, rank, order, elegance, classification.

classic *(SYN.)* masterpiece.

classification *(SYN.)* order, category, class, arrangement, ordering, grouping.

classify *(SYN.)* arrange, class, order, sort, grade, group.

clause *(SYN.)* condition, paragraph, limitation, article.

claw *(SYN.)* hook, talon, nail.

clean *(SYN.)* mop, tidy, neat, dustless, clear, unsoiled, immaculate, unstained, untainted, pure, dust, vacuum. *(ANT.)* stain, soil, pollute, soiled, impure, dirty, stain.

cleanse *(SYN.)* mop, purify, wash, sweep. *(ANT.)* stain, soil, dirty.

clear *(SYN.)* fair, sunny, cloudless, transparent, apparent, limpid, distinct, intelligible, evident. *(ANT.)* obscure, unclear, muddled, confused, dark, cloudy, blocked.

clearly *(SYN.)* plainly, obviously, evidently, definitely. *(ANT.)* questionably, dubiously.

clemency *(SYN.)* forgiveness, charity, compassion, grace, mercy, leniency, pity. *(ANT.)* punishment, vengeance, retribution.

clerical *(SYN.)* ministerial, pastoral, priestly, celestial, holy, sacred, secretarial.

clerk *(SYN.)* typist, office worker, office girl, saleslady, salesperson, salesclerk.

clever *(SYN.)* apt, dexterous, quick, adroit, quick-witted, talented, bright, skillful, witty, ingenious, smart. *(ANT.)* unskilled, slow, stupid, backward, maladroit, bungling, dull, clumsy.

client *(SYN.)* patron.

cliff *(SYN.)* scar, tor, bluff, crag, precipice, escarpment.

climate *(SYN.)* aura, atmosphere, air, ambience.

climax *(SYN.)* apex, culmination, peak, summit, consummation, height, acme. *(ANT.)* depth, base, anticlimax, floor.

climb *(SYN.)* mount, scale. *(ANT.)* descend.

clip *(SYN.)* snip, crop, cut, mow, clasp.

cloak *(SYN.)* conceal, cover, disguise, clothe, cape, guard, envelop, hide, mask. *(ANT.)* divulge, expose, reveal, bare, unveil.

clod *(SYN.)* wad, hunk, gobbet, lump, chunk, clot, gob, dunce, dolt, oaf, fool.

clog *(SYN.)* crowd, congest, cram, overfill, stuff.

cloister *(SYN.)* monastery, priory, hermitage, abbey.

close *(SYN.)* adjacent, adjoining, immediate, unventilated, stuffy, abutting.
(ANT.) afar, faraway, removed, distant.

closet *(SYN.)* cabinet, locker, wardrobe, cupboard.

cloth *(SYN.)* fabric, goods, material, textile.

clothe *(SYN.)* garb, dress, apparel.
(ANT.) strip, undress.

clothes *(SYN.)* array, attire, apparel, clothing, dress, garb, dress, garments, raiment, drapery, vestments.
(ANT.) nudity, nakedness.

cloud *(SYN.)* fog, mist, haze, mass, collection, obscure, dim, shadow.

club *(SYN.)* society, association, set, circle, organization, bat, cudgel, stick, blackjack.

clue *(SYN.)* sign, trace, hint, suggestion.

clumsy *(SYN.)* bungling, inept, rough, unpolished, bumbling, awkward, ungraceful, gauche, ungainly, unskillful, untoward.
(ANT.) polished, skillful, neat, graceful, dexterous, adroit.

cluster *(SYN.)* batch, clutch, group, bunch, gather, pack, assemble, crowd.

clutch *(SYN.)* grip, grab, seize, hold.

coalition *(SYN.)* combination, association, alliance, confederacy, entente, league, treaty.
(ANT.) schism, separation, divorce.

coarse *(SYN.)* unpolished, vulgar, refined, rough, smooth, impure, rude, crude, gruff, gross, cultivated, delicate, cultured.
(ANT.) delicate, smooth, refined, polished, genteel, cultivated, suave, fine, cultured.

coast *(SYN.)* seaboard, seashore, beach, shore, drift, glide, ride.

coax *(SYN.)* urge, persuade, wheedle, cajole.
(ANT.) force, bully, coerce.

coddle *(SYN.)* pamper, baby, spoil, indulge.

code *(SYN.)* crypt, cryptogram, cipher.

coerce *(SYN.)* constrain, compel, enforce, force, drive, oblige, impel.
(ANT.) prevent, persuade, convince, induce.

coercion *(SYN.)* emphasis, intensity, energy, dint, might potency, power, vigor, strength, compulsion, force, constraint, violence.
(ANT.) impotence, frailty, feebleness, weakness, persuasion.

cognizance *(SYN.)* apprehension, erudition, acquaintance, information, learning, knowledge, lore, science, scholarship, understanding.
(ANT.) illiteracy, misunderstanding, ignorance.

cognizant *(SYN.)* conscious, aware, apprised informed, mindful, observant, perceptive.
(ANT.) unaware, ignorant, oblivious, insensible.

coherent *(SYN.)* logical, intelligible, sensible, rational.

coincide *(SYN.)* acquiesce, agree, accede, assent, consent, comply, correspond, concur, match, tally, harmonize, conform.
(ANT.) differ, disagree, protest, contradict.

coincidence *(SYN.)* accident, chance.
(ANT.) plot, plan, prearrangement, scheme.

coincident *(SYN.)* identical, equal, equivalent, distinguishable, same, like.
(ANT.) distinct, contrary, disparate, opposed.

coincidental *(SYN.)* unpredicted, unexpected, chance, unforeseen, accidental, fortuitous.

cold *(SYN.)* cool, freezing, chilly, frigid, icy, frozen, wintry, arctic, unfriendly, indifferent, phlegmatic, stoical, passionless, chill,

unemotional, heartless, unfeeling.
(ANT.) hot, torrid, fiery, burning, ardent, friendly, temperate, warm, passionate.

collapse (SYN.) descend, decrease, diminish, fail, downfall, failure, decline, fall, drop, sink, subside, topple.
(ANT.) soar, steady, limb, mount, arise.

colleague (SYN.) companion, attendant, comrade, associate, crony, co-worker, mate, friend, partner.
(ANT.) enemy, stranger, adversary.

collect (SYN.) assemble, amass, concentrate, pile, accumulate, congregate, obtain, heap, gather, solicit, secure, procure, raise, get, mass, hoard, consolidate.
(ANT.) divide, dole, assort, dispel, distribute, disperse.

collected (SYN.) cool, calm, composed, peaceful, imperturbable, placid, sedate, quiet.
(ANT.) excited, violent, aroused, agitated.

collection (SYN.) amount, conglomeration, sum, entirely, aggregation, hoard, accumulation, pile, store, aggregate, total, whole.
(ANT.) part, unit, particular, element, ingredient.

collide (SYN.) hit, smash, crash, strike.

collision (SYN.) conflict, combat, duel, battle, encounter, crash, smash, fight, contention, struggle, discord.
(ANT.) concord, amity, harmony, consonance.

collusion (SYN.) combination, cabal, intrigue, conspiracy, plot, treason, treachery.

color (SYN.) hue, paint, pigment, complexion, dye, shade, tone, tincture, stain, tint, tinge.
(ANT.) paleness, transparency, achromatism.

colorful (SYN.) impressive, vivid, striking, full-color,

multicolored, offbeat, weird, unusual.
(ANT.) flat, dull, uninteresting.

colossal (SYN.) enormous, elephantine, gargantuan, huge, immense, gigantic, prodigious.
(ANT.) little, minute, small, miniature, diminutive, microscopic, tiny.

combat (SYN.) conflict, duel, battle, collision, encounter, fight, contest, oppose, war, contention, struggle, discord.
(ANT.) consonance, harmony, concord, yield, surrender, succumb, amity.

combination (SYN.) association, confederacy, alliance, entente, league, compounding, mixture, blend, composite, federation, mixing, compound, blending, union.
(ANT.) separation, division, schism, divorce.

combine (SYN.) adjoin, associate, accompany, conjoin, connect, link, mix, blend, couple, unite, join.
(ANT.) detach, disjoin, divide, separate, disconnect.

come (SYN.) near, approach, reach, arrive, advance.
(ANT.) depart, leave, go.

comedian (SYN.) comic, wit, humorist, gagman, wag.

comely (SYN.) charming, elegant, beauteous, beautiful, fine, lovely, pretty, handsome.
(ANT.) hideous, repulsive, foul, unsightly.

come-on (SYN.) lure, inducement, enticement, temptation, premium.

comfort (SYN.) contentment, ease, enjoyment, relieve, consolation, relief, cheer, console, calm, satisfaction, soothe, encourage, succor, luxury, solace.
(ANT.) depress, torture, discomfort, upset, misery, disturb, agitate, affliction, discompose, uncertainty, suffering.

comfortable *(SYN.)* pleasing, agreeable, convenient, cozy, welcome, acceptable, relaxed, restful, cozy, gratifying, easy, contented, rested, satisfying, pleasurable.
(ANT.) miserable, distressing, tense, strained, troubling, edgy, uncomfortable.

comical *(SYN.)* droll, funny, humorous, amusing, ludicrous, witty, ridiculous, odd, queer.
(ANT.) sober, solemn, sad, serious, melancholy.

command *(SYN.)* class, method, plan regularity, rank, arrangement, series, sequence, point, aim, conduct, manage, guide, bid, system, succession, bidding, direct, order, demand, direction, rule, dictate, decree.
(ANT.) consent, obey, misdirect, distract, deceive, misguide, license, confusion.

commandeer *(SYN.)* take, possession, seize, confiscate, appropriate.

commanding *(SYN.)* imposing, masterful, assertive, authoritative, positive.

commence *(SYN.)* open, start.
(ANT.) stop, end, terminate, finish.

commend *(SYN.)* laud, praise, applaud, recommend.
(ANT.) censure, blame, criticize.

commendable *(SYN.)* deserving, praise-worthy.
(ANT.) bad, deplorable, lamentable.

commendation *(SYN.)* approval, applause, praise, recommendation, honor, medal.
(ANT.) criticism, condemnation, censure.

commensurate *(SYN.)* keep, celebrate, observe, honor, commend, extol, glorify, laud, praise, honor.
(ANT.) decry, disgrace, disregard, overlook, profane, dishonor.

comment *(SYN.)* assertion, declaration, annotation, explanation, review, commen-

tary, report, remark, observation, utterance, criticism, statement.

commerce *(SYN.)* business, engagement, employment, art, trade, marketing, enterprise, occupation.
(ANT.) hobby, pastime, avocation.

commission *(SYN.)* board, committee, command, permit, order, permission, delegate, authorize, deputize, entrust.

commit *(SYN.)* perpetrate, perform, obligate, do, commend, consign, relegate, bind, delegate, empower, pledge, entrust, authorize, trust.
(ANT.) neglect, mistrust, release, free, miscarry, fail, loose.

commitment *(SYN.)* duty, promise, responsibility, pledge.

committee *(SYN.)* commission, bureau, board, delegate, council.

commodious *(SYN.)* appropriate, accessible, adapted, favorable, handy, fitting, timely.
(ANT.) inconvenient, troublesome, awkward.

commodity *(SYN.)* article, merchandise, wares, goods.

common *(SYN.)* ordinary, popular, familiar, mean, low, general, vulgar, communal, mutual, shared, natural, frequent, prevalent, joint, conventional, plain, usual, universal.
(ANT.) odd, exceptional, scarce, noble, extraordinary, different, separate, outstanding, rare, unusual, distinctive, refined.

commonplace *(SYN.)* common, usual, frequent, ordinary, everyday.
(ANT.) distinctive, unusual, original.

commonsense *(SYN.)* perceptible, alive, apprehensible, aware, awake, cognizant, conscious, comprehending, perceptible.

(ANT.) unaware, impalpable, imperceptible.

commotion *(SYN.)* confusion, chaos, disarray, ferment, disorder, stir, tumult, agitation.

(ANT.) tranquillity, peace, certainty, order.

communicable *(SYN.)* infectious, virulent, catching, transferable, contagious.

(ANT.) hygienic, noncommunicable, healthful.

communicate *(SYN.)* convey, impart, inform, confer, disclose, reveal, relate, tell, advertise, publish, transmit, publicize, divulge.

(ANT.) withhold, hide, conceal.

communication *(SYN.)* disclosure, transmission, declaration, announcement, publication, message, report, news, information.

communion *(SYN.)* intercourse, fellowship, participation, association, sacrament, union.

(ANT.) nonparticipation, alienation.

community *(SYN.)* public, society, city, town, village.

compact *(SYN.)* contracted, firm, narrow, snug, close, constricted, packed, vanity, treaty, agreement, tense, taught, tight, niggardly, parsimonious, compressed.

(ANT.) slack, open, loose, relaxed, unconfined, unfretted, sprawling, lax.

companion *(SYN.)* attendant, comrade, consort, friend, colleague, partner, crony, mate, associate.

(ANT.) stranger, enemy, adversary.

companionship *(SYN.)* familiarity, cognizance, acquaintance, fellowship.

(ANT.) unfamiliarity, inexperience, ignorance.

company *(SYN.)* crew, group, band, party, throng, house, assemblage, troop, fellowship, association, business, concern, partnership, companionship, firm.

(ANT.) seclusion, individual, solitude, dispersion.

comparable *(SYN.)* allied, analogous, alike, akin, like, correlative, parallel.

(ANT.) opposed, incongruous, dissimilar, unalike, different, divergent.

compare *(SYN.)* discriminate, match, differentiate, contrast, oppose.

comparison *(SYN.)* likening, contrasting, judgment.

compartment *(SYN.)* division, section.

compassion *(SYN.)* mercy, sympathy, pity, commiseration, condolence.

(ANT.) ruthlessness, hardness, brutality, inhumanity, cruelty.

compassionate *(SYN.)* sympathizing, benign, forbearing, good, tender, affable, humane, indulgent, kind, sympathetic, kindly.

(ANT.) inhuman, merciless, unkind, cold-hearted, unsympathetic, cruel.

compatible *(SYN.)* consistent, agreeing, conforming, accordant, congruous, harmonious, cooperative, agreeable, constant, consonant, correspondent.

(ANT.) discrepant, paradoxical, disagreeable, contradictory.

compel *(SYN.)* drive, enforce, coerce, constrain, force, oblige, impel.

(ANT.) induce, coax, prevent, wheedle, persuade, cajole, convince.

compensate *(SYN.)* remunerate, repay, reimburse, recompense, balance.

compensation *(SYN.)* fee, earnings, pay, payment, recompense, allowance, remuneration, remittance, settlement, stipend, repayment, salary, wages.

(ANT.) present, gratuity, gift.

compete *(SYN.)* rival, contest, oppose, vie.

(ANT.) reconcile, accord.

00

competence (SYN.) skill, ability, capability.

competent (SYN.) efficient, clever, capable, able, apt, proficient, skillful, fitted, qualified.
(ANT.) inept, incapable, unfitted, awkward, incompetent, inadequate.

competition (SYN.) contest, match, rivalry, tournament.

competitor (SYN.) rival, contestant, opponent.
(ANT.) ally, friend, colleague.

complain (SYN.) lament, murmur, protest, grouch, grumble, regret, moan, remonstrate, whine, repine.
(ANT.) rejoice, praise, applaud, approve.

complaint (SYN.) protest, objection, grievance.

complement (SYN.) supplement, complete.
(ANT.) clash, conflict.

complete (SYN.) consummate, entire, ended, full, thorough, finished, full, whole, concluded, over, done, terminate, total, undivided.
(ANT.) unfinished, imperfect, incomplete, start, partial, failure, defeat.

complex (SYN.) sophisticated, compound, intricate, involved, perplexing, elaborate, complicated.
(ANT.) basic, simple, rudimentary, uncompounded, uncomplicated, plain.

complexion (SYN.) paint, pigment hue, color, dye, stain, tincture, tinge, tint, shade.
(ANT.) paleness, transparency, achromatism.

compliant (SYN.) meek, modest, lowly, plain, submissive, simple, unostentatious, unassuming, unpretentious.
(ANT.) proud, vain, arrogant, haughty, boastful.

complicated (SYN.) intricate, involved, complex, compound, perplexing.
(ANT.) simple, plain, uncompounded.

compliment (SYN.) eulogy, flattery, praise, admiration, honor, adulation, flatter, commendation, tribute.
(ANT.) taunt, affront, aspersion, insult, disparage, criticism.

complimentary (SYN.) gratis, free.

comply (SYN.) assent, consent, accede, acquiesce, coincide, conform, concur, tally.
(ANT.) differ, dissent, protest, disagree.

component (SYN.) division, fragment, allotment, moiety, apportionment, scrap, portion, section, share, segment, ingredient, organ.
(ANT.) whole, entirety.

comport (SYN.) carry, conduct, behave, act, deport, interact, operate, manage.

compose (SYN.) forge, fashion, mold, make, construct, create, produce, shape, form, constitute, arrange, organize, make up, write, invent, devise, frame.
(ANT.) misshape, dismantle, disfigure, destroy.

composer (SYN.) author, inventor, creator, maker, originator.

composition (SYN.) paper, theme, work, essay, compound, mixture, mix.

composure (SYN.) calmness, poise, control, self-control, self-possession.
(ANT.) anger, rage, turbulence, agitation.

compound (SYN.) blend, confound, jumble, consort, aggregate, complicated.
(ANT.) segregate, separate, divide, simple, sort.

comprehension (SYN.) insight, perception, understanding, awareness.
(ANT.) misconception, insensibility.

compress (SYN.) press, compact, squeeze, pack, crowd.
(ANT.) spread, stretch, expand.

compulsion (SYN.) might,

energy, potency, strength.
(ANT.) persuasion, impotence, frailty.

compulsory (SYN.) required, obligatory, necessary.
(ANT.) elective, optional, free, unrestricted.

compute (SYN.) count, calculate, determine, figure.
(ANT.) conjecture, guess, miscalculate.

comrade (SYN.) attendant, companion, colleague.
(ANT.) stranger, enemy.

con (SYN.) cheat, bamboozle, trick, swindle.

conceal (SYN.) disguise, cover, hide, mask, screen, secrete, veil, withhold.
(ANT.) reveal, show, disclose.

concede (SYN.) permit, suffer, tolerate, grant, give, admit, acknowledge, allow, yield.
(ANT.) forbid, contradict, protest, refuse, deny, negate.

conceit (SYN.) pride, vanity, complacency, conception.
(ANT.) humility, meekness, humbleness, modesty.

conceited (SYN.) proud, arrogant, vain, smug.
(ANT.) humble, modest, self-effacing.

conceive (SYN.) design, create, imagine, understand, devise, concoct, perceive, frame, grasp, invent.
(ANT.) imitate, reproduce.

concentrate (SYN.) localize, focus, condense, ponder, meditate, center, scrutinize.
(ANT.) scatter, diffuse, dissipate, disperse.

concept (SYN.) fancy, conception, image, notion, idea, sentiment, thought.
(ANT.) thing, matter, substance, entity.

conception (SYN.) consideration, deliberation, fancy.

concession (SYN.) admission, yielding, granting.
(ANT.) insistence, demand.

concise (SYN.) pity, neat, brief, compact, succinct.
(ANT.) wordy, lengthy, verbose, prolix.

conclude (SYN.) decide,

achieve, close, complete, end, finish, terminate, arrange, determine, settle.
(ANT.) start, begin.

conclusion (SYN.) end, finale, termination, deduction, close, settlement, decision.
(ANT.) commencement, inception, opening, start.

concord (SYN.) agreement, unison, understanding, accordance, stipulation.
(ANT.) disagreement, discord, dissension.

concrete (SYN.) solid, firm, precise, definite, specific.
(ANT.) undetermined, vague, general.

concur (SYN.) agree, assent, consent, accede.
(ANT.) dissent, protest, differ.

condemn (SYN.) denounce, reproach, blame, upbraid.
(ANT.) condone, forgive, absolve, praise.

condense (SYN.) shorten, reduce, abridge, abbreviate, concentrate, digest.
(ANT.) enlarge, increase, swell, expand.

condition (SYN.) circumstance, state, situation, case, plight, requirement.

conduct (SYN.) control, deportment, supervise, manage, behavior, deed, actions.

confess (SYN.) avow, acknowledge, admit, concede.
(ANT.) disown, renounce, deny, conceal.

confidence (SYN.) firmness, self-reliance, assurance, faith, trust, pledge, declaration, self-confidence, reliance, self-assurance.
(ANT.) distrust, shyness, mistrust, bashfulness.

confident (SYN.) certain, sure, dauntless, self-assured.
(ANT.) uncertain, timid, shy.

confine (SYN.) enclose, restrict, hinder, fence, limit.
(ANT.) release, expose, free, expand, open.

confirm acknowledge, establish, settle, substantiate, approve, fix, verify, assure.
(ANT.) disclaim, deny.

confirmation (SYN.) demonstration, experiment, test, trail, verification.
(ANT.) fallacy, invalidity.

conflict (SYN.) duel, combat, fight, collision, discord, encounter, interference, inconsistency, contention.
(ANT.) consonance, harmony, amity.

confiscate (SYN.) capture, catch, gain, purloin, steal.

conflagration (SYN.) flame, glow, heat, warmth, fervor.
(ANT.) apathy, cold, quiescence.

conform (SYN.) adapt, comply, yield, submit, obey, adjust, agree, fit, suit.
(ANT.) misapply, misfit, rebel, vary, disagree, disturb.

conformity (SYN.) congruence, accord, agreement.

confound (SYN.) confuse, baffle, perplex, puzzle.

confront (SYN.) confront, defy, hinder, resist, thwart.
(ANT.) submit, agree, support.

confuse (SYN.) confound, perplex, mystify, dumbfound, baffle, puzzle.
(ANT.) explain, instruct, edify, illumine, enlighten.

congregate (SYN.) gather, foregather, meet, convene.
(ANT.) scatter, dispel, disperse, dissipate.

congress (SYN.) parliament, legislature, assembly.

conjecture (SYN.) law, supposition, theory.
(ANT.) proof, fact, certainty.

conjunction (SYN.) combination, junction, connection.
(ANT.) separation, disconnection, diversion.

connect (SYN.) adjoin, link, combine, relate, join, attach, unite, associate, attribute.
(ANT.) detach, separate, disjoin, untie, dissociation.

conquest (SYN.) triumph, victory, achievement.
(ANT.) surrender, failure.

conscientious (SYN.) upright, straight, honest.
(ANT.) careless, irresponsible.

consecrated (SYN.) holy, divine, devout, spiritual.
(ANT.) evil, worldly, secular.

consent (SYN.) permission, leave, agree, let, assent, agreement, license, permit.
(ANT.) refusal, opposition, denial, dissent, prohibition.

consequence (SYN.) outcome, issue, result, effect, significance, importance.
(ANT.) impetus, cause.

consequential (SYN.) significant, important, weighty.
(ANT.) trivial, unimportant, minor, insignificant.

conservative (SYN.) conventional, reactionary, cautious, moderate, careful.
(ANT.) radical, liberal, rash, foolhardy, reckless.

consider (SYN.) heed, ponder, contemplate, examine, study, weigh, reflect, think.
(ANT.) ignore, overlook, disdain, disregard, neglect.

considerate (SYN.) careful, considerate, heedful, prudent, kind, thoughtful, polite, introspective, reflective.
(ANT.) thoughtless, heedless, inconsiderate, selfish, rash.

consistent (SYN.) conforming, accordant, compatible.
(ANT.) paradoxical, discrepant, contrary, antagonistic, opposed, eccentric, incon

consolation (SYN.) enjoyment, sympathy, relief, ease, contentment, comfort.
(ANT.) discomfort, suffering, discouragement, torture.

console (SYN.) solace, comfort, sympathize with.
(ANT.) worry, annoy, upset, disturb, distress.

consolidate (SYN.) blend, combine, conjoin, fuse, mix, merge, unite.
(ANT.) decompose, separate, analyze, disintegrate.

conspicuous (SYN.) distinguished, clear, manifest.
(ANT.) hidden, obscure, neutral, common.

conspire (SYN.) plan, intrigue, plot, scheme.

constancy (SYN.) devotion, faithfulness, accuracy, pre

cision, exactness.
(ANT.) faithlessness, treachery, perfidy.

constant (SYN.) continual, invariable, abiding, permanent, faithful, invariant, true, ceaseless, enduring.
(ANT.) fickle, irregular, wavering, off-and-on, infrequent, occasional.

constantly (SYN.) eternally, ever, evermore, forever.
(ANT.) rarely, sometimes, never, occasionally.

consternation (SYN.) apprehension, dismay, alarm.
(ANT.) bravery, courage, boldness, assurance.

constitute (SYN.) compose, found, form, establish, organize, create, appoint, delegate, authorize.

constitution (SYN.) law, code, physique, health, vitality.

constrain (SYN.) necessity, indigence, need, want.
(ANT.) luxury, freedom, uncertainty.

construct (SYN.) build, form, erect, make, fabricate, raise.
(ANT.) raze, demolish.

constructive (SYN.) useful, helpful, valuable.
(ANT.) ruinous, destructive.

construe (SYN.) explain, interpret, solve, render.
(ANT.) distort, confuse, misconstrue.

consult (SYN.) discuss, chatter, discourse, gossip, confer, report, rumor, deliberate, speech, talk.
(ANT.) writing, correspondence, silence.

consume (SYN.) engulf, absorb, use up, use, expend, exhaust, devour, devastate.
(ANT.) emit, expel, exude, discharge.

contagious (SYN.) infectious, virulent, communicable.
(ANT.) noncommunicable, healthful, hygienic.

contain (SYN.) embody, hold, embrace, include, accommodate, repress, restrain.
(ANT.) emit, encourage, yield, discharge.

contaminate (SYN.) corrupt, sully, taint, defile, soil, pollute, dirty, infect, poison.
(ANT.) purify.

contemplative (SYN.) simultaneous, meditative.
(ANT.) inattentive, indifferent, thoughtless.

contempt (SYN.) detestation, malice, contumely, disdain.
(ANT.) respect, reverence, admiration, esteem, awe.

contemptible (SYN.) base, mean, vile, vulgar, nasty, low, detestable, selfish.
(ANT.) generous, honorable, noble, exalted, admirable.

contend (SYN.) dispute, combat, contest, assert, claim, argue, maintain.

content (SYN.) pleased, happy, contented, satisfied.
(ANT.) restless, dissatisfied, discontented.

contented (SYN.) delighted, fortunate, gay, happy, joyous, lucky, merry.
(ANT.) gloomy, blue.

contention (SYN.) combat, duel, struggle, discord.
(ANT.) concord, harmony, amity, consonance.

contentment (SYN.) delight, happiness, gladness, pleasure, satisfaction.
(ANT.) misery, sorrow, grief, sadness, despair.

contest (SYN.) dispute, debate, competition.
(ANT.) allow, concede, agree.

continence (SYN.) forbearance, temperance.
(ANT.) self-indulgence, excess, intoxication.

contingency (SYN.) likelihood, possibility, occasion.

continue (SYN.) proceed, extend, endure, persist, resume, renew, recommence.
(ANT.) check, cease, discontinue, stop, suspend.

continuous (SYN.) continuing, uninterrupted, ceaseless, unceasing, incessant.
(ANT.) intermittent, irregular, sporadic.

contract (SYN.) condense, diminish, reduce, bargain.

(ANT.) lengthen, extend, swell, expand, elongate.

contradict *(SYN.)* gainsay, counter, oppose, confute, dispute.
(ANT.) verify, confirm, agree, support.

contradictory *(SYN.)* inconsistent, conflicting, incompatible, paradoxical, unsteady.
(ANT.) congruous, consistent, correspondent.

contribute *(SYN.)* grant, give, donate, bestow, provide, offer.
(ANT.) deny, withhold.

contrition *(SYN.)* grief, regret, self-reproach.
(ANT.) self-satisfaction, complacency.

control *(SYN.)* govern, regulate, rule, command, dominate, direct, manage.
(ANT.) ignore, forsake, follow, submit, abandon.

controversy *(SYN.)* disagreement, dispute, debate.
(ANT.) agreement, harmony, accord, concord, decision.

convenience *(SYN.)* accessibility, aid, benefit, help, service, availability.
(ANT.) inconvenience.

conventional *(SYN.)* common, regular, usual, everyday, habitual, routine.
(ANT.) exotic, unusual, bizarre, extraordinary.

conversation *(SYN.)* colloquy, dialogue, chat, parley.

converse *(SYN.)* jabber, talk, argue, comment, harangue, plead, rant, spout, discuss, chat, talk, speak, reason.

conversion *(SYN.)* alteration, change, mutation, modification, metamorphosis.

convert *(SYN.)* change, alter, alter, turn, transform, shift, modify, exchange, win over.
(ANT.) establish, stabilize, settle, retain.

convey *(SYN.)* carry, bear, communicate, transport, transmit, support, sustain.
(ANT.) drop, abandon.

conveyance *(SYN.)* van, car, train, truck, plane.

conviction *(SYN.)* opinion, position, view, faith, belief, confidence, feeling.
(ANT.) doubt, heresy, incredulity, denial.

convince *(SYN.)* persuade, assure, exhort, induce.
(ANT.) deter, compel, restrain, dissuade.

convivial *(SYN.)* jolly, social, jovial, gregarious.
(ANT.) solemn, stern, unsociable.

convoy *(SYN.)* with, attend, chaperone.
(ANT.) avoid, desert, quit, leave.

cooperate *(SYN.)* unite, combine, help, contribute.

coordinate *(SYN.)* attune, harmonize, adapt, match.

copious *(SYN.)* ample, abundant, bountiful, overflowing, plentiful, profuse, rich.
(ANT.) scant, scarce, insufficient, meager, deficient.

cordial *(SYN.)* polite, friendly, affable, genial, earnest, gracious, warm, ardent, warmhearted, hearty, sincere.
(ANT.) unfriendly, cool, aloof, hostile, ill-tempered.

core *(SYN.)* midpoint, heart, kernel, center, middle.
(ANT.) outskirts, border, surface, outside, boundary, rim.

corpse *(SYN.)* cadaver, carcass, remains, body, form.
(ANT.) spirit, soul, mind.

corpulent *(SYN.)* obese, portly, chubby, stout.
(ANT.) slim, thin, slender, lean, gaunt.

correct *(SYN.)* true, set right, faultless, impeccable, proper, accurate, precise.
(ANT.) condone, aggravate, false, inaccurate, wrong, untrue, faulty.

correction *(SYN.)* order, improvement, regulation, instruction, amendment.
(ANT.) turbulence, chaos.

correspond *(SYN.)* compare, match, agree, suit, fit, write.
(ANT.) differ, diverge, vary.

corridor *(SYN.)* hallway, hall,

foyer, passage, lobby.

corrode *(SYN.)* erode.

corrupted *(SYN.)* crooked, dishonest, impure, spoiled.

cost *(SYN.)* price, value, damage, charge, loss, sacrifice, penalty, worth.

couch *(SYN.)* davenport, sofa.

counsel *(SYN.)* guidance, attorney, lawyer, counselor, hint, imply, opinion, advice. *(ANT.)* declare, dictate, insist.

countenance *(SYN.)* visage, face, aspect, support, appearance, approval. *(ANT.)* forbid, prohibit.

counterfeit *(SYN.)* false, fraudulent, pretended, pretend, sham, imitate, forgery. *(ANT.)* authentic, natural, real, genuine, true.

couple *(SYN.)* team, pair, accompany, associate, attach. *(ANT.)* detach, separate, disjoin, disconnect.

courage *(SYN.)* fearlessness, boldness, chivalry, fortitude, mettle, spirit, daring. *(ANT.)* fear, timidity.

course *(SYN.)* passage, advance, path, road, progress.

courteous *(SYN.)* civil, respectful, polite, genteel, well-mannered, gracious. *(ANT.)* discourteous, rude, uncivil, impolite, boorish.

courtesy *(SYN.)* graciousness, politeness, respect. *(ANT.)* discourtesy, rudeness.

covenant *(SYN.)* agreement, concord, harmony, unison. *(ANT.)* variance, discord, dissension, difference.

cover *(SYN.)* clothe, conceal, disguise, curtain, guard, envelop, mask, cloak, shield, hide, screen, protect. *(ANT.)* bare, expose, reveal.

covert *(SYN.)* potential, undeveloped, concealed. *(ANT.)* visible, manifest.

covetous *(SYN.)* grasping, greedy, acquisitive. *(ANT.)* generous.

cowardice *(SYN.)* dread, dismay, fright, dismay, panic, terror, timidity. *(ANT.)* courage, bravery.

crack *(SYN.)* snap, break.

cracker *(SYN.)* wafer, biscuit.

craggy *(SYN.)* rough, rugged, irregular, uneven. *(ANT.)* level, sleek, smooth, fine, polished.

crank *(SYN.)* cross, irritable, bad-tempered, testy. *(ANT.)* cheerful, happy.

crash *(SYN.)* smash, shatter.

craving *(SYN.)* relish appetite, desire, liking, longing. *(ANT.)* renunciation, distaste, disgust.

create *(SYN.)* fashion, form, generate, engender, formulate, make, originate. *(ANT.)* disband, abolish, terminate, destroy, demolish.

credit *(SYN.)* believe, accept, belief, trust, faith, merit. *(ANT.)* doubt, reject, question, distrust.

credulous *(SYN.)* trusting, naive, believing, gullible. *(ANT.)* suspicious.

creed *(SYN.)* belief, precept, credo, faith, teaching. *(ANT.)* practice, deed, conduct, performance.

criminal *(SYN.)* unlawful, crook, gangster, outlaw, illegal, convict, delinquent.

crisis *(SYN.)* conjuncture, emergency, pass, pinch, acme, climax, contingency. *(ANT.)* calm, normality, stability, equilibrium.

crisp *(SYN.)* crumbling, delicate, frail, brittle. *(ANT.)* calm, normality.

criterion *(SYN.)* measure, law, rule, principle, gauge, proof. *(ANT.)* fancy guess, chance, supposition.

critic *(SYN.)* reviewer, judge, commentator, censor, defamer, slanderer.

critical *(SYN.)* exact, fastidious, caviling, faultfinding, accurate, condemning. *(ANT.)* shallow, uncritical, approving, insignificant, trivial.

criticize *(SYN.)* examine, analyze, inspect, blame, censure, appraise, evaluate. *(ANT.)* neglect, overlook, approve.

critique *(SYN.)* criticism, inspection, review.

cross *(SYN.)* mix, mingle, traverse, interbreed, annoyed, irritable, cranky, testy, angry, mean.
(ANT.) cheerful.

crude *(SYN.)* rude, graceless, unpolished, green, harsh, rough, coarse, ill-prepared.
(ANT.) finished, refined, polished, cultured, genteel.

cruel *(SYN.)* ferocious, mean, heartless, unmerciful.
(ANT.) humane, forbearing, kind, compassionate.

crumb *(SYN.)* jot, grain, mite, particle, shred.
(ANT.) mass, bulk, quantity.

crunch *(SYN.)* champ, gnaw, nibble, pierce.

crush *(SYN.)* smash, break.

cryptic *(SYN.)* puzzling, mysterious, enigmatic, secret, vague, obscure, occult.

cull *(SYN.)* elect, choose, pick.
(ANT.) reject, refuse.

culpable *(SYN.)* guilty.
(ANT.) innocent.

culprit *(SYN.)* delinquent, felon, offender.

culture *(SYN.)* humanism, upbringing, cultivation, breeding, education, learning.
(ANT.) illiteracy, vulgarity, ignorance.

cumbersome *(SYN.)* bulky, clumsy, awkward.
(ANT.) handy.

cunning *(SYN.)* clever, wily, crafty, foxy, skillful, tricky, ingenious, foxiness, ability.
(ANT.) gullible, honest, naive, openness, straightforward.

cure *(SYN.)* help, treatment, heal, medicine, restorative.

curious *(SYN.)* interrogative, interested, peculiar, queer, nosy, peeping, prying.
(ANT.) unconcerned, incurious, ordinary, indifferent.

current *(SYN.)* up-to-date, contemporary, present.
(ANT.) antiquated, old, bygone, ancient, past.

curse *(SYN.)* ban, oath, denounce, swear, condemn.
(ANT.) boon, blessing.

dab *(SYN.)* coat, pat, smear.

dabble *(SYN.)* splatter, toy, splash, fiddle, putter.

daft *(SYN.)* crazy, foolish.

daily *(SYN.)* every day, diurnal, regularly.

dainty *(SYN.)* slender, pleasing, delicate, frail, pleasant.
(ANT.) uncouth, vulgar, coarse, tough.

damage *(SYN.)* spoil, deface, impair, mar, hurt, injury.
(ANT.) repair, benefit, mend, rebuild, improve, ameliorate.

dame *(SYN.)* woman, lady.

damp *(SYN.)* humid, dank, moisture, wetness.
(ANT.) arid, dry.

dandle *(SYN.)* jounce, joggle, bounce, jiggle, nestle.

dandy *(SYN.)* coxcomb, fop, swell, great, fine, wonderful.
(ANT.) rotten, terrible, awful, miserable, slob.

danger *(SYN.)* jeopardy, risk, threat, hazard, uncertainty.
(ANT.) safety, immunity, security, defense.

dappled *(SYN.)* spotted, flecked, brindled, variegated.
(ANT.) uniform, solid.

dare *(SYN.)* brave, call, question, defy, risk, challenge.

daring *(SYN.)* foolhardy, chivalrous, rash, fearless, courageous, intrepid, valiant, courage, bravery, brave.
(ANT.) timid, cowardice, timidity, cautious.

dark *(SYN.)* somber, obscure, gloomy, black, unilluminated, dim, evil, hidden, dismal, mournful.
(ANT.) lucid, light, happy, cheerful, illuminated.

darn *(SYN.)* repair, mend.

dash *(SYN.)* pound, thump, beat, smite, buffet, thrash, smash, break, scurry, run.
(ANT.) stroke, hearten, encourage, defend.

dastardly *(SYN.)* meanspirited, craven, cowardly, mean, rotten, villainous.
(ANT.) heroic, brave, highminded, courageous.

data *(SYN.)* information, statistics, proof, facts.

daub *(SYN.)* coat, grease, soil, scribble, cover, stain, smear.

daunt *(SYN.)* discourage, dishearten, intimidate.
(ANT.) enspirit, encourage.

dauntless *(SYN.)* fearless, brave, bold, courageous, intrepid, valiant.
(ANT.) fearful, timid.

dawn *(SYN.)* sunrise, start, outset, daybreak, origin.
(ANT.) dusk, sunset, nightfall, end, conclusion, finish.

daze *(SYN.)* perplex, stun, puzzle, bewilder, upset, confuse, ruffle, confusion.

dazzle *(SYN.)* surprise, stun, astonish, impress, bewilder.

dead *(SYN.)* departed, lifeless, deceased, insensible, inanimate, dull, defunct, gone.
(ANT.) animate, functioning, active, living, alive, stirring.

deaf *(SYN.)* stone-deaf, unhearing, unheeding, unaware, unheedful, stubborn.
(ANT.) aware, conscious.

deal *(SYN.)* act, treat, attend, cope, barter, trade, bargain, apportion, give, distribute.

dear *(SYN.)* valued, esteemed, expensive, beloved, costly, darling, high-priced, loved.
(ANT.) hateful, reasonable, inexpensive, cheap.

death *(SYN.)* decease, extinction, demise, passing.
(ANT.) life.

debase *(SYN.)* lower, degrade, alloy, adulterate, defile, abase, pervert, corrupt.
(ANT.) restore, improve, vitalize, enhance.

debate *(SYN.)* wrangle, discuss, plead, argue, discussion, contend, argument.
(ANT.) agreement, reject, accord, ignore, spurn.

debonair *(SYN.)* urbane, sophisticated, refined.

debris *(SYN.)* rubbish, litter, junk, wreckage, refuse, detritus, ruins, trash, residue.

debt *(SYN.)* amount due, liability, obligation.

decay *(SYN.)* decrease, spoil, ebb, decline, waste, disintegrate, wane, dwindle,

wither, rot, putrefy, die.
(ANT.) progress, rise, increase, grow, flourish.

deceit *(SYN.)* duplicity, cheat, fraud, chicanery, trick, cunning, deception, guile, beguilement, deceitfulness.
(ANT.) truthfulness, openness, forthrightness, honesty.

deceive *(SYN.)* cheat, defraud, hoodwink, mislead, swindle.

decent *(SYN.)* befitting, fit, suitable, becoming, respectable, adequate, seemly, fitting, tolerable, decorous.
(ANT.) vulgar, gross, improper, unsuitable, indecorous, indecent, coarse.

decide *(SYN.)* resolve, determine, terminate, conclude, close, settle, adjudicate.
(ANT.) waver, hesitate, vacillate, doubt, suspend.

decipher *(SYN.)* render, unravel, construe, solve.
(ANT.) misconstrue, distort, misinterpret, confuse.

decision *(SYN.)* resolution, determination, settlement.

decisive *(SYN.)* determined, firm, decided, unhesitating.

declare *(SYN.)* assert, promulate, affirm, tell, broadcast.
(ANT.) deny, withhold, conceal, suppress.

decline *(SYN.)* descend, decay, dwindle, refuse, incline.
(ANT.) accept, ascend, ameliorate, increase.

decorate *(SYN.)* trim, paint, deck, enrich, color, beautify.
(ANT.) uncover, mar, deface, defame, debase.

decrease *(SYN.)* lessen, wane, deduct, diminish, curtail.
(ANT.) expansion, increase, enlarge, expand, grow.

decree *(SYN.)* order, edict, statute, declaration.

decrepit *(SYN.)* feeble, puny, weakened, infirm, enfeebled, tumble-down.
(ANT.) strong, forceful, vigorous, energetic, lusty.

decry *(SYN.)* lower, belittle, derogate, minimize.
(ANT.) praise, commend, magnify, aggrandize.

dedicate *(SYN.)* sanctify, consecrate, hallow, devote.

dedicated *(SYN.)* disposed, true, affectionate, fond.
(ANT.) indisposed, detached, untrammeled, disinclined.

deduct *(SYN.)* lessen, shorten, abate, remove, eliminate, curtail, subtract.
(ANT.) grow, enlarge, add, increase, amplify, expand.

deep *(SYN.)* bottomless, low, unplumbed, acute, obscure, involved, absorbed.
(ANT.) shallow.

deface *(SYN.)* spoil, impair, damage, mar, hurt, scratch, mutilate, disfigure, injure.
(ANT.) mend, benefit, repair.

defamation *(SYN.)* invective, reproach, upbraiding, abuse, insult, outrage.
(ANT.) respect, approval, laudation, commendation.

default *(SYN.)* loss, omission, lack, failure, want.
(ANT.) victory, achievement, sufficiency, success.

defeat *(SYN.)* quell, vanquish, beat, overcome, overthrow, subdue, frustrate, spoil.
(ANT.) submit, retreat, cede, yield, surrender, capitulate.

defect *(SYN.)* shortcoming, fault, omission, blemish, imperfection, forsake, leave.
(ANT.) perfection, flawlessness, support, join.

defend *(SYN.)* screen, espouse, justify, protect, vindicate, fortify, assert, guard, safeguard, shield.
(ANT.) oppose, assault, submit, attack, deny.

defense *(SYN.)* resistance, protection, bulwark, fort, barricade, trench, rampart.

defer *(SYN.)* postpone, delay.
(ANT.) speed, hurry, expedite.

defiant *(SYN.)* rebellious, antagonistic, obstinate.
(ANT.) yielding, submissive.

deficient *(SYN.)* lacking, short, incomplete, defective, scanty, insufficient, inadequate.
(ANT.) enough, ample, sufficient, adequate.

defile *(SYN.)* pollute, march,

corrupt, dirty, file, debase.
(ANT.) purify.

define *(SYN.)* describe, fix, establish, label, designate, set, name, explain.

definite *(SYN.)* fixed, prescribed, certain, specific, exact, determined, distinct.
(ANT.) indefinite, confused, undetermined, equivocal.

definition *(SYN.)* sense, interpretation, meaning.

deft *(SYN.)* handy, adroit, clever, adept, dexterous, skillful, skilled.
(ANT.) inept, clumsy, maladroit, awkward.

defunct *(SYN.)* lifeless, dead, departed, expired, extinct, spiritless, inanimate.
(ANT.) living, stirring.

defy *(SYN.)* hinder, oppose, withstand, attack, resist, confront, challenge, flout.
(ANT.) yield, allow, relent, surrender, submit, accede.

degenerate *(SYN.)* dwindle, decline, weaken.
(ANT.) ascend, ameliorate, increase, appreciate.

degree *(SYN.)* grade, amount, step, measure, rank, honor.

deign *(SYN.)* condescend.

dejected *(SYN.)* depressed, downcast, sad, disheartened, blue, discouraged.
(ANT.) cheerful, happy.

delectable *(SYN.)* tasty, delicious, savory, delightful.
(ANT.) unsavory, distasteful, unpalatable, acrid.

delegate *(SYN.)* emissary, envoy, ambassador, representative, commission.

delete *(SYN.)* cancel, remove.
(ANT.) add.

deleterious *(SYN.)* evil, unwholesome, base, sinful, bad, wicked, immoral, destructive, injurious, hurtful.
(ANT.) moral, excellent, reputable, healthful, healthy, helpful, constructive, good.

deliberate *(SYN.)* studied, willful, intended, contemplated, premeditated, planned, methodical.
(ANT.) fortuitous, hasty, ac-

cidental.

delicate (SYN.) frail, critical, slender, dainty, pleasing, fastidious, exquisite, precarious, demanding, sensitive, savory, fragile, weak.
(ANT.) tough, strong, coarse, clumsy, hearty, hale, vulgar.

delicious (SYN.) tasty, luscious, delectable, sweet.
(ANT.) unsavory, distasteful, unpalatable, unpleasant.

delight (SYN.) joy, bliss, gladness, pleasure, ecstasy, happiness, rapture.
(ANT.) revolt, sorrow, annoyance, displeasure, disgust, displease, revulsion, misery.

delirious (SYN.) raving, mad, giddy, frantic, hysterical.

deliver (SYN.) impart, publish, rescue, commit, communicate, free, address, offer, save, give, liberate.
(ANT.) restrict, confine, capture, enslave, withhold.

deluge (SYN.) overflow, flood.

delusion (SYN.) mirage, fantasy, phantasm, vision, dream, illusion, phantom.
(ANT.) substance, actuality.

delve (SYN.) dig, look, search, scoop, explore, hunt.

demand (SYN.) claim, inquire, ask, need, require, obligation, requirement, ask for.
(ANT.) tender, give, present, waive, relinquish, offer.

demean (SYN.) comport, bear, operate, carry, act, manage.

demeanor (SYN.) manner, way, conduct, actions.

demented (SYN.) insane, crazy, mad, mental.

demolish (SYN.) ruin, devastate, ravage, annihilate, wreck, destroy, raze, exterminate, obliterate.
(ANT.) erect, make, save, construct, preserve, build.

demonstrate (SYN.) evince, show, prove, display, illustrate, describe, explain, manifest, exhibit.
(ANT.) hide, conceal.

demur (SYN.) waver, falter, delay, stutter, doubt, vacillate, hesitate, scruple.

(ANT.) proceed, decide, resolve, continue.

demure (SYN.) meek, shy, modest, diffident, retiring, bashful, coy.

den (SYN.) cave, lair, cavern.

denial (SYN.) disallowance, proscription, refusal.

denounce (SYN.) condemn, blame, reprove, reprehend, censure, reproach, upbraid.
(ANT.) condone, approve, forgive, commend, praise.

dense (SYN.) crowded, slow, close, obtuse, compact, dull, stupid, compressed, thick.
(ANT.) sparse, quick, dispersed, clever, dissipated, empty, smart, bright.

dent (SYN.) notch, impress, pit, nick.

deny (SYN.) refuse, withhold, dispute, disavow, forbid.
(ANT.) confirm, affirm, admit, confess, permit, allow, concede, assert.

depart (SYN.) quit, forsake, withdraw, renounce, desert, relinquish, die, perish.
(ANT.) tarry, remain, come, abide, stay, arrive.

depict (SYN.) explain, recount, describe, portray, characterize, relate, narrate.

deplore (SYN.) repine, lament, bemoan, wail, bewail, weep.

deport (SYN.) exile, eject, oust, banish, expel, dismiss, ostracize, dispel, exclude.
(ANT.) receive, admit, shelter, accept, harbor.

deposit (SYN.) place, put, bank, save, store, sediment, dregs, addition, entry.
(ANT.) withdraw, withdrawal.

depreciate (SYN.) dwindle, decrease, decay, belittle, disparage, weaken, minimize.
(ANT.) ascend, ameliorate, praise, increase, applaud.

depress (SYN.) deject, dishearten, sadden, dampen, devaluate, devalue, lessen, lower, cheapen, reduce, dispirit, discourage, sink.
(ANT.) exalt, cheer, exhilarate.

derision (SYN.) irony, satire, banter, raillery, sneering, gibe, ridicule.

derivation (SYN.) source, birth, inception, start, beginning, spring, commencement, foundation, origin.
(ANT.) issue, end, outcome, harvest, product.

descend (SYN.) wane, lower, move, slope, incline, decline, slant, sink.
(ANT.) increase, appreciate, ameliorate, ascend.

descendant (SYN.) child, issue, progeny, offspring.

describe (SYN.) portray, picture, recount, depict, relate, characterize, represent.

description (SYN.) history, record, recital, account, computation, chronicle.
(ANT.) misrepresentation, confusion, caricature.

desecration (SYN.) profanation, insult, defamation, reviling, abuse, maltreatment, aspersion, perversion.
(ANT.) respect, commendation, approval, laudation.

desert (SYN.) forsake, wilderness, resign, abjure, abandon, wasteland, waste, leave, surrender, abdicate, quit, barren, uninhabited.
(ANT.) uphold, defend, stay, maintain, accompany, join.

design (SYN.) drawing, purpose, outline, devise, intend, draw, contrive, draft, cunning, plan, artfulness, delineation, scheming, sketch.
(ANT.) candor, accident, result, chance.

designate (SYN.) manifest, indicate, show, specify, denote, reveal, name, appoint.
(ANT.) divert, mislead, conceal, falsify, distract.

desirable (SYN.) coveted, wanted.

desire (SYN.) longing, craving, yearning, appetite, lust, long for, crave, covet, want.
(ANT.) hate, aversion, loathing, abomination, detest.

desist (SYN.) cork, stop, cease, hinder, terminate, abstain, halt, interrupt, seal, arrest.
(ANT.) promote, begin, speed,

proceed, start.

desolate (SYN.) forlorn, waste, bare, lonely, abandoned, wild, deserted, uninhabited, empty, sad, miserable.
(ANT.) crowded, teeming, populous, happy, cheerful, fertile, attended.

despair (SYN.) discouragement, pessimism.
(ANT.) elation, optimism, hope, joy, confidence.

desperate (SYN.) reckless, determined, despairing, wild, daring, hopeless, despondent, audacious.
(ANT.) optimistic, composed, hopeful, collected, calm.

despicable (SYN.) vulgar, offensive, base, vile, contemptible, selfish, low, mean, worthless, nasty.
(ANT.) noble, exalted, admirable, generous, worthy, dignified.

despise (SYN.) hate, scorn, detest, loathe, disdain, abhor, condemn, dislike.
(ANT.) honor, love, approve, like, admire.

despoil (SYN.) plunder, rob.

despondent (SYN.) sad, dismal, depressed, somber, ejected, melancholy, doleful, sorrowful.
(ANT.) joyous, cheerful, merry, happy.

despot (SYN.) tyrant, ruler, oppressor, dictator.

despotic (SYN.) authoritative, unconditional, absolute, tyrannous, entire.
(ANT.) dependent, conditional, qualified.

destiny (SYN.) fate, portion, outcome, consequence, result, fortune, doom, lot.

destitute (SYN.) poor, penurious, needy, impecunious, impoverished, indigent.
(ANT.) opulent, wealthy, affluent, rich.

destroyed (SYN.) rent, smashed, interrupted, flattened, wrecked, broken.
(ANT.) whole, repaired, integral, united.

destruction (SYN.) ruin, de-

vastation, extinction.
(ANT.) beginning, creation.

detach (SYN.) deduct, remove, subtract, curtail, divide, shorten, decrease.
(ANT.) hitch, grow, enlarge, increase, connect, amplify, attack, expand.

detail (SYN.) elaborate, commission, part, itemize, portion, division, fragment, assign, circumstance.

detain (SYN.) impede, delay, hold back, retard, arrest, restrain, stay.
(ANT.) quicken, hasten, expedite, forward, precipitate.

detect (SYN.) discover, reveal, find, ascertain, determine, learn, originate, devise.
(ANT.) hide, screen, lose, cover, mask.

determinant (SYN.) reason, incentive, source, agent, principle, inducement.
(ANT.) result, effect, consequence, end.

determine (SYN.) decide, settle, end, conclude, ascertain, induce, fix, verify, resolve, establish.

detest (SYN.) loathe, hate, despise.
(ANT.) savor, appreciate, like, love.

detriment (SYN.) injury, disadvantage, damage.
(ANT.) benefit.

develop (SYN.) evolve, unfold, enlarge, amplify, expand, create, grow, reveal, unfold, mature, elaborate.
(ANT.) wither, contract, degenerate, stunt, deteriorate, compress.

development (SYN.) growth, expansion, progress, unraveling, elaboration, evolution, maturing, unfolding.
(ANT.) compression, abbreviation, curtailment.

deviate (SYN.) deflect, stray, divert, diverge, wander, sidetrack, digress.
(ANT.) preserve, follow, remain, continue, persist.

device (SYN.) tool, utensil, means, channel, machine,

agent, vehicle, gadget, apparatus, tools, instrument.
(ANT.) preventive, impediment, obstruction.

devise (SYN.) create, concoct, invent, originate.

devote (SYN.) assign, dedicate, give, apply.
(ANT.) withhold, relinquish, ignore, withdraw.

devotion (SYN.) piety, zeal, ardor, loyalty, dedication, religiousness, consecration.
(ANT.) unfaithfulness, aversion, alienation, indifference.

devour (SYN.) consume, gulp, gorge, waste, eat, ruin.

devout (SYN.) sacred, religious, spiritual, holy, theological, pietistic, pious.
(ANT.) profane, skeptical, atheistic, secular, impious.

dexterity (SYN.) talent, capability, qualification, aptness, skill, ability.
(ANT.) unreadiness, incapacity, disability.

dexterous (SYN.) clever, adroit, handy, deft, facile, skillful, skilled, proficient.
(ANT.) awkward, clumsy.

dialect (SYN.) slang, jargon, cant, speech, idiom, tongue, diction, vernacular.
(ANT.) nonsense, drivel, babble, gibberish.

dialogue (SYN.) interview, chat, discussion, conference, exchange, talk.

diary (SYN.) memo, account, journal, words.

dicker (SYN.) haggle, bargain, negotiate.

dictate (SYN.) deliver, speak, record, command, order.

dictator (SYN.) oppressor, tyrant, despot, persecutor, overlord, autocrat.

die (SYN.) fade, wane, cease, depart, wither, decay, decline, sink, expire, perish.
(ANT.) live, begin, grow, survive, flourish.

difference (SYN.) inequality, variety, disparity, discord, distinction, dissension.
(ANT.) harmony, similarity, identity, agreement, likeness,

compatibility, kinship.

different *(SYN.)* unlike, various, distinct, miscellaneous, divergent, sundry, contrary, differing, diverse, variant. *(ANT.)* similar, congruous, same, alike, identical.

differentiate *(SYN.)* separate, discriminate, distinguish, perceive, detect, recognize. *(ANT.)* confuse, omit, mingle, confound, overlook.

diffuse *(SYN.)* spread, sparse, scattered, scanty, dispersed. *(ANT.)* concentrated.

dig *(SYN.)* burrow, excavate, appreciate, understand.

digest *(SYN.)* consume, eat, reflect on, study, shorten.

dignified *(SYN.)* serious, solemn, noble, stately.

dignify *(SYN.)* honor, elevate. *(ANT.)* shame, degrade, humiliate.

dignity *(SYN.)* stateliness, distinction, bearing.

digress *(SYN.)* divert, wander, bend, stray, deflect. *(ANT.)* preserve, continue, remain, follow, persist.

dilate *(SYN.)* increase, widen, amplify, enlarge, augment. *(ANT.)* shrink, contract, restrict, abridge.

dilemma *(SYN.)* fix, strait, condition, scrape, difficulty. *(ANT.)* ease, calmness, satisfaction, comfort.

diligent *(SYN.)* patient, busy, hard-working, active, perseverant, assiduous. *(ANT.)* unconcerned, indifferent, apathetic, lethargic.

dim *(SYN.)* pale, shadowy, faint, faded, unclear, vague, darken, dull, indistinct. *(ANT.)* brighten, brilliant, bright, illuminate, glaring.

dimension *(SYN.)* size, importance, measure, extent.

diminish *(SYN.)* suppress, lower, decrease, shrink, wane, abate, reduce, lessen. *(ANT.)* enlarge, revive, amplify, increase.

diminutive *(SYN.)* small, wee, tiny, little, minute. *(ANT.)* large, big, great, gigantic, huge.

din *(SYN.)* tumult, clamor, sound, babble, outcry, row. *(ANT.)* quiet, stillness, hush.

dine *(SYN.)* lunch, eat, sup, feed.

dingy *(SYN.)* dull, dark, dismal, dirty, drab, murky. *(ANT.)* cheerful, bright.

dip *(SYN.)* immerse, plunge, submerge, wet, swim.

diplomacy *(SYN.)* knack, dexterity, skill, address, poise, tact, finesse. *(ANT.)* vulgarity, blunder, awkwardness, incompetence.

diplomatic *(SYN.)* politic, adroit, tactful, discreet. *(ANT.)* rude, churlish, gruff, boorish, impolite, coarse.

dire *(SYN.)* horrible, terrible, appalling, fearful, harrowing, grievous, ghastly, awful. *(ANT.)* lovely, enchanting, fascinating, beautiful.

direct *(SYN.)* rule, manage, bid, order, level, command, conduct, regulate, point. *(ANT.)* swerving, untruthful, misguide, distract, indirect.

direction *(SYN.)* way, order, course, instruction, tendency, management, route, trend, guidance.

dirt *(SYN.)* pollution, soil, filthiness, filth. *(ANT.)* cleanliness, cleanness.

disability *(SYN.)* inability, weakness, handicap, incapacity, injury, unfitness, incompetence, impotence. *(ANT.)* power, ability, strength, capability.

disadvantage *(SYN.)* drawback, hindrance, handicap, inconvenience, obstacle. *(ANT.)* advantage, benefit, convenience.

disagree *(SYN.)* quarrel, dispute, differ, conflict. *(ANT.)* agree.

disappear *(SYN.)* end, fade out, vanish. *(ANT.)* emerge, appear.

disappoint *(SYN.)* fail, displease, mislead, dissatisfy. *(ANT.)* please, satisfy, gratify.

disapprove *(SYN.)* object to,

disfavor, oppose.
(ANT.) approve.

disarm (SYN.) paralyze, demilitarize.

disaster (SYN.) casualty, mishap, misfortune, catastrophe, accident, adversity.
(ANT.) fortune, advantage.

disavow (SYN.) reject, revoke, disclaim, retract, disown.
(ANT.) recognize.

disband (SYN.) scatter, split, dismiss, separate.

disbelief (SYN.) doubt, incredulity, skepticism.
(ANT.) certainty, credulity.

discard (SYN.) scrap, reject.

discern (SYN.) distinguish, see, descry, separate, differentiate, perceive.
(ANT.) omit, confuse, overlook, mingle, confound.

discernment (SYN.) perception, sharpness, intelligence, perspicacity, acuity.
(ANT.) dullness, stupidity.

discharge (SYN.) remove, relieve, dismiss, banish, unburden, shoot, fire, explosion, eject, detonation.
(ANT.) retain, employ, enlist, hire, accept, recall, detain.

disciple (SYN.) learner, follower, student, adherent, supporter, scholar, pupil.
(ANT.) guide, leader.

discipline (SYN.) training, order, instruction, drill, restraint, regulation.
(ANT.) carelessness, sloppiness, confusion, negligence, messiness, chaos, turbulence.

disclaim (SYN.) retract, reject, deny, renounce, disavow.
(ANT.) recognize.

disclose (SYN.) show, divulge, betray, uncover, discover, reveal, expose.
(ANT.) hide, cloak, mask, cover, obscure, conceal.

disconnect (SYN.) divide, separate, unhook.
(ANT.) connect, bind, attach, unify, engage.

disconsolate (SYN.) depressed, downcast, sorrowful, dejected, dismal, sad.
(ANT.) delightful, merry, glad,

cheerful, happy.

discontent (SYN.) displeased, disgruntled, unhappy, dissatisfied, vexed.

discontinue (SYN.) postpone, delay, adjourn, stay, stop, defer, suspend, end, cease.
(ANT.) prolong, persist, continue, start, begin, proceed.

discord (SYN.) disagreement, conflict.
(ANT.) concord, accord, agreement.

discourage (SYN.) hamper, obstruct, restrain, block, dishearten, retard, check, dispirit, thwart, depress.
(ANT.) expedite, inspire, encourage, promote, inspirit, assist, further.

discourteous (SYN.) gruff, rude, vulgar, blunt, impolite, saucy, uncivil.
(ANT.) stately, courtly, civil, dignified, genteel.

discover (SYN.) find out, invent, expose, ascertain, devise, reveal, learn, determine, detect.
(ANT.) hide, screen, cover, conceal, lose.

discredit (SYN.) disbelieve, dishonor, doubt, disgrace.

discreet (SYN.) politic, discriminating, judicious, adroit, prudent, cautious.
(ANT.) incautious, rude, coarse, boorish, tactless.

discrepant (SYN.) incompatible, wavering, contrary.
(ANT.) correspondent, compatible, consistent.

discriminating (SYN.) exact, particular, critical, accurate.
(ANT.) unimportant, shallow, insignificant, superficial.

discrimination (SYN.) perspicacity, discernment, racism, wisdom, bias, sagacity, intolerance, prejudice.
(ANT.) thoughtlessness, senselessness, arbitrariness.

discuss (SYN.) gossip, plead, discourse, blab, lecture, talk, chat, spout, mutter.

disease (SYN.) malady, disorder, ailment, illness, affliction, infirmity, complaint.

(ANT.) *soundness, health, vigor.*

disentangle (SYN.) unwind, untie, clear, unravel, unknot, unsnarl, untangle.

disfigured (SYN.) deformed, marred, defaced, scarred.

disgrace (SYN.) odium, chagrin, shame, mortification, embarrassment.
(ANT.) *renown, glory, respect, praise, dignity, honor.*

disgraceful (SYN.) ignominious, shameful, discreditable, disreputable, scandalous, dishonorable.
(ANT.) *renowned, esteemed, respectable, honorable.*

disguise (SYN.) excuse, simulation, pretension, hide.
(ANT.) *show, reality, actuality, display, reveal, sincerity, fact.*

disgust (SYN.) offend, repulse, nauseate, revolt.
(ANT.) *admiration, liking.*

disgusting (SYN.) repulsive, nauseating, revolting, nauseous, repugnant.

dish (SYN.) serve, container, give, receptacle.

dishonest (SYN.) crooked, impure, unsound, false, contaminated, venal, corrupt.
(ANT.) *upright, honest, straightforward.*

dishonor (SYN.) disrepute, scandal, indignity, chagrin, mortification, shame, obloquy, defamation.
(ANT.) *renown, glory, praise, honor, dignity.*

disinclined (SYN.) unwilling, reluctant, loath.

disingenuous (SYN.) tricky, deceitful, scheming, dishonest, underhanded.

disintegrate (SYN.) decompose, dwindle, spoil, decay, wane, ebb, decline, rot.
(ANT.) *increase, flourish, rise.*

disinterested (SYN.) unbiased, open-minded, neutral, impartial, unprejudiced.

dislike (SYN.) aversion, dread, reluctance, abhorrence.
(ANT.) *devotion, affection, enthusiasm, attachment.*

disloyal (SYN.) false, treasonable, apostate, unfaithful, recreant, treacherous.
(ANT.) *true, devoted, constant, loyal.*

dismal (SYN.) dark, lonesome, somber, bleak, dull, sad, doleful, sorrowful.
(ANT.) *lively, gay, happy, lighthearted, charming, cheerful.*

dismantle (SYN.) take apart, wreck, disassemble.

dismay (SYN.) disturb, bother, dishearten, horror, alarm, bewilder, frighten, scare.
(ANT.) *encourage, hearten.*

dismiss (SYN.) remove, discharge, discard, release.
(ANT.) *retain, detain, engage, hire, accept, recall.*

disobedient (SYN.) refractory, forward, unruly, insubordinate, defiant, rebellious.
(ANT.) *submissive, compliant, obedient.*

disobey (SYN.) invade, break, violate, infringe, defile.

disorder (SYN.) tumult, chaos, jumble, confusion.
(ANT.) *organization, neatness, system, order.*

disorganization (SYN.) jumble, confusion, muddle.
(ANT.) *system, order.*

disorganized (SYN.) muddled, confused, indistinct, bewildered, mixed.
(ANT.) *organized, lucid, clear.*

disown (SYN.) deny, renounce, reject, repudiate, forsake, disinherit.

disparaging (SYN.) belittling, deprecatory, discrediting.

disparage (SYN.) undervalue, depreciate, lower, belittle.
(ANT.) *exalting, praise, aggrandize, magnify.*

disparagement (SYN.) lowering, decrying, undervaluing, belittling, minimizing.
(ANT.) *praise, exalting, aggrandizement.*

dispassionate (SYN.) calm, cool, composed, controlled, unemotional.

dispatch (SYN.) throw, impel, transmit, emit, cast, finish, report, message, send, speed, achieve, conclude, communication.

(ANT.) reluctance, get, retain, bring, slowness, hold.

dispel *(SYN.)* disseminate, scatter, disperse, separate.

(ANT.) collect, accumulate, gather.

dispense *(SYN.)* deal, give, allot, assign, apportion, mete, distribute, grant, allocate.

(ANT.) refuse, withhold, confiscate, retain, keep.

disperse *(SYN.)* dissipate, scatter, disseminate, diffuse, separate, dispel.

(ANT.) collect, amass, gather, assemble, accumulate.

dispirited *(SYN.)* downhearted, unhappy, dejected, disheartened, sad.

(ANT.) cheerful, happy, optimistic.

displace *(SYN.)* remove, transport, lodge, shift.

(ANT.) retain, leave, stay.

display *(SYN.)* parade, exhibit, show, expose, reveal, demonstrate, showing.

(ANT.) hide, cover, conceal.

displeasure *(SYN.)* dislike, disapproval, dissatisfaction, distaste, discontentment.

disposal *(SYN.)* elimination, adjustment, removal, release, arrangement.

dispose *(SYN.)* settle, adjust.

disposition *(SYN.)* behavior, character, deed, deportment, action, manner, bearing, temperament, nature.

dispossess *(SYN.)* eject, expel, evict, oust, dislodge.

disprove *(SYN.)* refute, deny, invalidate, controvert.

dispute *(SYN.)* squabble, debate, argument, controversy, contention, disagreement, bicker, contest.

(ANT.) harmony, concord, agreement, allow, concur.

disregard *(SYN.)* slight, omit, ignore, inattention, oversight, skip, neglect.

(ANT.) regard, include.

disrepair *(SYN.)* ruin, decay, dilapidation, destruction.

disreputable *(SYN.)* dishonored, notorious, dis-

honorable, disgraced.

disrespectful *(SYN.)* fresh, impertinent, rude, impolite.

(ANT.) polite, respectful, courteous.

dissect *(SYN.)* examine, cut.

disseminate *(SYN.)* publish, circulate, spread, broadcast.

dissent *(SYN.)* objection, challenge, disagreement, protest, remonstrance, difference, nonconformity.

(ANT.) assent, acceptance, compliance, agreement.

dissertation *(SYN.)* thesis, treatise, disquisition.

dissimilar *(SYN.)* diverse, unlike, various, distinct, contrary, sundry, different.

(ANT.) same, alike, similar, congruous.

dissimulation *(SYN.)* pretense, deceit, sanctimony, hypocrisy, cant.

(ANT.) honesty, candor, openness, frankness, truth.

dissipate *(SYN.)* misuse, squander, dwindle, consume, waste, lavish.

(ANT.) save, conserve, preserve, accumulate.

dissolve *(SYN.)* liquefy, end, cease, melt, fade, disappear.

distant *(SYN.)* stiff, cold, removed, far, afar, unfriendly, remote, far-away, separated, aloof, reserved.

(ANT.) nigh, friendly, close, cordial, near.

distasteful *(SYN.)* disagreeable, unpleasant, objectionable.

distend *(SYN.)* swell, widen, magnify, expand, enlarge.

distinct *(SYN.)* plain, evident, lucid, visible, apparent, different, separate, individual, obvious, manifest, clear.

(ANT.) vague, indistinct, uncertain, obscure, ambiguous.

distinction *(SYN.)* importance, peculiarity, trait, honor, fame, characteristic, repute, quality, renown.

(ANT.) nature, substance, essence, being.

distinctive *(SYN.)* odd, exceptional, rare, individual, ec-

centric, special, strange.
(ANT.) ordinary, general, common, normal.
distinguish (SYN.) recognize, differentiate, divide, classify, descry, discern, separate, perceive, detect.
(ANT.) mingle, conjoin, blend, found, omit, confuse.
distinguished (SYN.) eminent, illustrious, renowned, celebrated, elevated, noted.
(ANT.) ordinary, common, unknown, undistinguished.
distort (SYN.) contort, falsify, twist, misrepresent.
distract (SYN.) occupy, bewilder, disturb, divert.
(ANT.) focus, concentrate.
distracted (SYN.) abstracted, preoccupied, absent.
(ANT.) attentive, attending, watchful, present.
distraction (SYN.) entertainment, confusion.
distress (SYN.) torment, misery, trouble, worry, pain, agony, torture, anguish, anxiety, disaster, wretchedness, peril, danger.
(ANT.) joy, solace, comfort, relief.
distribute (SYN.) deal, sort, allot, mete, classify, share, issue, dole, apportion, allocate, dispense, group.
district (SYN.) domain, place, territory, country, region.
distrust (SYN.) scruple, unbelief, suspect, mistrust.
(ANT.) faith, conviction, trust, belief, determination.
disturb (SYN.) perturb, vex, confuse, worry, agitate, derange, unsettle, perplex.
(ANT.) quiet, order, calm, settle, pacify, soothe.
disturbance (SYN.) disorder, commotion, confusion, riot, fight, brawl.
(ANT.) calm, tranquillity, serenity.
diverge (SYN.) fork, separate.
(ANT.) converge, join, merge.
diverse (SYN.) unlike, various, different, several.
divert (SYN.) detract, amuse, confuse, distract, deflect.

(ANT.) tire, bore, weary.
divide (SYN.) share, split, detach, cleave, apportion, sunder, part, distribute, allocate, disunite, estrange.
(ANT.) merge, unite, convene, join, gather, combine.
divine (SYN.) holy, supernatural, godlike, transcendent, celestial, heavenly.
(ANT.) mundane, wicked, blasphemous, profane.
division (SYN.) partition, separation, sharing, section, segment, part, portion.
(ANT.) union, agreement.
divorce (SYN.) disjoin, disconnect, separate, divide.
divulge (SYN.) discover, release, expose, show, betray, reveal, admit, disclose.
(ANT.) hide, conceal, cloak.
dizzy (SYN.) staggering unsteady, giddy, light-headed.
(ANT.) rational, clearheaded, unconfused.
do (SYN.) effect, conduct, perform, work, suffice, accomplish, finish, transact, serve, discharge, execute, complete, carry on, make, settle, conclude, fulfill.
docile (SYN.) pliant, tame, complaint, teachable, obedient, submissive, yielding.
(ANT.) unruly, obstinate, ungovernable, mulish.
doctor (SYN.) heal, treat, medic, remedy, cure.
doctrine (SYN.) tenet, precept, belief, dogma, teaching, principle, creed.
(ANT.) deed, practice, conduct, perform.
document (SYN.) report, minute, memorial, vestige, account, note, trace.
doing (SYN.) feat, performance, act, deed, action, accomplishment, transaction.
(ANT.) intention, inactivity, cessation, inhibition.
doleful (SYN.) dark, depressed, sad, dismal, sorrowful, unhappy, morose, lonesome, mournful.
(ANT.) gay, lively, cheerful, joyous.

domain (SYN.) place, division, region, territory, empire, realm, quarter, dominion, bailiwick, jurisdiction, land.

domestic (SYN.) family, tame, native, servant, homemade, household, internal.
(ANT.) alien, foreign, outside.

domesticate (SYN.) train, tame, housebreak, teach.

domicile (SYN.) dwelling, residence, home, abode.

dominate (SYN.) control, manage, rule, influence, subjugate, command, govern, direct, regulate.
(ANT.) follow, ignore, abandon, submit, forsake.

domination (SYN.) mastery, ascendancy, transcendence.

don (SYN.) wear, slip on.

donation (SYN.) gift, bequest, present, benefaction, grant, contribution, offering.
(ANT.) earnings, purchase, deprivation, loss.

done (SYN.) complete, concluded, finished terminated.

doom (SYN.) fortune, issue, result, destruction, destiny, consequence, fate, outcome, destine, ruin, death, lot.

doomed (SYN.) fated, predestined, foreordained.

dormant (SYN.) unemployed, inert, lazy, unoccupied, idle.
(ANT.) working, employed, occupied, active, industrious.

dose (SYN.) quantity, amount, portion.

dote (SYN.) indulge, treasure, coddle, pamper, spoil.
(ANT.) ignore.

double (SYN.) copy, fold, duplicate.

doubt (SYN.) distrust, incredulity, suspicion, hesitation, uncertainty, question, scruple, ambiguity, skepticism, suspect, mistrust, unbelief, suspense.
(ANT.) conviction, belief, determination, trust, certainty.

doubtful (SYN.) uncertain, unsettled, dubious, questionable, undetermined.

doubtless (SYN.) certainly,

undoubtedly, assuredly, positively, unquestionably.

dour (SYN.) gloomy, sulky, crabbed, morose, fretful.
(ANT.) joyous, pleasant, amiable, merry.

douse (SYN.) immerse, dip, dunk, extinguish.

dowdy (SYN.) messy, unkempt, untidy, sloppy, shabby, frowzy.

downcast (SYN.) sad, disheartened, unhappy, dejected, dispirited, discourage, depressed, glum.

dowry (SYN.) endowment, gift, settlement, talent.

drab (SYN.) flat, dull, lifeless, unattractive.

draft (SYN.) air, induction, wind, drawing, outline.

drag (SYN.) heave, pull, tug, crawl, draw, tarry, tow, haul, delay.

drain (SYN.) empty, deprive, dry, filter, spend, tap, exhaust, waste, sap, use.
(ANT.) fulfill, fill.

drama (SYN.) show, play, production, piece.

drape (SYN.) flow, cover, hang.

drastic (SYN.) severe, rough, extreme, violent, tough, intense.

draw (SYN.) tug, obtain, trace, lure, drag, attract, persuade, induce, haul, write, remove, extend, stretch, take out, allure, pull, prolong, extract, tow, draft, delineate, unsheathe, lure, depict, sketch.
(ANT.) shorten, contract, propel, alienate, drive.

dread (SYN.) awe, horror, fear, terror, alarm, reverence, apprehension.
(ANT.) courage, boldness, assurance, confidence.

dreadful (SYN.) dire, inspiring, ghastly, appalling, horrid, impressive, terrible.
(ANT.) fascinating, beautiful, enjoyable, enchanting, lovely.

dream (SYN.) fantasy, wish, hope, vision, daydream, reverie, imagine, fantasize.

dream up (SYN.) cook up,

create, think up, concost.

dreary (SYN.) dull, sad, bleak, lonesome, gloomy, chilling. (ANT.) lively, hopeful, gay, cheerful, bright, joyous.

drench (SYN.) wet, bathe, flood, soak, saturate.

dress (SYN.) garb, frock, gown, clothing, costume, apparel, attire, wardrobe, wear, don, robe, raiment. (ANT.) undress, strip, disrobe.

dribble (SYN.) fall, drip, leak, slaver, slobber.

drift (SYN.) roam, tendency, meander, sail, float, direction, wander, intention.

drifter (SYN.) hobo, tramp.

drill (SYN.) employment, lesson, task, use, activity, operation, training. (ANT.) relaxation, indolence, rest, idleness, repose.

drink (SYN.) gulp, swallow, imbibe, beverage.

drip (SYN.) dribble, drop.

drive (SYN.) impel, coerce, oblige, force, push, direct, constrain, journey, urge, enforce, trip, handle, ride.

droll (SYN.) laughable, funny, amusing, witty, comical. (ANT.) sober, sad, solemn, melancholy.

drone (SYN.) buzz, hum, loafer, idler, nonworker.

drool (SYN.) drivel, slaver, dribble, spit, gibber, jabber.

droop (SYN.) dangle, weaken, hang, sink, fail, settle, sag. (ANT.) stand, tower, extend, rise, straighten.

drop (SYN.) droop, dribble, topple, collapse, downward, drip, trickle, tumble, gob, slip, decrease, fall, dismiss. (ANT.) ascend, mount, steady, arise, soar.

drown (SYN.) sink, inundate, submerge, immerse.

drowsy (SYN.) dozing, torpid, soothing, dreamy, sleepy, comatose, lethargic. (ANT.) alert, awake, sharp, keen, acute.

drub (SYN.) wallop, thrash, beat, thump, cane, flog, rout, outclass, overcome.

drudgery (SYN.) toil, travail, effort, task, labor. (ANT.) recreation, indolence, leisure.

drug (SYN.) remedy, medicine, stupefy, anesthetize.

drunk (SYN.) tight, intoxicated, soused, drunken, inebriated, sozzled, tipsy.

dry (SYN.) thirsty, dehydrated, vapid, plain, arid, parched, barren, waterless, dull, desiccated, tiresome. (ANT.) fresh, wet, soaked, fascinating, attractive, lively.

dubious (SYN.) unsure, uncertain, undecided, hesitant, spurious, unreliable, puzzling, ambiguous. (ANT.) decided, fixed, irrefutable, definite, genuine, authentic, trustworthy.

due (SYN.) payable, unpaid, owing, owed, expected.

dues (SYN.) assessment, fees, cost, levy, admission, fare, toll, demand, contribution.

duffer (SYN.) bungler, slouch, blunderer, novice, incompetent, fumbler, lummox. (ANT.) master, expert, pro.

duplicate (SYN.) replica, replicate, facsimile, copy, twin, transcript. (ANT.) prototype.

durable (SYN.) constant, firm, fixed, unchangeable, enduring, abiding, lasting. (ANT.) unstable, temporary, perishable, transitory.

duration (SYN.) time, term, epoch, interim.

dutiful (SYN.) docile, faithful. (ANT.) disobedient, willful, unruly, headstrong.

dwell (SYN.) inhabit, roost, settle, abide, live, reside.

dwindle (SYN.) wane, decrease, diminish, fade. (ANT.) enlarge, wax, increase, grow, gain.

dying (SYN.) failing, expiring, waning, passing, final. (ANT.) thriving, flourishing.

dynamic (SYN.) active, forceful, kinetic, energetic. (ANT.) sleepy, stable, inert, ineffectual, listless.

eager (SYN.) avid, hot, anxious, fervent, enthusiastic, impatient, ardent.
(ANT.) unconcerned, apathetic, impassioned, dull, uninterested, indifferent.

early (SYN.) betimes, opportune, first, beforehand, advanced, soon, shortly.
(ANT.) retarded, late, tardy, belated, overdue.

earmark (SYN.) peculiarity, characteristic, brand, sign, stamp, trademark.

earn (SYN.) attain, win, get, achieve, obtain, gain.
(ANT.) lose, waste, consume.

earnest (SYN.) sincere, decided, determined, intent, serious, eager, resolute.
(ANT.) indifferent, frivolous.

earnings (SYN.) wages, pay, salary, income.

earth (SYN.) globe, dirt, land, world, turf, soil, sod.

earthy (SYN.) earthlike, coarse, earthen, crude, unrefined, vulgar.

ease (SYN.) lighten, alleviate, pacify, soothe, allay, comfort, contentedness.
(ANT.) worry, disturb, confound, aggravate.

easygoing (SYN.) calm, mild, complacent, relaxed, unconcerned, serene.
(ANT.) severe, demanding, stern, strict, harsh.

eat (SYN.) consume, swallow, dine, corrode, chew, lunch.

eavesdrop (SYN.) spy, listen, snoop, overhear.

eccentric (SYN.) odd, irregular, unusual, abnormal.
(ANT.) ordinary, conventional, normal.

eccentricity (SYN.) kink, idiosyncracy, whim, freak, caprice, foible, quirk, oddness, strangeness.
(ANT.) normality, conventionality, ordinariness.

ecclesiastical (SYN.) religious, churchly, clerical.

echelon (SYN.) rank, level, grade, place, status.

echo (SYN.) response, imitation, suggestion, trace, reaction, imitate, repeat.

eclectic (SYN.) selective, diverse, broad, liberal.
(ANT.) limited, narrow, rigid, confined.

eclipse (SYN.) conceal, screen, hide, cover, obscure, overcast, veil.

economical (SYN.) saving, thrifty, careful, frugal, provident, sparing.
(ANT.) wasteful, extravagant, lavish, improvident, prodigal.

ecstasy (SYN.) frenzy, gladness, delight, madness, joy, glee, exaltation, pleasure, trance, rapture.
(ANT.) misery, melancholy, sadness.

ecstatic (SYN.) overjoyed, thrilled, delighted, happy.

edge (SYN.) margin, brim, verge, brink, border, keenness, extremity, boundary, trim, periphery, hem, rim.
(ANT.) dullness, center, bluntness.

edict (SYN.) declaration, order, ruling, decree, pronouncement, command.

edifice (SYN.) construction, building, establishment.

edit (SYN.) check, revise, correct, amend.

educate (SYN.) instruct, teach, school, train.

education (SYN.) training, development, knowledge, learning, cultivation, schooling, instruction, study.

eerie (SYN.) weird, fearful, ghastly, spooky, strange.

effect (SYN.) produce, consequence, evoke, cause, make, complete, outcome.

effective (SYN.) efficient, practical, productive.
(ANT.) useless, wasteful, ineffective.

effort (SYN.) labor, endeavor, pains, essay, trial, exertion, struggle, strain, try, attempt, strife, toil.

egg (SYN.) stir, ovum, incite, urge, arouse, embryo.

egghead (SYN.) scholar, intellectual, pedant.

egoism (SYN.) self-interest,

conceit, pride, selfishness.
(ANT.) *modesty, generosity, selflessness.*

eject (SYN.) expel, remove, oust, eliminate.

elaborate (SYN.) detail, develop, decorated, decorative, ornate, complex.
(ANT.) *simplify, simple, unadorned.*

elastic (SYN.) yielding, flexible, adaptable, pliable.

elated (SYN.) delighted, rejoicing, overjoyed, jubilant.
(ANT.) *sad, unhappy.*

elect (SYN.) pick, appoint.

electrify (SYN.) shock, charge, stir, upset, generate, agitate.

elegant (SYN.) tasteful, refined, cultivated, choice, polished, superior, fine.
(ANT.) *crude, coarse, unpolished, tasteless.*

elementary (SYN.) simple, primary, basic, uncomplicated, initial, beginning.
(ANT.) *involved, complex, sophisticated, complicated.*

elevate (SYN.) raise, lift.
(ANT.) *lower, drop.*

elf (SYN.) devil, fairy, imp.

eligible (SYN.) fit, suitable.

eliminate (SYN.) expel, eject, remove, dislodge, extirpate, erase, oust.
(ANT.) *admit, involve.*

elite (SYN.) nobility, upperclass, aristocracy, gentry.
(ANT.) *mob, proletariat.*

elongate (SYN.) extend, prolong, lengthen.

eloquent (SYN.) expressive, fluent, articulate, glib.
(ANT.) *inarticulate.*

elude (SYN.) escape, miss, avoid, dodge.
(ANT.) *add, include.*

emaciated (SYN.) wasted, thin, starved, withered, shriveled, gaunt, shrunken, drawn, undernourished.

emancipate (SYN.) liberate, free, deliver, save.
(ANT.) *restrain.*

embankment (SYN.) shore, dam, bank, fortification.

embargo (SYN.) prohibition, restriction, restraint.

embarrass (SYN.) discomfit, rattle, distress, hamper, fluster, entangle, abash, mortify, hinder, perplex, confuse, shame, trouble.
(ANT.) *relieve, encourage.*

embassy (SYN.) ministry, legation, consulate.

embed (SYN.) root, inset, enclose, plant.

embellish (SYN.) adorn, decorate, ornament.

embezzle (SYN.) pilfer, misuse, rob, misappropriate, steal, take.

embitter (SYN.) provoke, arouse, alienate, anger.

emblem (SYN.) token, mark, symbol, badge.

embody (SYN.) comprise, cover, embrace, include.

embrace (SYN.) espouse, accept, receive, comprehend, contain, welcome, comprise, cover, clasp, include.
(ANT.) *spurn, reject, bar, exclude, repudiate.*

embroider (SYN.) decorate, adorn, stitch, trim, overstate, embellish, ornament, exaggerate, magnify.

emergency (SYN.) strait, pass, crisis, urgency, predicament, pinch.

emissary (SYN.) envoy, minister, delegate, agent, spy.

emit (SYN.) expel, breathe, shoot, hurl, ooze, vent.

emotion (SYN.) passion, turmoil, perturbation, affection, sentiment, feeling, trepidation, agitation.
(ANT.) *dispassion, indifference, tranquillity, calm.*

emotional (SYN.) ardent, passionate, stirring, zealous, impetuous, overwrought.
(ANT.) *tranquil, calm, placid.*

emphasis (SYN.) accent, stress, insistence.

emphatic (SYN.) positive, definite, forceful, energetic.
(ANT.) *lax, quiet, unforceful.*

employ (SYN.) avail, use, devote, apply, utilize, engage, sign, hire, retain.
(ANT.) *reject, discard.*

employee (SYN.) laborer,

worker, servant.
(ANT.) boss, employer.

employer *(SYN.)* owner, boss, manager, superintendent.
(ANT.) employee, worker.

employment *(SYN.)* occupation, work, business, position, job, service.
(ANT.) leisure, idleness, slothfulness.

empower *(SYN.)* enable, sanction, permit, warrant.

empty *(SYN.)* void, devoid, unfilled, barren, unoccupied, unfurnished, vacant, blank.
(ANT.) supplied, full, occupied.

enact *(SYN.)* legislate, portray, pass, stage, represent.

enchant *(SYN.)* charm, titillate, fascinate, bewitch, delight, thrill, captivate.
(ANT.) tire, bore.

encircle *(SYN.)* comprise, include, bound, encompass.

enclose *(SYN.)* envelop, confine, bound, surround, encompass, encircle.
(ANT.) open, exclude, distend, expose, develop.

encompass *(SYN.)* include, surround, encircle.

encounter *(SYN.)* battle, meet, oppose, run into, face.

encourage *(SYN.)* incite, favor, cheer, impel, countenance, inspirit, exhilarate, animate, hearten, embolden.
(ANT.) deter, dispirit, deject, dissuade.

encroach *(SYN.)* interfere, trespass, intrude, infringe.

encumber *(SYN.)* hamper, load, burden.

end *(SYN.)* completion, object, close, aim, result, conclusion, finish, extremity, intent, halt, stop, limit, purpose, cessation, expiration.
(ANT.) opening, start, introduction, beginning, launch, inception.

endanger *(SYN.)* imperil, hazard, risk.
(ANT.) secure.

endear *(SYN.)* allure, charm.

endeavor *(SYN.)* strive, struggle, exertion, attempt, try.

endless *(SYN.)* constant, nonstop, continuous, incessant, everlasting.

endorse *(SYN.)* approve, accept, sign, confirm, pass.

endow *(SYN.)* provide, furnish, bestow, give.
(ANT.) divest.

endure *(SYN.)* experience, undergo, sustain, last, bear, continue, remain, undergo, persist, brook, tolerate.
(ANT.) wane, die, perish, succumb, fail.

enemy *(SYN.)* foe, antagonist, rival, opponent, competitor, adversary, opposition.
(ANT.) colleague, ally, friend, accomplice.

energy *(SYN.)* strength, vim, force, power, stamina, vigor.
(ANT.) feebleness, lethargy.

enervate *(SYN.)* enfeeble, weaken, debilitate, exhaust, devitalize.
(ANT.) invigorate.

enfold *(SYN.)* clasp, surround, wrap, embrace, hug.

enforce *(SYN.)* make, drive, compel, execute, force.

engage *(SYN.)* absorb, occupy, employ, hold, involve, hire, agree, engross, retain, promise, commit, entangle.
(ANT.) fire, disengage, discharge, dismiss.

engaged *(SYN.)* affianced, betrothed, busy, occupied.

engaging *(SYN.)* fascinating, appealing, enticing, interesting, tempting, lovely, beguiling, charming, enchanting.
(ANT.) ordinary, boring.

engender *(SYN.)* develop, breed, cause, generate.

engineer *(SYN.)* direct, conduct, guide, lead, manage.

engrave *(SYN.)* print, cut, impress, inscribe, carve.

engross *(SYN.)* engage, enthrall, occupy, fascinate.

engulf *(SYN.)* flood, swallow.

enhance *(SYN.)* better, uplift, improve.

enigma *(SYN.)* mystery, stumper, riddle.

enigmatic *(SYN.)* perplexing, confusing, puzzling, baffling, mystifying.

enjoy (SYN.) savor, like, relish.

enjoyment (SYN.) pleasure, delight, gratification.
(ANT.) abhorrence, displeasure.

enlarge (SYN.) widen, distend, amplify, broaden, extend, increase, augment, expand.
(ANT.) diminish, shrink, contract, decrease, wane, restrict.

enlighten (SYN.) inform, illuminate, clarify, teach, instruct.
(ANT.) confuse.

enlist (SYN.) enroll, prompt, join, induce, enter, register.
(ANT.) quit, leave, abandon.

enliven (SYN.) inspire, brighten, stimulate.

enmity (SYN.) antagonism, hatred, animosity, malignity, ill-will, antipathy, hostility, unfriendliness.
(ANT.) love, like, friendliness.

enormity (SYN.) heinousness, wickedness, barbarity.

enormous (SYN.) vast, huge, colossal, immense, gargantuan, elephantine, gigantic, stupendous, large.
(ANT.) small, slight, tiny, minute, infinitesimal, diminutive, little.

enough (SYN.) ample, adequate, sufficient, plenty.
(ANT.) inadequate, insufficient.

enrage (SYN.) anger, provoke, madden, inflame.
(ANT.) appease, soothe, calm.

enrich (SYN.) better, improve.

enroll (SYN.) record, list, recruit, register, enlist, write, induct.
(ANT.) quit, leave, abandon.

enshrine (SYN.) bury, entomb.

ensign (SYN.) banner, colors, flag, officer.

enslave (SYN.) keep, hold.

ensue (SYN.) arise, succeed, follow, result.

ensure (SYN.) guarantee, assure, protect, defend, cover.

entangle (SYN.) confuse, snare, involve, ravel, snarl, tangle, trap.

enter (SYN.) join, go inside.

enterprise (SYN.) fete, deed, venture, project, adventure, undertaking, ambition, business, exploit.

enterprising (SYN.) energetic, resourceful.
(ANT.) lazy, indolent, sluggish, unresourceful.

entertain (SYN.) cheer, gladden, hold, consider, please, contemplate, divert, amuse, harbor, fascinate, interest.
(ANT.) repulse, tire, bore, disgust, annoy.

enthrall (SYN.) captivate, fascinate, enchant, charm.

enthusiasm (SYN.) fervor, fanaticism, zeal, ardor, intensity, devotion, excitement, eagerness, fervency.
(ANT.) indifference, ennui, apathy, unconcern, detachment.

enthusiastic (SYN.) earnest, zealous, eager.
(ANT.) aloof, indifferent, unconcerned.

entice (SYN.) lure, attract, seduce.

entire (SYN.) complete, intact, whole, undivided.
(ANT.) divided, separated, incomplete, partial.

entirely (SYN.) altogether, thoroughly, wholly, solely.

entitle (SYN.) call, label, name, empower, allow, authorize, license, title.

entourage (SYN.) train, company, retinue, escort.

entrance (SYN.) inlet, portal, doorway, fascinate, entry, intrigue, door, thrill.
(ANT.) exit.

entreat (SYN.) implore, beg.

entreaty (SYN.) plea, appeal.

entrust (SYN.) commit, charge, assign, delegate, consign, commission.

enumerate (SYN.) count, tally, list, number.

enunciate (SYN.) announce, express, speak, state.

envelop (SYN.) embrace, cover, conceal, surround.

environment (SYN.) neighborhood, habitat, surroundings, setting.

envision *(SYN.)* picture, imagine, visualize.

envoy *(SYN.)* delegate, emissary, representative, agent.

envy *(SYN.)* covetousness, jealousy, spitefulness, covet. *(ANT.)* indifference, generosity.

epicure *(SYN.)* gourmand, gourmet, connoisseur, gastronome, epicurean.

epidemic *(SYN.)* prevalent, scourge, plague, catching, widespread, pestilence, infectious.

episode *(SYN.)* happening, affair, occurrence, event.

epoch *(SYN.)* age.

equal *(SYN.)* even, uniform, like, alike, equitable, same, identical, commensurate, equivalent, regular, parallel. *(ANT.)* different, unequal, irregular, uneven.

equilibrium *(SYN.)* stability, steadiness, balance.

equip *(SYN.)* fit, rig, provide, outfit, prepare, furnish.

equipment *(SYN.)* utensils, material, apparatus.

equitable *(SYN.)* square, rightful, fair, due, just, fit. *(ANT.)* partial, biased, unjust, uneven.

equity *(SYN.)* impartiality, fairness, justness, justice, fairmindedness.

equivalent *(SYN.)* match, rival, equal, like, replacement.

equivocal *(SYN.)* oblique, ambiguous, vague, indeterminate, uncertain, obscure. *(ANT.)* clear, precise, explicit, certain, clear-cut, definite.

equivocate *(SYN.)* temporize, evade, hedge, quibble, fudge, waffle, straddle.

era *(SYN.)* epoch, cycle, age, time, period.

eradicate *(SYN.)* remove, demolish, eliminate.

erase *(SYN.)* obliterate, remove, cancel. *(ANT.)* add, include.

erect *(SYN.)* upright, build, straight, raise, construct. *(ANT.)* flat, horizontal, raze, flatten, demolish.

erection *(SYN.)* building, construction, raising.

erode *(SYN.)* rust, consume, disintegrate.

erotic *(SYN.)* carnal, fleshy, amatory, prurient, lewd, wanton, passionate.

err *(SYN.)* slip, misjudge.

errand *(SYN.)* chore, duty, task, exercise.

errant *(SYN.)* roving, rambling, wandering, vagrant.

erratic *(SYN.)* irregular, abnormal, uneven, occasional, sporadic, changeable, unsteady, odd, eccentric. *(ANT.)* regular, steady, normal, ordinary.

erroneous *(SYN.)* wrong, mistaken, incorrect, inaccurate, false, untrue. *(ANT.)* true, right, correct.

error *(SYN.)* inaccuracy, fault, slip, oversight, fallacy, mistake, blunder.

erudite *(SYN.)* sage, wise, learned, deep, profound.

erupt *(SYN.)* vomit.

escapade *(SYN.)* caper, antic, stunt, trick, prank.

escape *(SYN.)* shun, avoid, flee, decamp, elude, flight, avert, departure, abscond. *(ANT.)* meet, confront, invite.

escort *(SYN.)* conduct, lead, attend, accompany, protection, guard, guide, convoy, usher, squire.

especially *(SYN.)* unusually, principally, mainly, particularly, primarily.

essay *(SYN.)* test, thesis, undertake, paper, try.

essence *(SYN.)* substance, character, nature, principle, odor, meaning, basis.

essential *(SYN.)* vital, intrinsic, basic, requisite, fundamental, indispensable, critical, requirement, necessity, necessary, important. *(ANT.)* dispensable, unimportant, inessential.

establish *(SYN.)* prove, fix, found, settle, institute, raise, verify, conform, form, sanction, ordain, begin. *(ANT.)* upset, discontinue, scatter, disperse, refute, abolish, unsettle.

esteem (SYN.) revere, deem, appreciate, honor, value, think, admire, respect, hold, prize, reverence, regard.
(ANT.) scorn, disdain, depreciate, disregard, contempt, abhor.

estimate (SYN.) calculate, gauge, judge, rate, evaluate, compute, value, figure.

estimation (SYN.) judgment, viewpoint, opinion.

etch (SYN.) stamp, engrave.

eternal (SYN.) undying, immortal, ceaseless, infinite, everlasting, deathless, perpetual, endless, timeless.
(ANT.) mortal, transient, finite, brief, temporary.

etiquette (SYN.) decorum, formality.

evacuate (SYN.) withdraw, depart, leave, vacate.

evade (SYN.) miss, avoid.
(ANT.) confront, meet, face.

evaluate (SYN.) value, appraise, assay.

evaporate (SYN.) disappear.
(ANT.) condense, appear.

even (SYN.) smooth, level, still, square, same, flat, balanced, equal, parallel.
(ANT.) irregular, bumpy, unbalanced, unequal.

eventually (SYN.) ultimately.

ever (SYN.) continuously, always, constantly.
(ANT.) never.

everlasting (SYN.) permanent, ceaseless, endless.

everyday (SYN.) commonplace, common, usual, ordinary, customary.
(ANT.) rare.

evidence (SYN.) grounds, clue, facts, testimony, data, sign.

evident (SYN.) apparent, clear, obvious, indubitable, plain, conspicuous, patent.
(ANT.) hidden, unclear, uncertain, obscure, concealed.

evil (SYN.) immoral, harmful, badness, sinful, injurious.
(ANT.) goodness, moral, useful, upright, virtuous, beneficial, virtue, advantageous.

evoke (SYN.) summon.

evolve (SYN.) grow, advance, develop, result, emerge.

exact (SYN.) correct, faultless, errorless, detailed, accurate.
(ANT.) inaccurate, inexact, faulty.

exalt (SYN.) erect, consecrate, raise, elevate, extol, dignify.
(ANT.) humble, degrade, humiliate.

example (SYN.) pattern, archetype, specimen, illustration, model, instance, prototype, sample.
(ANT.) rule, concept.

exceedingly (SYN.) extremely, very, especially, unusually.

excel (SYN.) better, beat.

excellence (SYN.) distinction.
(ANT.) poorness, inferiority.

excellent (SYN.) wonderful, fine, marvelous, superior.
(ANT.) poor, terrible, bad.

except (SYN.) omitting, barring, but, reject, excluding, save, exclude.

excess (SYN.) surplus, intemperance, extravagance, immoderation, profusion, abundant, profuse.
(ANT.) want, sparse, lack, dearth.

exchange (SYN.) barter, interchange, substitute, trade, change, swap.

excite (SYN.) arouse, incite, agitate, stimulate, awaken.
(ANT.) lull, quiet, bore, pacify.

exclaim (SYN.) vociferate, cry, call out, cry out, ejaculate.

exclude (SYN.) omit, restrain, hinder, bar, except, prevent.
(ANT.) welcome, involve, embrace, admit, accept, include.

exclusive (SYN.) restricted, limited, restrictive, choice, selective, fashionable.
(ANT.) common, general, ordinary, unrestricted.

excuse (SYN.) exculpate, forgive, remit, acquit, free, pardon, condone, explanation, overlook, exempt, reason, justify, absolve.
(ANT.) revenge, punish, convict.

execute (SYN.) complete, accomplish, do, achieve, kill.

exertion *(SYN.)* attempt, effort, strain, endeavor.

exhaust *(SYN.)* drain, tire, empty, wear out, use, finish.
(ANT.) renew, refresh.

exhaustive *(SYN.)* comprehensive, thorough, extensive.
(ANT.) incomplete.

exhibit *(SYN.)* demonstrate, display, reveal, betray, present, show, flaunt.
(ANT.) hide conceal, disguise.

exhilarate *(SYN.)* gladden, refresh, cheer, excite.

exhort *(SYN.)* advise, coax, press, urge, prompt.

exile *(SYN.)* expulsion, proscription, deportation, ostracism, expatriation, deport, extradition, expel.
(ANT.) retrieval, welcome, recall, admittance.

exist *(SYN.)* stand, live, be.

exit *(SYN.)* leave, depart.

exodus *(SYN.)* leaving, exit, parting, departure.

exorbitant *(SYN.)* unreasonable, outrageous, overpriced, preposterous.
(ANT.) normal, reasonable.

expand *(SYN.)* unfold, enlarge, broaden, spread, inflate, swell, grow.
(ANT.) contract, shrivel.

expect *(SYN.)* await, think, hope, anticipate.

expedition *(SYN.)* trek, speed, trip, haste, voyage, journey.

expel *(SYN.)* exile, dislodge, discharge, excommunicate, oust, eject, dismiss, banish.
(ANT.) favor, recall, invite.

expense *(SYN.)* charge, cost, payment, price.

experience *(SYN.)* occurrence, episode, sensation, happening, existence, background, feeling, living, encountering.

experienced *(SYN.)* expert, qualified, accomplished, skilled, practiced.
(ANT.) untutored, inexperienced, naive.

experiment *(SYN.)* trial, test, prove, research, examine, try, verify.

expire *(SYN.)* terminate, die,

cease, perish, pass, end.
(ANT.) commence, continue.

explain *(SYN.)* illustrate, decipher, expound, clarify, resolve, define, unravel, elucidate, unfold, justify.
(ANT.) darken, baffle, obscure.

explanation *(SYN.)* definition, description, interpretation, account, reason, justification, excuse.

explicit *(SYN.)* lucid, definitive, specific, express, clear.
(ANT.) vague, implicit, ambiguous.

explosion *(SYN.)* bang, boom, blowup, flare-up, blast, detonation, outbreak, convulsion, furor, tantrum.

exponent *(SYN.)* explicator, spokesman, supporter, expounder, interpreter.

expose *(SYN.)* uncover, display, bare, open, unmask.
(ANT.) hide, conceal, mask, covered.

express *(SYN.)* voice, tell, send, say, ship, declare, state, precise, specific, swift.

expression *(SYN.)* declaration, statement, look.

expressive *(SYN.)* suggestive, meaningful, telling, significant, thoughtful.
(ANT.) unthinking, meaningless, nondescript.

expulsion *(SYN.)* ejection, discharge, removal.

expunge *(SYN.)* blot out, erase, cancel, obliterate, delete, efface, remove.

expurgate *(SYN.)* cleanse, purge, censor, edit, emasculate, abridge, blip.

extant *(SYN.)* subsisting, remaining, surviving, present.
(ANT.) lost, defunct, extinct, vanished.

extend *(SYN.)* lengthen, stretch, increase, offer, give, grant, magnify, expand.
(ANT.) abbreviate, shorten, curtail.

extension *(SYN.)* expansion, increase, stretching, enlargement.

extensive *(SYN.)* vast, wide,

spacious, broad.
(ANT.) narrow, cramped, confined, restricted.

extent (SYN.) length, degree, range, amount, measure, size, compass, reach, magnitude, scope, expanse, area.

extenuating (SYN.) exculpating, excusable, qualifying, justifying, softening.

exterminate (SYN.) slay, kill, destroy.

external (SYN.) outer, exterior, outside.
(ANT.) inner, internal, inside, interior.

externals (SYN.) images, effects, look, appearance, veneer, aspect.

extinct (SYN.) lost, dead, gone, vanished.
(ANT.) present, flourishing, alive, extant.

extinction (SYN.) eclipse, annihilation, obliteration, death, extirpation.

extinguish (SYN.) suppress, smother, quench.

extol (SYN.) laud, eulogize, exalt, praise.
(ANT.) denounce, belittle, discredit, disparage.

extra (SYN.) surplus, spare, additional.

extract (SYN.) remove, withdraw, essence.
(ANT.) penetrate, introduce.

extraordinary (SYN.) unusual, wonderful, marvelous, peculiar, noteworthy, remarkable, uncommon.
(ANT.) commonplace, ordinary, usual.

extravagant (SYN.) excessive, exaggerated, lavish, wasteful, extreme.
(ANT.) prudent, frugal, thrifty, economical, provident.

extreme (SYN.) excessive, overdone, outermost, limit, greatest, utmost, furthest, endmost, extravagant.
(ANT.) reasonable, modest.

exuberant (SYN.) buoyant, ebullient, vivacious.
(ANT.) sad, depressed.

eye (SYN.) watch, view, stare, look, inspect, glance.

fable (SYN.) legend, parable, myth, fib, falsehood, fiction.

fabled (SYN.) legendary, famous, famed, historic.

fabric (SYN.) goods, textile, material, cloth, yard goods.

fabricate (SYN.) assemble, make, construct, produce.
(ANT.) raze, destroy, demolish.

fabrication (SYN.) deceit, lie, falsehood, untruth, forgery.
(ANT.) verity, reality, actuality, truth, fact.

fabulous (SYN.) amazing, marvelous, unbelievable, fantastic, astounding, astonishing, striking.
(ANT.) ordinary, commonplace, credible, proven.

facade (SYN.) deception, mask, front, show, pose, veneer, guise, affectation.

face (SYN.) cover, mug, front, assurance, countenance, audacity, visage, expression.
(ANT.) rear, shun, avoid, evade, back.

facet (SYN.) perspective, view, side, phase.

facetious (SYN.) jocular, pungent, humorous, funny, clever, droll, witty, jesting, playful.
(ANT.) sober, serious, grave.

face to face (SYN.) opposing, confronting.

facile (SYN.) simple, easy, quick, uncomplicated, clever, fluent, skillful.
(ANT.) complex, difficult, complicated, laborious, hard, ponderous, painstaking.

facilitate (SYN.) help, speed, expedite, ease, promote, accelerate.

facilities (SYN.) aid, means, resources, conveniences.

facility (SYN.) ability, skill, ease, skillfulness.
(ANT.) effort, difficulty, labor.

facsimile (SYN.) reproduction, likeness.

fact (SYN.) reality, deed, certainty, act, incident, circumstance, event, truth.
(ANT.) falsehood, fiction, delusion.

faction (SYN.) clique, party.

factitious (SYN.) false, sham, artificial, spurious, unnatural, affected.
(ANT.) natural, real, genuine.

factor (SYN.) part, certain.

factory (SYN.) installation, plant, mill.

factual (SYN.) true, correct, accurate. sure, genuine.
(ANT.) incorrect, erroneous, fabricated.

faculty (SYN.) power, capacity, talent, staff, gift, ability, skill.

fad (SYN.) fashion, vogue, mania, rage.

faddish (SYN.) ephemeral, modish, temporary, passing.
(ANT.) lasting, permanent, classic.

fade (SYN.) pale, bleach, weaken, dim, decline, sink, discolor, fail, diminish.

fagged (SYN.) exhausted, tired, weary, jaded, pooped.

fail (SYN.) neglect, weaken, flunk, miss, decline, disappoint, fade.
(ANT.) succeed, achieve, accomplish.

failing (SYN.) fault, foible, imperfection, frailty, defect, peccadillo, shortcoming.
(ANT.) steadiness, strength.

failure (SYN.) miscarriage, omission, decline, deficiency, fiasco, lack, dereliction, failing, unsuccessfulness, loss, default, want, insufficiency, decay.
(ANT.) conquest, accomplishment, success, triumph, victory, achievement.

faint (SYN.) timid, faded, languid, half-hearted, dim, feeble, indistinct, weak.
(ANT.) strong, sharp, forceful, glaring, clear, distinct, conspicuous, brave.

faint-hearted (SYN.) shy, cowardly, timid, bashful.
(ANT.) fearless, brave, stouthearted, courageous.

fair (SYN.) pale, average, light, sunny, mediocre, bright, just, clear, lovely, market, blond, honest, equitable, impartial, reasonable.
(ANT.) ugly, fraudulent, foul, outstanding, dishonorable.

fairly (SYN.) equally, evenly, rather, impartially, passably, justly, somewhat.

fair-minded (SYN.) reasonable, fair, just, open-minded, honest, impartial.
(ANT.) bigoted, narrow-minded, unjust, close-minded, partisan.

fairness (SYN.) equity, justice, evenhandedness, honesty.
(ANT.) favoritism, partiality.

fairy (SYN.) leprechaun, gnome, elf, pixie, sprite.

faith (SYN.) dependence, trust, reliance, creed, loyalty, doctrine, confidence, dogma, tenet.
(ANT.) mistrust, disbelief.

faithful (SYN.) staunch, true, devoted, trusty, loyal, constant, credible, steadfast, strict, trustworthy, accurate.
(ANT.) untrustworthy, faithless, inaccurate, wrong, false, disloyal, erroneous.

faithless (SYN.) treacherous, unfaithful, disloyal, perfidious, untrue.
(ANT.) loyal, true, constant.

fake (SYN.) falsify, distort, pretend, feign, fraud, counterfeit, cheat, false, artificial, imitation, forgery, mock.
(ANT.) honest, real, genuine, authentic.

falderal (SYN.) foolery, jargon, nonsense, gibberish, blather, balderdash.

fall (SYN.) drop, decline, diminish, droop, topple, decrease, sink, hang, descend, subside, plunge.
(ANT.) soar, climb, steady, rise, ascend.

fallacious (SYN.) untrue, false, wrong, erroneous, deceptive, illusory, delusive.
(ANT.) accurate, exact, real.

fallacy (SYN.) mistake, error, illusion, sophism, misconception, deception.

fall back (SYN.) retreat, recede, retire, withdraw.
(ANT.) progress, gain,

prosper, proceed.

fallow *(SYN.)* idle, unprepared, inactive.
(ANT.) prepared, productive, cultivated.

false *(SYN.)* incorrect, wrong, deceitful, fake, imitation.
(ANT.) genuine, loyal, true.

falsehood *(SYN.)* untruth, lie, fib, story.
(ANT.) truth.

falsify *(SYN.)* misquote, distort, misstate, mislead, adulterate.

falter *(SYN.)* stumble, tremble, waver, hesitate.

fame *(SYN.)* distinction, glory, mane, eminence, credit, reputation, renown, acclaim, notoriety.
(ANT.) infamy, anonymity, disrepute.

famed *(SYN.)* known, renowned, famous.
(ANT.) obscure, unknown, anonymous.

familiar *(SYN.)* informal, intimate, close, acquainted, amicable, knowing, sociable, affable, aware, known.
(ANT.) unfamiliar, affected, reserved.

familiarity *(SYN.)* sociability, acquaintance, frankness, intimacy, knowledge.
(ANT.) distance, ignorance, reserve, presumption, constraint, haughtiness.

family *(SYN.)* kin, tribe, group, relatives.

famine *(SYN.)* want, starvation, need.
(ANT.) excess, plenty.

famous *(SYN.)* distinguished, noted, glorious, illustrious, famed, celebrated.
(ANT.) obscure, hidden, unknown.

fan *(SYN.)* arouse, spread, admirer, enthusiast, devotee, stir, whip, follower.

fanatic *(SYN.)* bigot, enthusiast, zealot.

fancy *(SYN.)* love, dream, ornate, imagine, suppose, imagination, taste, fantasy, ornamented, elaborate, think.
(ANT.) plain, simple, un-

adorned.

fantastic *(SYN.)* strange, unusual, odd, wild, unimaginable, incredible, unbelievable, bizarre, capricious.
(ANT.) ordinary, staid.

fantasy *(SYN.)* illusion, dream, whim, delusion, mirage, daydream, fancy.
(ANT.) bore.

far *(SYN.)* removed, much, distant, remote, estranged.
(ANT.) close, near.

fare *(SYN.)* prosper, eat, passenger, thrive, toll, progress.

farewell *(SYN.)* good-by, valediction, departure, leaving.
(ANT.) welcome, greeting.

farm *(SYN.)* grow, harvest, cultivate, ranch, hire, charter, plantation.

fascinate *(SYN.)* charm, enchant, bewitch, attract.

fashion *(SYN.)* create, shape, style, mode, make, custom, form, manner, method, way.

fashionable *(SYN.)* chic, smart, stylish, modish, elegant, voguish.
(ANT.) dowdy, unfashionable.

fast *(SYN.)* fleet, firm, quick, swift, inflexible, stable, secure, expeditious, rapid.
(ANT.) insecure, sluggish, unstable, loose, slow, unsteady.

fasten *(SYN.)* secure, bind, tie.
(ANT.) open, loose, free, release.

fastidious *(SYN.)* choosy, selective, discriminating, picky.

fat *(SYN.)* stout, plump, chubby, pudgy, obese, oily, fleshy, greasy, fatty, portly, corpulent, paunchy, wide.
(ANT.) gaunt, emaciated, thin, slender.

fatal *(SYN.)* killing, lethal, doomed, disastrous, deadly, fateful, mortal.
(ANT.) nonfatal.

fate *(SYN.)* end, fortune, doom, issue, destiny, necessity, portion, result, lot, chance, luck, outcome.

father *(SYN.)* cause, sire, breed, originate, founder.

fatherly *(SYN.)* protective, paternal, kind, paternalistic.

fathom (SYN.) penetrate, understand, interpret.

fatigue (SYN.) weariness, lassitude, exhaustion, enervation, languor, tiredness.
(ANT.) rejuvenation, energy.

fault (SYN.) defect, flaw, mistake, imperfection, shortcoming, error, weakness, responsibility, omission.
(ANT.) perfection.

faultfinding (SYN.) carping, censorious, critical, caviling.

faulty (SYN.) imperfect, broken, defective, damaged.
(ANT.) flawless, perfect, whole.

favor (SYN.) rather, resemble, liking, service, prefer, approval, like, support, patronize, benefit.
(ANT.) deplore, disapprove.

favorite (SYN.) prized, pet, choice, darling, treasured.

fear (SYN.) horror, terror, fright, trepidation, alarm, anxiety, dread.
(ANT.) fearlessness, courage.

fearless (SYN.) bold, brave, courageous, gallant, dauntless, confident.
(ANT.) timid, fearful, cowardly.

feast (SYN.) dinner, banquet, barbecue.

feat (SYN.) performance, act, operation, accomplishment, achievement, doing.
(ANT.) intention, deliberation, cessation.

feature (SYN.) trait, quality, characteristic, highlight.

fee (SYN.) payment, pay, remuneration.

feeble (SYN.) faint, puny, exhausted, impair, delicate, weak, enervated, frail, powerless, forceless, sickly.
(ANT.) strong, forceful, powerful, vigorous, stout.

feed (SYN.) satisfy, food, fodder, forage.

feel (SYN.) sense, experience.

feeling (SYN.) opinion, sensibility, tenderness, affection, impression, belief, sensation, sympathy, thought.
(ANT.) fact, anesthesia, insensibility.

fellowship (SYN.) clan, society, brotherhood, fraternity, camaraderie, companionship, comradeship.
(ANT.) dislike, discord, distrust, enmity.

feminine (SYN.) womanly, girlish, ladylike, female, maidenly, womanish.
(ANT.) masculine, male, virile.

ferocious (SYN.) savage, fierce, wild, blood-thirsty.
(ANT.) playful, gentle, harmless, calm.

fertile (SYN.) rich, fruitful, teeming, plenteous, bountiful, prolific, luxuriant.
(ANT.) unproductive, barren, sterile.

festival (SYN.) feast, banquet, regalement, celebration.

festive (SYN.) joyful, gay, joyous, merry, gala, jovial.
(ANT.) sad, gloomy, mournful, morose.

fetching (SYN.) charming, attractive, pleasing, captivating, winsome.

feud (SYN.) dispute, quarrel, strife, argument, conflict.
(ANT.) amity, understanding, harmony.

fiber (SYN.) line, strand, thread, string.

fickle (SYN.) unstable, capricious, restless, changeable, inconstant, variable.
(ANT.) stable, constant, trustworthy, steady, reliable.

fiction (SYN.) fabrication, romance, falsehood, tale, allegory, narrative, fable.
(ANT.) verity, reality, fact.

fictitious (SYN.) invented, make-believe, imaginary, fabricated, unreal.
(ANT.) real, true, genuine, actual, proven.

fidelity (SYN.) fealty, devotion, precision, allegiance, exactness, constancy, accuracy, faithfulness, loyalty.
(ANT.) treachery, disloyalty.

fiendish (SYN.) devilish, demonic, diabolical, savage.

fierce (SYN.) furious, wild,

savage, violent, ferocious.
(ANT.) *calm, meek, mild, gentle, placid.*

fight (SYN.) contend, scuffle, struggle, battle, wrangle, combat, brawl, quarrel, dispute, war, skirmish, conflict.

figure (SYN.) design, pattern, mold, shape, form, frame, reckon, calculate.

fill (SYN.) glut, furnish, store, stuff, occupy, gorge, pervade, content, stock, fill up, supply, sate, replenish.
(ANT.) *void, drain, exhaust, deplete, empty.*

filthy (SYN.) foul, polluted, dirty, stained, unwashed.
(ANT.) *pure, clean, unspoiled.*

final (SYN.) ultimate, decisive, concluding, ending, terminal, last, conclusive.
(ANT.) *inaugural, rudimentary, beginning, initial, incipient, first, original.*

find (SYN.) observe, detect.

fine (SYN.) thin, pure, choice, small, elegant, dainty, splendid, handsome, delicate, nice, powdered, beautiful, minute, exquisite, subtle, pretty, refined.
(ANT.) *thick, coarse, rough, blunt, large.*

finicky (SYN.) fussy, meticulous, finical, fastidious.

finish (SYN.) consummate, close, get done, terminate, accomplish, conclude, execute, perform, complete.
(ANT.) *open, begin, start, beginning.*

fire (SYN.) vigor, glow, combustion, passion, burning, conflagration, ardor, flame, blaze, intensity, fervor.
(ANT.) *apathy, cold.*

firm (SYN.) solid, rigid, inflexible, stiff, unchanging, steadfast, dense, hard, unshakable, compact, business, company.
(ANT.) *weak, limp, soft.*

first (SYN.) chief, primary, initial, pristine, beginning, foremost, primeval, earliest, prime, primitive, original.
(ANT.) *subordinate, last, least,*

hindmost, latest.

fit (SYN.) adjust, suit, suitable, accommodate, conform, robust, harmonize, belong, seizure, spasm, attack, suited, appropriate, healthy.
(ANT.) *misfit, disturb.*

fitful (SYN.) variable, restless, fickle, capricious, unstable.
(ANT.) *trustworthy, stable, constant.*

fitting (SYN.) apt, due, suitable, proper.
(ANT.) *improper, unsuitable.*

fix (SYN.) mend, regulate, affix, set, tie, repair, attach, settle, link, bind, determine, establish, define, place, rectify, stick, limit, adjust.
(ANT.) *damage, change, mistreat, displace, alter, disturb.*

fixation (SYN.) fetish, obsession, infatuation.

flair (SYN.) style, dash, flamboyance, drama, gift, knack.

flamboyant (SYN.) showy, flashy, ostentatious, gaudy.

flash (SYN.) flare, flame, wink, twinkling, instant, gleam.

flashy (SYN.) tawdry, tasteless, pretentious, garish.

flat (SYN.) vapid, stale, even, smooth, tasteless, horizontal, dull, level, insipid, uninteresting, lifeless, boring.
(ANT.) *tasty, racy, hilly, savory, stimulating, interesting, broken, sloping.*

flattery (SYN.) compliment, praise, applause, blarney.

flaunt (SYN.) exhibit, show off, display, parade.
(ANT.) *conceal, hide, disguise.*

flavor (SYN.) tang, taste, savor, essence, quality, character, season, spice.

flaw (SYN.) spot, imperfection, blemish, fault.

flee (SYN.) fly, abscond, hasten, escape, run away, decamp, evade.
(ANT.) *remain, appear, stay.*

fleece (SYN.) filch, rob, purloin, swindle, defraud, pilfer, cheat.

fleet (SYN.) rapid, swift, quick.
(ANT.) *unhurried, sluggish, slow.*

fleshy *(SYN.)* overweight, chubby, stocky, plump, obese, stout.
(ANT.) spare, underweight.

flexible *(SYN.)* lithe, resilient, pliable, tractable, complaint, elastic, yielding, adaptable, agreeable, supple, pliant, easy, ductile.
(ANT.) hard, unbending, firm, brittle, inflexible, rigid, fixed.

flighty *(SYN.)* giddy, light-headed, frivolous.
(ANT.) solid, responsible, steady.

flimsy *(SYN.)* wobbly, weak, frail, fragile, unsteady, delicate, thin.
(ANT.) durable, stable, firm.

fling *(SYN.)* pitch, throw, toss, fun, celebration, party.

flippant *(SYN.)* disrespectful, sassy, insolent, brazen, rude.
(ANT.) courteous, polite, mannerly.

flit *(SYN.)* flutter, scurry, dart.

flock *(SYN.)* gathering, group, flight, swarm, herd, school.

flog *(SYN.)* thrash, lash, strike.

flood *(SYN.)* overflow, inundate, cascade.

florid *(SYN.)* gaudy, ornate, embellished.
(ANT.) spare, simple, plain, unadorned.

flourish *(SYN.)* succeed, grow, prosper, wave, thrive.
(ANT.) wither, wane, die, decline.

flout *(SYN.)* disdain, scorn, spurn, ignore, taunt, ridicule, mock.

flow *(SYN.)* proceed, abound, spout, come, stream, run, originate, emanate, result, pour, squirt, issue, gush.

fluctuate *(SYN.)* vary, oscillate, change, waver, hesitate.
(ANT.) persist, stick, adhere.

fluent *(SYN.)* graceful, glib.

fluster *(SYN.)* rattle, flurry, agitate, upset, perturb, quiver, vibrate.

fly *(SYN.)* flee, mount, shoot, decamp, hover, soar, flit, flutter, sail, escape, rush, spring, glide, abscond, dart.
(ANT.) sink, descend, plummet.

fog *(SYN.)* haze, mist, cloud, daze, confusion, stupor.

foible *(SYN.)* frailty, weakness, failing, shortcoming, kink.

fold *(SYN.)* lap, double, overlap, clasp, pleat, tuck.

follow *(SYN.)* trail, observe, succeed, ensue, obey, chase.
(ANT.) elude, cause, precede, avoid, flee.

follower *(SYN.)* supporter, devotee, henchman, adherent, partisan, disciple, successor.
(ANT.) master, head, chief, dissenter.

fond *(SYN.)* affectionate, loving, attached, tender.
(ANT.) hostile, cool, distant, unfriendly.

food *(SYN.)* viands, edibles, feed, repast, nutriment, sustenance, diet, bread.
(ANT.) want, hunger, drink, starvation.

foolish *(SYN.)* senseless, irrational, crazy, silly, brainless.
(ANT.) sane, sound, sensible, reasonable, prudent.

forbearance *(SYN.)* moderation, abstinence, abstention.
(ANT.) greed, excess, intoxication.

forbid *(SYN.)* disallow, prevent, ban, prohibit, taboo.
(ANT.) approve, let, allow.

force *(SYN.)* energy, might, violence, vigor, intensity, dint, power, constraint.
(ANT.) weakness, frailty, persuasion, feebleness, impotence, ineffectiveness.

forceful *(SYN.)* dynamic, vigorous, energetic, potent, drastic, intense.
(ANT.) lackadaisical, insipid.

foregoing *(SYN.)* above, former, preceding, previous.
(ANT.) later, coming, below, follow.

foreign *(SYN.)* alien, strange, exotic, different, unfamiliar.
(ANT.) commonplace, ordinary.

foresee *(SYN.)* forecast, expect, anticipate, surmise.

forest *(SYN.)* grove, woodland, wood, copse, woods.

forever *(SYN.)* evermore, always, everlasting, hereafter.
(ANT.) fleeting, temporarily.

forgo *(SYN.)* relinquish, release, surrender, waive.
(ANT.) keep, retain, safeguard.

forlorn *(SYN.)* pitiable, desolate, dejected, woeful.
(ANT.) optimistic, cherished, cheerful.

form *(SYN.)* frame, compose, fashion, arrange, construct, make up, devise, create, invent, mold, shape, forge.
(ANT.) wreck, dismantle, destroy.

formal *(SYN.)* exact, stiff, correct, outward, conformist, conventional, affected.
(ANT.) heartfelt, unconstrained, easy.

former *(SYN.)* earlier, previous, prior.

formidable *(SYN.)* alarming, frightful, imposing, terrible, terrifying, dire.
(ANT.) weak, unimpressive, ordinary.

forsake *(SYN.)* abandon, desert, forgo, quit, discard.

forthright *(SYN.)* honest, direct, candid, outspoken, blunt sincere, plain, explicit.

fortify *(SYN.)* bolster strengthen, buttress, barricade.

fortuitous *(SYN.)* successful, benign, lucky, happy.
(ANT.) unlucky, condemned, persecuted.

fortunate *(SYN.)* happy, auspicious, fortuitous, successful, favored, advantageous, benign, charmed, lucky, felicitous, blessed, propitious.
(ANT.) ill-fated, cheerless, unlucky, unfortunate, cursed.

forward *(SYN.)* leading, front, promote, elevate, advance, first, ahead, onward, further, foremost, aggrandize.
(ANT.) withhold, hinder, retreat, oppose.

foul *(SYN.)* base, soiled, dirty, mean, unclean, polluted, wicked, rainy, stormy.
(ANT.) pure, neat, wholesome, clean.

foundation *(SYN.)* support, root, base, underpinning, bottom, substructure.
(ANT.) top, cover, building.

fraction *(SYN.)* fragment, part, section, morsel, share.

fragile *(SYN.)* delicate, frail, weak, breakable, infirm, brittle, feeble.
(ANT.) tough, hardy, sturdy, strong, stout, durable.

fragment *(SYN.)* scrap, piece, bit, remnant, part, splinter.

fragrance *(SYN.)* odor, smell.

fragrant *(SYN.)* aromatic.

frail *(SYN.)* feeble, weak, delicate, breakable, fragile.
(ANT.) sturdy, strong.

frame *(SYN.)* support, framework, skeleton, molding, border, mount.

frank *(SYN.)* honest, candid, open, unreserved, direct, sincere, straightforward.
(ANT.) tricky, dishonest.

frantic *(SYN.)* frenzied, raving, panicky.
(ANT.) composed, stoic.

fraud *(SYN.)* deception, guile, swindle, deceit, artifice, imposture, trick, cheat.
(ANT.) sincerity, fairness, integrity.

fray *(SYN.)* strife, fight, battle, struggle, tussle, combat, brawl, melee, skirmish.
(ANT.) truce, agreement.

freak *(SYN.)* curiosity, abnormality, monster, oddity.

free *(SYN.)* munificent, clear, autonomous, immune, open, freed, bountiful, liberated, unfastened, immune, emancipated, unconfined, bounteous.
(ANT.) stingy, clogged, illiberal, confined.

freedom *(SYN.)* independence, privilege, familiarity, unrestraint, liberty, exemption, liberation, immunity.
(ANT.) servitude, constraint, bondage, slavery, necessity.

frequent *(SYN.)* usual, habitual, common, often, customary, general.
(ANT.) unique, rare, solitary, uncommon, exceptional, in-

frequent, scanty.

fresh (SYN.) recent, new, additional, modern, further, refreshing, natural, brisk, novel, inexperienced, late.
(ANT.) stagnant, decayed, musty, faded.

fret (SYN.) worry, grieve, anguish.

fretful (SYN.) testy, irritable, touchy, peevish, shorttempered.
(ANT.) calm.

friend (SYN.) crony, supporter, ally, companion, intimate, associate, advocate, comrade, mate, patron.
(ANT.) stranger, adversary.

friendly (SYN.) sociable, kindly, affable, genial, companionable, social.
(ANT.) hostile, antagonistic, reserved.

friendship (SYN.) knowledge, familiarity, fraternity, acquaintance, intimacy, fellowship, comradeship, cognizance.
(ANT.) unfamiliarity, ignorance.

fright (SYN.) alarm, fear, panic, terror.

frighten (SYN.) scare, horrify, daunt, affright, appall, terrify, alarm, terrorize, astound, dismay, startle.
(ANT.) soothe, compose, reassure.

frigid (SYN.) cold, wintry, icy, glacial, arctic, freezing.

frolic (SYN.) play, romp, frisk, gambol.

front (SYN.) facade, face, start, beginning, border.
(ANT.) rear, back.

frugal (SYN.) parsimonious, saving, stingy, provident.
(ANT.) extravagant, wasteful, self-indulgent, intemperate.

fruitful (SYN.) fertile, rich, bountiful, teeming, fecund, productive, luxuriant.
(ANT.) lean, barren, sterile.

fruitless (SYN.) barren, futile, vain, sterile, unproductive.
(ANT.) fertile, productive.

frustrate (SYN.) hinder, defeat, thwart, circumvent,

outwit, foil, baffle.
(ANT.) fulfill, accomplish.

fulfill (SYN.) do, effect, complete, accomplish, realize.

full (SYN.) baggy, crammed, entire, satiated, flowing, perfect, gorged, soaked.
(ANT.) lacking, partial, empty, depleted.

fullness (SYN.) glut, repletion, satisfaction, overload.
(ANT.) need, want, hunger, lack, insufficiency, privation, emptiness.

full-scale (SYN.) major, all-out, lavish, comprehensive, unlimited, maximum.
(ANT.) indifferent, partial, minor.

fulsome (SYN.) disgusting, repulsive, nauseating, repellent, revolting.

fume (SYN.) gas, steam, smoke, rage, rave, vapor.

fun (SYN.) merriment, pleasure, enjoyment, gaiety.

function (SYN.) operation, activity, affair, ceremony, gathering, party.

fundamental (SYN.) basic, essential, primary.

funny (SYN.) odd, droll, ridiculous, queer, farcical, laughable, comic, curious, amusing, humorous, witty.
(ANT.) solemn, sad, sober, melancholy.

furnish (SYN.) yield, give, endow, fit, produce, equip, afford, decorate, supply.
(ANT.) divest, denude, strip.

furthermore (SYN.) moreover, also, further.

furtive (SYN.) surreptitious, secret, hidden, clandestine.
(ANT.) honest, open.

fury (SYN.) wrath, anger, frenzy, rage, violence.
(ANT.) calmness, serenity.

fuss (SYN.) commotion, bother, pester.

futile (SYN.) pointless, idle, vain, useless, worthless.
(ANT.) weighty, important, worthwhile, serious, valuable.

future (SYN.) approaching, imminent, coming.
(ANT.) former, past.

gab *(SYN.)* jabber, babble, chatter, prattle, gossip.

gabble *(SYN.)* chatter, babble, jabber, blab, prate, gaggle, prattle, blather.

gabby *(SYN.)* chatty, talkative, wordy, verbose.

gad *(SYN.)* wander, roam, rove, ramble, meander.

gadabout *(SYN.)* gypsy, wanderer, rambler.

gadget *(SYN.)* contrivance, device, doodad, jigger, thing.

gaffe *(SYN.)* blunder, boner, mistake, gaucherie, error.

gag *(SYN.)* witticism, crack, jest, joke.

gaiety *(SYN.)* joyousness, cheerfulness, joyfulness, light-heartedness, high-spiritedness.

(ANT.) melancholy, sadness, depression.

gain *(SYN.)* acquire, avail, account, good, interest, attain, favor, achieve, get, secure, advantage, earn, profit, procure, service, obtain.

(ANT.) trouble, lose, calamity, forfeit, handicap, lose.

gainful *(SYN.)* lucrative, rewarding, profitable, beneficial, payable, productive.

(ANT.) unproductive, unprofitable.

gainsay *(SYN.)* refute, contradict, controvert, deny, refuse, inpugn, contravene.

(ANT.) maintain, aver, affirm.

gait *(SYN.)* stride, walk, tread.

gala *(SYN.)* ball, party, carnival, fete.

gale *(SYN.)* burst, surge.

gall *(SYN.)* nerve, audacity, impudence, annoy, vex, anger, provoke, irritate.

gallant *(SYN.)* bold, brave, courageous, valorous, valiant, noble, polite, fearless, heroic, chivalrous.

gallantry *(SYN.)* valor, daring, courage, prowess, heroism, manliness, dauntlessness, graciousness, attentiveness, coquetry, gentleness.

(ANT.) poltroonery, timidity, cowardice, craveness.

gallery *(SYN.)* passageway,

hall, aisle, hallway, passage.

galling *(SYN.)* vexing, irritating, annoying, distressful.

galore *(SYN.)* abounding, plentiful, profuse, rich.

gamble *(SYN.)* game, wager, bet, hazard, risk, venture.

game *(SYN.)* fun, contest, merriment, pastime, match, play, amusement, recreation, diversion.

(ANT.) labor, hardship, work, business.

gangster *(SYN.)* crook, hoodlum, gunman, criminal.

gap *(SYN.)* cavity, chasm, pore, gulf, aperture, abyss, interval, space, hole, void, pore, break, opening.

gape *(SYN.)* ogle, stare, gawk.

garb *(SYN.)* clothing, dress, vesture, array, attire, clothes, drapery, apparel.

(ANT.) nudity, nakedness.

garbage *(SYN.)* refuse, waste.

garbled *(SYN.)* twisted, confused.

gargantuan *(SYN.)* colossal, monumental, giant, huge, large, enormous.

garments *(SYN.)* drapery, dress, garb, apparel, array, attire, clothes, vesture, raiment, clothing.

(ANT.) nakedness, nudity.

garnish *(SYN.)* decorate, embellish, trim, adorn, enrich, beautify, deck, ornament.

(ANT.) expose, strip, uncover, defame.

garrulous *(SYN.)* chatty, glib, verbose, talkative, communicative, voluble.

(ANT.) silent, uncommunicative, laconic, reticent, taciturn.

gash *(SYN.)* lacerate, slash, pierce, cut, hew, slice.

gasp *(SYN.)* pant, puff, wheeze.

gather *(ANT.)* assemble, collect, garner, harvest, reap, deduce, judge, amass, congregate, muster, cull, glean.

(ANT.) scatter, disperse, distribute, disband, separate.

gathering *(SYN.)* meeting, crowd, throng, company.

gaudy (SYN.) showy, flashy, loud, bold.

gaunt (ANT.) lank, diaphanous, flimsy, gauzy, narrow, rare, scanty, meager, gossamer, emaciated, scrawny, tenuous, thin, fine, lean, skinny, spare, slim.
(ANT.) wide, fat, thick, broad.

gay (SYN.) merry, lighthearted, joyful, cheerful, sprightly, jolly, happy, joyous, gleeful, jovial, colorful, bright.
(ANT.) glum, mournful, sad, depressed, sorrowful, somber.

gaze (SYN.) look, stare, view, watch, examine, observe, glance, behold, discern, seem, see, survey, witness.
(ANT.) hide, overlook, avert.

geld (SYN.) neuter, alter, spay, castrate.

gem (SYN.) jewel, semiprecious stone.

general (SYN.) ordinary, universal, usual, common, customary, regular, vague, miscellaneous, indefinite.
(ANT.) definite, particular, exceptional, singular, rare, particular, precise, exact.

generally (SYN.) ordinarily, usually, customarily, normally, mainly.
(ANT.) seldom, infrequently.

generation (SYN.) age, date, era, period, seniority, senescence, senility.
(ANT.) infancy, youth, childhood.

generosity (SYN.) magnanimity, benevolence, humanity, kindness, philanthropy, tenderness, altruism.
(ANT.) selfishness, malevolence, cruelty, inhumanity.

generous (SYN.) giving, liberal, unselfish, magnanimous, bountiful, munificent, charitable, big, noble, beneficent.
(ANT.) greedy, stingy, selfish, covetous.

genesis (SYN.) birth, root, creation, source, origin.

genius (SYN.) intellect, adept, intellectual, sagacity, proficient, creativity, ability, inspiration, faculty.

gaudy (ANT.) dullard, stupidity, dolt, shallowness, moron, ineptitude, obtuseness.

genre (SYN.) chaste, order, set, elegance, class, excellence, kind, caste.

genteel (SYN.) cultured, polished, polite, refined.
(ANT.) discourteous, churlish.

gentle (SYN.) peaceful, placid, tame, serene, relaxed, docile, benign, soothing, calm, soft, mild, amiable, friendly.
(ANT.) nasty, harsh, rough, fierce, mean.

genuine (SYN.) real, true, unaffected, authentic, sincere, bona fide, unadulterated, legitimate, actual, veritable.
(ANT.) false, sham, artificial, fake, counterfeit, bogus, pretended, insincere, sham.

genus (SYN.) kind, race, species, type, variety.

germ (SYN.) pest, virus, contamination, disease, pollution, taint, infection.

germinate (SYN.) vegetate, pullulate, sprout, develop.

gesture (SYN.) omen, signal, symbol, emblem, indication, note, token, symptom.

get (SYN.) obtain, receive, attain, gain, achieve, acquire, procure, earn, fetch, carry, remove, prepare, take.
(ANT.) lose, surrender, forfeit, leave, renounce.

ghastly (SYN.) frightful, horrible, horrifying, frightening, grisly, hideous.

ghost (SYN.) phantom, spook, apparition, specter, trace, hint, vestige, spirit.

ghoulish (SYN.) weird, eerie, horrifying, gruesome, sinister, scary.

giant (SYN.) monster, colossus, mammoth, superman.
(ANT.) small, tiny, dwarf, runt, midget, infinitesimal.

gibe (SYN.) sneer, jeer, mock, scoff, boo, hoot, hiss.
(ANT.) approve.

giddy (SYN.) reeling, dizzy, flighty, silly, scatterbrained.
(ANT.) serious.

gift (SYN.) endowment, favor,

gratuity, bequest, talent, charity, present.
(ANT.) purchase, loss, ineptitude, deprivation, earnings.

gigantic (SYN.) huge, colossal, immense, large, vast, elephantine, gargantuan.
(ANT.) small, tiny, minute, diminutive, little.

giggle (SYN.) chuckle, jeer, laugh, roar, snicker, titter, cackle, guffaw, mock.

gild (SYN.) cover, coat, paint, embellish, sweeten, retouch.

gingerly (SYN.) gentle, cautiously, carefully, gently.
(ANT.) roughly.

gird (SYN.) wrap, tie, bind, belt, encircle, surround, get set, prepare.
(ANT.) untie.

girl (SYN.) female, lass, miss.

girth (SYN.) measure, size, width, dimensions, expanse.

gist (SYN.) connotation, explanation, purpose, significance, acceptation.
(ANT.) redundancy.

give (SYN.) bestow, contribute, grant, impart, provide, donate, confer, deliver, present, furnish, yield, develop.
(ANT.) withdraw, take, retain, keep, seize.

glad (SYN.) happy, cheerful, gratified, delighted, joyous, merry, pleased, exulting.
(ANT.) sad, depressed, dejected, melancholy, unhappy, morose, somber.

gladiator (SYN.) battler, fighter, competitor, combatant, contender, contestant.

glamorous (SYN.) spellbinding, fascinating, alluring.

glamour (SYN.) charm, allure, attraction, magnetism.

glance (SYN.) eye, gaze, survey, view, examine, inspect, discern, look, see, witness.
(ANT.) hide, miss, avert, overlook.

glare (SYN.) flash, dazzle, stare, glower, glow, shine.

glaring (SYN.) flagrant, obvious, blatant, prominent.

glass (SYN.) cup, tumbler, goblet, pane.

glaze (SYN.) buff, luster, cover, wax, gloss, coat, polish.

gleam (SYN.) flash, glimmer, glisten, shimmer, sparkle.

glean (SYN.) reap, gather, select, harvest, pick, separate.

glee (SYN.) mirth, joy, gladness, enchantment, delight, cheer, bliss, elation.
(ANT.) depression, misery, dejection.

glen (SYN.) ravine, valley.

glib (SYN.) smooth, suave, flat, plain, polished, sleek.
(ANT.) rough, rugged, blunt, harsh, bluff.

glide (SYN.) sweep, sail, fly, flow, slip, coast, cruise, move easily, skim, slide.

glimmer (SYN.) blink, shimmer, flicker, indication, hint, clue, suggestion.

glimpse (SYN.) notice, glance, peek, see, impression, look.

glint (SYN.) flash, gleam, peek, glance, glimpse, sparkle, glitter.

glisten (SYN.) shimmer, shine, glimmer, twinkle, glitter, glister, sparkle.

globe (SYN.) orb, ball, world, earth, map, universe.

gloom (SYN.) bleakness, despondency, misery, sadness, woe, darkness, dejection.
(ANT.) joy, mirth, exultation, cheerfulness, light, happiness, brightness, frivolity.

gloomy (SYN.) despondent, dismal, glum, somber, sorrowful, sad, dejected, disconsolate, dim, dark.
(ANT.) happy, merry, cheerful, high-spirited, bright, sunny.

glorify (SYN.) enthrone, exalt, honor, revere, adore, dignify, enshrine, consecrate, praise, worship, laud.
(ANT.) mock, dishonor, debase, abuse.

glorious (SYN.) exalted, high, noble, splendid, supreme, elevated, lofty, celebrated, renowned, famed, magnificent, grand, proud.
(ANT.) ridiculous, low, base.

glory (SYN.) esteem, praise, respect, reverence, admira-

tion, honor, dignity.
(*ANT.*) *dishonor, disgrace, contempt, reproach, derision.*
gloss (*SYN.*) luster, shine, glow, sheen.
glossy (*SYN.*) smooth, glistening, shiny, sleek, polished.
(*ANT.*) *matte, dull.*
glow (*SYN.*) beam, glisten, radiate, shimmer, sparkle.
glower (*SYN.*) scowl, stare, frown, glare.
(*ANT.*) *beam, grin, smile.*
glowing (*SYN.*) fiery, intense, passionate, zealous, enthusiastic, ardent, eager.
(*ANT.*) *cool, indifferent, apathetic.*
glue (*SYN.*) bind, fasten, cement, paste.
glum (*SYN.*) morose, sulky, fretful, crabbed, sullen, dismal, dour, moody.
(*ANT.*) *joyous, merry, amiable.*
glut (*SYN.*) gorge, sate, content, furnish, fill, pervade, satiate, stuff, replenish.
(*ANT.*) *empty, exhaust, deplete, void.*
glutton (*SYN.*) pig, hog, greedy eater.
gluttony (*SYN.*) ravenousness, piggishness, devouring.
(*ANT.*) *satisfaction, fullness.*
gnarled (*SYN.*) twisted, knotted, rugged, knobby.
go (*SYN.*) proceed, depart, flee, move, vanish, exit, leave, suit, harmonize, pass.
(*ANT.*) *stay, arrive, enter, stand, come.*
goad (*SYN.*) incite, prod, drive, urge, push, shove, jab, provoke, stimulate.
goal (*SYN.*) craving, destination, desire, longing, objective, finish, end, passion.
godlike (*SYN.*) holy, supernatural, heavenly, celestial, divine, transcendent.
(*ANT.*) *profane, wicked, blasphemous, diabolical.*
godly (*SYN.*) pious, religious, holy, pure, divine, spiritual, righteous, saintly.
golden (*SYN.*) shining, metallic, bright, fine, superior, nice, excellent, valuable.

(*ANT.*) *dull, inferior.*
good (*SYN.*) honest, sound, valid, cheerful, honorable, worthy, conscientious, moral, genuine, humane, kind, fair, useful, skillful, adequate, friendly, genial.
(*ANT.*) *bad, imperfect, vicious, undesirable, unfriendly, unkind, evil.*
good-hearted (*SYN.*) good, kind, thoughtful, kindhearted, considerate.
(*ANT.*) *evil-hearted.*
good-humored (*SYN.*) pleasant, good-natured, cheerful, sunny, amiable.
(*ANT.*) *petulant, cranky.*
goodness (*SYN.*) good, honesty, integrity, virtue.
(*ANT.*) *sin, evil, dishonesty, corruption, badness.*
goods (*SYN.*) property, belongings, holdings, possessions, merchandise, wares.
good will (*SYN.*) agreeability, harmony, willingness.
gore (*SYN.*) impale, penetrate, puncture, gouge.
gorge (*SYN.*) ravine, devour, stuff, gobble, valley, defile, pass, cram, fill.
gorgeous (*SYN.*) grand, ravishing, glorious, stunning, brilliant, divine.
(*ANT.*) *homely, ugly, squalid.*
gory (*SYN.*) bloody.
gossamer (*SYN.*) dainty, fine, filmy, delicate, sheer.
gossip (*SYN.*) prate, rumor, prattle, hearsay, meddler, tattler, chatter.
gouge (*SYN.*) scoop, dig, carve, burrow, excavate, chisel, notch.
govern (*SYN.*) manage, oversee, reign, preside over, supervise, direct, command, regulate, determine, influence, guide, rule.
(*ANT.*) *assent, submit, acquiesce, obey.*
government (*SYN.*) control, direction, rule, command.
governor (*SYN.*) controller, administrator, director.
gown (*SYN.*) garment, robe, frock, dress, costume, attire

grab *(SYN.)* snatch, grip, clutch, seize, grasp, capture, pluck.

grace *(SYN.)* charm, beauty, handsomeness, loveliness, dignify, fairness, honor, distinguish, sympathy, attractiveness, elegance, clemency, excuse, pardon.
(ANT.) eyesore, homeliness, deformity, ugliness, disfiguration.

graceful *(SYN.)* elegant, fluid, natural, supple, beautiful, comely, flowing, lithe.
(ANT.) clumsy, awkward, gawky, ungainly, deformed.

gracious *(SYN.)* warm-hearted, pleasing, friendly, engaging, agreeable, kind, amiable, kindly, nice, good, courteous.
(ANT.) surly, hateful, churlish, rude, disagreeable, impolite, thoughtless, discourteous, ill-natured.

grade *(SYN.)* kind, rank, elegance, denomination, sort, arrange, category, classify, rate, group, place, mark.

gradual *(SYN.)* deliberate, sluggish, dawdling, slow, moderate, easy, delaying.
(ANT.) quick, swift, fast, speedy, rapid.

graduate *(SYN.)* pass, finish, advance.

graft *(SYN.)* fraud, theft, cheating, bribery, dishonesty, transplant, corruption.

grain *(SYN.)* speck, particle, plant, bit, seed, temper, fiber, character, texture, markings, nature, tendency.

grand *(SYN.)* great, elaborate, splendid, royal, stately, noble, considerable, outstanding, distinguished, impressive, prominent, majestic, fine, dignified.
(ANT.) unassuming, modest, insignificant, unimportant, humble.

grandeur *(SYN.)* resplendence, majesty, distinction, glory.

grandiose *(SYN.)* grand, lofty, magnificent, stately, noble, pompous.
(ANT.) lowly, ordinary, common, undignified, humble.

grandstand *(SYN.)* bleachers, gallery.

granite *(SYN.)* stone, rock.

grant *(SYN.)* confer, allocate, deal, divide, mete, appropriation, assign, benefaction, distribute, allowance, donate, award, mete out, deal out.
(ANT.) refuse, withhold, confiscate, keep.

granular *(SYN.)* grainy, sandy, crumbly, rough, gritty.

graph *(SYN.)* design, plan, stratagem, draw up, chart, sketch, cabal, machination, outline, plot, scheme, diagram.

graphic *(SYN.)* vivid, lifelike, significant, meaningful, pictorial, descriptive.

grapple *(SYN.)* grip, seize, clutch, clasp, grasp, fight, struggle.

grasp *(SYN.)* clutch, grip, seize, apprehend, capture, snare, hold, clasp, comprehend, reach, grab, understand, grapple, possession, control.
(ANT.) release, lose, throw, liberate.

grasping *(SYN.)* possessive, greedy, selfish, acquisitive, mercenary.
(ANT.) liberal, unselfish, generous.

grate *(SYN.)* file, pulverize, grind, scrape, scratch, annoy, irritate.

grateful *(SYN.)* beholden, obliged, appreciative, thankful, indebted.
(ANT.) ungrateful, unappreciative, grudging, thankless.

gratify *(SYN.)* charm, gladden, please.
(ANT.) frustrate.

gratifying *(SYN.)* contentment, solace, relief, comfort, ease, succor.
(ANT.) suffering, torment, affliction, discomfort, torture, misery.

grating (SYN.) harsh, rugged, severe, stringent, coarse, gruff, strict.
(ANT.) smooth, mild, gentle, soft.

gratis (SYN.) complimentary, free.

gratitude (SYN.) gratefulness, thankfulness, appreciation.
(ANT.) ungratefulness.

gratuity (SYN.) tip, bonus, gift, donation.

grave (SYN.) sober, grim, earnest, serious, important, momentous, sedate, solemn, somber, imposing, vital, essential, staid, consequential, thoughtful.
(ANT.) light, flighty, trivial, insignificant, unimportant, trifling, merry, frivolous.

gravel (SYN.) stones, pebbles, grain.

gravitate (SYN.) incline, tend, lean, approach, toward.

gravity (SYN.) concern, importance, seriousness, pull, movement.
(ANT.) triviality.

graze (SYN.) scrape, feed, rub, brush, contact, skim.

grease (SYN.) fat, oil, lubrication.

greasy (SYN.) messy, buttery, waxy, fatty.

great (SYN.) large, numerous, eminent, illustrious, big, gigantic enormous, immense, vast, weighty, fine, important, countless, prominent, vital, huge, grand.
(ANT.) minute, common, menial, ordinary, diminutive, small, paltry, unknown.

greed (SYN.) piggishness, lust, desire, greediness, avarice.
(ANT.) unselfishness, selflessness.

greedy (SYN.) selfish, devouring, ravenous, avaricious, covetous, rapacious.
(ANT.) full, generous, munificent, giving.

green (SYN.) inexperienced, modern, novel, recent, further, naive, fresh, natural.
(ANT.) hackneyed, musty, decayed, faded, stagnant.

greet (SYN.) hail, accost, meet, address, talk to, speak to, welcome, approach.
(ANT.) pass by, avoid.

gregarious (SYN.) outgoing, civil, affable, communicative, hospitable, sociable.
(ANT.) inhospitable, antisocial, disagreeable, hermitic.

grief (SYN.) misery, sadness, tribulation, affliction, heartache, woe, trial, anguish.
(ANT.) happiness, solace, consolation, comfort, joy.

grievance (SYN.) injury, wrong, injustice, detriment, complaint, damage, prejudice, evil, objection.
(ANT.) improvement, benefit, repair.

grieve (SYN.) lament, brood over, mourn, weep, wail, sorrow, distress, bemoan.
(ANT.) revel, carouse, celebrate, rejoice, gladden.

grievous (SYN.) gross, awful, outrageous, shameful, lamentable, regrettable.
(ANT.) agreeable, pleasurable.

grill (SYN.) cook, broil, question, interrogate, barbecue, grating, gridiron.

grim (SYN.) severe, harsh, strict, merciless, fierce, horrible, inflexible, adamant, ghastly, frightful, unyielding.
(ANT.) pleasant, lenient, relaxed, amiable, congenial, smiling.

grimace (SYN.) expression, scowl, mope.

grimy (SYN.) unclean, grubby, soiled.

grin (SYN.) beam, smile, smirk.

grind (SYN.) mill, mash, powder, crush, crumble, pulverize, smooth, grate.

grip (SYN.) catch, clutch, apprehend, trap, arrest, grasp, hold, bag, suitcase, lay hold of, clench, command, control.
(ANT.) release, liberate, lose, throw.

gripe (SYN.) protest, lament,

complaint.

grit *(SYN.)* rub, grind, grate, sand, gravel, pluck, courage, stamina.

groan *(SYN.)* sob, wail, howl, moan, whimper, wail, complain.

groggy *(SYN.)* dazed, dopy, stupefied, stunned, drugged, unsteady.
(ANT.) alert.

groom *(SYN.)* tend, tidy, preen, curry, spouse, consort.

groove *(SYN.)* furrow, channel, track, routine, slot, scratch.

groovy *(SYN.)* marvelous, delightful, wonderful.

grope *(SYN.)* fumble, feel around.

gross *(SYN.)* glaring, coarse, indelicate, obscene, bulky, great, total, whole, brutal, grievous, aggregate, earthy, rude, vulgar, entire, enormous, plain, crass.
(ANT.) appealing, delicate, refined, proper, polite, cultivated, slight, comely, trivial, decent.

grotesque *(SYN.)* strange, weird, odd, incredible, fantastic, monstrous, absurd, freakish, bizarre, peculiar, deformed.

grotto *(SYN.)* tunnel, cave, hole, cavern.

grouch *(SYN.)* protest, remonstrate, whine, complain, grumble, murmur.
(ANT.) praise, applaud, rejoice, approve.

ground *(SYN.)* foundation, presumption, surface, principle, underpinning.
(ANT.) implication, superstructure.

groundless *(SYN.)* baseless, unfounded, unwarranted.

grounds *(SYN.)* garden, lawns, dregs, foundation, leftovers, reason, sediment, cause.

group *(SYN.)* crowd, clock, party, troupe, swarm, bunch, brook, assembly, lot, collection, pack, horde.
(ANT.) disassemble.

grouse *(SYN.)* mutter, grumble, gripe, scold, growl.

grovel *(SYN.)* creep, crawl, cower, cringe, slouch, stoop.

groveling *(SYN.)* dishonorable, lowly, sordid, vile, mean, abject, despicable, ignoble.
(ANT.) lofty, noble, esteemed.

grow *(SYN.)* extend, swell, advance, develop, enlarge, enlarge, germinate, mature, expand, flower, raise.
(ANT.) wane, shrink, atrophy, decay, diminish, contract.

growl *(SYN.)* complain, snarl, grumble, gnarl, roar.

grown-up *(SYN.)* full-grown, adult, of age, mature, big.
(ANT.) little, childish, budding, junior.

growth *(SYN.)* expansion, development, unfolding, maturing, progress, elaboration, evolution.
(ANT.) degeneration, deterioration, curtailment, abbreviation, compression.

grudge *(SYN.)* malevolence, malice, resentment, bitterness, spite, animosity.
(ANT.) kindness, love, benevolence, affection, good will, friendliness, toleration.

grudgingly *(SYN.)* reluctantly, unwillingly, under protest, involuntarily.

grueling *(SYN.)* taxing, exhausting, excruciating, trying, arduous, grinding.
(ANT.) effortless, easy, light, simple.

gruesome *(SYN.)* hideous, frightful, horrible, loathsome, ghastly, horrifying.
(ANT.) agreeable, soothing, delightful, charming.

guarantee *(SYN.)* bond, pledge, token, warrant, earnest, surety, bail, commitment, promise, secure.

guarantor *(SYN.)* voucher, sponsor, warrantor, signatory, underwriter, surety.

guaranty *(SYN.)* warranty, token, deposit, earnest.

guard *(SYN.)* protect, shield, veil, cloak, conceal, disguise, envelop, preserve, hide.

(ANT.) unveil, expose, ignore, neglect, bare, reveal, disregard, divulge.

guardian *(SYN.)* curator, keeper, protector, custodian, patron, watchdog.

guess *(SYN.)* estimate, suppose, think, assume, reason, believe, reckon, speculate. *(ANT.) know.*

guest *(SYN.)* caller, client, customer, patient, visitor. *(ANT.) host.*

guide *(SYN.)* manage, supervise, conduct, direct, lead, steer, escort, pilot, show. *(ANT.) follower, follow.*

guild *(SYN.)* association, union, society.

guile *(SYN.)* deceitfulness, fraud, wiliness, trick, deceit. *(ANT.) sincerity, openness, honesty, truthfulness, candor, frankness.*

guileless *(SYN.)* open, innocent, naive, sincere, simple, candid. *(ANT.) treacherous, plotting.*

guilt *(SYN.)* sin, blame, misstep, fault, offense.

guilty *(SYN.)* culpable, to blame, responsible, at fault, criminal, blameworthy. *(ANT.) blameless, innocent, guiltless.*

gulch *(SYN.)* gorge, valley, gully, ravine, canyon.

gullible *(SYN.)* trustful, naive, innocent, unsuspecting, deceivable, unsuspicious. *(ANT.) skeptical, sophisticated.*

gully *(SYN.)* ditch, gorge, ravine, valley, gulch, gulf.

gulp *(SYN.)* devour, swallow, gasp, repress, choke.

gush *(SYN.)* pour, spurt, stream, rush out, spout, flood, flush, chatter, babble.

gust *(SYN.)* blast, wind, outbreak, outburst, eruption.

gutter *(SYN.)* ditch, groove, drain, channel, trench.

gymnasium *(SYN.)* playground, arena, court, athletic field.

gymnastics *(SYN.)* drill, exercise, acrobatics, calisthenics.

habit *(SYN.)* usage, routine, compulsion, use, wont, custom, disposition, practice, addiction, fashion.

habitation *(SYN.)* abode, domicile, lodgings.

habitual *(SYN.)* general, usual, common, frequent, persistent, customary, routine, regular, often. *(ANT.) solitary, unique, exceptional, ususual, rare, scanty, occasional.*

habituated *(SYN.)* used, accustomed, adapted, acclimated, comfortable, familiarized, addicted.

hack *(SYN.)* cleave, chop, slash, hew, slice, pick, sever.

hackneyed *(SYN.)* stale, stereotyped, trite, commonplace, ordinary, banal, common, unique. *(ANT.) novel, stimulating, modern, fresh, creative.*

hag *(SYN.)* beldam, crone, vixen, granny, ogress, harridan, virage.

haggard *(SYN.)* drawn, careworn, debilitated, spent. *(ANT.) bright, fresh, cleareyed, animated.*

haggle *(SYN.)* dicker, bargain.

hail *(SYN.)* welcome, approach, accost, speak to, address, greet. *(ANT.) pass by, avoid.*

hairdresser *(SYN.)* beautician.

hairless *(SYN.)* shorn, glabrous, bald, baldpated. *(ANT.) hirsute, hairy, unshaven.*

hair-raising *(SYN.)* horrifying, exciting, alarming, thrilling, startling, frightful, scary.

hairy *(SYN.)* bearded, shaggy, hirsute, bewhiskered.

hale *(SYN.)* robust, well, wholesome, hearty, healthy, sound, salubrious. *(ANT.) noxious, frail, diseased, delicate, infirm.*

half-baked *(SYN.)* crude, premature, makeshift, illogical.

half-hearted *(SYN.)* uncaring, indifferent, unenthusiastic. *(ANT.) eager, enthusiastic, earnest.*

half-wit *(SYN.)* dope, simpleton, nitwit, dunce, idiot.

hall *(SYN.)* corridor, lobby, passage, hallway, vestibule.

hallow *(SYN.)* glorify, exalt, dignify, aggrandize, consecrate, elevate, ennoble, raise, erect.
(ANT.) dishonor, humiliate, debase, degrade.

hallowed *(SYN.)* holy, sacred, beatified, sacrosanct, blessed, divine.

hallucination *(SYN.)* fantasy, mirage, dream, vision, phantasm, appearance.

halt *(SYN.)* impede, obstruct, terminate, stop, hinder, desist, check, arrest, abstain.
(ANT.) start, begin, proceed, speed, beginning, promote.

halting *(SYN.)* imperfect, awkward, stuttering, faltering, hobbling, doubtful, limping.
(ANT.) decisive, confident, smooth, graceful, facile.

hammer *(SYN.)* beat, bang, whack, pound, batter, drive.

hamper *(SYN.)* prevent, impede, thwart, restrain, hinder, obstruct.
(ANT.) help, assist, encourage, facilitate.

hamstrung *(SYN.)* disabled, helpless, paralyzed.

hand *(SYN.)* assistant, helper, support, aid, farmhand.

handicap *(SYN.)* retribution, penalty, disadvantage, forfeiture, hindrance.
(ANT.) reward, pardon, compensation, remuneration.

handily *(SYN.)* readily, skillfully, easily, dexterously, smoothly, adroitly, deftly.

handkerchief *(SYN.)* bandanna, scarf.

handle *(SYN.)* hold, touch, finger, clutch, grip, manipulate, feel, grasp, control, oversee, direct, treat, steer, supervise, run, regulate.

hand out *(SYN.)* disburse, distribute, deal, mete.

hand over *(SYN.)* release, surrender, deliver, yield, present, fork over.

handsome *(SYN.)* lovely, pretty, fair, comely, beautiful, charming, elegant, good-looking, large, generous, liberal, beauteous, fine.
(ANT.) repulsive, ugly, unattractive, stingy, small, mean, homely, foul, hideous.

handy *(SYN.)* suitable, adapted, appropriate, favorable, fitting, near, ready, close.
(ANT.) inopportune, troublesome, awkward.

hang *(SYN.)* drape, hover, dangle, suspend, kill, sag, execute, lynch.

hang in *(SYN.)* continue, endure, remain, persevere, resist, persist.

hang-up *(SYN.)* inhibition, difficulty, snag, hindrance.

hanker *(SYN.)* wish, yearn, long, desire, pine, thirst.

haphazard *(SYN.)* aimless, random, purposeless, indiscriminate, accidental.
(ANT.) determined, planned, designed, deliberate.

hapless *(SYN.)* ill-fated, unfortunate, jinxed, luckless.

happen *(SYN.)* occur, take place, bechance, betide, transpire, come to pass, chance, befall.

happening *(SYN.)* episode, event, scene, incident, affair, experience, phenomenon.

happiness *(SYN.)* pleasure, gladness, delight, beatitude, bliss, contentment, satisfaction, joy, joyousness.
(ANT.) sadness, sorrow, misery, grief.

happy *(SYN.)* gay, joyous, cheerful, fortunate, glad, merry, contented, satisfied, lucky, blessed, pleased.
(ANT.) gloomy, morose, sad, sorrowful, miserable, inconvenient, unlucky, depressed.

happy-go-lucky *(SYN.)* easygoing, carefree, unconcerned.
(ANT.) prudent, responsible, concerned.

harangue *(SYN.)* oration, diatribe, lecture, tirade.

harass *(SYN.)* badger, irritate, molest, pester, taunt, torment, provoke, tantalize,

worry, aggravate, annoy, nag, plague, vex.
(ANT.) please, soothe, comfort, delight, gratify.

harbinger (SYN.) sign, messenger, proclaim.

harbor (SYN.) haven, port, anchorage, cherish, entertain, protect, shelter.

hard (SYN.) difficult, burdensome, arduous, rigid, puzzling, cruel, strict, unfeeling.
(ANT.) fluid, brittle, effortless, gentle, tender, easy, simple, plastic, soft, lenient, flabby.

hard-boiled (SYN.) unsympathetic, tough, harsh.

hardship (SYN.) ordeal, test, effort, affliction, misfortune, trouble, experiment.
(ANT.) consolation, alleviation.

hardy (SYN.) sturdy, strong, tough, vigorous.
(ANT.) frail, decrepit, feeble, weak, fragile.

harm (SYN.) hurt, mischief, misfortune, mishap, damage, wickedness, cripple.
(ANT.) favor, kindness, benefit, boon.

harmful (SYN.) damaging, injurious, mischievous, detrimental, hurtful, deleterious.
(ANT.) helpful, salutary, profitable, advantageous.

harmless (SYN.) protected, secure, snag, dependable, certain, painless, innocent.
(ANT.) perilous, hazardous, insecure, dangerous, unsafe.

harmonious (SYN.) tuneful, melodious, congenial.
(ANT.) dissonant, discordant, disagreeable.

harmony (SYN.) unison, bargain, contract, stipulation, pact, agreement, accordance, concord, accord.
(ANT.) discord, dissension, difference, variance.

harness (SYN.) control, yoke.

harry (SYN.) vex, pester, harass, bother, plague.

harsh (SYN.) jarring, gruff, rugged, severe, stringent, blunt, grating, unpleasant.
(ANT.) smooth, soft, gentle, melodious, soothing, easy.

harvest (SYN.) reap, gather, produce, yield, crop, gain, acquire, fruit, result, reaping, proceeds, glean, garner.
(ANT.) plant, squander, lose.

haste (SYN.) speed, hurry, rush, rapidity, flurry.
(ANT.) sloth, sluggishness.

hasten (SYN.) hurry, sprint, quicken, rush, precipitate, accelerate, scurry, run.
(ANT.) retard, tarry, detain, linger, dawdle, delay, hinder.

hasty (SYN.) quick, swift, irascible, lively, nimble, brisk, active, speedy, impatient, testy, sharp, fast, rapid.
(ANT.) slow, dull, sluggish.

hat (SYN.) helmet, bonnet.

hatch (SYN.) breed, incubate.

hate (SYN.) loathe, detest, despise, disfavor, hatred, abhorrence, abominate.
(ANT.) love, cherish, admire, like.

hatred (SYN.) detestation, dislike, malevolence, enmity, aversion, animosity.
(ANT.) friendship, affection, attraction.

haughty (SYN.) proud, stately, vainglorious, arrogant, disdainful, overbearing.
(ANT.) meek, ashamed, lowly.

haul (SYN.) draw, pull, drag.

have (SYN.) own, possess, seize, hold, control, occupy, acquire, undergo, maintain, experience, receive, gain.
(ANT.) surrender, abandon, renounce, lose.

havoc (SYN.) devastation, ruin, destruction.

hazard (SYN.) peril, chance, dare, risk, offer, conjecture.
(ANT.) safety, defense, protection, immunity.

hazardous (SYN.) perilous, precarious, threatening, unsafe, dangerous, critical.
(ANT.) protected, secure, safe.

hazy (SYN.) uncertain, unclear, ambiguous, dim.
(ANT.) specific, clear, lucid, precise, explicit.

head (SYN.) leader, summit, top, culmination, director,

chief, master, commander.
(ANT.) foot, base, bottom, follower, subordinate.
heady (SYN.) thrilling, intoxicating, exciting.
healthy (SYN.) wholesome, hale, robust, sound, well, vigorous, strong, hearty, healthful, hygienic.
(ANT.) noxious, diseased, unhealthy, delicate, frail, infirm, injurious.
heap (SYN.) collection, mound, increase, store, stack, pile, gather, accumulate, amass, accrue.
(ANT.) dissipate, scatter, waste, diminish, disperse.
hear (SYN.) heed, listen, detect, harken, perceive.
heart (SYN.) middle, center, sympathy, nucleus, midpoint, sentiment, core.
(ANT.) outskirts, periphery, border, rim, boundary.
heartache (SYN.) anguish, mourning, sadness, sorrow, affliction, distress, grief.
(ANT.) happiness, joy, solace, comfort, consolation.
heartbroken (SYN.) distressed, forlorn, mean, paltry, worthless, contemptible, wretched, crestfallen, disconsolate, low.
(ANT.) noble, fortunate, contented, significant.
hearten (SYN.) encourage, favor, impel, urge, promote, sanction, animate, cheer, exhilarate, cheer.
(ANT.) deter, dissuade, deject, discourage, dispirit.
heartless (SYN.) mean, cruel, ruthless, hardhearted.
(ANT.) sympathetic, kind.
heart-rending (SYN.) heartbreaking, depressing.
hearty (SYN.) warm, earnest, ardent, cordial, sincere, gracious, sociable.
(ANT.) taciturn, aloof, cool.
heat (SYN.) hotness, warmth, temperature, passion, ardor, zeal, inflame, cook.
(ANT.) cool, chill, coolness, freeze, coldness, chilliness, iciness, cold.

heated (SYN.) vehement, fiery, intense, passionate.
heave (SYN.) boost, hoist.
heaven (SYN.) empyrean, paradise.
heavenly (SYN.) superhuman, god-like, blissful, saintly, holy, divine, celestial.
(ANT.) wicked, mundane, profane, blasphemous.
heavy (SYN.) weighty, massive, gloomy, serious, ponderous, cumbersome, trying, burdensome, harsh, grave.
(ANT.) brisk, light, animated.
heckle (SYN.) torment, harass, tease, hector, harry.
heed (SYN.) care, alertness, circumspection, consider, watchfulness, study, attention, notice, regard.
(ANT.) negligence, oversight, over look, neglect, ignore, disregard, indifference.
heedless (SYN.) sightless, headlong, rash, unmindful, deaf, unseeing, oblivious, ignorant, blind.
(ANT.) perceiving, sensible, aware, calculated.
height (SYN.) zenith, peak, summit, tallness, mountain, acme, apex, elevation, altitude, prominence.
(ANT.) base, depth, anticlimax.
heighten (SYN.) increase, magnify, annoy, chafe, intensify, amplify, aggravate, provoke, irritate.
(ANT.) soothe, mitigate, palliate, soften, appease.
heinous (SYN.) abominable, grievous, atrocious.
hello (SYN.) greeting, good evening, good afternoon, good morning.
(ANT.) farewell, good-bye, so long.
help (SYN.) assist, support, promote, relieve, abet, succor, back, uphold, further, remedy, encourage, aid, facilitate, mitigate.
(ANT.) afflict, thwart, resist, hinder, impede.
helper (SYN.) aide, assistant, supporter.

helpful *(SYN.)* beneficial, serviceable, wholesome, useful, profitable, advantageous, good, salutary.
(ANT.) harmful, injurious, useless, worthless, destructive, deleterious, detrimental.

helpfulness *(SYN.)* assistance, cooperation, usefulness.
(ANT.) antagonism, hostility, opposition.

helpless *(SYN.)* weak, feeble, dependent, disabled, inept, unresourceful, incapable.
(ANT.) resourceful, enterprising.

helplessness *(SYN.)* impotence, feebleness, weakness, incapacity, ineptitude, invalidism, shiftless.
(ANT.) power, strength, might, potency.

helter-skelter *(SYN.)* haphazardly, chaotically, irregularly.

hem *(SYN.)* bottom, border, edge, rim, margin, pale, verge, flounce, boundary.

hem in *(SYN.)* enclose, shut in, confine, restrict, limit.

hence *(SYN.)* consequently, thence, therefore, so, accordingly.

herald *(SYN.)* harbinger, crier, envoy, forerunner, precursor, augury, forecast.

herculean *(SYN.)* demanding, heroic, titanic, mighty, prodigious, laborious, arduous.

herd *(SYN.)* group, pack, drove, crowd, flock, gather.

heretic *(SYN.)* nonconformist, sectarian, unbeliever, sectary, schismatic, apostate.

heritage *(SYN.)* birthright, legacy, patrimony.

hermit *(SYN.)* recluse, anchorite, eremite.

hero *(SYN.)* paladin, champion, idol.

heroic *(SYN.)* bold, courageous, fearless, gallant, valiant, valorous, brave, chivalrous, adventurous, dauntless, intrepid, magnanimous.
(ANT.) fearful, weak, cringing, timid, cowardly.

heroism *(SYN.)* valor, bravery, gallant, dauntless, bold, courageous, fearless.

hesitant *(SYN.)* reluctant, unwilling, disinclined, loath, slow, averse.
(ANT.) willing, inclined, eager, ready, disposed.

hesitate *(SYN.)* falter, waver, pause, doubt, demur, delay, vacillate, wait, stammer, stutter, scruple.
(ANT.) proceed, resolve, continue, decide, persevere.

hesitation *(SYN.)* distrust, scruple, suspense, uncertainty, unbelief, ambiguity, doubt, incredulity, skepticism.
(ANT.) determination, belief, certainty, faith, conviction.

hidden *(SYN.)* undeveloped, unseen dormant, concealed, quiescent, latent, potential, inactive.
(ANT.) visible, explicit, conspicuous, evident.

hide *(SYN.)* disguise, mask, suppress, withhold, veil, cloak, conceal, screen, camouflage, pelt, skin, leather, cover.
(ANT.) reveal, show, expose, disclose, uncover, divulge.

hideous *(SYN.)* frightful, ugly, shocking, frightening, horrible, terrible, horrifying, terrifying, grisly, gross.
(ANT.) lovely, beautiful, beauteous.

high *(SYN.)* tall, eminent, exalted, elevated, high-pitched, sharp, lofty, proud, shrill, raised, strident, prominent, important, powerful, expensive, dear, high-priced, costly, grave, serious, extreme, towering.
(ANT.) low, mean, tiny, stunted, short, base, lowly, deep, insignificant, unimportant, inexpensive, reasonable, trivial, petty, small.

highly *(SYN.)* extremely, very, extraordinarily, exceedingly.

high-minded *(SYN.)* lofty, noble, honorable.

(ANT.) *dishonorable, base.*

high-priced (SYN.) dear, expensive, costly.
(ANT.) *economical, cheap.*

high-strung (SYN.) nervous, tense, wrought-up, intense.
(ANT.) *calm.*

highway (SYN.) parkway, speedway, turnpike, superhighway, freeway.

hilarious (SYN.) funny, side-splitting, hysterical.
(ANT.) *depressing, sad.*

hinder (SYN.) hamper, impede, block, retard, stop, resist, thwart, obstruct, check, prevent, interrupt, delay, slow, restrain.
(ANT.) *promote, further, assist, expedite, advance, facilitate.*

hindrance (SYN.) interruption, delay, interference, obstruction, obstacle, barrier.

hinge (SYN.) rely, depend, pivot.

hint (SYN.) reminder, allusion, suggestion, clue, tip, taste, whisper, implication, intimate, suspicion, mention, insinuation.
(ANT.) *declaration, affirmation, statement.*

hire (SYN.) employ, occupy, devote, apply, enlist, lease, rent, charter, rental, busy, engage, utilize, retain, let, avail.
(ANT.) *reject, banish, discard, fire, dismiss, discharge.*

history (SYN.) narration, relation, computation, record, account, chronicle, detail, description, narrative, annal, tale, recital.
(ANT.) *confusion, misrepresentation, distortion, caricature.*

hit (SYN.) knock, pound, strike, hurt, pummel, beat, come upon, find, discover, blow, smite.

hitch (SYN.) tether, fasten, harness, interruption, hindrance, interference.

hoard (SYN.) amass, increase, accumulate, gather, save, secret, store, cache, store, accrue, heap.
(ANT.) *dissipate, scatter, waste, diminish, squander, spend, disperse.*

hoarse (SYN.) deep, rough, husky, raucous, grating, harsh.
(ANT.) *clear.*

hoax (SYN.) ploy, ruse, wile, device, cheat, deception, antic, imposture, stratagem, stunt, guile, fraud.
(ANT.) *openness, sincerity, candor, exposure, honesty.*

hobby (SYN.) diversion, pastime, avocation.
(ANT.) *vocation, profession.*

hoist (SYN.) heave, lift, elevate, raise, crane, elevator.

hold (SYN.) grasp, occupy, possess, curb, contain, stow, carry, adhere, have, clutch, keep, maintain, clasp, grip.
(ANT.) *vacate, relinquish, surrender, abandon.*

holdup (SYN.) heist, robbery, stickup, delay, interruption.

hole (SYN.) cavity, void, pore, opening, abyss, chasm, gulf, aperture, tear, pit, burrow.

hollow (SYN.) unfilled, vacant, vain, meaningless, flimsy, false, hole, cavity.
(ANT.) *sound, solid, genuine, sincere, full.*

holy (SYN.) devout, divine, blessed, consecrated, sacred, spiritual, pious, sainted, religious, saintly, hallowed.
(ANT.) *worldly, sacrilegious, unconsecrated, evil, profane.*

home (SYN.) dwelling, abode, residence, seat, quarters, house, habitat.

homely (SYN.) uncommonly, disagreeable, ill-natured, unattractive, deformed, surly, repellent, spiteful.
(ANT.) *fair, handsome, pretty, attractive, comely, beautiful.*

honest (SYN.) sincere, trustworthy, truthful, fair, ingenuous, candid, conscientious, moral, upright, open, just, straightfoward.
(ANT.) *fraudulent, tricky, deceitful, dishonest, lying.*

honor (SYN.) esteem, praise,

worship, admiration, homage, glory, respect, admire.
(ANT.) scorn, dishonor, despise, neglect, abuse, shame, derision, disgrace.

honorable (SYN.) fair, noble, creditable, proper, reputable, honest, admirable, true, trusty, eminent.
(ANT.) infamous, disgraceful, shameful, dishonorable.

honorary (SYN.) gratuitous, complimentary.

hoodlum (SYN.) crook, gangster, criminal, hooligan.

hope (SYN.) expectation, faith, optimism, anticipation, expectancy.
(ANT.) pessimism, despair, despondency.

hopeless (SYN.) desperate, incurable, disastrous.
(ANT.) promising, hopeful.

horde (SYN.) host, masses, press, rabble, swarm, multitude, crowd, populace.

horizontal (SYN.) even, level, plane, flat, straight.
(ANT.) upright, vertical.

horrendous (SYN.) awful, horrifying, terrible, dreadful.
(ANT.) splendid, wonderful.

horrible (SYN.) awful, dire, ghastly, horrid, repulsive, frightful, appalling, horrifying, dreadful, ghastly.
(ANT.) enjoyable, enchanting, beautiful, lovely, fascinating.

horrid (SYN.) repulsive, terrible, appalling, dire, awful, frightful, fearful, shocking.
(ANT.) fascinating, enchanting, enjoyable, lovely.

horror (SYN.) dread, awe, hatred, loathing, foreboding, alarm, apprehension.
(ANT.) courage, boldness, assurance, confidence.

hospital (SYN.) infirmary, clinic, sanatorium, rest home, sanitarium.

hospitality (SYN.) warmth, liberality, generosity, graciousness, welcome.

hostile (SYN.) unfriendly, opposed, antagonistic, inimical, adverse, warlike.
(ANT.) friendly, favorable,

amicable, cordial.

hot (SYN.) scorching, fervent, fiery, impetuous, scalding, heated, sizzling, blazing, frying, roasting, warm.
(ANT.) indifferent, apathetic, bland, frigid, cold, freezing, cool, phlegmatic.

hotbed (SYN.) sink, nest, well, den, nursery, cradle, source, incubator, seedbed.

hotel (SYN.) hostel, motel, inn, hostelry.

hourly (SYN.) frequently, steadily, constantly, unfailingly, perpetually, ceaselessly, continually.
(ANT.) occasionally, seldom.

house (SYN.) building, residence, abode, dwelling.

housebreaker (SYN.) robber, thief, prowler, cracksman.

housing (SYN.) lodgings, shelter, dwelling, lodgment.

hovel (SYN.) cabin, hut, sty, shack, shed.

hover (SYN.) hang, drift, poise, stand by, linger, impend, waver, hand around.

hub (SYN.) pivot, center, core, heart, axis, basis, focus.

hubbub (SYN.) uproar, tumult, commotion, clamor.
(ANT.) peacefulness, stillness, silence, quiet, quiescence.

huddle (SYN.) mass, herd, bunch, crowd, cram, gather, shove, flock, ball.

hue (SYN.) pigment, tint, shade, dye, complexion, paint, color, tone, tincture.
(ANT.) transparency, achromatism, paleness.

huffy (SYN.) sensitive, vulnerable, testy, offended, thin-skinned, touchy, irascible.
(ANT.) tough, placid, stolid, impassive.

hug (SYN.) embrace, coddle, caress, kiss, pet, press, clasp, fondle, cuddle.
(ANT.) tease, vex, spurn, buffet, annoy.

huge (SYN.) great, immense, vast, ample, big, capacious, extensive, gigantic, enormous, vast, tremendous.
(ANT.) short, small, mean,

little, tiny.

hulking *(SYN.)* massive, awkward, bulky, ponderous.

hum *(SYN.)* whir, buzz, whizz, purr, croon, murmur, intone, vibrate.

human *(SYN.)* manlike, hominid, mortal, fleshly, individual, person, tellurian.

humanist *(SYN.)* scholar, sage, savant.

humanitarianism *(SYN.)* good will, beneficence, philanthropy, humanism.

humble *(SYN.)* modest, crush, mortify, simple, shame, subdue, meek, abase, break, plain, submissive, compliant, unpretentious.
(ANT.) praise, arrogant, exalt, illustrious, boastful, honor.

humbly *(SYN.)* deferentially, meekly, respectfully, unassumingly, diffidently, modestly, subserviently.
(ANT.) insolently, proudly, grandly, arrogantly.

humid *(SYN.)* moist, damp, misty, muggy, wet, watery.
(ANT.) parched, dry.

humiliate *(SYN.)* corrupt, defile, depress, pervert, abase, degrade, disgrace.
(ANT.) restore, raise, improve.

humiliation *(SYN.)* chagrin, dishonor, ignominy.
(ANT.) honor, praise, dignity, renown.

humor *(SYN.)* jocularity, wit, irony, joking, amusement, facetiousness, joke, disposition, waggery, fun, clowning.
(ANT.) sorrow, gravity, seriousness.

hunger *(SYN.)* desire, longing, zest, craving, liking, passion.
(ANT.) satiety, repugnance, disgust, distaste.

hunt *(SYN.)* pursuit, investigation, examination, inquiry.
(ANT.) cession, abandonment.

hurried *(SYN.)* rushed, hasty, swift, headlong, slipshod, careless, impulsive.
(ANT.) deliberate, slow, dilatory, thorough.

hurry *(SYN.)* quicken, speed, ado, rush, accelerate, run, hasten, race, urge, bustle.
(ANT.) retard, tarry, hinder, linger, dawdle, delay.

hurt *(SYN.)* damage, harm, grievance, detriment, pain, injustice, injure, abuse, distress, disfigured, mar.
(ANT.) improvement, repair, compliment, help, praise.

hurtle *(SYN.)* charge, collide, rush, crash, lunge, bump.

husband *(SYN.)* spouse, mate.

husk *(SYN.)* shell, hull, pod, skin, covering, crust, bark.

hustle *(SYN.)* hasten, run, hurry, speed.

hut *(SYN.)* cottage, shanty, cabin, shed.

hutch *(SYN.)* box, chest, locker, trunk, coffer, bin.

hybrid *(SYN.)* mule, mixture, crossbreed, cross, mongrel, mutt, composite.

hypercritical *(SYN.)* faultfinding, captious, censorious.
(ANT.) lax, easygoing, indulgent, lenient, tolerant.

hypnotic *(SYN.)* soothing, opiate, sedative, soporific, entrancing, spellbinding, arresting, charming, engaging, gripping.

hypnotize *(SYN.)* entrance, dazzle, mesmerize, fascinate, spellbind.

hypocrisy *(SYN.)* pretense, deceit, dissembling, fakery, feigning, pharisaism, sanctimony, cant, dissimulation.
(ANT.) openness, candor, truth, directness, forthrightness, honesty, frankness.

hypocrite *(SYN.)* cheat, deceiver, pretender, dissembler, fake, charlatan.

hypocritical *(SYN.)* dissembling, two-faced, insincere, dishonest, duplicitous, deceitful, phony.
(ANT.) heartfelt, true, genuine, honest.

hypothesis *(SYN.)* law, theory, supposition, conjecture.
(ANT.) proof, fact, certainty.

hypothetical *(SYN.)* conjectural, speculative.
(ANT.) actual.

idea (SYN.) conception, image, opinion, sentiment, thought, impression.
(ANT.) thing, matter, entity, object, substance.

ideal (SYN.) imaginary, supreme, unreal, visionary, exemplary, utopian.
(ANT.) imperfect, actual, material, real, faulty.

identify (ANT.) recollect, apprehend, perceive, remember, confess, acknowledge.
(ANT.) ignore, forget, overlook, renounce, disown.

idiom (SYN.) language, speech, vernacular, lingo, dialect, jargon, slang.
(ANT.) babble, gibberish, drivel, nonsense.

idiot (SYN.) buffoon, harlequin, dolt, jester, dunce, blockhead, imbecile, numbskull, simpleton, oaf.
(ANT.) philosopher, genius, scholar, sage.

idle (SYN.) unemployed, dormant, lazy, inactive, unoccupied, indolent, slothful.
(ANT.) occupied, working, employed, active, industrious, busy, engaged.

ignoble (SYN.) dishonorable, ignominious, lowly, menial, vile, sordid, vulgar, abject.
(ANT.) righteous, lofty, honored, esteemed, noble.

ignorant (SYN.) uneducated, untaught, uncultured, illiterate, uninformed.
(ANT.) cultured, literate, educated, erudite, informed, cultivated, schooled, learned.

ignore (SYN.) omit, slight, disregard, overlook, neglect.
(ANT.) notice, regard, include.

ill (SYN.) diseased, ailing, indisposed, morbid, infirm, unwell, unhealthy, sick.
(ANT.) robust, strong, healthy, well, sound, fit.

illegal (SYN.) prohibited, unlawful, criminal, illicit.
(ANT.) permitted, lawful, honest, legal, legitimate.

illiberal (SYN.) fanatical, bigoted, intolerant, narrow-minded, dogmatic.
(ANT.) progressive, liberal.

illicit (SYN.) illegitimate, criminal, outlawed, unlawful, prohibited, illegal.
(ANT.) legal, honest, permitted, lawful, licit.

illness (SYN.) complaint, infirmity, ailment, disorder.
(ANT.) healthiness, health, soundness, vigor.

illogical (SYN.) absurd, irrational, preposterous.

illuminate (SYN.) enlighten, clarify, irradiate, illustrate, light, lighten, explain, interpret, elucidate, brighten.
(ANT.) obscure, confuse, darken, obfuscate, shadow.

illusion (SYN.) hallucination, vision, phantom, delusion, fantasy, dream, mirage.
(ANT.) substance, actuality.

illusive (SYN.) fallacious, delusive, false, specious.
(ANT.) real, truthful, authentic, genuine, honest.

illustrate (SYN.) decorate, illuminate, adorn, show, picture, embellish.

illustrious (SYN.) prominent, eminent, renowned, famed, great, vital, elevated, noble, excellent, dignified, gigantic, enormous, immense.
(ANT.) menial, common, minute, diminutive, small, obscure, ordinary, little.

image (SYN.) reflection, likeness, idea, representation, notion, picture, conception.

imaginary (SYN.) fanciful, fantastic, unreal, whimsical.
(ANT.) actual, real.

imagine (SYN.) assume, surmise, suppose, conceive, dream, pretend, conjecture.

imbecile (SYN.) idiot, numbskull, simpleton, blockhead, harlequin, nincompoop.
(ANT.) scholar, genius, philosopher, sage.

imbibe (SYN.) absorb, consume, assimilate, engulf, engage, occupy, engross.
(ANT.) dispense, exude, discharge, emit.

imitate (SYN.) duplicate,

mimic, follow, reproduce, mock, counterfeit, copy.
(ANT.) invent, distort, alter.
imitation (SYN.) replica, reproduction copy, duplicate, facsimile, transcript.
(ANT.) prototype, original.
immaculate (SYN.) clean, spotless, unblemished.
(ANT.) dirty.
immature (SYN.) young, boyish, childish, youthful, childlike, puerile, girlish.
(ANT.) old, senile, aged, elderly, mature.
immediately (SYN.) now, presently, instantly, promptly, straightway, directly, instantaneously, forthwith.
(ANT.) sometime, hereafter, later, shortly, distantly.
immense (SYN.) enormous, large, gigantic, huge, colossal, elephantine, great.
(ANT.) small, diminutive, little, minuscule, minute.
immensity (SYN.) hugeness, enormousness, vastness.
immerse (SYN.) plunge, dip, dunk, sink, submerge, engage, absorb, engross.
(ANT.) uplift, elevate, recover.
immigration (SYN.) settlement, colonization.
(ANT.) exodus, emigration.
imminent (SYN.) impending, menacing, threatening.
(ANT.) retreating, afar, distant, improbable, remote.
immoral (SYN.) sinful, wicked, corrupt, bad, indecent, profligate, unprincipled.
(ANT.) pure, high-minded, chaste, virtuous, noble.
immortal (SYN.) infinite, eternal, timeless, undying, perpetual, ceaseless.
(ANT.) mortal, transient, finite, ephemeral, temporal.
immune (SYN.) easy, open, autonomous, unobstructed, free, emancipated, clear, independent, unrestricted.
(ANT.) confined, impeded, restricted, subject.
impact (SYN.) striking, contact, collision.
impair (SYN.) harm, injure,

spoil, deface, destroy, hurt, damage, mar.
(ANT.) repair, mend, ameliorate, enhance, benefit.
impart (SYN.) convey, disclose, inform, tell, reveal, transmit, notify, confer, divulge, communicate, relate.
(ANT.) withhold, conceal.
impartial (SYN.) unbiased, just, honest, fair, reasonable, equitable.
(ANT.) fraudulent, dishonorable, partial.
impartiality (SYN.) indifference, unconcern, impartiality, neutrality, disinterestedness, insensibility.
(ANT.) passion, ardor, fervor, affection.
impede (SYN.) hamper, hinder, retard, thwart, check, encumber, interrupt, bar, clog, delay, obstruct, block, frustrate, restrain, stop.
(ANT.) assist, promote, help, advance, further.
impediment (SYN.) barrier, bar, block, difficulty, check, hindrance, obstruction.
(ANT.) assistance, help, aid, encouragement.
impel (SYN.) oblige, enforce, coerce, force, constrain.
(ANT.) induce, prevent, convince, persuade.
impending (SYN.) imminent, nigh, threatening, overhanging, approaching, menacing.
(ANT.) remote, improbable, afar, distant, retreating.
imperative (SYN.) critical, instant, important, necessary, serious, urgent, cogent, compelling, crucial, pressing, impelling, importunate.
(ANT.) trivial, insignificant, unimportant, petty.
imperfection (SYN.) flaw, shortcoming, vice, defect, blemish, failure, mistake.
(ANT.) correctness, perfection, completeness.
imperil (SYN.) jeopardize, risk, endanger, hazard, risk.
(ANT.) guard, insure.
impersonal (SYN.) objective, detached, disinterested.

(ANT.) personal.

impersonate *(SYN.)* mock, simulate, imitate, ape, counterfeit, copy, duplicate.
(ANT.) invent, diverge, distort.

impertinent *(SYN.)* rude, offensive, insolent, disrespectful, arrogant, brazen, impudent, insulting, contemptuous, abusive.
(ANT.) polite, respectful, considerate, courteous.

impetuous *(SYN.)* rash, heedless, quick, hasty, careless, passionate, impulsive.
(ANT.) cautious, reasoning, careful, prudent, calculating.

implicate *(SYN.)* reproach, accuse, blame, involve, upbraid, condemn, incriminate, rebuke, censure.
(ANT.) exonerate, acquit.

implore *(SYN.)* beg, pray, request, solicit, crave, entreat, beseech, ask, supplicate.
(ANT.) give, cede, bestow, favor, grant.

imply *(SYN.)* mean, involve, suggest, connote, hint, mention, indicate, insinuate.
(ANT.) state, assert, declare, express.

important *(SYN.)* critical, grave, influential, momentous, pressing, relevant, prominent, essential, material, famous, principle, famed, sequential, notable, significant, illustrious.
(ANT.) unimportant, trifling, petty, trivial, insignificant, secondary, irrelevant.

imposing *(SYN.)* lofty, noble, majestic, magnificent, august, dignified, grandiose, high, grand, impressive, pompous, stately.
(ANT.) ordinary, undignified, humble, common, lowly.

imposition *(SYN.)* load, onus, burden.

impregnable *(SYN.)* safe, invulnerable, unassailable.
(ANT.) vulnerable.

impress *(SYN.)* awe, emboss, affect, mark, imprint, indent, influence.

impression *(SYN.)* influence, indentation, feeling, opinion, mark, effect, depression, guess, thought, belief.
(ANT.) fact, insensibility.

impromptu *(SYN.)* casual, unprepared, extemporaneous.

improper *(SYN.)* unfit, unsuitable, inappropriate, indecent, unbecoming.
(ANT.) fitting, proper, appropriate.

improve *(SYN.)* better, reform, refine, ameliorate, amend, help, upgrade.
(ANT.) debase, vitiate, impair, corrupt, damage.

imprudent *(SYN.)* indiscreet, thoughtless, desultory, lax, neglectful, remiss, careless, inattentive, heedless, inconsiderate, reckless, ill-advised, irresponsible.
(ANT.) careful, meticulous, accurate.

impudence *(SYN.)* boldness, insolence, rudeness, sauciness, assurance, effrontery, impertinence, presumption.
(ANT.) politeness, truckling, subserviency, diffidence.

impulse *(SYN.)* hunch, whim, fancy, urge, caprice, surge.

impulsive *(SYN.)* passionate, rash, spontaneous, heedless, careless, hasty, quick.
(ANT.) reasoning, calculating, careful, prudent, cautious.

inability *(SYN.)* incompetence, incapacity, handicap, disability, impotence.
(ANT.) power, strength, ability, capability.

inaccurate *(SYN.)* false, incorrect, mistaken, untrue, askew, wrong, awry, erroneous, fallacious.
(ANT.) right, accurate, true, correct.

inactive *(SYN.)* lazy, unemployed, indolent, motionless, still, inert.
(ANT.) employed, working, active, industrious, occupied.

inadequate *(SYN.)* insufficient, lacking, short, incomplete, defective, scanty.
(ANT.) satisfactory, enough, adequate, ample, sufficient.

inadvertent (SYN.) careless, negligent, unthinking.

inane (SYN.) trite, insipid, banal, absurd, silly, commonplace, vapid, foolish.
(ANT.) stimulating, novel, fresh, original, striking.

inanimate (SYN.) deceased, spiritless, lifeless, gone, dull, mineral, departed.
(ANT.) living, stirring, alive, animate.

inattentive (SYN.) absent-minded, distracted, abstracted, preoccupied.
(ANT.) watchful, attending, attentive.

inaugurate (SYN.) commence, begin, open, originate, start, arise, launch, enter.
(ANT.) end, terminate, close, complete, finish.

incentive (SYN.) impulse, stimulus, inducement.
(ANT.) discouragement.

inception (SYN.) origin, start, source, opening, beginning, outset, commencement.
(ANT.) end, termination, close, completion.

incessant (SYN.) perennial, uninterrupted, continual, ceaseless, continuous, unremitting, eternal, constant.
(ANT.) rare, occasional, periodic, interrupted.

incident (SYN.) happening, situation, occurrence, circumstance, condition.

incidental (SYN.) casual, contingent, trivial, undesigned.
(ANT.) intended, fundamental, planned, calculated.

incinerate (SYN.) sear, char, blaze, scald, singe, consume.
(ANT.) quench, put out, extinguish.

incisive (SYN.) neat, succinct, terse, brief, compact, condensed, summary, concise.
(ANT.) wordy, prolix, verbose.

incite (SYN.) goad, provoke, urge, arouse, encourage.
(ANT.) quiet, bore, pacify, soothe.

inclination (SYN.) bent, preference, desire, slope, affection, bent, bias, disposi-

tion, bending, penchant.
(ANT.) nonchalance, apathy, distaste, reluctance, disinclination, repugnance.

include (SYN.) contain, hold, accommodate, embody, encompass, involve, comprise.
(ANT.) omit, exclude, discharge.

incomparable (SYN.) peerless, matchless, unequaled.

incompetency (SYN.) inability, weakness, handicap, impotence, disability.
(ANT.) strength, ability, power, capability.

incongruous (SYN.) inconsistent, contrary, incompatible, irreconcilable, contradictory, unsteady, incongruous.
(ANT.) consistent, compatible, correspondent.

inconsiderate (SYN.) unthinking, careless, unthoughtful.
(ANT.) logical, consistent.

inconsistency (SYN.) discord, variance, contention.
(ANT.) harmony, concord, amity, consonance.

inconsistent (SYN.) fickle, wavering, variable, changeable, contrary, unstable, illogical, contradictory.
(ANT.) unchanging, steady, logical, stable, uniform.

inconspicuous (SYN.) retiring, unnoticed, unostentatious.
(ANT.) obvious, conspicuous.

inconstant (SYN.) fickle, shifting, changeable, fitful, vacillating, unstable, wavering.
(ANT.) stable, constant, steady, uniform, unchanging.

inconvenient (SYN.) awkward, inappropriate, untimely.
(ANT.) handy, convenient.

incorrect (SYN.) mistaken, wrong, erroneous.
(ANT.) proper, accurate.

increase (SYN.) amplify, enlarge, grow, magnify, multiply, augment, enhance, expand, intensify, swell, raise.
(ANT.) diminish, reduce, atrophy, shrink, shrinkage.

incredible (SYN.) improbable, unbelievable.
(ANT.) plausible, credible,

believable.

incriminate *(SYN.)* charge, accuse, indict, arraign.
(ANT.) release, exonerate, acquit, absolve, vindicate.

incrimination *(SYN.)* imputation, indictment, accusation, charge, arraignment.
(ANT.) exoneration, pardon, exculpation.

indecent *(SYN.)* impure, obscene, coarse, dirty, filthy, smutty, gross, disgusting.
(ANT.) modest, refined, decent, pure.

indeed *(SYN.)* truthfully, really, honestly, surely.

indefinite *(SYN.)* unsure, uncertain, vague, confused.
(ANT.) decided, definite, equivocal.

independence *(SYN.)* liberation, privilege, freedom, immunity, familiarity.
(ANT.) necessity, constraint, compulsion, reliance, dependence, bondage, servitude.

indestructible *(SYN.)* enduring, lasting, permanent, unchangeable, abiding.
(ANT.) unstable, temporary, transitory, ephemeral.

indicate *(SYN.)* imply, denote, signify, specify, intimate, designate, symbolize, show.
(ANT.) mislead, falsify, distract, conceal, falsify.

indication *(SYN.)* proof, emblem, omen, sign, symbol, token, mark, portent.

indict *(SYN.)* charge, accuse, incriminate, censure.
(ANT.) acquit, vindicate, absolve, exonerate.

indigence *(SYN.)* necessity, destitution, poverty, want, need, privation, penury.
(ANT.) wealth, abundance, plenty, riches, affluence.

indigenous *(SYN.)* inborn, native, inherent, domestic.

indigent *(SYN.)* wishing, covetous, demanding, lacking, requiring, wanting.

indignant *(SYN.)* irritated, irate, angry, aroused.
(ANT.) calm, serene, content.

indignity *(SYN.)* insolence, insult, abuse, affront, offense.
(ANT.) homage, apology, salutation.

indirect *(SYN.)* winding, crooked, devious, roundabout, cunning, tricky.
(ANT.) straightforward, direct, straight, honest.

indiscretion *(SYN.)* imprudence, folly, absurdity.
(ANT.) prudence, sense, wisdom, judgment.

indispensable *(SYN.)* necessary, fundamental, basic, essential, important, intrinsic.
(ANT.) optional, expendable, peripheral, extrinsic.

indistinct *(SYN.)* cloudy, dark, mysterious, vague, blurry, ambiguous, cryptic, dim, obscure, enigmatic, abstruse, hazy, blurred.
(ANT.) clear, lucid, bright, distinct.

individual *(SYN.)* singular, specific, unique, distinctive, single, particular, undivided, human, apart, different, special, separate.
(ANT.) universal, common, general, ordinary.

individuality *(SYN.)* symbol, description, mark, kind, character, repute, class, standing, sort, nature, disposition, reputation, sign.

indolent *(SYN.)* slothful, lazy, idle, inactive, slow, sluggish, torpid, supine, inert.
(ANT.) diligent, active, assiduous, vigorous, alert.

indomitable *(SYN.)* insurmountable, unconquerable, invulnerable, impregnable.
(ANT.) weak, puny, powerless, vulnerable.

induce *(SYN.)* evoke, cause, influence, persuade, effect, make, originate, prompt, incite, create.

inducement *(SYN.)* incentive, motive, purpose, stimulus, reason, impulse, cause, principle, spur, incitement.
(ANT.) result, attempt, action, effort, deed.

induct *(SYN.)* instate, establish, install.

indulge (SYN.) humor, satisfy, gratify.

indulgent (SYN.) obliging, pampering, tolerant, easy.

indurate (SYN.) impenitent, hard, insensible, tough, obdurate, callous, unfeeling.
(ANT.) soft, compassionate, tender, sensitive.

industrious (SYN.) hard-working, perseverant, busy, active, diligent, assiduous, careful, patient.
(ANT.) unconcerned, indifferent, lethargic, careless, apathetic, lazy, indolent, shiftless.

inebriated (SYN.) drunk, tight, drunken, intoxicated, tipsy.
(ANT.) sober, clearheaded, temperate.

ineffective (SYN.) pliant, tender, vague, wavering, defenseless, weak, inadequate, poor, irresolute, frail, decrepit, delicate, vacillating, assailable, vulnerable.
(ANT.) sturdy, robust, strong, potent, powerful.

inept (SYN.) clumsy, awkward, improper, inappropriate.
(ANT.) adroit, dexterous, adept, appropriate, proper, apt, fitting.

inequity (SYN.) wrong, injustice, grievance, injury.
(ANT.) righteousness, lawfulness, equity, justice.

inert (SYN.) lazy, dormant, slothful, inactive, idle, indolent, motionless, unmoving, fixed, static.
(ANT.) working, active, industrious, occupied.

inertia (SYN.) indolence, torpidity, idleness, slothfulness, sluggishness, supineness.
(ANT.) assiduousness, activity, alertness, diligence.

inevitable (SYN.) definite, fixed, positive, sure, undeniable, indubitable, certain, assured, unquestionable, secure.
(ANT.) uncertain, probable, doubtful, questionable.

inexpensive (SYN.) low-priced, cheap, inferior, mean, beggarly, common, poor, shabby, modest, economical.
(ANT.) expensive, costly, dear.

inexperienced (SYN.) naive, untrained, uninformed.
(ANT.) experienced, skilled, sophisticated, trained, seasoned.

inexplicable (SYN.) hidden, mysterious, obscure, secret, dark, cryptic, enigmatical, incomprehensible, occult, recondite, inscrutable, dim.
(ANT.) plain, simple, clear, obvious, explained.

infamous (SYN.) shocking, shameful, scandalous.

infantile (SYN.) babyish, naive, immature, childish.
(ANT.) mature, grownup, adult.

infect (SYN.) pollute, poison, contaminate, defile, sully, taint.
(ANT.) purify, disinfect.

infection (SYN.) virus, poison, ailment, disease, pollution, pest, germ, taint, contamination, contagion.

infectious (SYN.) contagious, virulent, catching, communicable, pestilential, transferable.
(ANT.) noncommunicable, hygienic, healthful.

infer (SYN.) understand, deduce, extract.

inference (SYN.) consequence, result, conclusion, corollary, judgment, deduction.
(ANT.) preconception, foreknowledge, assumption, presupposition.

inferior (SYN.) secondary, lower, poorer, minor, subordinate, mediocre.
(ANT.) greater, superior, better, higher.

infinite (SYN.) immeasurable, interminable, unlimited, unbounded, eternal, boundless, illimitable, immense, endless, vast, innumerable, numberless, limitless.

(ANT.) confined, limited, bounded, circumscribed, finite.

infinitesimal *(SYN.)* minute, microscopic, tiny, sub-microscopic.
(ANT.) gigantic, huge, enormous.

infirm *(SYN.)* feeble, impaired, decrepit, forceless, languid, puny, powerless, enervated, weak, exhausted.
(ANT.) stout, vigorous, forceful, lusty, strong.

infirmity *(SYN.)* disease, illness, malady, ailment, sickness, disorder, complaint.
(ANT.) soundness, health, vigor, healthiness.

inflame *(SYN.)* fire, incite, excite, arouse.
(ANT.) soothe, calm.

inflammation *(SYN.)* infection, soreness, irritation.

inflammatory *(SYN.)* instigating, inciting, provocative.

inflate *(SYN.)* expand, swell, distend.
(ANT.) collapse, deflate.

inflexible *(SYN.)* firm, stubborn, headstrong, immovable, unyielding, uncompromising, dogged, contumacious, determined, obstinate, rigid, unbending, unyielding, steadfast.
(ANT.) submissive, compliant, docile, amenable, yielding, flexible, giving, elastic.

inflict *(SYN.)* deliver, deal, give, impose, apply.

influence *(SYN.)* weight, control, effect, sway.

influenced *(SYN.)* sway, affect, bias, control, actuate, impel, stir, incite.

influential *(SYN.)* important, weighty, prominent, significant, critical, decisive, momentous, relevant, material, pressing, consequential, grave.
(ANT.) petty, irrelevant, mean, trivial, insignificant.

inform *(SYN.)* apprise, instruct, tell, notify, advise, acquaint, enlighten, impart, warn, teach, advise, relate.
(ANT.) delude, mislead, distract, conceal.

informal *(SYN.)* simple, easy, natural, unofficial, familiar.
(ANT.) formal, distant, reserved, proper.

informality *(SYN.)* friendship, frankness, liberty, acquaintance, sociability, intimacy, unreserved.
(ANT.) presumption, constraint, reserve, distance, haughtiness.

information *(SYN.)* knowledge, data, intelligence, facts.

informative *(SYN.)* educational, enlightening, instructive.

informer *(SYN.)* tattler, traitor, betrayer.

infrequent *(SYN.)* unusual, rare, occasional, strange.
(ANT.) commonplace, abundant, usual, ordinary, customary, frequent, numerous.

ingenious *(SYN.)* clever, skillful, talented, adroit, dexterous, quick-witted, bright, smart, witty, sharp, apt, resourceful, imaginative, inventive, creative.
(ANT.) dull, slow, awkward, bungling, unskilled, stupid.

ingenuity *(SYN.)* cunning, inventiveness, resourcefulness, aptitude, faculty, cleverness, ingenuousness.
(ANT.) ineptitude, clumsiness, dullness, stupidity.

ingenuous *(SYN.)* open, sincere, honest, candid, straightforward, plain, frank, truthful, free, naive, simple, innocent, unsophisticated.
(ANT.) scheming, sly, contrived, wily.

ingredient *(SYN.)* component, element, constituent.

inhabit *(SYN.)* fill, possess, absorb, dwell, occupy, live.
(ANT.) relinquish, abandon, release.

inherent *(SYN.)* innate, native, congenital, inherent, intrinsic, inborn, inbred, natural,

real.
(ANT.) extraneous, acquired, external, extrinsic.

inhibit (SYN.) curb, constrain, hold back, restrain, bridle, hinder, repress, suppress, stop, limit.
(ANT.) loosen, aid, incite, encourage.

inhuman (SYN.) merciless, cruel, brutal, ferocious, savage, ruthless, malignant, barbarous, barbaric, bestial.
(ANT.) kind, benevolent, forbearing, gentle, compassionate, merciful, humane, humane.

inimical (SYN.) hostile, warlike, adverse, antagonistic, opposed, unfriendly.
(ANT.) favorable, amicable, cordial.

iniquitous (SYN.) baleful, immoral, pernicious, sinfu.,
(ANT.) moral, good, excellent, honorable, reputable.

iniquity (SYN.) injustice, wrong, grievance.
(ANT.) lawful, equity, righteousness, justice.

initial (SYN.) original, first, prime, beginning, earliest.
(ANT.) latest, subordinate, last, least, hindmost, final.

initiate (SYN.) institute, enter, arise, inaugurate.
(ANT.) terminate, complete, end, finish, close, stop.

initiative (SYN.) enthusiasm, energy, vigor, enterprise.

injure (SYN.) harm, wound, abuse, dishonor, damage, hurt, impair, spoil.
(ANT.) praise, ameliorate, help, preserve, compliment.

injurious (SYN.) detrimental, harmful, mischievous, damaging, hurtful, deleterious.
(ANT.) profitable, helpful, advantageous, salutary, beneficial, useful.

injury (SYN.) harm, detriment, damage, injustice, wrong, prejudice, grievance.
(ANT.) repair, benefit, improvement.

injustice (SYN.) unfairness, grievance, iniquity, wrong.

(ANT.) righteousness, justice, equity, lawfulness.

innate (SYN.) native, inherent, congenital, innate, real, inborn, natural, intrinsic.
(ANT.) extraneous, acquired, external, extrinsic.

innocent (SYN.) pure, sinless, blameless, innocuous, lawful, naive, faultless, virtuous.
(ANT.) guilty, corrupt, sinful, culpable, sophisticated, wise.

innocuous (SYN.) naive, pure, innocent, blameless, virtuous, lawful, faultless.
(ANT.) sinful, corrupt, unrighteous, culpable, guilty.

inquire (SYN.) ask, solicit, invite, demand, claim, entreat, interrogate, query, beg.
(ANT.) dictate, insist, reply, command, order.

inquiry (SYN.) investigation, quest, research, examination, interrogation.
(ANT.) inattention, inactivity, disregard, negligence.

inquisitive (SYN.) meddling, peeping, nosy, interrogative, peering, searching, prying.
(ANT.) unconcerned, indifferent, incurious.

insane (SYN.) deranged, mad, foolish, idiotic, demented.
(ANT.) sane, rational, reasonable, sound, sensible.

insensitive (SYN.) unfeeling, impenitent, callous, hard.
(ANT.) soft, compassionate, tender, sensitive.

insight (SYN.) intuition, acumen, penetration.
(ANT.) obtuseness.

insignificant (SYN.) trivial, paltry, petty, small, frivolous, unimportant.
(ANT.) momentous, serious, important, weighty.

insist (SYN.) command, demand, require.

insolence (SYN.) boldness, presumption, sauciness, effrontery, audacity.
(ANT.) politeness, truckling, diffidence, subserviency.

insolent (SYN.) arrogant, impertinent, insulting, rude.
(ANT.) respectful, courteous,

polite, considerate.

inspect *(SYN.)* observe, discern, eye, behold, glance, scan, stare, survey, view.
(ANT.) overlook, miss, avert.

inspection *(SYN.)* examination, retrospect, survey.

inspiration *(SYN.)* creativity, aptitude, genius, originality.
(ANT.) dullard, moron, shallowness, ineptitude, stupidity.

instance *(SYN.)* occasion, illustration, occurrence.

instant *(SYN.)* flash, moment.

instantaneous *(SYN.)* hasty, sudden unexpected, rapid, abrupt, immediate.
(ANT.) slowly, anticipated.

instantly *(SYN.)* now, presently, directly, forthwith, immediately, rapidly.
(ANT.) sometime, distantly, hereafter, later, shortly.

institute *(SYN.)* ordain, establish, raise, form, organize, begin, initiate.
(ANT.) overthrow, upset, demolish, abolish, unsettle.

instruct *(SYN.)* teach, tutor, educate, inform, school, instill, train, inculcate, drill.
(ANT.) misinform, misguide.

instrument *(SYN.)* channel, device, utensil, tool, agent, medium, agent, implement.
(ANT.) obstruction, hindrance, preventive.

insubordinate *(SYN.)* rebellious, unruly, defiant, disorderly, disobedient, undutiful, refractory, intractable.
(ANT.) obedient, compliant, submissive, dutiful.

insufficient *(SYN.)* limited, deficient, inadequate.
(ANT.) ample, protracted, abundant, big, extended.

insulation *(SYN.)* quarantine, segregation, seclusion, withdrawal, isolation, loneliness, alienation, solitude.
(ANT.) union, communion, association, connection.

insult *(SYN.)* insolence, offense, abuse, dishonor, affront, insult, indignity, offend, humiliate, outrage.
(ANT.) compliment, homage,

apology, salutation, praise.

integrated *(SYN.)* mingled, mixed, combined, interspersed, desegregated, nonsectarian, interracial.
(ANT.) separated, divided, segregated.

integrity *(SYN.)* honesty, openness, trustworthiness, fairness, candor, justice, rectitude, sincerity, soundness, wholeness, honor, principle, virtue.
(ANT.) fraud, deceit, cheating, trickery, dishonesty.

intellect *(SYN.)* understanding, judgment.

intellectual *(SYN.)* intelligent.

intelligence *(SYN.)* reason, sense, intellect, understanding, mind, ability, skill.
(ANT.) passion, emotion.

intelligent *(SYN.)* clever, smart, knowledgeable, well-informed, alert, discerning, astute, quick, enlightened, smart, bright, wise.
(ANT.) insipid, obtuse, dull, stupid, slow, foolish, unintelligent, dumb.

intend *(SYN.)* plan, prepare, scheme, contrive, outline, design, sketch, plot, project.

intense *(SYN.)* brilliant, animated, graphic, lucid, bright, expressive, vivid, deep, profound, concentrated, serious, earnest.
(ANT.) dull, vague, dusky, dim, dreary.

intensify *(SYN.)* accrue, augment, amplify, enlarge, enhance, extend, expand, grow, magnify, multiply.
(ANT.) reduce, decrease, contract, diminish.

intent *(SYN.)* purpose, design, objective, intention, aim.
(ANT.) accidental, result, chance.

intensity *(SYN.)* force, potency, power, toughness, activity, durability, fortitude, vigor, stamina.
(ANT.) weakness, feebleness, infirmity, frailty.

intention *(SYN.)* intent, purpose, objective, plan, expec-

tation, aim, object.
(ANT.) chance, accident.

intentional (SYN.) deliberate, intended, studied, willful, contemplated, premeditated, designed, voluntary, purposeful, planned.
(ANT.) fortuitous, accidental, chance.

intentionally (SYN.) purposefully, deliberately.
(ANT.) accidentally.

interest (SYN.) attention, concern, care, advantage, benefit, profit, ownership, credit, attract, engage, amuse.
(ANT.) apathy, weary, disinterest.

interested (SYN.) affected, concerned.
(ANT.) unconcerned, indifferent, uninterested.

interesting (SYN.) engaging, inviting, fascinating.
(ANT.) boring, tedious, uninteresting, wearisome.

interfere (SYN.) meddle, monkey, interpose, interrupt, tamper, butt in, intervene.

interference (SYN.) prying, intrusion, meddling, obstacle, obstruction.

interior (SYN.) internal, inmost, inner, inward, inside, center.
(ANT.) outer, adjacent, exterior, external, outside.

interject (SYN.) intrude, introduce, inject, interpose.
(ANT.) avoid, disregard.

interminable (SYN.) immense, endless, immeasurable, unlimited, vast, unbounded, boundless, eternal, infinite.
(ANT.) limited, bounded, circumscribed, confined.

internal (SYN.) inner, interior, inside, intimate, private.
(ANT.) outer, external, surface.

interpose (SYN.) arbitrate, inject, intervene, meddle, insert, interject, introduce, intercede, intrude, interfere.
(ANT.) overlook, avoid, disregard.

interpret (SYN.) explain, solve, translate, construe,

elucidate, decode, explicate, unravel, define, understand.
(ANT.) misinterpret, falsify, confuse, distort, misconstrue.

interrogate (SYN.) quiz, analyze, inquire, audit, question, contemplate, assess, dissect, notice, scan, review, view, check, survey, scrutinize, examine.
(ANT.) overlook, omit, neglect, disregard.

interrupt (SYN.) suspend, delay, postpone, defer, adjourn, stay, discontinue, intrude, interfere.
(ANT.) prolong, persist, continue, maintain, proceed.

interval (SYN.) pause, gap.

intervene (SYN.) insert, intercede, meddle, introduce, interpose, mediate, interfere, interrupt, intrude.
(ANT.) avoid, disregard.

intimacy (SYN.) fellowship, friendship, acquaintance, frankness, familiarity, unreserved, liberty.
(ANT.) presumption, distance, haughtiness, constraint, reserve.

intimate (SYN.) chummy, confidential, friendly, loving, affectionate, close, familiar, personal, private, secret.
(ANT.) conventional, formal, ceremonious, distant.

intimation (SYN.) reminder, implication, allusion, hint.
(ANT.) declaration, statement, affirmation.

intolerant (SYN.) fanatical, narrow-minded, prejudice.
(ANT.) tolerant, radical, liberal, progressive.

intoxicated (SYN.) inebriated, tipsy, drunk, tight, drunken.
(ANT.) sober, temperate, clearheaded.

intrepid (SYN.) brave, fearless, insolent, abrupt, rude, pushy, adventurous, daring.
(ANT.) timid, bashful, flinching, cowardly, retiring.

intricate (SYN.) compound, perplexing, complex, involved, complicated.
(ANT.) simple, plain.

intrigue *(SYN.)* design, plot, cabal, machination..

intrinsic *(SYN.)* natural, inherent, inbred, congenital.
(ANT.) extraneous, acquired, external, extrinsic.

introduce *(SYN.)* acquaint, submit, present, offer.

introduction *(SYN.)* preamble, prelude, beginning, prologue, start, preface.
(ANT.) finale, conclusion, end, epilogue, completion.

intrude *(SYN.)* invade, attack, encroach, trespass.
(ANT.) vacate, evacuate, abandon, relinquish.

intruder *(SYN.)* trespasser, thief, prowler, robber.

intuition *(SYN.)* insight, acumen, perspicuity, penetration, discernment.

invade *(SYN.)* intrude, violate, infringe, attack, penetrate, encroach, trespass.
(ANT.) vacate, abandon, evacuate, relinquish.

invalidate *(SYN.)* annul, cancel, abolish, revoke.
(ANT.) promote, restore, sustain, establish, continue.

invaluable *(SYN.)* priceless, precious, valuable.
(ANT.) worthless.

invasion *(SYN.)* assault, onslaught, aggression, attack.
(ANT.) surrender, opposition, resistance, defense.

invective *(SYN.)* insult, abuse, disparagement, upbraiding.
(ANT.) laudation, plaudit, commendation.

invent *(SYN.)* devise, fabricate, conceive, contrive, create.
(SYN.) reproduce, copy.

inventive *(SYN.)* fanciful, poetical, clever, creative.
(ANT.) unromantic, literal, dull, prosaic.

invert *(SYN.)* upset, turn about, transpose.
(ANT.) maintain, stabilize, endorse.

investigate *(SYN.)* look, probe, search, scour, inspect, study.

invisible *(SYN.)* indistinguishable, unseen, imperceptible.
(ANT.) evident, visible, seen, perceptible.

invite *(SYN.)* bid, ask, encourage, request, urge.

involuntary *(SYN.)* reflex, uncontrolled, automatic.
(SYN.) voluntary, willful.

involve *(SYN.)* include, embrace, entangle, envelop.
(ANT.) separate, disconnect, extricate, disengage.

involved *(SYN.)* compound, intricate, complicated, complex, perplexing.
(ANT.) plain, uncompounded, simple.

ire *(SYN.)* indignation, irritation, wrath, anger, animosity, fury, passion.
(ANT.) peace, patience, conciliation, self-control.

irk *(SYN.)* irritate, bother, disturb, pester, trouble, vex, tease, chafe, annoy.
(ANT.) console, soothe, accommodate, gratify.

irrelevant *(SYN.)* foreign, unconnected, remote, alien.
(ANT.) germane, relevant, akin, kindred.

irresolute *(SYN.)* frail, pliant, vacillating, ineffective, wavering, weak, yielding, fragile.
(ANT.) robust, potent, sturdy, strong, powerful.

irritable *(SYN.)* hasty, hot, peevish, testy, irascible, choleric, excitable, touchy.
(ANT.) composed, agreeable, tranquil, calm.

irritate *(SYN.)* irk, molest, bother, annoy, tease, disturb, inconvenience, vex.
(ANT.) console, gratify, accommodate, soothe, pacify.

irritable *(SYN.)* peevish, testy, sensitive, touchy.
(ANT.) happy, cheerful.

isolate *(SYN.)* detach, segregate, separate.
(ANT.) happy, cheerful.

isolated *(SYN.)* lone, single, alone, desolate, secluded, solitary, deserted, sole.
(ANT.) surrounded, accompanied.

issue *(SYN.)* flow, result, come, emanate, originate, abound, copy, distribute.

jab *(SYN.)* thrust, poke, nudge, prod, shove, jolt, boost, tap, slap, rap, thwack.

jabber *(SYN.)* mumble, gossip, prattle, chatter, gab, palaver.

jacent *(SYN.)* level, flatness, plane, proneness, recline.

jackal *(SYN.)* puppet, drone, legman, flunky, tool, servility, vassal.

jackass *(SYN.)* fool, idiot, dope, dunce, ignoramus, imbecile, ninny, simpleton.

jacket *(SYN.)* wrapper, envelope, coat, sheath, cover, casing, folder, skin.

jade *(SYN.)* hussy, wanton, trollop, harlot, common.

jaded *(SYN.)* exhausted, bored, tired, fatigued, satiated, weary, hardened.

jag *(SYN.)* notch, snag, protuberance, barb, dent, cut.

jagged *(SYN.)* crooked, bent, ragged, pointy, notched. *(ANT.)* smooth.

jail *(SYN.)* stockade, prison, reformatory, penitentiary.

jailbird *(SYN.)* convict, parolee, con, inmate, prisoner.

jargon *(SYN.)* speech, idiom, dialect, vernacular, diction. *(ANT.)* gibberish, babble, nonsense, drivel.

jaunt *(SYN.)* journey, trip, tour, excursion, outing.

jealous *(SYN.)* covetous, desirous of, envious.

jealousy *(SYN.)* suspicion, envy, resentfulness, greed. *(ANT.)* tolerance, indifference, geniality, liberality.

jeer *(SYN.)* taunt, mock, scoff, deride, make fun of, gibe. *(ANT.)* flatter, praise, compliment, laud.

jerk *(SYN.)* quiver, twitch, shake, spasm, jolt, yank.

jest *(SYN.)* mock, joke, tease, fun, witticism, quip.

jester *(SYN.)* fool, buffoon, harlequin, clown. *(ANT.)* sage, genius, scholar, philosopher.

jet *(SYN.)* squirt, spurt, gush, inky, coal-black, nozzle.

jetty *(SYN.)* pier, breakwater, bulwark, buttress.

jewel *(SYN.)* ornament, gemstone, gem, bauble, stone.

jilt *(SYN.)* abandon, get rid of, reject, desert, forsake, leave.

job *(SYN.)* toil, business, occupation, post, chore, stint.

jobless *(SYN.)* idle, unoccupied, inactive, unemployed.

jocularity *(SYN.)* humor, wit, joke, facetiousness. *(ANT.)* sorrow, gravity.

jocund *(SYN.)* mirthful, cheerful, merry, gay, jovial.

jog *(SYN.)* gait, trot, sprint.

join *(SYN.)* conjoin, unite, attach, accompany, associate. *(ANT.)* separate, disconnect, split, sunder, part, divide.

joint *(SYN.)* link, union, connection, junction, coupling. *(ANT.)* divided, separate.

joke *(SYN.)* game, jest, caper, prank, anecdote, quip.

joker *(SYN.)* wisecracker, humorist, comedian, trickster, comic, jester, wit, punster.

jolly *(SYN.)* merry, joyful, gay, happy, sprightly, pleasant, jovial, gleeful, spirited. *(ANT.)* mournful, depressed, sullen, glum.

jolt *(SYN.)* sway, waver, startle, rock, jar, totter, jerk, bounce, bump, shake.

josh *(SYN.)* poke fun at, kid, tease, ridicule.

jostle *(SYN.)* shove, push, bump, thrust.

jounce *(SYN.)* bounce, jolt, bump, jostle, jar, shake.

journal *(SYN.)* account, diary, chronicle, newspaper.

journey *(SYN.)* tour, passage, cruise, voyage, pilgrimage, jaunt, trip, outing.

joust *(SYN.)* tournament, contest, skirmish, competition.

jovial *(SYN.)* good-natured, kindly, merry, good-humored, good-hearted, joyful. *(ANT.)* solemn, sad, serious.

joy *(SYN.)* pleasure, glee, bliss, elation, mirth, felicity, rapture, delight, transport. *(ANT.)* grief, depression, unhappiness, sorrow, misery, gloom, sadness, affliction.

joyful *(SYN.)* gay, lucky, op-

portune, cheerful, happy, blissful, jovial, merry, gleeful, delighted, glad.
(ANT.) gloomy, sad, blue, solemn, serious, grim, morose, glum, depressed.

joyous *(SYN.)* jolly, gay, blithe, merry, gleeful, cheerful.
(ANT.) sad, gloomy, sorrowful, melancholy.

jubilant *(SYN.)* exulting, rejoicing, overjoyed, triumphant, gay, elated.
(ANT.) dejected.

jubilee *(SYN.)* gala, holiday, celebration, festival, fete.

judge *(SYN.)* umpire, think, estimate, decide, arbitrator, condemn, decree, critic, appreciate, adjudicator, determine, arbiter, magistrate.

judgment *(SYN.)* wisdom, perspicacity, discernment, decision, common sense, estimation, verdict, understanding, intelligence.
(ANT.) thoughtlessness, senselessness, arbitrariness.

judicial *(SYN.)* legal, judicatory, forensic.

jug *(SYN.)* bottle, jar, flask, flagon, pitcher.

juice *(SYN.)* broth, liquid, sap, distillation, serum, fluid.

jump *(SYN.)* leap, caper, skip, bound, jerk, vault, hop.

junction *(SYN.)* coupling, joining, union, crossroads.
(ANT.) separation.

junior *(SYN.)* secondary, inferior, minor, lower, younger.

junk *(SYN.)* rubbish, scraps, trash, waste, dump, discard.

just *(SYN.)* fair, trustworthy, precise, exact, candid, upright, honest, impartial.
(ANT.) tricky, dishonest, unjust, corrupt, lying, deceitful.

justice *(SYN.)* justness, rectitude, equity, law, fairness.
(ANT.) unfairness, inequity, wrong, partiality.

justify *(SYN.)* uphold, excuse, defend, acquit, exonerate.
(ANT.) convict.

juvenile *(SYN.)* puerile, youthful, childish, babyish.
(ANT.) old, aged, adult.

kaiser *(SYN.)* czar, caesar, caliph, mogul, padishah, tycoon, khan, landamman, cazique.

kavass *(SYN.)* badel, macebearer, constable.

keck *(SYN.)* vomit, belch.

keen *(SYN.)* clever, cunning, acute, penetrating, exact, severe, shrewd, wily, astute, sharp, bright, intelligent, smart, witty, cutting, fine.
(ANT.) stupid, shallow, dull, blunted, slow, bland, gentle.

keep *(SYN.)* maintain, retain, observe, protect, confine, sustain, continue, preserve, execute, celebrate, save, guard, restrain, obey.
(ANT.) abandon, disobey, dismiss, discard, ignore, lose, reject, neglect.

keeper *(SYN.)* warden, jailer, ranger, gaoler, guard, turnkey, watchman, escort.

keeping *(SYN.)* congeniality, uniformity, consentaneousness, conformance, congruity, union.

keepsake *(SYN.)* reminder, memorial, relic, souvenir, memento, hint.

keg *(SYN.)* container, drum, tub, barrel, receptacle, reservatory, capsule, cask.

kelpie *(SYN.)* sprite, nixie, naiad, pixy.

kelson *(SYN.)* bottom, sole, toe, foot, root, keel.

kempt *(SYN.)* neat, trim, tidy, spruce, cleaned.

ken *(SYN.)* field, view, vision, range, scope.

kennel *(SYN.)* swarm, flock, covy, drove, herd, pound.

kerchief *(SYN.)* neckcloth, hankerchief, scarf, headpiece, babushka.

kern *(SYN.)* peasant, carle, serf, tike, fyke, countryman.

kernel *(SYN.)* marrow, pith, backbone, soul, heart, core.

ketch *(SYN.)* lugger, cutter, clipper, ship, barge, sloop.

kettle *(SYN.)* pan, caldron, vat, pot, teapot, vessel, receptacle, receiver, tureen.

key *(SYN.)* opener, explanation, tone, lead, cause, source, note, pitch, answer.

keynote *(SYN.)* core, model, theme, pattern, standard.

keystone *(SYN.)* backbone, support.

khan *(SYN.)* master, czar, kaiser, padishah, caesar.

kick *(SYN.)* punt, remonstrate, boot.

kickback *(SYN.)* repercussion, backfire, rebound.

kickoff *(SYN.)* beginning, commencement, outset.

kid *(SYN.)* joke, tease, fool, jest, tot, child.

kidnap *(SYN.)* abduct, snatch.

kill *(SYN.)* execute, put to death, slay, butcher, assassinate, murder, cancel, destroy, slaughter, finish, end, annihilate, massacre.
(ANT.) save, protect, animate, resuscitate, vivify.

killing *(SYN.)* massacre, genocide, slaughter, carnage, butchery, blood-shed.

killjoy *(SYN.)* wet blanket, sourpuss, party-pooper.

kin *(SYN.)* relatives, family, folks, relations.

kind *(SYN.)* humane, affable, compassionate, benevolent, merciful, tender, sympathetic, breed, indulgent, forbearing, kindly, race, good, thoughtful, character.
(ANT.) unkind, cruel, merciless, severe, mean, inhuman.

kindle *(SYN.)* fire, ignite, arouse, excite, set afire, stir up, inflame, trigger, move, provoke, light.
(ANT.) pacify, extinguish, calm.

kindly *(SYN.)* warm, kindhearted, warm-hearted.
(ANT.) mean, cruel.

kindred *(SYN.)* family, relations, relatives, consanguinity, kinsfolk, affinity.
(ANT.) strangers, disconnection.

kinetic *(SYN.)* forceful, vigorous, active, dynamic, energetic, mobile.

king *(SYN.)* sovereign, ruler, chief, monarch, potentate.

kingdom *(SYN.)* realm, empire, monarchy, domain.

kingly *(SYN.)* kinglike, imperial, regal, royal, majestic.

kink *(SYN.)* twist, curl, quirk, complication.

kinship *(SYN.)* lineage, blood, family, stock, relationship.

kismet *(SYN.)* fate, end, fortune, destiny.

kiss *(SYN.)* pet, caress, fondle, cuddle, osculate, embrace.
(ANT.) vex, spurn, annoy, tease, buffet.

kit *(SYN.)* outfit, collection, furnishings, gear, set, equipment, rig.

knack *(SYN.)* cleverness, readiness, deftness, ability, adroitness, skillfulness.
(ANT.) inability, clumsiness, awkwardness, ineptitude.

knave *(SYN.)* rogue, rascal, villain, scoundrel.

knead *(SYN.)* combine, massage, blend.

knife *(SYN.)* sword, blade.

knightly *(SYN.)* valiant, courageous, gallant, chivalrous.

knit *(SYN.)* unite, join, mend, fasten, connect, combine.

knock *(SYN.)* thump, tap, rap, strike, hit, jab, punch, beat.

knockout *(SYN.)* stunning, overpowering, stupefying.

knot *(SYN.)* cluster, gathering, collection, group, crowd.

know *(SYN.)* perceive, comprehend, apprehend, recognize, understand, discern.
(ANT.) doubt, suspect, dispute, ignore.

knowing *(SYN.)* sage, smart, wise, clever, sagacious.

knowledge *(SYN.)* information, wisdom, erudition, lore, cognizance, learning, apprehension.
(ANT.) misunderstanding, ignorance, stupidity, illiteracy.

knurl *(SYN.)* gnarl, knot, projection, burl, node, lump.

kosher *(SYN.)* permitted, okay, fit, proper, acceptable.

kowtow *(SYN.)* stoop, bend, kneel, genuflect, bow.

kudos *(SYN.)* acclaim, praise, approbation, approval.

label *(SYN.)* mark, tag, title, name, marker, sticker, ticket, docket, identity.

labor *(SYN.)* toil, travail, effort, task, childbirth, work, workingmen, strive, exertion, employment, drudgery, endeavor.
(ANT.) recreation, indolence, idleness, leisure.

laboratory *(SYN.)* lab, workroom, workshop.

laborer *(SYN.)* wage earner, helper, worker, coolie, blue-collar worker.

laborious *(SYN.)* tiring, difficult, hard, burdensome, industrious, painstaking.
(ANT.) simple, easy, relaxing.

labyrinth *(SYN.)* maze, tangle.

lace *(SYN.)* openwork, fancywork, embroidery, edging.

laceration *(SYN.)* cut, wound, puncture, gash, lesion.

lack *(SYN.)* want, need, shortage, dearth, scarcity.
(ANT.) profusion, quantity, plentifulness.

lacking *(SYN.)* insufficient, short, deficient, incomplete.
(ANT.) satisfactory, enough, ample, sufficient, adequate.

lackluster *(SYN.)* dull, pallid, flat, lifeless, drab, dim.

laconic *(SYN.)* short, terse, compact, brief, curt.

lacquer *(SYN.)* polish, varnish, gild.

lad *(SYN.)* youth, boy, fellow, stripling.

lady *(SYN.)* matron, woman.

ladylike *(SYN.)* feminine, womanly, female.
(ANT.) masculine, male, virile, manly.

lag *(SYN.)* dawdle, loiter, linger, poke, dilly-dally, straggle, delay, tarry.

laggard *(SYN.)* dallier, idler, lingerer, slowpoke, dawdler.

lair *(SYN.)* retreat, burrow, den, nest, mew, hole.

lame *(SYN.)* feeble, maimed, disabled, crippled, deformed, hobbling inadequate, halt.
(ANT.) vigorous, convincing, plausible, athletic, robust,
agile, sound.

lament *(SYN.)* deplore, wail, bemoan, bewail, regret, grieve, mourning.
(ANT.) celebrate, rejoice.

lamp *(SYN.)* light, beam, illumination, shine, insight, knowledge, understanding.
(ANT.) shadow, darkness, obscurity.

lance *(SYN.)* cut, pierce, perforate, stab, puncture, impale, knife.

land *(SYN.)* earth, continent, ground, soil, domain, estate, arrive, descend, country, island, region, alight, shore.

landlord *(SYN.)* owner, landholder, landowner.

landmark *(SYN.)* keystone, monument, cornerstone.

lane *(SYN.)* alley, way, road, path, aisle, pass, channel.

language *(SYN.)* dialect, tongue, speech, lingo, jargon, cant, diction, idiom, patter, phraseology.
(ANT.) nonsense, babble.

languid *(SYN.)* feeble, drooping, irresolute, debilitated, dull, lethargic, weak, faint.
(ANT.) forceful, strong, vigorous.

languish *(SYN.)* decline, sink, droop, wither, waste, fail.
(ANT.) revive, rejuvenate, refresh, renew.

languor *(SYN.)* weariness, depression, torpor, inertia.

lanky *(SYN.)* skinny, gaunt, lean, scrawny, slender, thin.
(ANT.) chunky, stocky, obese, fat.

lapse *(SYN.)* decline, sink.

larceny *(SYN.)* pillage, robbery, stealing, theft, burglary, plunder.

large *(SYN.)* great, vast, colossal, ample, extensive, capacious, sizable, broad, massive, grand, immense, big.
(ANT.) tiny, little, short, small.

largely *(SYN.)* chiefly, mainly, principally, mostly.

lark *(SYN.)* fling, frolic, play, fun, spree, joke, revel.

lascivious *(SYN.)* lecherous, raunchy, lustful, wanton.

lash *(SYN.)* thong, whip, rod, cane, blow, strike, hit, beat.

lasso *(SYN.)* lariat, rope, noose, snare.

last *(SYN.)* terminal, final, ultimate, remain, endure, end, conclusive, hindmost, continue, extreme.
(ANT.) first, initial, beginning, opening, starting, foremost.

latch *(SYN.)* clasp, hook, fastener, lock, closing, seal.

late *(SYN.)* overdue, tardy, behind, advanced, delayed.
(ANT.) timely, early.

latent *(SYN.)* potential, undeveloped, unseen, dormant, secret, concealed, inactive, hidden, obscured.
(ANT.) visible, evident, conspicuous, explicit, manifest.

lather *(SYN.)* suds, foam, froth.

lateral *(SYN.)* sideways, glancing, tangential, marginal.

lattice *(SYN.)* grating, screen, framework, grid.

laud *(SYN.)* commend, praise, extol, glorify, compliment.
(ANT.) criticize, belittle.

laudable *(SYN.)* creditable, praiseworthy

laudation *(SYN.)* applause, commendation, acclaim, extolling, glorification.
(ANT.) criticizing, condemnation, reproach, disparagement, censure.

laugh *(SYN.)* chuckle, giggle, snicker, cackle, titter, grin, smile, roar, jeer.

launch *(SYN.)* drive, fire, propel, start, begin, originate, set afloat, initiate.
(ANT.) finish, stop, terminate.

launder *(SYN.)* bathe, wash, scrub, scour.

laurels *(SYN.)* glory, distinction, recognition, award.

lavatory *(SYN.)* toilet, washroom, bathroom, latrine.

lavish *(SYN.)* squander, waste, dissipate, scatter, abundant, free, plentiful, liberal, extravagant, ample, wear out.
(ANT.) economize, save, conserve, accumulate, sparing.

law *(SYN.)* decree, formula, statute, act, rule, ruling, standard, principle.

lawful *(SYN.)* legal, permissible, allowable, legitimate, authorized, constitutional.
(ANT.) prohibited, criminal, illicit, illegal, illegitimate.

lawless *(SYN.)* uncivilized, uncontrolled, wild, savage.
(ANT.) obedient, law-abiding.

lax *(SYN.)* slack, loose, careless, vague, lenient, lazy.
(ANT.) firm, rigid.

lay *(SYN.)* mundane, worldly, temporal, place, dispose, laic, arrange, location, put, set, ballad, deposit, position, song, secular.
(ANT.) spiritual, unworldly, mislay, disarrange, ecclesiastical, religious.

layout *(SYN.)* plan, arrangement, design.

lazy *(SYN.)* slothful, supine, idle, inactive, sluggish, inert.
(ANT.) alert, ambitious, forceful, diligent, active, assiduous.

leach *(SYN.)* remove, extract, seep, dilute, wash out.

lead *(SYN.)* regulate, conduct, guide, escort, direct, supervise, command, come first.
(ANT.) follow.

leader *(SYN.)* master, ruler, captain, chief, commander, principal, director, head.
(ANT.) follower, servant, disciple, subordinate, attendant.

leading *(SYN.)* dominant, foremost, principal, first, main, primary.

league *(SYN.)* entente, partnership, association, confederacy, coalition, society.
(ANT.) separation, schism.

leak *(SYN.)* dribble, flow, drip, opening, perforation.

lean *(SYN.)* rely, tilt, slim, slender, slope, incline, tend, trust, bend, narrow, sag.
(ANT.) rise, heavy, fat, erect, straighten, portly, raise.

leaning *(SYN.)* trend, proclivity, bias, tendency, bent, predisposition.
(ANT.) disinclination, aversion.

leap *(SYN.)* vault, skip, caper, dive, hurdle, jump, bound, start, hop, plunge.

learn *(SYN.)* gain, find out, memorize, acquire.

learned *(SYN.)* erudite, knowing, enlightened, deep, wise, discerning, scholarly, intelligent, educated, sagacious. *(ANT.)* simple, uneducated, ignorant, illiterate, unlettered, foolish.

learning *(SYN.)* science, education, lore, apprehension, wisdom, knowledge. *(ANT.)* misunderstanding, ignorance, stupidity.

lease *(SYN.)* charter, let, rent.

leash *(SYN.)* chain, strap, shackle, collar.

least *(SYN.)* minutest, smallest, tiniest, trivial, minimum, fewest, slightest. *(ANT.)* most.

leave *(SYN.)* give up, retire, desert, abandon, withdraw, relinquish, will, depart, quit, liberty, renounce, go, permission, freedom, forsake. *(ANT.)* come, stay, arrive, remain, abide.

lecherous *(SYN.)* lustful, sensual, carnal, lascivious.

lecture *(SYN.)* talk, discussion, lesson, instruct, speech. *(ANT.)* meditation, correspondence.

leech *(SYN.)* barnacle, bloodsucker, parasite.

leer *(SYN.)* eye, grimace, ogle, wink, squint.

leftovers *(SYN.)* scraps, remains, residue.

legal *(SYN.)* legitimate, rightful, honest, allowable, allowed, permissible, lawful. *(ANT.)* illicit, illegal, prohibited.

legalize *(SYN.)* authorize, ordain, approve, sanction.

legate *(SYN.)* envoy, agent, representative, emissary.

legend *(SYN.)* saga, fable, allegory, myth, parable, tale, story, folklore, fiction. *(ANT.)* history, facts.

legendary *(SYN.)* fictitious, traditional, mythical.

legion *(SYN.)* outfit, unit, troop, regiment, company.

legislation *(SYN.)* resolution, ruling, lawmaking, regulation, enactment.

legislator *(SYN.)* statesman, congressman, senator, politician, lawmaker.

legitimate *(SYN.)* true, real, bona fide, lawful, proper, right, valid, correct, unadulterated, authentic, legal. *(ANT.)* ounterfeit, artificial.

leisure *(SYN.)* respite, intermission, ease, relaxation, rest, calm, tranquillity. *(ANT.)* motion, commotion, tumult, agitation.

leisurely *(SYN.)* sluggish, laggard, unhurried, relaxed, casual, dawdling, slow. *(ANT.)* hurried, swift, pressed, rushed, forced, fast, speedy.

lend *(SYN.)* entrust, advance.

length *(SYN.)* reach, measure, extent, distance, span, longness, stretch.

lengthen *(SYN.)* stretch, prolong, draw, reach, increase, grow. *(ANT.)* shrink, contract, shorten.

leniency *(SYN.)* grace, pity, compassion, mildness, charity, mercy, clemency. *(ANT.)* vengeance, punishment, cruelty.

lenient *(SYN.)* tender, humane, clement, tolerant, compassionate, mild, kind. *(ANT.)* unfeeling, pitiless, brutal, remorseless.

leprechaun *(SYN.)* gnome, imp, goblin, fairy, elf, sprite.

lesion *(SYN.)* wound, blemish, sore, trauma, injury.

less *(SYN.)* fewer, smaller, reduced, negative, stinted. *(ANT.)* more.

lessen *(SYN.)* shorten, reduce, decline, instruction, teaching, remove, decrease. *(ANT.)* swell, grow, enlarge, increase, expand, multiply.

lesson *(SYN.)* exercise, session, class, assignment.

let *(SYN.)* admit, hire out, contract, allow, permit, consent,

leave, grant, rent.
(ANT.) deny.

lethal (SYN.) mortal, dangerous, deadly, fatal.

lethargic (SYN.) sluggish, logy, slow, listless, phlegmatic.
(ANT.) vivacious, energetic.

lethargy (SYN.) numbness, stupor, daze, insensibility.
(ANT.) wakefulness, liveliness, activity, readiness.

letter (SYN.) note, letter, mark, message, character, symbol, sign, memorandum.

letup (SYN.) slowdown, slackening, lessening, abatement.

level (SYN.) smooth, even, plane, equivalent, uniform, equalize, raze, demolish.
(ANT.) uneven, sloping, hilly.

level-headed (SYN.) reasonable, sensible, calm, collected, cool.

levity (SYN.) humor, triviality, giddiness, hilarity, fun.

levy (SYN.) tax, duty, tribute, rate, assessment, exaction, charge, custom.
(ANT.) wages, remuneration.

lewd (SYN.) indecent, smutty, course, gross, disgusting.
(ANT.) pure, decent, refined.

liability (SYN.) indebtedness, answerability, vulnerability.

liable (SYN.) answerable, responsible, likely, exposed to, subject, amenable.
(ANT.) immune, exempt, independent.

liaison (SYN.) union, coupling, link, connection.

liar (SYN.) fibber, falsifier, storyteller, fabricator.

libel (SYN.) slander, calumny, vilification, aspersion.
(ANT.) defense, praise, applause.

liberal (SYN.) large, generous, unselfish, tolerant, kind, unprejudiced, lavish, plentiful, ample, abundant.
(ANT.) restricted, conservative, confined.

liberality (SYN.) kindness, philanthropy, beneficence, humanity, altruism.
(ANT.) selfishness, cruelty, malevolence.

liberate (SYN.) emancipate, loose, release, let go, deliver, free, discharge.
(ANT.) subjugate, oppress, jail, confine, restrict.

liberated (SYN.) loose, frank, emancipated, careless, liberal, freed, autonomous.
(ANT.) subject, clogged, restricted.

liberty (SYN.) permission, independence, autonomy, license, privilege.
(ANT.) constraint, imprisonment, bondage, captivity.

license (SYN.) liberty, freedom, liberation, permission, exemption, authorization, warrant, allow, consent, permit, sanction.
(ANT.) servitude, constraint, bondage.

lie (SYN.) untruth, fib, illusion, delusion, falsehood, fiction, equivocation, prevarication, repose, location, recline, similitude.
(ANT.) variance, truth, difference.

life (SYN.) sparkle, being, spirit, vivacity, animation, biography, energy, liveliness, vigor.
(ANT.) demise, lethargy, death, languor.

light (SYN.) brightness, illumination, beam, gleam, ignite, burn, dawn, incandescence, flame, airy, unsubstantial, dainty, luminosity, shine, radiance.
(ANT.) darken, gloom, shadow, extinguish.

lighten (SYN.) diminish, unburden, reduce, brighten.

lighthearted (SYN.) carefree, merry, gay, cheerful, happy.
(ANT.) somber, sad.

like (SYN.) fancy, esteem, adore, love, admire, care for, prefer, cherish.
(ANT.) disapprove, loathe, hate, dislike.

likely (SYN.) liable, reasonable, probable.

likeness (SYN.) similarity, resemblance, portrait.
(ANT.) difference.

likewise *(SYN.)* besides, as well, also, too, similarly.

limb *(SYN.)* arm, leg, member, appendage, part, bough.

limelight *(SYN.)* spotlight, notice, notoriety, fame.

limit *(SYN.)* terminus, bound, extent, confine, border, restriction, boundary, restraint, edge, frontier.
(ANT.) endlessness, vastness.

limn *(SYN.)* depict, portray, sketch, paint, illustrate.

limp *(SYN.)* soft, flabby, drooping, walk, limber, supple, flexible, hobble.
(ANT.) stiff.

limpid *(SYN.)* clear, open, transparent, unobstructed.
(ANT.) cloudy.

line *(SYN.)* row, file, series, array, sequence, wire, seam, wrinkle, crease, division.

lineage *(SYN.)* race, family, tribe, nation, strain, folk.

linger *(SYN.)* wait, rest, bide, delay, dwadle, stay, loiter, remain, tarry.
(ANT.) leave, expedite.

lingo *(SYN.)* vernacular, dialect, language, jargon.

link *(SYN.)* unite, connector, loop, couple, attach, connective, connection.
(ANT.) separate, disconnect.

lip *(SYN.)* edge, brim, rim.

liquor *(SYN.)* spirits, alcohol, drink, booze.

lissom *(SYN.)* nimble, quick, lively, flexible, agile.

list *(SYN.)* roll, register, slate, enumeration, series.

listen *(SYN.)* overhear, attend to, heed, hear, list, hearken.
(ANT.) ignore, scorn, disregard, reject.

listless *(SYN.)* uninterested, tired, lethargic, unconcerned, apathetic.
(ANT.) active.

literal *(SYN.)* exact, verbatim, precise, strict, faithful.

literature *(SYN.)* books, writings, publications.

lithe *(SYN.)* supple, flexible, bending, limber, pliable.
(ANT.) stiff.

litter *(SYN.)* rubbish, trash,

scatter, clutter, strew, debris, rubble, disorder.

little *(SYN.)* tiny, petty, miniature, diminutive, puny, wee, brief, bit, trivial.
(ANT.) huge, large, big, long, immense.

liturgy *(SYN.)* ritual, sacrament, worship.

live *(SYN.)* dwell, reside, abide, survive, exist, alive, occupy, stay, active.
(ANT.) die.

livelihood *(SYN.)* keep, support, subsistence, job, trade, profession, vocation.

livid *(SYN.)* furious, pale.

living *(SYN.)* support, livelihood, existent, alive.

load *(SYN.)* oppress, trouble, burden, weight, freight, afflict, encumber, pack, shipment, cargo, lade, tax.
(ANT.) lighten, console, unload, mitigate, empty, ease.

loafer *(SYN.)* loiterer, bum, idler, sponger, deadbeat.

loan *(SYN.)* credit, advance.

loathe *(SYN.)* dislike, despise, hate, abhor, detest.
(ANT.) love, approve, like, admire.

loathsome *(SYN.)* foul, vile, detestable, revolting, abominable, atrocious.
(ANT.) pleasant, commendable, alluring, agreeable.

lob *(SYN.)* toss, hurl, pitch, throw, heave.

lobby *(SYN.)* foyer, entry, entrance, vestibule, passageway, entryway.

locality *(SYN.)* nearness, neighborhood, district.
(ANT.) remoteness.

locate *(SYN.)* discover, find, unearth, site, situate, place.

located *(SYN.)* found, residing, positioned, situated.

location *(SYN.)* spot, locale, station, locality, situation, place, area, site, vicinity, position, zone, region.

lock *(SYN.)* curl, hook, bolt, braid, ringlet, plait, close, latch, tuft, fastening, bar.
(ANT.) open.

locket *(SYN.)* case, lavaliere,

pendant.

locomotion (SYN.) movement, travel, transit, motion.

lodge (SYN.) cabin, cottage, room, reside, dwell, live, occupy, inhabit, abide, board.

lodger (SYN.) guest, tenant, boarder, occupant.

lofty (SYN.) high, stately, grandiose, towering, elevated, exalted, sublime.

(ANT.) undignified, lowly, common.

log (SYN.) lumber, wood, board, register, record, album, account, journal.

logical (SYN.) strong, effective, telling, convincing, reasonable, sensible, rational, sane, sound, cogent.

(ANT.) crazy, illogical, irrational, unreasonable, weak.

loiter (SYN.) idle, linger, wait, stay, tarry, dilly-dally.

loll (SYN.) hang, droop, recline, relax.

lone (SYN.) lonely, sole, unaided, single, deserted, isolated, secluded, apart.

(ANT.) surrounded, accompanied.

loner (SYN.) recluse, outsider, hermit.

loneliness (SYN.) solitude, isolation, seclusion, alienation.

lonely (SYN.) unaided, isolated, single, solitary, lonesome, unaccompanied, deserted, alone, desolate.

(ANT.) surrounded, attended.

lonesome (SYN.) secluded, remote, unpopulated, barren, empty, desolate.

long (SYN.) lengthy, prolonged, elongated, extended, lingering, drawn out, lasting, protracted, extensive, length, prolix, far-reaching, extended.

(ANT.) terse, concise, abridged, short.

long-standing (SYN.) persistent, established.

long-winded (SYN.) boring, dull, wordy.

(ANT.) curt, terse.

look (SYN.) gaze, witness, seem, eye, behold, see, watch, scan, view, appear, stare, discern, glance, examine, examination, peep, expression.

(ANT.) overlook, hide, avert, miss.

loom (SYN.) emerge, appear, show up.

loop (SYN.) noose, spiral, fastener.

loose (SYN.) untied, unbound, lax, vague, unrestrained, dissolute, limp, undone, baggy, disengaged, indefinite, slack, careless.

(ANT.) restrained, steady, fastened, secure, tied, firm, fast, definite, inhibited.

loosen (SYN.) untie, loose, unchain.

(ANT.) tie, tighten, secure.

loot (SYN.) booty, plunder, take, steal, rob, sack, rifle, ravage, devastate.

lope (SYN.) run, race, bound, gallop.

lopsided (SYN.) unequal, twisted, uneven, askew, distorted.

loquacious (SYN.) garrulous, wordy, profuse, chatty, verbose.

lord (SYN.) peer, ruler, proprietor, master, owner.

lore (SYN.) learning, knowledge, wisdom, stories, legends beliefs, teachings.

lose (SYN.) misplace, flop, fail, sacrifice, forfeit, mislay, vanish, surrender.

(ANT.) succeed, locate, place, win, discover, find.

loss (SYN.) injury, damage, want, hurt, need, bereavement, trouble, death, failure, deficiency.

lost (SYN.) dazed, wasted, astray, forfeited, preoccupied, used, adrift, bewildered, missing, distracted, consumed, misspent, absorbed, confused, mislaid, gone, destroyed.

(ANT.) found, anchored.

lot (SYN.) result, destiny, bunch, many, amount, fate, cluster, group, sum, portion, outcome, number, doom, issue.

lotion (SYN.) cosmetic, balm, cream.

lottery (SYN.) chance, drawing, raffle.

loud (SYN.) vociferous, noisy, resounding, shrill, blaring, roaring, deafening.
(ANT.) soft, inaudible, murmuring, subdued, quiet.

lounge (SYN.) idle, loaf, laze, sofa, couch, davenport, relax, rest, lobby, salon, divan.

louse (SYN.) scoundrel, knave, cad, rat.

lousy (SYN.) revolting, grimy, rotten, dirty, disgusting.

lovable (SYN.) charming, attractive, delightful, amiable, sweet, cuddly.

love (SYN.) attachment, endearment, affection, adoration, liking, devotion, warmth, tenderness, friendliness, adore, worship, like, cherish, fondness.
(ANT.) loathing, detest, indifference, dislike, hate, hatred.

loveliness (SYN.) grace, pulchritude, charm, attractiveness, comeliness.
(ANT.) ugliness, eyesore, disfigurement, deformity.

lovely (SYN.) handsome, fair, charming, pretty, attractive, delightful, beautiful.
(ANT.) ugly, unsightly, homely, foul, hideous.

lover (SYN.) fiance, suitor, courter, sweetheart, beau.

loving (SYN.) close, intimate, confidential, affectionate.
(ANT.) formal, conventional, ceremonious, distant.

low (SYN.) mean, vile, despicable, vulgar, abject, groveling, lesser.
(ANT.) righteous, lofty, esteemed, noble.

lower (SYN.) subordinate, minor, secondary, quiet, soften, disgrace, degrade.
(ANT.) greater, superior, increase, better.

lowly (SYN.) humble, base, low, mean, common, aver-

age, simple, modest.
(ANT.) royal, noble.

loyal (SYN.) earnest, ardent, addicted, inclined, faithful, devoted, prone, fond, patriotic, dependable, true.
(ANT.) indisposed, detached, disloyal, traitorous, untrammeled.

loyalty (SYN.) devotion, steadfastness, constancy, faithfulness, fidelity, patriotism, allegiance.
(ANT.) treachery, falseness, disloyalty.

lubricate (SYN.) oil, grease, anoint.

lucent (SYN.) radiant, beaming, vivid, illuminated, lustrous.

lucid (SYN.) plain, visible, clear, intelligible, unmistakable, transparent, limpid, translucent, open, shining, light, explicit, understandable, clear-cut.
(ANT.) unclear, vague, obscure.

luck (SYN.) chance, fortunate, fortune, lot, fate, fluke, destiny, karma.
(ANT.) misfortune.

lucky (SYN.) favored, favorable, auspicious, fortunate, successful, benign.
(ANT.) unlucky, condemned, unfortunate, persecuted.

lucrative (SYN.) well-paying, profitable, high-paying, productive, beneficial.

luggage (SYN.) bags, valises, baggage, suitcases, trunks.

lugubrious (SYN.) mournful, sad, gloomy, somber.

lukewarm (SYN.) unenthusiastic, tepid, spiritless, detached, apathetic, mild.

lull (SYN.) quiet, calm, soothe, rest, hush, stillness, pause, break, intermission, recess.

luminous (SYN.) beaming, lustrous, shining, glowing, alight, clear, radiant.
(ANT.) murky, dull, dark.

lummox (SYN.) yokel, oaf, bumpkin, clown, klutz.

lump (SYN.) swelling, protuberance, mass, chunk,

hunk, bump.

lunacy (SYN.) derangement, madness, aberration, psychosis, craziness.
(ANT.) stability, rationality.

lunge (SYN.) charge, stab, attack, push.

lurch (SYN.) topple, sway, toss, roll, rock, tip, pitch.

lure (SYN.) draw, tug, drag, entice, attraction, haul, attract, temptation, persuade, pull, draw on, allure.
(ANT.) drive, alienate, propel.

lurid (SYN.) sensational, terrible, melodramatic, startling.

lurk (SYN.) sneak, hide, prowl, slink.

luscious (SYN.) savory, delightful, juicy, sweet, pleasing, delectable, palatable, delicious, tasty.
(ANT.) unsavory, nauseous, acrid.

lush (SYN.) tender, succulent, ripe, juicy.

lust (SYN.) longing, desire, passion, appetite, craving, aspiration, urge.
(ANT.) hate, aversion, loathing, distaste.

luster (SYN.) radiance, brightness, glister, honor, fame, effulgence, gloss, sheen, shine, gleam, glow, glitter, brilliance, splendor.
(ANT.) dullness, obscurity, darkness.

lustful (SYN.) amorous, sexy, desirous, passionate, wanton.

lusty (SYN.) healthy, strong, mighty, powerful, sturdy, strapping, hale, hardy, rugged, hefty, robust.
(ANT.) weak.

luxuriant (SYN.) abundant, flourishing, dense, lush, rich.

luxurious (SYN.) rich, deluxe.
(ANT.) simple, crude, sparse.

luxury (SYN.) frills, comfort, extravagance, grandeur.
(ANT.) poverty.

lyric (SYN.) musical, text, words, libretto.

lyrical (SYN.) poetic, musical.

macabre (SYN.) grim, horrible, gruesome.

machine (SYN.) motor, mechanism, device, contrivance.

macilent (SYN.) gaunt, lean, lank, meager, emaciated.

maculation (SYN.) irisation, striae, iridescence.

mad (SYN.) incensed, crazy, insane, angry, furious, delirious, provoked.
(ANT.) sane, calm, healthy, rational, lucid, cheerful.

madam (SYN.) dame, woman, lady, matron, mistress.

maelstrom (SYN.) surge, rapids, eddy, riptide.

magical (SYN.) mystical, marvelous, magic, miraculous.

magician (SYN.) conjuror, sorcerer, wizard, witch, artist, trickster.

magnanimous (SYN.) giving, bountiful, beneficent.
(ANT.) stingy, greedy, selfish.

magnate (SYN.) leader, bigwig, tycoon, chief, giant.

magnetic (SYN.) pulling, attractive, alluring, drawing, enthralling, seductive.

magnificent (SYN.) rich, lavish, luxurious, splendid, wonderful, impressive.
(ANT.) simple, plain.

magnify (SYN.) heighten, exaggerate, amplify, expand, stretch, caricature, increase.
(ANT.) compress understate, depreciate, belittle.

maid (SYN.) chambermaid, servant, maidservant.

maiden (SYN.) original, foremost, first, damsel, lass.
(ANT.) accessory, secondary.

maim (SYN.) disable, cripple, hurt, wound, injure, mangle.

main (SYN.) essential, chief, highest, principal, first, leading, cardinal.
(ANT.) supplemental, subordinate.

maintain (SYN.) claim, support, uphold, defend, vindicate, sustain, continue.
(ANT.) neglect, oppose, discontinue, resist, deny.

majestic (SYN.) magnificent, stately, noble, august, grand,

imposing, sublime, lofty.
(ANT.) *humble, lowly, undignified, common, ordinary.*

majesty (SYN.) grandeur, dignity, nobility, splendor, distinction, eminence.

major (SYN.) important, superior, larger, chief, greater.
(ANT.) *minor.*

make (SYN.) execute, cause, produce, establish, assemble, create, shape, compel, build, fabricate.
(ANT.) *break, undo, demolish.*

malady (SYN.) disease, illness, sickness, ailment, infirmity, disorder, affliction.
(ANT.) *vigor, healthiness, health.*

malaise (SYN.) anxiety, apprehension, dissatisfaction, uneasiness, nervousness.

male (SYN.) masculine, virile.
(ANT.) *female, womanly, feminine.*

malcontent (SYN.) displeased, ill-humored, querulous.

malevolence (SYN.) spite, malice, enmity, rancor.
(ANT.) *love, affection, toleration, kindness.*

malfunction (SYN.) flaw, breakdown, snag, glitch.

malice (SYN.) spite, grudge, enmity, ill will, malignity, animosity, rancor, grudge.
(ANT.) *love, affection, toleration, benevolence, charity.*

malicious (SYN.) hostile, malignant, virulent, bitter, rancorous, evilminded, malevolent, spiteful, wicked.
(ANT.) *kind, benevolent, affectionate.*

malign (SYN.) misuse, defame, revile, abuse, asperse, misapply.
(ANT.) *praise, cherish, protect, honor.*

malignant (SYN.) harmful, deadly, mortal, destructive, hurtful, malicious.
(ANT.) *benign, harmless.*

malingerer (SYN.) quitter, idler, gold-brick.

malleable (SYN.) meek, tender, soft, lenient.
(ANT.) *tough, rigid, unyielding, hard.*

malodorous (SYN.) reeking, fetid, smelly, noxious, vile, rancid, offensive.

malpractice (SYN.) wrongdoing, misdeed, abuse, malfeasance, error.

mammoth (SYN.) enormous, gigantic, gargantuan.
(ANT.) *minuscule, tiny, small.*

man (SYN.) person, human being, soul, individual, fellow, male, gentleman.
(ANT.) *woman.*

manageable (SYN.) willing, obedient, docile, controllable, tractable, submissive, governable, untroublesome.
(ANT.) *recalcitrant, unmanageable, wild.*

management (SYN.) regulation, administration, supervision, direction.

manager (SYN.) overseer, superintendent, supervisor, director, boss.

mandate (SYN.) order, injunction, command, referendum, dictate, writ, directive.

mandatory (SYN.) compulsory, required, obligatory, imperative, necessary.
(ANT.) *optional.*

mangle (SYN.) tear apart, cut, maim, wound, mutilate, injure, break.

mangy (SYN.) shoddy, frazzled, seedy, threadbare, shabby, ragged, sordid.

manhandle (SYN.) maltreat, maul, abuse, ill-treat.

mania (SYN.) insanity, enthusiasm, craze, desire.

manic (SYN.) excited, hyped up, agitated.

manifest (SYN.) open, evident, lucid, clear, distinct, unobstructed, cloudless, apparent, intelligible.
(ANT.) *vague, overcast, unclear, cloudy, hidden.*

manifold (SYN.) various, many, multiple, numerous, abundant, copious, profuse.
(ANT.) *few.*

manipulate (SYN.) manage, feel, work, operate, handle, touch, maneuver.

manly (SYN.) strong, brave, masculine, manful, courageous, stalwart.

manner (SYN.) air, demeanor, way, behavior, fashion.

manor (SYN.) land, mansion, estate, domain, villa, castle, property, palace.

mantle (SYN.) serape, garment, overgarment, cover, cloak, wrap.

manual (SYN.) directory, guidebook, handbook, physical, laborious, menial.

manufacture (SYN.) construct, make, assemble, fabricate.

manuscript (SYN.) copy, writing, composition, document.

many (SYN.) numerous, various, divers, multitudinous, sundry, multifarious, several, manifold.
(ANT.) infrequent, meager, few, scanty.

map (SYN.) sketch, plan, chart, graph, itinerary.

mar (SYN.) spoil, hurt, damage, impair, harm, deface, injure.
(ANT.) repair, benefit, mend.

march (SYN.) promenade, parade, pace, hike, walk.

marginal (SYN.) unnecessary, nonessential, borderline.
(ANT.) essential.

marine (SYN.) naval, oceanic, nautical, ocean, maritime.

mariner (SYN.) seafarer, gob, seaman, sailor.

maritime (SYN.) shore, coastal, nautical.

mark (SYN.) stain, badge, stigma, vestige, sign, feature, label, characteristic, trace.

market (SYN.) supermarket, marketplace, plaza.

maroon (SYN.) desert, leave behind, forsake, abandon.

marriage (SYN.) wedding, matrimony, nuptials, espousal, union, alliance.
(ANT.) divorce, celibacy, separation.

marrow (SYN.) center, core, gist, essential, soul.

marsh (SYN.) bog, swamp, mire, everglade, estuary.

marshal (SYN.) adjutant, officer, order, arrange, rank.

martial (SYN.) warlike, combative, militant, belligerent.
(ANT.) peaceful.

martyr (SYN.) victim, sufferer, tortured, torment, plague, harass, persecute.

marvel (SYN.) phenomenon, wonder, miracle, astonishment, sensation.

marvelous (SYN.) rare, wonderful, extraordinary, unusual, exceptional, miraculous, wondrous.
(ANT.) usual, common, ordinary. commonplace.

masculine (SYN.) robust, manly, virile, strong, bold.
(ANT.) weak, emasculated, feminine, female.

mash (SYN.) mix, pulverize, crush, grind, crumble.

mask (SYN.) veil, disguise, cloak, secrete, withhold, hide, cover, protection, protector, camouflage.
(ANT.) uncover, reveal, disclose, show, expose.

masquerade (SYN.) pretend, disguise, pose, impersonate, costume party.

mass (SYN.) society, torso, body, remains, association, carcass, bulk, company, pile.
(ANT.) spirit, mind, intellect.

massacre (SYN.) butcher, murder, carnage, slaughter, execute, slay, genocide.
(ANT.) save, protect, vivify, animate.

mastery (SYN.) sway, domination, transcendence, ascendancy, influence, jurisdiction, prestige.

mat (SYN.) cover, rug, pallet, bedding, pad.

match (SYN.) equivalent, equal, contest, balance, resemble, peer, mate.

mate (SYN.) friend, colleague, associate, partner, companion, comrade.
(ANT.) stranger, adversary.

material (SYN.) sensible, momentous, bodily, palpable, important, physical.
(ANT.) metaphysical, spiritual, insignificant, mental.

materialize *(SYN.)* take shape, finalize, embody, incarnate, emerge, appear.

matrimony *(SYN.)* marriage, wedding, espousal, union.
(ANT.) virginity, divorce.

matrix *(SYN.)* template, stamp, negative, stencil, mold, form, die, cutout.

matted *(SYN.)* tangled, clustered, rumpled, shaggy, knotted, gnarled, tousled.

matter *(SYN.)* cause, thing, substance, occasion, material, moment, topic, stuff, consequence, affair.
(ANT.) spirit, immateriality.

mature *(SYN.)* ready, matured, complete, ripe, consummate, mellow, aged, seasoned, full-grown.
(ANT.) raw, crude, undeveloped, young, immature.

mausoleum *(SYN.)* shrine, tomb, vault.

maybe *(SYN.)* feasibly, perchance, perhaps, possibly.
(ANT.) definitely.

mayhem *(SYN.)* brutality, viciousness, ruthlessness.

maze *(SYN.)* complex, labyrinth, network, muddle, confusion, snarl, tangle.

meadow *(SYN.)* field, pasture, lea, range, grassland.

meager *(SYN.)* sparse, scanty, mean, frugal, deficient, slight, paltry, inadequate.
(ANT.) ample, plentiful, abundant, bountiful.

mean *(SYN.)* sordid, base, intend, plan, propose, expect, indicate, denote, say, signify.
(ANT.) dignified, noble, openhanded, kind, generous.

meaning *(SYN.)* gist, connotation, intent, purport, drift, signification, explanation, purpose, significance.

measure *(SYN.)* law, bulk, rule, criterion, size, volume, weight, standard, dimension, breadth, depth, test.
(ANT.) guess, chance, supposition.

mechanism *(SYN.)* device, contrivance, tool, machine.

medal *(SYN.)* decoration, award, badge, medallion, reward, ribbon, prize, honor.

meddle *(SYN.)* tamper, interpose, pry, snoop, intrude, interrupt, interfere.

mediate *(SYN.)* settle, intercede, umpire, intervene, negotiate, arbitrate, referee.

medicinal *(SYN.)* helping, healing, remedial, therapeutic, corrective.

medicine *(SYN.)* drug, medication, remedy, cure, prescription, potion.

meditate *(SYN.)* remember, muse, think, judge, mean, conceive, contemplate, consider, picture, reflect.

medium *(SYN.)* modicum, average, middling, median.
(ANT.) extreme.

medley *(SYN.)* hodgepodge, mixture, assortment.

meek *(SYN.)* subdued, dull, tedious, flat, docile, domesticated, tame, domestic.
(ANT.) spirited, exciting, savage, wild.

meet *(SYN.)* fulfill, suffer, find, collide, gratify, engage, connect, converge.
(ANT.) scatter, disperse, separate, cleave.

melancholy *(SYN.)* disconsolate, dejected, despondent, glum, somber, pensive.
(ANT.) happy, cheerful, merry.

meld *(SYN.)* unite, mix, combine, fuse, merge, blend, commingle, amalgamate.

melee *(SYN.)* battle royal, fight, brawl, free-for-all.

mellow *(SYN.)* mature, ripe, aged, cured, full-flavored, sweet, smooth, melodious,.
(ANT.) unripened, immature.

melodious *(SYN.)* lilting, musical, lyric, dulcet, mellifluous, tuneful, melodic.

melody *(SYN.)* strain, concord, music, air, song, tune, harmony.

melt *(SYN.)* dissolve, liquefy, blend, fade out, vanish, dwindle, disappear, thaw.
(ANT.) freeze, harden, solidify.

member *(SYN.)* share, part, allotment, moiety, element,

concern, interest, lines, faction, role, apportionment.
(ANT.) whole.

membrane *(SYN.)* layer, sheath, tissue.

memento *(SYN.)* keepsake, token, reminder, trophy, sign, souvenir.

memoirs *(SYN.)* diary, reflections, experiences, autobiography, journal.

memorable *(SYN.)* important, historic, significant, unforgettable, noteworthy, momentous, impressive.
(ANT.) passing, forgettable, transitory, commonplace.

memorandum *(SYN.)* letter, mark, token, note, indication, remark, message.

memorial *(SYN.)* monument, souvenir, memento, remembrance, ritual, testimonial.

memory *(SYN.)* renown, reminiscence, recollection.
(ANT.) oblivion.

menace *(SYN.)* warning, threat, intimidation, warn, threaten, imperil, forebode.

menagerie *(SYN.)* collection, zoo, kennel.

mend *(SYN.)* restore, better, refit, sew, remedy, patch, correct, repair, rectify, improve, reform, recover.
(ANT.) deface, rend, destroy.

mendacious *(SYN.)* dishonest, false, lying, deceitful, deceptive, tricky.
(ANT.) honest, truthful, sincere, creditable.

mendicant *(SYN.)* ragamuffin, vagabond, beggar.

menial *(SYN.)* unskilled, lowly, degrading, tedious, humble, routine.

mental *(SYN.)* reasoning, intellectual, rational, thinking, conscious, thoughtful.
(ANT.) physical.

mentality *(SYN.)* intellect, reason, understanding, liking, disposition, judgment, brain, inclination, faculties.
(ANT.) materiality, corporeality.

mention *(SYN.)* introduce, refer to, reference, allude,

enumerate, speak of.

mentor *(SYN.)* advisor, tutor, sponsor, guru, teacher, counselor, master, coach.

mercenary *(SYN.)* sordid, corrupt, venal, covetous, grasping, avaricious, greedy.
(ANT.) liberal, generous.

merchandise *(SYN.)* stock, wares, goods, sell, commodities, promote, staples.

merchant *(SYN.)* retailer, dealer, trader, storekeeper, salesman, businessman.

merciful *(SYN.)* humane, kindhearted, tender, clement, sympathetic, forgiving, tolerant, forbearing, lenient, compassionate.
(ANT.) remorseless, cruel, unjust, mean, harsh, unforgiving, vengeful, brutal.

merciless *(SYN.)* carnal, ferocious, brute, barbarous, gross, ruthless, cruel, remorseless, bestial, savage, rough, pitiless, inhuman.
(ANT.) humane, courteous, merciful, openhearted, kind, civilized.

mercurial *(SYN.)* fickle, unstable, volatile, changeable, inconstant, capricious.

mercy *(SYN.)* grace, consideration, kindness, clemency, mildness, forgiveness, pity, sympathy, leniency.
(ANT.) punishment, retribution, cruelty, vengeance.

mere *(SYN.)* only, simple, scant, bare.
(ANT.) substantial, considerable.

merely *(SYN.)* only, barely, simply.

meretricious *(SYN.)* gaudy, sham, bogus, tawdry, flashy, garish.

merge *(SYN.)* unify, fuse, combine, unite, commingle.
(ANT.) separate, decompose, analyze.

merger *(SYN.)* cartel, union, conglomerate, trust, incorporation, combine.

meridian *(SYN.)* climax, summit, pinnacle, zenith, peak, acme, apex.

merit (SYN.) worthiness, earn, goodness, power, value, virtue, goodness, quality, deserve, excellence, worth.
(ANT.) fault, lose, consume.

merited (SYN.) proper, deserved, suitable, adequate, earned.
(ANT.) unmerited, improper.

meritorious (SYN.) laudable, excellent, good, praiseworthy, deserving.

merry (SYN.) hilarious, lively, festive, mirthful, blithe, gay, cheery, joyful, jolly, happy, gleeful, jovial, cheerful.
(ANT.) sorrowful, doleful, morose, gloomy, sad, melancholy.

mesh (SYN.) grid, screen, net, complex.

mesmerize (SYN.) enthrall, transfix, spellbind, charm, fascinate, hypnotize.

mess (SYN.) dirtiness, untidiness, disorder, confusion, muddle, trouble, jumble, difficulty, predicament.

message (SYN.) letter, annotation, memo, symbol, indication, sign, note, communication, memorandum, observation, token.

messenger (SYN.) bearer, agent, runner, courier, liaison, delegate, page.

messy (SYN.) disorderly, dirty, confusing, confused, disordered, sloppy, slovenly.
(ANT.) orderly, neat, tidy.

metallic (SYN.) grating, harsh, clanging, brassy, brazen.

metamorphosis (SYN.) transfiguration, change, alteration, rebirth, mutation.

mete (SYN.) deal, assign, apportion, divide, give, allocate, allot, measure.
(ANT.) withhold, keep, retain.

meteoric (SYN.) flashing, blazing, swift, brilliant, spectacular, remarkable.

meter (SYN.) record, measure, gauge.

method (SYN.) order, manner, plan, way, mode, technique, fashion, approach, design, procedure.

(ANT.) disorder.

methodical (SYN.) exact, definite, ceremonious, stiff, accurate, distinct, unequivocal.
(ANT.) easy, loose, informal, rough.

meticulous (SYN.) precise, careful, exacting, fastidious, fussy, perfectionist.

metropolitan (SYN.) civic, city, municipal.

mettle (SYN.) intrepidity, resolution.
(ANT.) fear, timidity, cowardice.

microscopic (SYN.) tiny, precise, fine, detailed, minute, infinitesimal, minimal.
(ANT.) general, huge, enormous.

middle (SYN.) midpoint, nucleus, center, midst, median, central, intermediate.
(ANT.) end, rim, outskirts, beginning, border, periphery.

middleman (SYN.) dealer, agent, distributor, broker, representative.

midget (SYN.) gnome, shrimp, pygmy, runt, dwarf.
(ANT.) giant.

midst (SYN.) center, heart, middle, thick.

midway (SYN.) halfway, midmost, inside, central, middle.

mien (SYN.) way, semblance, manner, behavior, demeanor, expression, deportment.

miff (SYN.) provoke, rile, chagrin, irk, irritate, affront, offend, annoy, exasperate.

might (SYN.) force, power, vigor, potency, ability, strength.
(ANT.) frailty, vulnerability, weakness.

mighty (SYN.) firm, fortified, powerful, athletic, potent, muscular, robust, strong, cogent.
(ANT.) feeble, weak, brittle, insipid, frail, delicate.

migrant (SYN.) traveling, roaming, straying, roving, rambling, transient, meandering.
(ANT.) stationary.

migrate (SYN.) resettle, move, emigrate, immigrate, relocate, journey.
(ANT.) stay, remain, settle.

migratory (SYN.) itinerant, roving, mobile, vagabond, unsettled, nomadic.

mild (SYN.) soothing, moderate, gentle, tender, bland, pleasant, kind, meek, calm, compassionate, temperate, peaceful, soft.
(ANT.) severe, turbulent, stormy, excitable, violent, harsh, bitter.

milieu (SYN.) environment, background, locale, setting, scene, circumstances.

militant (SYN.) warlike, belligerent, hostile, fighting, aggressive, combative.
(ANT.) peaceful.

military (SYN.) troops, army, soldiers.

millstone (SYN.) load, impediment, burden, encumbrance, hindrance.

mimic (SYN.) simulate, duplicate, copy, imitate, mock, counterfeit, simulate.
(ANT.) invent, distort, alter.

mind (SYN.) intelligence, psyche, disposition, intention, understanding, intellect, spirit, brain, inclination, mentality, soul, wit.
(ANT.) matter, corporeality.

mindful (SYN.) alert, aware, watchful, cognizant, watchful, sensible, heedful.

mingle (SYN.) unite, coalesce, fuse, merge, combine, amalgamate, unify, conjoin, mix, blend, commingle.
(ANT.) analyze, sort, disintegrate.

miniature (SYN.) small, little, tiny, midget, minute, minuscule, wee, petite.
(ANT.) outsize.

minimize (SYN.) shorten, deduct, belittle, decrease, reduce, curtail, lessen,

diminish, subtract.
(ANT.) enlarge, increase, amplify.

minimum (SYN.) lowest, least, smallest, slightest.
(ANT.) maximum.

minister (SYN.) pastor, clergyman, vicar, parson, curate, preacher, prelate, chaplain, cleric, deacon, reverend.

minor (SYN.) poorer, lesser, petty, youth, inferior, secondary, smaller, unimportant, lower.
(ANT.) higher, superior, major, greater.

minority (SYN.) youth, childhood, immaturity.

minstrel (SYN.) bard, musician.

mint (SYN.) stamp, coin, strike, punch.

minus (SYN.) lacking, missing, less, absent, without.

minute (SYN.) tiny, particular, fine, precise, jiffy, instant, moment, wee, exact, detailed, microscopic.
(ANT.) large, general, huge, enormous.

miraculous (SYN.) spiritual, wonderful, marvelous, incredible, preternatural.
(ANT.) natural, common, plain, everyday, human.

mirage (SYN.) vision, illusion, fantasy, dream, phantom.
(ANT.) reality, actuality.

mirror (SYN.) glass, reflector.

mirth (SYN.) joy, glee, jollity, joyousness, gaiety, joyfulness, laughter, merriment.
(ANT.) sadness, gloom.

misappropriate (SYN.) embezzle, steal, purloin, plunder, cheat, filch.

miscarriage (SYN.) omission, want, decay, fiasco, default, deficiency, loss, abortion.
(ANT.) success, sufficiency, achievement.

miscellaneous (SYN.) diverse, motley, indiscriminate, assorted, sundry, heterogeneous, mixed, varied.
(ANT.) classified, selected, homogeneous, alike, ordered.

mischief *(SYN.)* injury, harm, damage, evil, ill, prankishness, rascality, roguishness.
(ANT.) kindness, boon.

mischievous *(SYN.)* roguish, prankish, naughty, playful.
(ANT.) well-behaved, good.

miscreant *(SYN.)* rascal, wretch, rogue, sinner, criminal, villain, scoundrel.

miscue *(SYN.)* blunder, fluff, mistake, error, lapse.

misdemeanor *(SYN.)* infringement, transgression, violation, offense, wrong.

miserable *(SYN.)* abject, forlorn, comfortless, low, worthless, pitiable, distressed, heartbroken.
(ANT.) fortunate, happy, contented, joyful, content, wealthy, honorable, lucky, noble, significant.

miserly *(SYN.)* stingy, greedy, acquisitive, tight, tightfisted, cheap, mean, parsimonious, avaricious.
(ANT.) bountiful, generous, spendthrift, munificent, extravagant, openhanded, altruistic.

misery *(SYN.)* suffering, woe, evil, agony, torment, trouble, distress, anguish, grief, unhappiness, anguish, tribulation, calamity, sorrow.
(ANT.) fun, pleasure, delight, joy.

misfit *(SYN.)* crank, loner, deviate, fifth wheel, individualist.

misfortune *(SYN.)* adversity, distress, mishap, calamity, accident, catastrophe, hardship, ruin, disaster, affliction.
(ANT.) success, blessing, prosperity.

misgiving *(SYN.)* suspicion, doubt, mistrust, hesitation, uncertainty.

mishap *(SYN.)* misfortune, casualty, accident, disaster, adversity, reverse.
(ANT.) intention, calculation.

misjudge *(SYN.)* err, mistake, miscalculate.

mislay *(SYN.)* misplace, lose.
(ANT.) discover, find.

mislead *(SYN.)* misdirect, deceive, deceive, delude.

miss *(SYN.)* lose, want, crave, yearn for, fumble, drop, error, slip, default, omit, lack.
(ANT.) suffice, have, achieve.

mission *(SYN.)* business, task, job, stint, work, errand, assignment, delegation.

mistake *(SYN.)* slip, misjudge, fault, blunder, misunderstand, confuse.
(ANT.) truth, accuracy.

mistaken *(SYN.)* false, amiss, incorrect, awry, wrong, misinformed, inaccurate.
(ANT.) true, correct, right.

mister *(SYN.)* young man, gentleman, esquire, fellow.

mistreat *(SYN.)* wrong, pervert, oppress, harm, maltreat, abuse.

mistrust *(SYN.)* suspect, doubt, distrust, question.
(ANT.) trust.

mite *(SYN.)* particle, mote, smidgen, trifle, iota.

mitigate *(SYN.)* soften, soothe, abate, assuage, relieve, allay, diminish.
(ANT.) irritate, agitate, increase.

mixture *(SYN.)* diversity, variety, strain, sort, change, kind, confusion.
(ANT.) likeness, sameness, homogeneity, monotony.

moan *(SYN.)* wail, groan, cry.

mob *(SYN.)* crowd, host, populace, swarm, riot, bevy.

mock *(SYN.)* taunt, jeer, deride, scoff, scorn, fleer, ridicule, tease, fake, imitation, sham, gibe, sneer.
(ANT.) praise, applaud, real, genuine, honor, authentic.

mode *(SYN.)* method, fashion, procedure, design, manner, technique, way, style.
(ANT.) disorder, confusion.

moderation *(SYN.)* sobriety, forbearance, self-control, restraint, continence.
(ANT.) greed, excess.

moderator *(SYN.)* referee, leader, arbitrator, chairman.

modern (SYN.) modish, current, recent, novel, fresh, contemporary, new.
(ANT.) old, antiquated, past, bygone, ancient.

modest (SYN.) unassuming, virtuous, bashful, meek, shy, humble, decent, demure.
(ANT.) forward, bold, ostentatious, conceited, immodest.

modesty (SYN.) decency, humility, propriety, simplicity, shyness.

modification (SYN.) alternation, substitution, variety, change, alteration.
(ANT.) uniformity, monotony.

module (SYN.) unit, measure, norm, dimension, component, gauge.

moiety (SYN.) part, scrap, share, allotment, piece, division, portion.

moisture (SYN.) wetness, mist, dampness, condensation.
(ANT.) aridity, dryness.

mold (SYN.) make, fashion, organize, produce, forge, constitute, create, combine.
(ANT.) wreck, dismantle, destroy, misshape.

molest (SYN.) irk, disturb, trouble, annoy, pester, bother, vex, inconvenience.
(ANT.) console, accommodate.

moment (SYN.) flash, jiffy, instant, twinkling, gravity, importance, consequence.

momentary (SYN.) concise, pithy, brief, curt, terse, laconic, compendious.
(ANT.) long, extended, prolonged.

momentous (SYN.) critical, serious, essential, grave.
(ANT.) unimportant, trifling, mean, trivial, tribial.

momentum (SYN.) impetus, push, thrust, force, impulse, drive, vigor, propulsion.

monarch (SYN.) ruler, king, queen, empress, emperor.

monastic (SYN.) withdrawn, dedicated, austere, unworldly, celibate, abstinent.

monastery (SYN.) convent, priory, abbey, hermitage.

monogram (SYN.) mark, stamp, signature.

monologue (SYN.) discourse, lecture, sermon, talk.

monomania (SYN.) obsessiveness, passion, single-mindedness, extremism.

monotonous (SYN.) dull, slow, tiresome, boring, humdrum.
(ANT.) interesting, riveting, quick, fascinating, exciting.

monster (SYN.) brute, beast, villain, demon, wretch.

monument (SYN.) remembrance, memento, commemoration, statue.

mood (SYN.) joke, irony, waggery, temper, disposition, temperament, sarcasm.
(ANT.) sorrow, gravity.

moor (SYN.) tether, fasten, tie, dock, anchor, bind.

moot (SYN.) unsettled, questionable, problematical, controversial, contestable.

mop (SYN.) wash, wipe, swab, scrub.

mope (SYN.) gloom, pout, whine, grumble, grieve, sulk, fret.
(ANT.) rejoice.

moral (SYN.) just, right, chaste, good, virtuous, pure, decent, honest, upright, ethical, righteous, honorable, scrupulous.
(ANT.) libertine, immoral, unethical, amoral, sinful.

morale (SYN.) confidence, spirit, assurance.

morals (SYN.) conduct, scruples, guide-lines, behavior, life style, standards.

morass (SYN.) fen, march, swamp, mire.

morbid (SYN.) sickly, unhealthy, ghastly, awful, horrible, shocking.
(ANT.) pleasant, healthy.

more (SYN.) further, greater, farther, extra, another.
(ANT.) less.

moron (SYN.) subnormal, dunce, blockhead, imbecile, retardate, simpleton.

morsel (SYN.) portion, fragment, bite, bit, scrap.
(ANT.) whole, all, sum.

mortal *(SYN.)* fatal, destructive, human, perishable.
(ANT.) superficial, divine.

mortified *(SYN.)* embarrassed, humiliated, ashamed.

mortuary *(SYN.)* morgue, crematory, funeral parlor.

most *(SYN.)* extreme, highest, supreme, greatest, majority.
(ANT.) least.

mostly *(SYN.)* chiefly, generally, largely, mainly, principally, especially.

motion *(SYN.)* change, activity, movement, proposition, action, signal, gesture.
(ANT.) stability, immobility, equilibrium, stillness.

motivate *(SYN.)* move, prompt, stimulate, induce, activate, propel, arouse.

motive *(SYN.)* inducement, purpose, cause, incentive, reason, incitement, idea.
(ANT.) deed, result, attempt.

motley *(SYN.)* heterogeneous, mixed, assorted, sundry, diverse, miscellaneous.
(ANT.) ordered, classified.

mound *(SYN.)* hillock, hill, heap, pile, knoll, dune.

mount *(SYN.)* scale, climb, increase, rise, prepare, ready, steed, horse, tower.
(ANT.) sink, descend.

mountain *(SYN.)* alp, mount, pike, peak, ridge, height.

mountebank *(SYN.)* faker, rascal, swindler, cheat.

mounting *(SYN.)* backing, pedestal, easel, support, framework, background.

mourn *(SYN.)* suffer, grieve, bemoan, sorrow, weep.
(ANT.) celebrate, carouse.

movement *(SYN.)* activity, effort, gesture, move, proposition, crusade, action.
(ANT.) stillness, immobility, equilibrium.

mow *(SYN.)* prune, cut, shave, crop, clip.

muff *(SYN.)* blunder, bungle, spoil, mess, fumble.

muffle *(SYN.)* soften, deaden, mute, quiet, drape, shroud.
(ANT.) louden, amplify.

mulish *(SYN.)* obstinate, stub-

born, tenacious, willful.

multiply *(SYN.)* double, treble, increase, triple, propagate, spread, expand.
(ANT.) lessen, decrease.

multitude *(SYN.)* crowd, throng, mass, swarm, host, mob, army, legion.
(ANT.) scarcity, handful.

mumble *(SYN.)* stammer, whisper, hesitate, mutter.
(ANT.) shout, yell.

munificent *(SYN.)* bountiful, full, generous, forthcoming.
(ANT.) voracious, insatiable, grasping, ravenous.

murder *(SYN.)* homicide, kill, slay, slaughter, butcher, killing, massacre, assassinate.
(ANT.) save, protect, vivify.

murky *(SYN.)* gloomy, dark, obscure, unclear.
(ANT.) cheerful, light.

muscle *(SYN.)* brawn, strength, power, fitness, vigor, vim, stamina.

muse *(SYN.)* ponder, brood, think, meditate, ruminate.

music *(SYN.)* symphony, harmony, consonance.

muss *(SYN.)* mess, disarray, rumple, litter, clutter.
(ANT.) fix, arrange.

musty *(SYN.)* mildewed, rancid, airless, dank, stale, decayed, rotten, funky.

mute *(SYN.)* quiet, noiseless, dumb, taciturn, hushed, uncommunicative, silent.
(ANT.) clamorous, noisy.

mutilate *(SYN.)* tear, cut, clip, amputate, lacerate, dismember, deform, castrate.

muzzle *(SYN.)* restrain, silence, bridle, bind, curb, suppress, gag, stifle, censor.

myopia *(SYN.)* incomprehension, folly, shortsightedness.

mystery *(SYN.)* riddle, difficulty, enigma, puzzle.
(ANT.) solution, key, answer.

mystify *(SYN.)* puzzle, confound, bewilder, stick, get.
(ANT.) enlighten, clarify.

myth *(SYN.)* fable, parable, allegory, fiction, tradition, lie, saga, legend, story
(ANT.) history.

nag *(SYN.)* badger, harry, provoke, tease, bother, annoy, molest, taunt, vex, torment.
(ANT.) please, comfort, soothe.

nail *(SYN.)* hold, fasten, secure, fix, seize, catch, snare.
(ANT.) release.

naive *(SYN.)* frank, unsophisticated, natural, artless, ingenuous, open, innocent.
(ANT.) worldly, cunning.

naked *(SYN.)* uncovered, unfurnished, nude, bare, open, unclothed, undressed.
(ANT.) covered, protected, dressed, clothed, concealed.

name *(SYN.)* title, reputation, appellation, style, fame, repute, renown, denomination, appoint, character.
(ANT.) anonymity, misnomer, hint, misname.

nap *(SYN.)* nod, doze, sleep, snooze, catnap, siesta.

narcissistic *(SYN.)* egotistical, egocentric, self-centered.

narrate *(SYN.)* recite, relate, declaim, detail, rehearse, deliver, review, tell.

narrative *(SYN.)* history, relation, account, record, chronicle, detail, recital.
(ANT.) distortion, caricature, misrepresentation.

narrow *(SYN.)* narrow-minded, illiberal, bigoted, fanatical, prejudiced, close.
(ANT.) progressive, liberal, wide.

nascent *(SYN.)* prime, introductory, emerging.

nasty *(SYN.)* offensive, malicious, selfish, mean, disagreeable, unpleasant, foul.
(ANT.) generous, dignified, noble, admirable, pleasant.

nation *(SYN.)* state, community, realm, nationality.

native *(SYN.)* domestic, inborn, inherent, natural, inbred, indigenous.
(ANT.) alien, stranger, foreigner, outsider, foreign.

natural *(SYN.)* innate, genuine, real, unaffected, characteristic, native, normal simple, inbred, inborn.

(ANT.) irregular, false, unnatural, formal, abnormal.

naturally *(SYN.)* typically, ordinarily, usually, indeed, surely, certainly.
(ANT.) artificially.

nature *(SYN.)* kind, disposition, reputation, character, repute, world, quality.

naughty *(SYN.)* unmanageable, insubordinate, disobedient, mischievous, unruly.
(ANT.) obedient, good, well-behaved.

nausea *(SYN.)* sickness, vomiting, upset, queasiness.

naval *(SYN.)* oceanic, marine, nautical, maritime.

navigate *(SYN.)* sail, cruise, pilot, guide, steer.

near *(SYN.)* close, nigh, dear, adjacent, familiar, at hand, impending, proximate.
(ANT.) removed, distant, far, remote.

nearly *(SYN.)* practically, close to, approximately.

neat *(SYN.)* trim, orderly, precise, clear, spruce, nice, dapper, smart, proficient.
(ANT.) unkempt, sloppy, dirty, slovenly, messy, sloppy.

nebulous *(SYN.)* fuzzy, indistinct, indefinite, clouded.
(ANT.) definite, distinct, clear.

necessary *(SYN.)* needed, expedient, unavoidable, required, essential.
(ANT.) optional, nonessential, contingent, casual.

necessity *(SYN.)* requirement, fate, destiny, constraint, requisite, prerequisite.
(ANT.) option, luxury, freedom, choice, uncertainty.

need *(SYN.)* crave, want, demand, claim, desire, covet, wish, lack, necessity.

needed *(SYN.)* necessary, indispensable, essential.
(ANT.) optional, contingent.

needle *(SYN.)* goad, badger, tease, nag, prod, provoke.

needless *(SYN.)* nonessential, unnecessary, superfluous, useless, purposeless.

needy *(SYN.)* poor, indigent,

impoverished penniless.
(ANT.) affluent, well-off, wealthy, well-to-do.

nefarious (SYN.) detestable, vicious, wicked, atrocious.

negate (SYN.) revoke, void, cancel, nullify.

neglect (SYN.) omission, default, heedlessness, carelessness, thoughtlessness, disregard, oversight.
(ANT.) diligence, do, protect, watchfulness, care, attention.

negligent (SYN.) imprudent, thoughtless, lax, careless, inattentive, indifferent.
(ANT.) careful, nice, accurate, meticulous.

negligible (SYN.) trifling, insignificant, trivial.
(ANT.) major, vital, important.

negotiate (SYN.) intervene, talk over, mediate, transact, umpire, referee, arbitrate.

neighborhood (SYN.) environs, nearness, locality, district, vicinity, area.
(ANT.) remoteness.

neighboring (SYN.) bordering, near, adjacent, next to, surrounding, adjoining.

neighborly (SYN.) friendly, sociable, amiable, affable, companionable, congenial.
(ANT.) distant, reserved, cool, unfriendly, hostile.

neophyte (SYN.) greenhorn, rookie, amateur, beginner, apprentice, tyro, student.

nepotism (SYN.) bias, prejudice, patronage.

nerve (SYN.) bravery, spirit, courage, boldness, rudeness, strength, stamina, bravado, daring.
(ANT.) frailty, cowardice, weakness.

nervous (SYN.) agitated, restless, excited, shy, timid, upset, disturbed, shaken, rattle, high-strung.
(ANT.) placid, courageous, confident, calm, tranquil, composed, bold.

nest (SYN.) den, refuge.

nestle (SYN.) cuddle, snuggle.

net (SYN.) snare, trap, mesh,

earn, gain, web, get, acquire, secure, obtain.

nettle (SYN.) irritate, vex, provoke, annoy, disturb, irk, needle, pester.

neurotic (SYN.) disturbed.

neutral (SYN.) nonpartisan, uninvolved, detached, impartial, cool, unprejudiced.
(ANT.) involved, biased, partisan.

neutralize (SYN.) offset, counteract, nullify, negate.

nevertheless (SYN.) notwithstanding, however, although, anyway, but.

new (SYN.) modern, original, newfangled, late, recent, novel, young, firsthand.
(ANT.) antiquated, old, ancient, obsolete, outmoded.

newborn (SYN.) baby, infant, cub, suckling.

news (SYN.) report, intelligence, information, copy, message, advice, tidings.

next (SYN.) nearest, following, closest, successive.

nice (SYN.) pleasing, pleasant, agreeable, thoughtful, satisfactory, friendly, enjoyable, gratifying, desirable, fine, good, cordial.
(ANT.) nasty, unpleasant, disagreeable, unkind, inexact, careless, thoughtless.

niche (SYN.) corner, nook, alcove, cranny, recess.

nick (SYN.) cut, notch, indentation, dash, score, mark.

nickname (SYN.) byname, sobriquet.

nigh (SYN.) close, imminent, near, adjacent, approaching, bordering, neighboring, impending.
(ANT.) removed, distant.

nightmare (SYN.) calamity, horror, torment, bad dream.

nil (SYN.) zero, none, nought, nothing.

nimble (SYN.) brisk, quick, active, supple, alert, lively, spry, light, fast, speedy, swift, agile.
(ANT.) slow, heavy, sluggish, clumsy.

nincompoop (SYN.) nitwit,

idiot, fool, moron, blockhead, ninny, idiot, simpleton.

nip *(SYN.)* bite, pinch, chill, cold, squeeze, crispness, sip, small.

nippy *(SYN.)* chilly, sharp, bitter, cold, penetrating.

nit-picker *(SYN.)* fussbudget, precise, purist, perfectionist.

nitty-gritty *(SYN.)* essentials, substance, essence.

noble *(SYN.)* illustrious, exalted, dignified, stately, eminent, lofty, grand, elevated, honorable, honest, virtuous, great, distinguished, majestic, important, prominent, magnificent, grandiose, aristocratic, upright, well-born.
(ANT.) vile, low, base, mean, dishonest, common, ignoble.

nocturnal *(SYN.)* nightly.

nod *(SYN.)* bob, bow, bend, tip, signal.

node *(SYN.)* protuberance, growth, nodule, cyst, lump, wen.

noise *(SYN.)* cry, sound, din, babel, racket, uproar, clamor, outcry, tumult, outcry, sounds, hubbub, bedlam, commotion, rumpus, clatter.
(ANT.) quiet, stillness, hush, silence, peace.

noisome *(SYN.)* repulsive, disgusting, revolting, obnoxious, malodorous, rotten.

noisy *(SYN.)* resounding, loud, clamorous, vociferous.
(ANT.) soft, dulcet, subdued, quiet, silent, peaceful.

nomination *(SYN.)* appointment, naming, choice, selection, designation.

nominee *(SYN.)* aspirant, contestant, candidate.

noncommittal *(SYN.)* neutral, tepid, undecided, cautious.

nonconformist *(SYN.)* protester, rebel, radical, dissenter, renegade, dissident.

nondescript *(SYN.)* unclassifiable, indescribable.

nonpareil *(SYN.)* unsur-passed, exceptional, paramount, unrivaled.

nonplus *(SYN.)* confuse, perplex, dumfound, mystify, confound, puzzle, baffle.
(ANT.) illumine, clarify, solve.

nonsense *(SYN.)* balderdash, rubbish, foolishness, folly, ridiculousness, stupidity.

nonsensical *(SYN.)* silly, preposterous, absurd, unreasonable, foolish, irrational, ridiculous, stupid, senseless.
(ANT.) sound, consistent, reasonable.

nonstop *(SYN.)* constant, continuous, unceasing, endless.

normal *(SYN.)* ordinary, uniform, natural, unvaried, customary, regular, healthy.
(ANT.) rare, erratic, unusual, abnormal.

normally *(SYN.)* regularly, frequently, customarily.

nosy *(SYN.)* inquisitive, meddling, prying, snooping.
(ANT.) unconcerned, incurious, uninterested.

note *(SYN.)* sign, annotation, letter, indication, observation, mark, symbol, comment, remark, token, message, memorandum.

noted *(SYN.)* renowned, glorious, celebrated, famous, illustrious, well-known.
(ANT.) unknown, hidden, infamous, ignominious.

notice *(SYN.)* heed, perceive, hold, mark, behold, descry, recognize, note, regard, see, sign, announcement, poster, note, warning.
(ANT.) overlook, disregard.

notify *(SYN.)* apprise, acquaint, instruct, tell, advise.
(ANT.) mislead, delude.

notion *(SYN.)* image, conception, sentiment, abstraction, thought, idea, fancy, understanding, opinion, concept.
(ANT.) thing, matter, substance, entity.

nourish *(SYN.)* strengthen, nurse, feed, supply, nurture, sustain, support.

nourishment (SYN.) nutriment, food, sustenance, support.
(ANT.) starvation, deprivation.

novel (SYN.) fiction, narrative, romance, invention, different, unusual, strange, firsthand, odd.
(ANT.) verity, history, truth, fact.

novice (SYN.) beginner, amateur, newcomer, learner, apprentice, dilettante.
(ANT.) expert, professional, adept, master.

now (SYN.) today, at once, right away, immediately, at this time, present.
(ANT.) later.

noxious (SYN.) poisonous, harmful, damaging, toxic, detrimental.
(ANT.) harmless.

nude (SYN.) naked, unclad, plain, open, defenseless, mere, bare, exposed.
(ANT.) dressed, concealed, protected, clothed, covered.

nuisance (SYN.) annoyance, bother, irritation, pest.

nullify (SYN.) abolish, cross out, delete, invalidate, obliterate, cancel, expunge.
(ANT.) perpetuate, confirm, enforce.

number (SYN.) quantity, sum, amount, volume, aggregate, figure, multitude, digit.
(ANT.) zero, nothing, nothingness.

numskull (SYN.) fool, nitwit, blockhead, ninny.

nuptials (SYN.) marriage, wedding, espousal, wedlock, matrimony.
(ANT.) virginity, divorce, celibacy.

nurse (SYN.) tend, care for, nourish, nurture, feed.

nurture (SYN.) hold dear, prize, bring up, rear, value.
(ANT.) dislike, disregard.

nutriment (SYN.) food, diet, sustenance, fare, edibles.
(ANT.) hunger, want.

nutrition (SYN.) nourishment, sustenance, food.

oaf (SYN.) boor, clod, clown, lummox, fool, lout, dunce.

oath (SYN.) promise, pledge, vow, profanity, curse, agreement, commitment.

obdurate (SYN.) insensible, callous, hard, tough, unfeeling, insensitive, impenitent.
(ANT.) soft, compassionate, tender.

obedience (SYN.) docility, submission, subservience, compliance, conformability.
(ANT.) rebelliousness, disobedience.

obedient (SYN.) dutiful, yielding, tractable, compliant.
(ANT.) rebellious, intractable, insubordinate, obstinate.

obese (SYN.) portly, fat, pudgy, chubby, plump, rotund, stout, thickset.
(ANT.) slim, gaunt, lean, thin, slender.

obey (SYN.) submit, yield, mind, comply, listen to.
(ANT.) resist, disobey.

object (SYN.) thing, aim, intention, design, end, objective, particular, mark.
(ANT.) assent, agree, concur, approve, acquiesce.

objective (SYN.) aspiration, goal, passion, desire, aim, hope, purpose, drift, design.
(ANT.) biased, subjective.

obligate (SYN.) oblige, require, pledge, bind, force.

obligation (SYN.) duty, bond, engagement, compulsion.
(ANT.) freedom, choice, exemption.

obliging (SYN.) considerate, helpful, thoughtful, well-meaning, accommodating.
(ANT.) discourteous.

obliterate (SYN.) terminate, destroy, eradicate, raze, extinguish, exterminate.
(ANT.) make, save, construct, establish, preserve.

oblivious (SYN.) sightless, unmindful, headlong, rash, blind, senseless, ignorant.
(ANT.) sensible, aware, calculated, perceiving, discerning.

oblong (SYN.) rectangular, elliptical, elongated.

obnoxious *(SYN.)* hateful, offensive, nasty, disagreeable, repulsive, loathsome, vile.

obscene *(SYN.)* indecent, filthy, impure, dirty, gross.
(ANT.) modest, pure, decent.

obscure *(SYN.)* cloudy, enigmatic, mysterious, abstruse, cryptic, dim, indistinct.
(ANT.) clear, famous, distinguished, noted, illumined.

obsequious *(SYN.)* fawning, flattering, ingratiating.

observance *(SYN.)* protocol, ritual, ceremony, rite, parade, pomp, solemnity.
(ANT.) omission.

observant *(SYN.)* aware, alert, careful, mindful, watchful, heedful, considerate.
(ANT.) unaware, indifferent.

observation *(SYN.)* attention, watching, comment, opinion, remark, notice.

observe *(SYN.)* note, behold, discover, notice, perceive, eye, detect, inspect, keep.
(ANT.) neglect, overlook, disregard, ignore.

observer *(SYN.)* examiner, overseer, lookout, spectator, bystander, witness.

obsession *(SYN.)* preoccupation, mania, compulsion, passion, fetish, infatuation.

obsolete *(SYN.)* old, out-of-date, ancient, archaic, extinct, old-fashioned.
(ANT.) modern, stylish, current, recent, fashionable.

obstacle *(SYN.)* block, hindrance, barrier, impediment, snag, check.
(ANT.) help, aid, assistance, encouragement.

obstinate *(SYN.)* firm, headstrong, immovable, stubborn, determined, dogged.
(ANT.) yielding, docile, amenable, submissive.

obstruct *(SYN.)* clog, barricade, impede, block, delay.
(ANT.) promote, clear, aid, help, open, further.

obtain *(SYN.)* get, acquire, secure, win, procure, attain, earn, gain, receive.
(ANT.) surrender, forfeit, lose, forego, miss.

obtrusive *(SYN.)* blatant, garish, conspicuous.

obtuse *(SYN.)* blunt, dull, slow-witted, unsharpened.
(ANT.) clear, interesting, lively, bright, animated.

obviate *(SYN.)* prevent, obstruct, forestall, preclude, intercept, avert, evade.

obvious *(SYN.)* plain, clear, evident, palpable, patent, self-evident, apparent.
(ANT.) concealed, hidden, abstruse, obscure.

obviously *(SYN.)* plainly, clearly, surely, evidently.

occasion *(SYN.)* occurrence, time, happening, excuse, opportunity, chance.

occasional *(SYN.)* random, irregular, sporadic, infrequent, periodically.
(ANT.) chronic, regular.

occasionally *(SYN.)* seldom, now and then, infrequently, sometimes, irregularly.
(ANT.) regularly, often.

occlude *(SYN.)* clog, obstruct, choke, throttle.

occupant *(SYN.)* tenant, lodger, boarder, dweller, resident, inhabitant.

occupation *(SYN.)* employment, business, enterprise, job, trade, vocation, work.
(ANT.) hobby, pastime, avocation.

occupy *(SYN.)* dwell, have, inhabit, absorb, hold, possess, fill, busy, keep.
(ANT.) relinquish, abandon, release.

occur *(SYN.)* take place, be chance, come about, befall.

occurrence *(SYN.)* episode, event, issue, end, result, consequence, happening.

ocean *(SYN.)* deep, sea, main.

odd *(SYN.)* strange, bizarre, eccentric, unusual, single, uneven, unique, queer.
(ANT.) matched, common, typical, normal, familiar.

odious *(SYN.)* obscene, depraved, vulgar, despicable, mean, wicked, sordid, foul, base, loathsome, vicious.

(ANT.) *decent, upright, laudable, attractive.*

odor (SYN.) fume, aroma, fragrance, redolence, smell, stink, scent, essence, stench.

odorous (SYN.) scented, aromatic, fragrant.

odyssey (SYN.) crusade, quest, journey, voyage.

offbeat (SYN.) uncommon, eccentric, strange.

off-color (SYN.) rude, improper, earthy, suggestive.

offend (SYN.) annoy, anger, vex, irritate, displease, provoke, hurt, grieve, pain, disgust, wound, horrify.
(ANT.) *flatter, please, delight.*

offender (SYN.) criminal, culprit, law-breaker, miscreant.

offense (SYN.) indignity, injustice, transgression, affront, outrage, misdeed, sin.
(ANT.) *morality, gentleness, innocence, right.*

offensive (SYN.) attacking, aggressive, unpleasant, revolting, disagreeable, nauseous.
(ANT.) *pleasing, defending, defensive, pleasant, attractive, agreeable.*

offer (SYN.) suggestion, overture, proposal, present, suggest, propose, try, submit.
(ANT.) *withdrawal, denial, rejection.*

offhand (SYN.) informal, unprepared, casual, impromptu, spontaneous.
(ANT.) *considered, planned.*

office (SYN.) position, job, situation, studio, berth, incumbency, capacity, headquarters, duty, task.

officiate (SYN.) regulate, administer, superintend, oversee, emcee.

offset (SYN.) compensate, counterbalance, cushion, counteract, neutralize, soften, balance.

offshoot (SYN.) outgrowth, addition, by-product, supplement, appendage, accessory, branch.

offspring (SYN.) issue, children, progeny, descendants.

often (SYN.) frequently, repeatedly, commonly, generally, many times, recurrently.
(ANT.) *seldom, infrequently, rarely, occasionally, sporadically.*

ogle (SYN.) gaze, stare, eye, leer.

ogre (SYN.) fiend, monster, devil, demon.

ointment (SYN.) lotion, pomade, balm, emollient.

old (SYN.) antique, senile, ancient, archaic, old-fashioned, superannuated, obsolete, venerable, antiquated, elderly, discontinued, abandoned, aged.
(ANT.) *new, youthful, recent, modern, young.*

old-fashioned (SYN.) outmoded, old, dated, ancient.
(ANT.) *modern, fashionable, current, new.*

olio (SYN.) potpourri, variety, mixture, jumble.

omen (SYN.) sign, gesture, indication, proof, portent, symbol, token, emblem, signal.

ominous (SYN.) unfavorable, threatening, sinister, menacing.

omission (SYN.) failure, neglect, oversight, default.
(ANT.) *inclusion, notice, attention, insertion.*

omit (SYN.) exclude, delete, cancel, eliminate, ignore, neglect, skip, leave out, drop, miss, bar, overlook, disregard.
(ANT.) *insert, notice, enter, include, introduce.*

omnipotent (SYN.) all-powerful, almighty, divine.

oncoming (SYN.) imminent, approaching, arriving, nearing.

onerous (SYN.) intricate, arduous, hard, perplexing, difficult, burdensome, puzzling.
(ANT.) *simple, easy, facile, effortless.*

one-sided (SYN.) unfair, partial, biased, prejudiced.
(ANT.) *impartial, neutral.*

ongoing *(SYN.)* advancing, developing, continuing, progressive.

onlooker *(SYN.)* witness, spectator, observer, bystander.

only *(SYN.)* lone, sole, solitary, single, merely, but, just.

onset *(SYN.)* commencement, beginning, opening, start, assault, attack, charge, offense, onslaught.
(ANT.) end.

onslaught *(SYN.)* invasion, aggression, attack, assault, offense, drive, criticism, onset, charge, denunciation.
(ANT.) vindication, defense, surrender, opposition, resistance.

onus *(SYN.)* load, weight, burden, duty.

onward *(SYN.)* ahead, forward, frontward.
(ANT.) backward.

ooze *(SYN.)* seep, leak, drip, flow, filter.

opacity *(SYN.)* obscurity, thickness, imperviousness.

opaque *(SYN.)* murky, dull, cloudy, filmy, unilluminated, dim, obtuse, indistinct, shadowy, dark, obscure.
(ANT.) light, clear, bright.

open *(SYN.)* uncovered, overt, agape, unlocked, passable, accessible, unrestricted, candid, plain, clear, exposed, unclosed, unobstructed, free, disengaged, frank, unoccupied, public, honest, ajar, available.

open *(SYN.)* unbar, unfold, exhibit, spread, unseal, expand, unfasten.
(ANT.) close, shut, conceal, hide.

open-handed *(SYN.)* kind, generous, charitable, lavish, extravagant, bountiful.
(ANT.) mean, stingy.

openhearted *(SYN.)* frank, honest, candid, sincere, ingenuous, straight-forward.
(ANT.) insincere, devious.

opening *(SYN.)* cavity, hole, void, abyss, aperture, chasm, pore, gap, loophole.

openly *(SYN.)* sincerely, frankly, freely.
(ANT.) secretly.

open-minded *(SYN.)* tolerant, fair, just, liberal, impartial, reasonable, unprejudiced.
(ANT.) prejudiced, bigoted.

operate *(SYN.)* comport, avail, behave, interact, apply, manage, utilize, demean, run, manipulate, employ, act, exploit, exert, exercise, practice, conduct.
(ANT.) neglect, waste.

operation *(SYN.)* effort, enterprise, mentality, maneuver, action, instrumentality, performance, working, proceeding, agency.
(ANT.) inaction, cessation, rest, inactivity.

operative *(SYN.)* busy, active, industrious, working, effective, functional.
(ANT.) inactive, dormant.

opiate *(SYN.)* hypnotic, tranquilizer, narcotic.

opinion *(SYN.)* decision, feeling, notion, view, idea, conviction, belief, judgment, sentiment, persuasion, impression.
(ANT.) knowledge, fact, misgiving, skepticism.

opinionated *(SYN.)* domineering, overbearing, arrogant, dogmatic, positive, magisterial, obstinate, pertinacious.
(ANT.) questioning, fluctuating, indecisive, skeptical, open-minded, indecisive.

opponent *(SYN.)* competitor, foe, adversary, contestant, enemy, rival, contender, combatant, antagonist.
(ANT.) comrade, team, ally, confederate.

oppose *(SYN.)* defy, resist, withstand, combat, bar, thwart, struggle, fight, contradict, hinder, obstruct.
(ANT.) submit, support, agree, cooperate, succumb.

opposed *(SYN.)* opposite, contrary, hostile, unlucky, antagonistic, disastrous.
(ANT.) lucky, benign, propitious, fortunate, favorable.

opposite *(SYN.)* reverse, contrary, different, unlike.
(ANT.) like, same, similar.

opposition *(SYN.)* combat, struggle, discord, collision, conflict, battle, fight.
(ANT.) harmony, amity, concord, consonance.

oppress *(SYN.)* harass, torment, vex, afflict, annoy, harry, pester, persecute.
(ANT.) encourage, support, comfort, assist, aid.

oppression *(SYN.)* cruelty, tyranny, persecution, injustice, despotism, brutality.
(ANT.) liberty, freedom.

oppressive *(SYN.)* difficult, stifling, burdensome, severe, domineering, harsh, unjust, overbearing.

oppressor *(SYN.)* bully, scourge, slave-driver.

opt *(SYN.)* choose, prefer, pick, select.

optimism *(SYN.)* faith, expectation, optimism, anticipation, trust, expectancy.
(ANT.) despair, pessimism, despondency.

optimistic *(SYN.)* happy, cheerful, bright, glad, pleasant, radiant, lighthearted.
(ANT.) pessimistic.

option *(SYN.)* preference, choice, selection, alternative, election.

opulence *(SYN.)* luxury, abundance, fortune, riches, wealth, plenty, affluence.
(ANT.) need, indigence, want, poverty.

opulent *(SYN.)* wealthy, rich, prosperous, well-off, affluent, well-heeled.

oracle *(SYN.)* authority, forecaster, wizard, seer, mastermind, clairvoyant.

oral *(SYN.)* voiced, sounded, vocalized, said, uttered.
(ANT.) recorded, written.

oration *(SYN.)* address, lecture, speech, sermon, discourse, recital, declamation.

orbit *(SYN.)* path, lap, course, circuit, revolution, revolve.

ordain *(SYN.)* constitute, create, order, decree, decide, dictate, comman.,
(ANT.) terminate, disband.

ordeal *(SYN.)* hardship, suffering, test, affliction, trouble, fortune, proof.
(ANT.) consolation, alleviation.

order *(SYN.)* plan, series, decree, instruction, command, system, method, aim, arrangement, class, injunction, mandate, instruct, requirement, dictate, bidding.
(ANT.) consent, license, confusion, disarray, irregularity, permission.

order *(SYN.)* guide, command, rule, direct, govern.
(ANT.) misguide, deceive, misdirect, distract.

orderly *(SYN.)* regulated, neat, well-organized, disciplined, methodical.
(ANT.) sloppy, messy, haphazard, disorganized.

ordinarily *(SYN.)* commonly, usually, generally, mostly, customarily, normally.

ordinary *(SYN.)* common, habitual, normal, typical, usual, conventional, familiar, accustomed, customary, everyday, inferior, plain.
(ANT.) uncommon, marvelous, extraordinary, remarkable, strange.

organization *(SYN.)* order, rule, system, arrangement, method, plan, regularity, scheme, mode, process.
(ANT.) irregularity, chaos, disarrangement, chance.

organize *(SYN.)* assort, arrange, plan, regulate, systematize, devise, categorize, classify, prepare.
(ANT.) jumble, disorder, disturb, confuse, scatter.

organized *(SYN.)* planned, neat, orderly, arranged.

orient *(SYN.)* align, fit, accustom, adjust.

orifice *SYN.)* vent, slot, opening, hole.

origin *(SYN.)* birth, foundation, source, start, commencement, inception, beginning, derivation, infancy.

(ANT.) product, issue, outcome, end.

original *(SYN.)* primary, fresh, new, initial, pristine, creative, first, primordial.
(ANT.) banal, trite, subsequent, derivative, later, modern, terminal.

originality *(SYN.)* unconventionality, genius, novelty, creativity, imagination.

originator *(SYN.)* creator, inventor, discoverer.
(ANT.) follower, imitator.

ornament *(SYN.)* decoration, ornamentation, adornment, trimming, garnish.

ornate *(SYN.)* florid, overdone, elaborate, showy, flowery.

orthodox *(SYN.)* customary, usual, conventional, correct, proper, accepted.
(ANT.) different, unorthodox.

oscillate *(SYN.)* vary, change, hesitate, waver, undulate, fluctuate, vacillate.
(ANT.) persist, resolve, adhere, stick, decide.

ostentatious *(SYN.)* flashy, showy, overdone, fancy, pretentious, garish.

ostracize *(SYN.)* hinder, omit, bar, exclude, blackball, expel, prohibit, shout out, prevent, except.
(ANT.) welcome, accept, include, admit.

other *(SYN.)* distinct, different, extra, further, new, additional, supplementary.

ought *(SYN.)* must, should, be obliged.

oust *(SYN.)* eject, banish, exclude, expatriate, ostracize, dismiss, exile, expel.
(ANT.) shelter, accept, receive, admit, harbor.

ouster *(SYN.)* expulsion, banishment, overthrow.

outburst *(SYN.)* outbreak, eruption, torrent, ejection, discharge.

outcast *(SYN.)* friendless, homeless, deserted, abandoned, forsaken, disowned, derelict, forlorn, rejected.

outcome *(SYN.)* fate, destiny, necessity, doom, portion, consequence, result, end.

outcry *(SYN.)* scream, protest, clamor, noise, uproar.

outdated *(SYN.)* old-fashioned, unfashionable, old.
(ANT.) stylish.

outfit *(SYN.)* garb, kit, gear, furnish, equip, rig, clothing.

outgoing *(SYN.)* leaving, departing, friendly, congenial, amicable.
(ANT.) unfriendly, incoming.

outgrowth *(SYN.)* effect, outcome, upshot, fruit, result, byproduct, development.

outing *(SYN.)* journey, trip, excursion, jaunt, expedition, junket.

outlandish *(SYN.)* peculiar, odd, weird, curious, strange, queer, exotic, bazaar.
(ANT.) ordinary, common.

outlaw *(SYN.)* exile, bandit, outcast, badman, convict, criminal, fugitive.

outlay *(SYN.)* expense, costs, spending, disbursement, expenditure, charge.

outlook *(SYN.)* viewpoint, view, prospect, opportunity, position, attitude, future.

outlying *(SYN.)* external, remote, outer, out-of-the-way, suburban, rural.

outnumber *(SYN.)* exceed.

output *(SYN.)* yield, crop, harvest, proceeds, productivity.

outrage *(SYN.)* aggression, transgression, vice, affront, atrocity, misdeed, trespass.
(ANT.) morality, right, gentleness, innocence.

outrageous *(SYN.)* shameful, shocking, disgraceful, insulting, nonsensical, absurd, ridiculous, bizarre, preposterous, offensive.
(ANT.) prudent, reasonable, sensible.

outright *(SYN.)* entirely, altogether, completely, quite, fully, thoroughly.

outset *(SYN.)* inception, origin, start, commencement, opening, source.
(ANT.) end, completion, termination, consummation.

outside *(SYN.)* covering, ex-

terior, surface, facade, externals, appearance.
(ANT.) *intimate, insider.*

outsider (SYN.) immigrant, stranger, foreigner, alien, newcomer, bystander.
(ANT.) *countryman, friend, acquaintance, neighbor, associate.*

outspoken (SYN.) rude, unrestrained, vocal, open, straight-foward, forthright.
(ANT.) *suave, tactful, shy, polished, polite, subtle.*

outstanding (SYN.) well-known, important, prominent, leading, eminent, distinguished, conspicuous.
(ANT.) *insignificant, unimportant.*

outward (SYN.) apparent, outside, exterior, visible.

outweigh (SYN.) predominate, supersede, dwarf.

outwit (SYN.) baffle, trick, outsmart, bewilder, outdo, outmaneuver, confuse.

oval (SYN.) egg-shaped, elliptical, ovular.

ovation (SYN.) fanfare, homage, applause, tribute, cheers, acclamation.

overall (SYN.) comprehensive, complete, general, extensive, wide-spread, entire.

overbearing (SYN.) domineering, masterful, autocratic, imperious, haughty.
(ANT.) *humble.*

overcast (SYN.) dim, shadowy, cloudy, murky, dark, mysterious, gloomy, somber, dismal, hazy, indistinct.
(ANT.) *sunny, bright, distinct, limpid, clear.*

overcome (SYN.) quell, beat, crush, surmount, rout, humble, conquer, subjugate.
(ANT.) *retreat, surrender, capitulate, cede, lose.*

overconfident (SYN.) egotistical, presumptuous, arrogant, conceited.

overdue (SYN.) tardy, advanced, slow, delayed, new.
(ANT.) *timely, early, beforehand.*

overflow (SYN.) run over, flood, spill, cascade.

overhaul (SYN.) recondition, rebuild, service, repair.

overhead (SYN.) high, above, aloft, expenses, costs.

overjoyed (SYN.) enchanted, delighted, ecstatic, enraptured, elated, blissful.
(ANT.) *depressed.*

overlap (SYN.) overhang, extend, superimpose.

overload (SYN.) burden, weight, oppress, afflict, weigh, trouble, encumber.
(ANT.) *ease, lighten, console, alleviate, mitigate.*

overlook (SYN.) miss, disregard, exclude, cancel, omit, skip, ignore, drop.
(ANT.) *notice, enter, include, introduce, insert.*

overly (SYN.) exceedingly, needlessly, unreasonably.

overpower (SYN.) overcome, conquer, defeat, surmount, vanquish, overwhelm.
(ANT.) *surrender.*

overrated (SYN.) exaggerated.

overrule (SYN.) disallow, nullify, cancel, override, repeal.

overrun (SYN.) spread, exceed, beset, infest, flood.

oversee (SYN.) direct, run, operate, administer, superintend, boss, manage.

overshadow (SYN.) dominate, control, outclass, surpass.

oversight (SYN.) omission, charge, superintendence, surveillance, inattention.
(ANT.) *scrutiny, care, attention, observation.*

overstep (SYN.) surpass, exceed, trespass, transcend, impinge, violate, intrude.

overt (SYN.) honest, candid, frank, plain, open, apparent, straightforward.

overture (SYN.) offer, bid, proposal, prelude, introduction, presentation.
(ANT.) *finale.*

overturn (SYN.) demolish, overcome, vanquish, upset.
(ANT.) *uphold, construct, build, preserve, conserve.*

owner (SYN.) landholder, partner, proprietor.

pace (SYN.) rate, gait, step.
pacific (SYN.) peaceful, calm, serene, undisturbed.
(ANT.) turbulent, wild, excited, frantic.
pacify (SYN.) appease, lull, relieve, quell, soothe, allay.
(ANT.) incense, inflame, arouse, excite.
pack (SYN.) prepare, stow, crowd, stuff, bundle, parcel.
packed (SYN.) filled, complete, plentiful, crammed, full, replete, gorged.
(ANT.) lacking, depleted, devoid, vacant, insufficient, partial, empty.
pain (SYN.) twinge, ache, anguish, paroxysm, suffering.
(ANT.) happiness, pleasure, comfort, relief, solace, ease.
painful (SYN.) hurting, galling, poignant, bitter, grievous, agonizing, aching.
(ANT.) sweet, pleasant.
painting (SYN.) image, picture, portrayal, scene, view, sketch, illustration.
pale (SYN.) colorless, white, pallid, dim, faint, whiten.
(ANT.) flushed, ruddy, bright.
panic (SYN.) fear, terror, fright, alarm, apprehension, trembling, horror, dread.
(ANT.) tranquillity, composure, calmness, serenity.
paper (SYN.) journal, newspaper, document, article.
parade (SYN.) procession, cavalcade, succession, train, file, cortege, retinue.
paradoxical (SYN.) unsteady, vacillating, wavering.
(ANT.) correspondent, compatible, congruous.
parallel (SYN.) allied, analogous, comparable, corresponding, akin, similar.
(ANT.) opposed, different, incongruous.
parcel (SYN.) packet, package, bundle.
parched (SYN.) dry, arid, thirsty, drained, dehydrated.
(ANT.) moist, damp.
pardon (SYN.) absolution, forgiveness, remission, acquittal, amnesty, excuse.

(ANT.) sentence, penalty, conviction, punishment.
pardon (SYN.) condone, overlook, remit, absolve, acquit, forgive, excuse, remit.
(ANT.) punish, chastise, accuse, condemn, convict.
parley (SYN.) interview, talk, conference, chat, dialogue.
parsimonious (SYN.) avaricious, miserly, penurious, stingy, acquisitive, greedy.
(ANT.) munificent, extravagant, bountiful, altruistic.
part (SYN.) piece, section, allotment, portion, segment, side, interest, lines, role, organ, party, moiety, section.
(ANT.) whole, entirety.
partake (SYN.) dispense, parcel, allot, assign, distribute, partition, appropriate.
(ANT.) condense, aggregate, combine.
partial (SYN.) unfinished, undone, incomplete, prejudiced, unfair.
participant (SYN.) associate, colleague, partner.
particle (SYN.) mite, crumb, scrap, atom, corpuscle, grain, speck, bit, spot.
(ANT.) quantity, bulk, mass.
particular (SYN.) peculiar, fastidious, individual, distinctive, singular.
(ANT.) general, rough, universal, comprehensive.
partisan (SYN.) follower, successor, adherent, attendant, henchman, devotee.
(ANT.) leader, master, head.
partition (SYN.) distribution, division, separation, screen.
(ANT.) unification, joining.
partner (SYN.) colleague, comrade, friend, crony, consort, associate, companion.
(ANT.) stranger, enemy, adversary.
pass (SYN.) proceed, continue, move, go, disregard, ignore, exceed, gap, permit.
(ANT.) note, consider, notice.
passable (SYN.) fair, average, mediocre, acceptable, adequate, satisfactory.
(ANT.) worst, excellent, first-

rate, exceptional.

passage *(SYN.)* section, passageway, corridor, section, voyage, tour, crossing.

passion *(SYN.)* feeling, affection, turmoil, sentiment, rapture, excitement, desire.
(ANT.) tranquillity, indifference, calm, restraint, dispassion, apathy, coolness.

passive *(SYN.)* relaxed, idle, stoical, enduring, inert, inactive, submissive.
(ANT.) dynamic, active, aggressive.

past *(SYN.)* done, finished, over, former.
(ANT.) future, present, ahead.

pastime *(SYN.)* match, amusement, diversion, fun, play, recreation, entertainment.
(ANT.) quiescence, labor, apathy.

patent *(SYN.)* conspicuous, apparent, obvious, clear, evident, unmistakable.
(ANT.) hidden, concealed, obscure.

path *(SYN.)* avenue, street, trail, walk, course, road.

pathetic *(SYN.)* piteous, sad, affecting, moving, poignant, pitiable, touching, pitiful.
(ANT.) funny, comical, ludicrous.

patience *(SYN.)* perseverance, composure, endurance, fortitude, long-suffering.
(ANT.) restlessness, nervousness, impatience, unquite, impetuosity.

pattern *(SYN.)* guide, example, original, model, design, figure, decoration.

pause *(SYN.)* falter, hesitate, waver, demur, doubt, scruple, delay, vacillate, hesitation, rest, interruption.
(ANT.) proceed, continue, decide, resolve, persevere, continuity, perpetuate.

pay *(SYN.)* earnings, salary, allowance, stipend, wages.
(ANT.) gratuity, present, gift.

peace *(SYN.)* hush, repose, serenity, tranquility, silence, stillness, calmness.
(ANT.) noise, tumult, agita-

tion, disturbance.

peaceable *(SYN.)* mild, calm, friendly, peaceful, amiable, gentle, pacific.
(ANT.) aggressive, hostile, warlike.

peaceful *(SYN.)* pacific, calm, undisturbed, quiet, serene, mild, placid, gentle.
(ANT.) noisy, violent, agitated, turbulent, disturbed, disrupted, riotous.

peak *(SYN.)* climax, culmination, summit, zenith, height.
(ANT.) depth, floor, base, anticlimax, base, bottom.

peculiar *(SYN.)* odd, eccentric, extraordinary, unusual, individual, particular, striking, rare, exceptional.
(ANT.) ordinary, common, normal, general, regular.

peculiarity *(SYN.)* characteristic, feature, mark, trait.

peer *(SYN.)* match, rival, equal, parallel, peep, glimpse, examine.

peevish *(SYN.)* ill-natured, irritable, waspish, touchy, petulant, snappish, fractious, ill-tempered, fretful.
(ANT.) pleasant, affable, good-tempered, genial.

penalty *(SYN.)* fine, retribution, handicap, punishment, forfeiture, forfeit.
(ANT.) remuneration, compensation, reward, pardon.

penchant *(SYN.)* disposition, propensity, tendency, partiality, inclination, bent.
(ANT.) justice, fairness, equity.

penetrating *(SYN.)* profound, recondite, abstruse, deep, solemn, piercing.
(ANT.) superficial, shallow, slight.

penitent *(SYN.)* remorseful, sorrowful, regretful, contrite, sorry, repentant.
(ANT.) remorseless, objurgate.

penniless *(SYN.)* poor, destitute, impecunious, needy, poverty-stricken.
(ANT.) rich, wealthy, affluent, opulent, prosperous, well-off.

pensive *(SYN.)* dreamy, medi-

tative, thoughtful, reflective.
(ANT.) *thoughtless, heedless, inconsiderate, precipitous.*

penurious (SYN.) avaricious, greedy, parsimonious, miserly, stingy, acquisitive.
(ANT.) *munificent, extravagant, bountiful, generous, altruistic.*

perceive (SYN.) note, conceive, see, comprehend, understand, discern, recognize, apprehend, notice, observe, distinguish.
(ANT.) *overlook, ignore, miss.*

perceptible (SYN.) sensible, appreciable, apprehensible.
(ANT.) *imperceptible, absurd.*

perception (SYN.) understanding, apprehension, conception, insight.
(ANT.) *misconception, ignorance, misapprehension, insensibility.*

perceptive (SYN.) informed, observant, apprised, cognizant, aware, conscious.
(ANT.) *unaware, ignorant, oblivious.*

perfect (SYN.) ideal, whole, faultless, immaculate, complete, superlative, absolute, unqualified, utter, sinless.
(ANT.) *incomplete, defective, imperfect, deficient.*

perform (SYN.) impersonate, pretend, act, play, do, accomplish, achieve.

performance (SYN.) parade, entertainment, demonstration, movie, show, production, ostentation, spectacle, presentation, offering.

perfunctory (SYN.) decorous, exact, formal, external, correct, affected, methodical.
(ANT.) *unconventional, easy, unconstrained, natural.*

perhaps (SYN.) conceivable, possible.
(ANT.) *absolutely, definitely.*

peril (SYN.) jeopardy, danger.
(ANT.) *safety, immunity, protection, defense, security.*

perilous (SYN.) menacing, risky, hazardous, critical.
(ANT.) *safe, firm, protected, secure.*

period (SYN.) era, age, interval, span, tempo, time.

periodical (SYN.) uniform, customary, orderly, systematic, regular, steady.
(ANT.) *exceptional, unusual, abnormal, rare, erratic.*

perish (SYN.) die, sink cease, decline, decay, depart, wane, wither, languish, expire, cease, pass away.
(ANT.) *grow, survive, flourish.*

permanent (SYN.) constant, fixed, changeless, unchangeable, lasting, indestructible, stable, continuing, longlived, persistent, persisting.
(ANT.) *unstable, transient, ephemeral, temporary, transitory, passing, inconstant.*

permeate (SYN.) penetrate, pervade, run through, diffuse, fill, saturate.

permissible (SYN.) allowable, fair, tolerable, admissible, justifiable, probable.
(ANT.) *inadmissible, irrelevant.*

permission (SYN.) authorization, liberty, permit, license.
(ANT.) *refusal, denial, opposition.*

permissive (SYN.) easy, tolerant, open-minded, unrestrictive.
(ANT.) *restrictive.*

permit (SYN.) let, tolerate, authorize, sanction, allow.
(ANT.) *refuse, resist, forbid, protest, object, prohibit.*

perpendicular (SYN.) standing, upright, vertical.
(ANT.) *horizontal.*

perpetrate (SYN.) commit, perform, do.
(ANT.) *neglect, fail, miscarry.*

perpetual (SYN.) everlasting, immortal, ceaseless, endless, timeless, undying.
(ANT.) *transient, mortal, finite, temporal ephemeral.*

perpetually (SYN.) continually, ever, incessantly, eternally, always, constantly.
(ANT.) *rarely, sometimes, never, occasionally, fitfully.*

perplex (SYN.) confuse, dumbfound, mystify, puzzle.

(ANT.) solve, explain, illumine, instruct, clarify.

perplexed *(SYN.)* confused, disorganized, mixed, bewildered, deranged.

(ANT.) plain, obvious, clear, lucid.

perplexing *(SYN.)* intricate, complex, involved, compound, complicated.

(ANT.) uncompounded, plain, simple.

persecute *(SYN.)* harass, hound, torment, worry, vex, torture, harry, afflict, annoy.

(ANT.) support, comfort, assist, encourage, aid.

persevere *(SYN.)* remain, abide, endure, last, persist.

(ANT.) vacillate, desist, discontinue, cease, waver, lapse.

perseverance *(SYN.)* persistency, constancy, pertinacity, steadfastness, tenacity.

(ANT.) sloth, cessation, laziness, idleness, rest.

persist *(SYN.)* endure, remain, abide, persevere, continue, last.

(ANT.) vacillate, waver, desist, cease, discontinue, stop.

persistence *(SYN.)* persistency, constancy, perseverance, tenacity.

(ANT.) cessation, rest, sloth, idleness.

persistent *(SYN.)* lasting, steady, obstinate, stubborn.

(ANT.) wavering, unsure, vacillating.

person *(SYN.)* human, individual, somebody, someone.

personality *(SYN.)* make-up, nature, disposition.

perspicacity *(SYN.)* intelligence, understanding, discernment, judgment, wisdom, sagacity.

(ANT.) thoughtlessness, stupidity, arbitrariness, senselessness.

persuade *(SYN.)* entice, coax, exhort, prevail upon, urge.

(ANT.) restrain, deter, compel, dissuade, coerce.

persuasion *(SYN.)* decision, notion, view, sentiment, conviction, belief, opinion.

(ANT.) knowledge, skepticism, fact.

persuasive *(SYN.)* winning, alluring, compelling, convincing, stimulating.

(ANT.) dubious, unconvincing.

pertinent *(SYN.)* apt, material, relevant, relating, applicable, to the point, germane, apropos, apposite.

(ANT.) unrelated, foreign, alien.

perturbed *(SYN.)* agitated, disturbed, upset, flustered.

pervade *(SYN.)* penetrate, saturate, fill, diffuse, infiltrate, run through.

perverse *(SYN.)* obstinate, ungovernable, sinful, contrary, fractious, peevish, forward.

(ANT.) docile, agreeable, obliging.

perversion *(SYN.)* maltreatment, outrage, desecration.

(ANT.) respect.

pervert *(SYN.)* deprave, humiliate, impair, debase, corrupt, degrade, defile.

(ANT.) improve, raise, enhance.

perverted *(SYN.)* wicked, perverse, sinful.

pest *(SYN.)* annoyance, nuisance, bother, irritant.

pester *(SYN.)* disturb, annoy, irritate, tease, bother, chafe, inconvenience, trouble, harass, torment, worry.

(ANT.) console, accommodate, gratify.

petition *(SYN.)* invocation, prayer, request, appeal, plea, application.

petty *(SYN.)* paltry, trivial, frivolous, small, unimportant, insignificant.

(ANT.) important, serious, weighty, momentous, vital, significant, generous.

petulant *(SYN.)* irritable, ill-natured, fretful, snappish.

(ANT.) pleasant, affable, good-tempered, genial.

phenomenon *(SYN.)* occurrence, fact, happening, incident.

philanthropy *(SYN.)* kindness,

benevolence, charity, generosity, tenderness, liberality, humanity, magnanimity.
(ANT.) *unkindness, inhumanity, cruelty, malevolence, selfishness.*

phlegmatic (SYN.) unfeeling, sluggish, slow, lazy.
(ANT.) *passionate, ardent, energetic.*

phony (SYN.) counterfeit, artificial, ersatz, fake, synthetic, unreal, spurious.
(ANT.) *real, genuine, natural, true.*

picture (SYN.) etching, image, representation, sketch, appearance, cinema, engraving, scene, view, illustration, likeness, drawing.

piece (SYN.) portion, bit, fraction, morsel, scrap, fragment, amount, part, quantity, unit, section, portion.
(ANT.) *sum, whole, entirety, all, total.*

pigment (SYN.) shade, tint, tincture, stain, tinge.
(ANT.) *transparency, paleness.*

pile (SYN.) accumulation, heap, collection, amass.

pilgrimage (SYN.) trip, tour, expedition.

pinnacle (SYN.) crown, zenith, head, summit, chief, apex.
(ANT.) *bottom, foundation, base, foot.*

pious (SYN.) devout, religious, spiritual, consecrated, divine, hallowed, holy, saintly, sacred.
(ANT.) *worldly, sacrilegious, evil, secular, profane.*

pitch (SYN.) throw, cast, toss, propel, hurl, fling, thrust.
(ANT.) *retain, draw, hold, pull, haul.*

piteous (SYN.) poignant, pitiable, sad, pathetic.
(ANT.) *funny, ludicrous, comical.*

pitfall (SYN.) lure, snare, wile, ambush, bait, intrigue, trick, trap, net, snare.

pitiable (SYN.) poignant, touching, moving, affecting.

(ANT.) *ludicrous, funny.*

pitiless (SYN.) unmerciful, mean, unpitying, merciless.
(ANT.) *gentle, kind.*

pity (SYN.) sympathy, commiseration, condolence, mercy, compassion, charity.
(ANT.) *ruthlessness, hardness, cruelty, inhumanity, brutality, vindictiveness.*

place (SYN.) lay, arrange, put, deposit, space, region, location, plot, area, spot.
(ANT.) *mislay, remove, disarrange, disturb, misplace.*

placid (SYN.) pacific, serene, tranquil, calm, imperturbable, composed, peaceful.
(ANT.) *wild, frantic, stormy, excited.*

plagiarize (SYN.) recite, adduce, cite, quote, paraphrase, repeat, extract.
(ANT.) *retort, contradict.*

plague (SYN.) hound, pester, worry, harass, annoy, persecute, vex, afflict, badger.
(ANT.) *encourage, aid, assist.*

plain (SYN.) candid, simple, flat, smooth, clear, evident, sincere, unpretentious, level, distinct, absolute, visible, open, frank, palpable.
(ANT.) *embellished, abstruse, abrupt, rough, broken, insincere, adorned, fancy.*

plan (SYN.) design, purpose, sketch, devise, invent, contrive, intend, draw, create.

plane (SYN.) level, airplane.

plastic (SYN.) pliable, moldable, supple, flexible.

plausible (SYN.) likely, practical, credible, feasible, possible, probable.
(ANT.) *impracticable.*

play (SYN.) entertainment, amusement, pastime, sport, game, fun, recreation, show.
(ANT.) *work, labor, boredom.*

plea (SYN.) invocation, request, appeal, entreaty, supplication, petition, suit.

plead (SYN.) beseech, defend, beg, appeal, ask, implore, argue, entreat.
(ANT.) *deprecate, deny, refuse.*

pleasant (SYN.) agreeable, welcome, suitable, charming, pleasing, amiable, gratifying, acceptable, pleasurable, enjoyable, nice.
(ANT.) offensive, disagreeable, obnoxious, unpleasant, horrid, sour, difficult, nasty.

please (SYN.) satisfy, suffice, fulfill, content, appease, gratify, satiate, compensate.
(ANT.) dissatisfy, annoy, tantalize, frustrate, displease.

pleasing (SYN.) luscious, melodious, sugary, delightful, agreeable, pleasant.
(ANT.) repulsive, sour, acrid, bitter, offensive, irritating.

pleasure (SYN.) felicity, delight, amusement, enjoyment gratification.
(ANT.) suffering, pain, vexation, trouble, affliction, discomfort, torment.

pledge (SYN.) promise, statement, assertion, declaration, assurance, agreement.

plenty (SYN.) fruitfulness, bounty, fullness, abundance.
(ANT.) want, scarcity, need.

pliable (SYN.) elastic, supple, resilient, ductile.
(ANT.) rigid, unbending, brittle, stiff.

plight (SYN.) dilemma, situation, difficulty, condition, fix, scrape, state.
(ANT.) satisfaction, ease, calmness.

plot (SYN.) design, plan, scheme, cabal, conspiracy, chart, machination.

plotting (SYN.) cunning, scheming, objective, artfulness, contrivance, purpose.
(ANT.) accident, chance, result, candor.

ploy (SYN.) ruse, guile, antic, deception, hoax, subterfuge.
(ANT.) honesty, sincerity, openness, exposure, candor.

plump (SYN.) obese, portly, corpulent, pudgy, stout.
(ANT.) slim, thin, gaunt, lean, slender.

plunder (SYN.) ravage, strip, sack, rob, pillage, raid, loot.

pogrom (SYN.) massacre, carnage, slaughter, butchery.

poignant (SYN.) pitiable, touching, affecting, impressive, sad, tender, moving.

point (SYN.) direct, level, spot.
(ANT.) distract, misguide, deceive.

pointed (SYN.) keen, sharp, quick, acute, cutting.
(ANT.) shallow, stupid, bland.

poise (SYN.) composure, self-equilibrium, carriage, calmness, balance, self-control.
(ANT.) rage, turbulence, agitation, anger, excitement.

poison (SYN.) corrupt, sully, taint, infect, befoul, defile.
(ANT.) purify, disinfect.

polished (SYN.) glib, diplomatic, urbane, refined, sleek, suave, slick.
(ANT.) rough, blunt, bluff.

polite (SYN.) civil, refined, well-mannered, accomplished, courteous, genteel, urbane, well-bred, cultivated.
(ANT.) uncouth, impertinent, rude, boorish, uncivil.

pollute (SYN.) contaminate, poison, taint, sully, infect, befoul, defile, dirty.
(ANT.) purify, disinfect, clean.

pompous (SYN.) high, magnificent, stately, august, dignified, grandiose, noble.
(ANT.) lowly, undignified, humble, common, ordinary.

ponder (SYN.) examined, study, contemplate, investigate, meditate, muse, weigh, deliberate, consider.

ponderous (SYN.) burdensome, trying, gloomy, serious, sluggish, massive, heavy, cumbersome, grievous, grave, dull, weighty.
(ANT.) light, animated, brisk.

poor (SYN.) penniless, bad, deficient, destitute, inferior, shabby, wrong, scanty, poverty-stricken, unfavorable, impoverished.
(ANT.) wealthy, prosperous, rich, fortunate, good.

poppycock (SYN.) rubbish, babble, twaddle, nonsense.

popular (SYN.) favorite, general, common, familiar,

well-liked, approved, accepted, celebrated, admired. (ANT.) unpopular, restricted.

pornographic (SYN.) impure, dirty, filthy, lewd, smutty, offensive, disgusting. (ANT.) refined, modest, pure.

portentous (SYN.) significant, critical, momentous. (ANT.) trivial.

portion (SYN.) share, bit, parcel, part, piece, section, segment, allotment. (ANT.) whole, bulk.

portly (SYN.) majestic, grand, impressive, dignified, stout, fat, heavy, obese. (ANT.) slender, thin, slim.

portrait (SYN.) painting, representation, picture, likeness.

portray (SYN.) depict, picture, represent, sketch, describe, delineate, paint. (ANT.) misrepresent, caricature, suggest.

pose (SYN.) model.

position (SYN.) caste, site, locality, situation, condition, standing, incumbency, office, bearing, posture, berth, place, job, pose, rank, attitude, location, place, spot, station, situation, occupation.

positive (SYN.) sure, definite, fixed, inevitable, undeniable, indubitable, assured, certain, unquestionable. (ANT.) uncertain, doubtful, questionable, probably, unsure, dubious, confused, negative, adverse.

positively (SYN.) unquestionably, surely, certainly, absolutely.

possess (SYN.) own, obtain, control, have, seize, hold, occupy, affect, hold, control. (ANT.) surrender, abandon, lose.

possessed (SYN.) entranced, obsessed, consumer, haunted, enchanted.

possession (SYN.) custody, ownership, occupancy.

possessions (SYN.) commodities, effects, goods, property, merchandise, wares, wealth, belongings, stock.

possible (SYN.) likely, practical, probable, feasible, plausible, credible. (ANT.) visionary, impossible, improbable.

possibility (SYN.) opportunity, chance, contingency, occasion. (ANT.) obstacle, disadvantage.

possible (SYN.) feasible, practical, practicable, doable.

possibly (SYN.) perhaps, maybe.

post (SYN.) position, job, berth, incumbency, situation, shaft, pole, fort, base.

postpone (SYN.) delay, stay, suspend, discontinue, defer, adjourn, interrupt. (ANT.) persist, prolong, maintain, continue, proceed.

postulate (SYN.) principle, adage, saying, proverb, truism, byword, aphorism, axiom, maxim.

potency (SYN.) effectiveness, capability, skillfulness, efficiency, competency. (ANT.) wastefulness, inability.

potent (SYN.) mighty, influential, convincing, effective. (ANT.) feeble, weak, powerless.

potential (SYN.) likely, possible, dormant, hidden, latent.

pouch (SYN.) container, bag, sack.

pound (SYN.) buffet, beat, punch, strike, thrash, defeat, subdue, pulse, smite, belabor, knock, thump, overpower, palpitate, rout, vanquish. (ANT.) fail, surrender, defend, shield.

pour (SYN.) flow.

pout (SYN.) brood, sulk, mope.

poverty (SYN.) necessity, need, want, destitution, indigence, distress. (ANT.) plenty, abundance, wealth, riches, affluence, richness, comfort.

power (SYN.) potency, might, authority, control, predominance, capability, faculty, validity, force, vigor, command, influence, talent, ability, dominion.
(ANT.) incapacity, fatigue, weakness, disablement, impotence, ineptitude.

powerful (SYN.) firm, strong, concentrated, enduring, forcible, robust, sturdy, tough, athletic, forceful, hale, impregnable, hardy, mighty, potent.
(ANT.) feeble, insipid, brittle, delicate, fragile, weak, ineffectual, powerless.

practical (SYN.) sensible, wise, prudent, reasonable, sagacious, sober, sound, workable, attainable.
(ANT.) stupid, unaware, impalpable, imperceptible, absurd, impractical.

practically (SYN.) almost, nearly.

practice (SYN.) exercise, habit, custom, manner, wont, usage, drill, tradition, performance, action, repetition.
(ANT.) inexperience, theory, disuse, idleness, speculation.

practiced (SYN.) able, expert, skilled.
(ANT.) inept.

prairie (SYN.) plain, grassland.

praise (SYN.) applaud, compliment, extol, laud, glorify, commend, acclaim, eulogize, flatter, admire, celebrate, commendation, approval.
(ANT.) criticize, censure, reprove, condemn, disparage, disapprove, criticism.

pray (SYN.) supplicate, importune, beseech, beg.

prayer (SYN.) plea, suit, appeal, invocation, supplication, petition, entreaty.

preach (SYN.) teach, urge, lecture.

preamble (SYN.) overture, prologue, beginning, introduction, prelude, start,
foreword, preface.
(ANT.) end, finale, completion, conclusion, epilogue.

precarious (SYN.) dangerous, perilous, threatening, menacing, critical, risky, unsafe, hazardous.
(ANT.) secure, firm, protected, safe.

precaution (SYN.) foresight, fore-thought, care.

precedence (SYN.) preference, priority.

precedent (SYN.) model, example.

precept (SYN.) doctrine, tenet, belief, creed, teaching, dogma.
(ANT.) practice, conduct, performance.

precious (SYN.) dear, useful, valuable, costly, esteemed, profitable, expensive, priceless, dear.
(ANT.) poor, worthless, mean, trashy.

precipice (SYN.) bluff, cliff.

precipitate (SYN.) swift, hasty, sudden.

precipitous (SYN.) unannounced, sudden, harsh, rough, unexpected, sharp, abrupt, hasty, craggy, steep.
(ANT.) expected, anticipated, gradual.

precise (SYN.) strict, exact, formal, rigid, definite, unequivocal, prim, ceremonious, distinct, accurate, correct.
(ANT.) loose, easy, vague, informal, careless, erroneous.

precisely (SYN.) specifically, exactly.

precision (SYN.) correction, accuracy.

preclude (SYN.) hinder, prevent, obstruct, forestall, obviate, thwart.
(ANT.) permit, aid, encourage, promote.

preclusion (SYN.) omission, exception.
(ANT.) standard, rule, inclusion.

predicament (SYN.) dilemma, plight, situation, condition, fix, difficulty.

(ANT.) *satisfaction, comfort, calmness.*

predict (SYN.) forecast, foretell.

prediction (SYN.) forecast, prophecy.

predilection (SYN.) attachment, inclination, affection, bent, desire, penchant, disposition, preference.

(ANT.) *repugnance, aversion, apathy, distaste, nonchalance.*

predominant (SYN.) highest, paramount, cardinal, foremost, main, first, leading, supreme, principal, essential, prevalent, dominant, prevailing.

(ANT.) *subsidiary, auxiliary, supplemental, minor, subordinate.*

predominate (SYN.) prevail, outweigh.

preface (SYN.) foreword, introduction, preliminary, prelude, prologue.

prefer (SYN.) select, favor, elect, fancy.

preference (SYN.) election, choice, selection, alternative, option.

prejudice (SYN.) bias, favoritism, unfairness, partiality.

prejudiced (SYN.) fanatical, narrow-minded, dogmatic, bigoted, intolerant.

(ANT.) *radical, liberal, progressive.*

preliminary (SYN.) introductory, preparatory, prelude, preface.

premature (SYN.) early, untimely, unexpected.

(ANT.) *timely.*

premeditated (SYN.) intended, voluntary, contemplated, designed, intentional, willful, deliberate, studied.

(ANT.) *fortuitous, accidental.*

premeditation (SYN.) intention, deliberation, forethought, forecast.

(ANT.) *hazard, accident, impromptu, extemporization.*

premise (SYN.) basis, presupposition, assumption, postulate, principle.

(ANT.) *superstructure, derivative, trimming, implication.*

preoccupied (SYN.) abstracted, distracted, absorbed, meditative, inattentive, absent, absent-minded.

(ANT.) *attentive, alert, conscious, present, attending, watchful.*

prepare (SYN.) contrive, furnish, ready, predispose, condition, fit, arrange, plan, qualify, make ready, get ready.

preposterous (SYN.) foolish, nonsensical, silly, contradictory, unreasonable, absurd, inconsistent, irrational.

(ANT.) *sensible, rational, consistent, sound, reasonable.*

prerequisite (SYN.) essential, requirement, necessity, demand.

prerogative (SYN.) grant, right, license, authority, privilege.

(ANT.) *violation, encroachment, wrong, injustice.*

prescribe (SYN.) order, direct, designate.

presence (SYN.) nearness, attendance, closeness, vicinity, appearance, bearing.

present (SYN.) donation, gift, today, now, existing, current, largess, donate, acquaint, introduce, being, give, gratuity, boon, grant.

(ANT.) *reject, accept, retain, receive.*

presentable (SYN.) polite, well-bred, respectable, well-mannered.

presently (SYN.) shortly, soon, directly, immediately.

preserve (SYN.) protect, save, conserve, maintain, secure, rescue, uphold, spare, keep, can, safeguard, defend, rescue.

(ANT.) *impair, abolish, destroy, abandon, squander, injure.*

preside (SYN.) officiate, direct, administrate.

press (SYN.) impel, shove, urge, hasten, push, compress, squeeze, hug, crowd, propel, force, drive, embrace, smooth, iron, insist on, pressure, promote jostle.

(ANT.) oppose, drag, retreat, ignore.

pressing (SYN.) impelling, insistent, necessary, urgent, compelling imperative, instant, serious, important, cogent, exigent, importunate.

(ANT.) unimportant, trifling, insignificant, petty, trivial.

pressure (SYN.) force, influence, stress, press, compulsion, urgency, constraint.

(ANT.) relaxation, leniency, ease.

prestige (SYN.) importance, reputation, weight, influence, renown, fame.

presume (SYN.) guess, speculate, surmise, imagine, conjecture, apprehend, believe, think, assume, suppose, deduce.

(ANT.) prove, ascertain, demonstrate, know, conclude.

presumption (SYN.) boldness, impertinence, insolence, rudeness, assurance, effrontery, impudence, assumption, audacity, supposition, sauciness.

(ANT.) politeness, truckling, diffidence.

presumptuous (SYN.) bold, impertinent, fresh, imprudent, rude, forward.

presupposition (SYN.) basis, principle, premise, assumption, postulate.

(ANT.) superstructure, derivative.

pretend (SYN.) feign, stimulate, act, profess, make believe, imagine, sham.

(ANT.) expose, reveal, display, exhibit.

pretense (SYN.) mask, pretext, show, affection, disguise, garb, semblance, simulation, fabrication, lie, excuse, falsification, deceit, subterfuge.

(ANT.) sincerity, actuality,

truth, fact, reality.

pretentious (SYN.) gaudy, ostentatious.

(ANT.) simple, humble.

pretty (SYN.) charming, handsome, lovely, beauteous, fair, comely, attractive, beautiful, elegant.

(ANT.) repulsive foul, unsightly, homely, plain, hideous.

prevail (SYN.) win, succeed, predominate, triumph.

(ANT.) yield, lose.

prevailing (SYN.) common, current, general, steady, regular, universal.

prevalent (SYN.) ordinary, usual, common, general, familiar, popular, prevailing, widespread, universal, frequent.

(ANT.) odd, scarce, extraordinary.

prevent (SYN.) impede, preclude, forestall, stop, block, check, halt, interrupt, deter, slow, obviate, hinder, obstruct.

(ANT.) expedite, help, allow, abet, aid, permit, encourage, promote.

previous (SYN.) former, anterior, preceding, prior, antecedent, earlier.

(ANT.) subsequent, following, consequent, succeeding, later.

prey (SYN.) raid, seize, victimize.

price (SYN.) worth, cost, expense, charge, value.

pride (SYN.) self-respect, vanity, glory, superciliousness, haughtiness, conceit, arrogance, self-importance, pretension, egotism, satisfaction, fulfillment, enjoyment, self-esteem.

(ANT.) modesty, shame, humbleness, lowliness, meekness, humility.

prim (SYN.) formal, puritanical, priggish, prudish.

primarily (SYN.) mainly, chiefly, firstly, essentially, originally.

(ANT.) secondarily.

primary *(SYN.)* first, principal, primeval, pristine, beginning, original, initial, fundamental, elementary, chief, foremost, earliest, main, prime.
(ANT.) subordinate, last, secondary, least, hindmost, latest.

prime *(SYN.)* first, primary, chief, excellent, best, superior, ready.

primeval *(SYN.)* fresh, primary, novel, inventive, creative, primordial, original, first, new, initial.
(ANT.) trite, modern, subsequent, banal, later, terminal, derivative.

primitive *(SYN.)* antiquated, early, primeval, prehistoric, uncivilized, uncultured, simple, pristine, old, aboriginal, unsophisticated, rude, rough, primary.
(ANT.) sophisticated, modish, civilized, cultured, cultivated, late.

primordial *(SYN.)* novel, creative, original, first, initial, new, primary.
(ANT.) trite, terminal, banal, modern, derivative, subsequent, later.

principal *(SYN.)* first, leading, main, supreme, predominant, chief, foremost, highest, prime, primary, leader, headmaster, paramount, essential, cardinal.
(ANT.) supplemental, secondary, auxiliary, accessory, minor, subordinate.

principle *(SYN.)* law, method, axiom, rule, propriety, regulation, maxim, formula, order, statute.
(ANT.) exception, hazard, chance.

print *(SYN.)* issue, reprint, publish, letter, sign, fingerprint, mark, picture, lithograph, engraving, etching.

prior *(SYN.)* previous, aforesaid, antecedent, sooner, earlier, preceding, former.
(ANT.) succeeding, following,

later, consequent, subsequent.

prison *(SYN.)* brig, jail, stockade.

pristine *(SYN.)* primordial, creative, first, original, fresh, inventive, novel, primary, initial.
(ANT.) trite, terminal, derivative, modern, banal, subsequent, plagiarized.

private *(SYN.)* concealed, hidden, secret, clandestine, unknown, personal, surreptitious, covert, individual, special.
(ANT.) exposed, known, closed, general, public, conspicuous, disclosed, obvious.

privation *(SYN.)* necessity, penury, destitution, need, poverty, want.
(ANT.) wealth, affluence, abundance, plenty, riches.

privilege *(SYN.)* liberty, right, advantage, immunity, freedom, license, favor.
(ANT.) restriction, inhibition, prohibition, disallowance.

prize *(SYN.)* compensation, bonus, award, premium, remuneration, reward, bounty, esteem, value, rate, recompense, requital.
(ANT.) charge, punishment, wages, earnings, assessment.

probable *(SYN.)* presumable, likely.

probe *(SYN.)* stretch, reach, investigate, examine, examination, scrutiny, scrutinize, inquire, explore, inquiry, investigation, extend.
(ANT.) miss, short.

problem *(SYN.)* dilemma, question, predicament, riddle, difficulty, puzzle.

procedure *(SYN.)* process, way, fashion, form, mode, conduct, practice, manner, habit, system, operation, management.

proceed *(SYN.)* progress, continue, issue, result, spring, thrive, improve, advance, emanate, rise.
(ANT.) retard, withhold,

withdraw, hinder, retreat, oppose.

proceeding *(SYN.)* occurrence, business, affair, deal, negotiation, transaction.

proceedings *(SYN.)* record, document.

proceeds *(SYN.)* result, produce, income, reward, intake, fruit, profit, store, yield, product, return, harvest, crop.

process *(SYN.)* method, course, system, procedure, operation, prepare, treat.

procession *(SYN.)* cortege, parade, sequence, train, cavalcade, succession.

proclaim *(SYN.)* declare, assert, make known, promulgate, state, assert, broadcast, express, announce, aver, advertise, tell, publish, profess.

proclamation *(SYN.)* declaration, announcement, promulgation.

procrastinate *(SYN.)* waver, vacillate, defer, hesitate, delay, postpone.

procreate *(SYN.)* generate, produce, beget, engender, originate, propagate, sire, create, father.

(ANT.) murder, destroy, abort, kill.

procure *(SYN.)* secure, gain, win, attain, obtain, get, acquire, earn.

(ANT.) lose.

prod *(SYN.)* goad, nudge, jab, push.

prodigious *(SYN.)* astonishing, enormous, immense, monstrous, remarkable, marvelous, huge, amazing, stupendous, monumental.

(ANT.) insignificant, commonplace.

produce *(SYN.)* harvest, reaping, bear, result, originate, bring about, store, supply, make, create, crop, proceeds, bring forth, because, breed, generate, cause, exhibit, show, demonstrate, fabricate, hatch, display, manufacture, exhibit, give, yield.

(ANT.) conceal, reduce, destroy, consume, waste, hide.

product *(SYN.)* outcome, result, output, produce, goods, commodity, stock.

productive *(SYN.)* fertile, luxuriant, rich, bountiful, fruitful, creative, fecund, teeming, plenteous, prolific.

(ANT.) wasteful, unproductive, barren, impotent, useless, sterile.

profanation *(SYN.)* dishonor, insult, outrage, aspersion, defamation, invective, misuse, abuse, reviling, maltreatment, desecration, perversion.

(ANT.) plaudit, commendation, laudation, respect, approval.

profane *(SYN.)* deflower, violate, desecrate, pollute, dishonor, ravish.

profess *(SYN.)* declare, assert, make known, state, protest, announce, aver, express, broadcast, avow, tell.

(ANT.) suppress, conceal, withhold.

profession *(SYN.)* calling, occupation, vocation, employment.

(ANT.) hobby, avocation, pastime.

proffer *(SYN.)* extend, tender, volunteer, propose, advance.

(ANT.) reject, spurn, accept, retain.

proficient *(SYN.)* competent, adept, clever, able, cunning, practiced, skilled, versed, ingenious, accomplished.

(ANT.) untrained, inexpert, bungling, awkward, clumsy.

profit *(SYN.)* gain, service, advantage, return, earnings, emolument, improvement, benefit, better, improve.

(ANT.) waste, loss, detriment, debit, lose, damage, ruin.

profitable *(SYN.)* beneficial, advantageous, helpful, wholesome, useful, gainful, favorable, beneficial, serviceable, salutary, productive, good.

(ANT.) harmful, destructive, injurious, deleterious, detrimental.

profligate *(SYN.)* corrupt, debased, tainted, unsound, vitiated, contaminated, crooked, depraved, impure.

profound *(SYN.)* deep, serious, knowing, wise, intelligent, knowledgeable, recondite, solemn, abstruse, penetrating.
(ANT.) trivial, slight, shallow.

profuse *(SYN.)* lavish, excessive, extravagant, improvident, luxuriant, prodigal, wasteful, exuberant, immoderate, plentiful.
(ANT.) meager, poor, economical, sparse, skimpy.

profusion *(SYN.)* immoderation, superabundance, surplus, extravagance, intemperance, superfluity.
(ANT.) lack, paucity, death, want, deficiency.

program *(SYN.)* record, schedule, plan, agenda, calendar.

progress *(SYN.)* advancement, betterment, advance, movement, improve, progression.
(ANT.) delay, regression, relapse, retrogression.

progression *(SYN.)* gradation, string, train, chain, arrangement, following.

prohibit *(SYN.)* hinder, forbid, disallow, obstruct, prevent.
(ANT.) help, tolerate, allow, sanction, encourage, permit.

project *(SYN.)* design, proposal, scheme, contrivance, throw, cast, device, plan.
(ANT.) production, accomplishment, performance.

prolong *(SYN.)* extend, increase, protract, draw, stretch, lengthen.
(ANT.) shorten.

promise *(SYN.)* assurance, guarantee, pledge, undertaking, agreement, bestowal.

promote *(SYN.)* advance, foster, encourage, assist.
(ANT.) obstruct, demote, hinder, impede.

prompt *(SYN.)* punctual, timely, exact, arouse, evoke, occasion, induce, urge, ineffect, cite, suggest, hint.
(ANT.) laggardly, slow, tardy, dilatory.

promptly *(SYN.)* immediately, instantly, straightway, forthwith, directly.
(ANT.) later, sometime, hereafter, distantly, shortly.

promulgate *(SYN.)* declare, known, protest, affirm, broadcast, profess, assert.
(ANT.) repress, conceal, withhold.

prone *(SYN.)* apt, inclined, disposed, likely.

pronounce *(SYN.)* proclaim, utter, announce, articulate.

proof *(SYN.)* evidence, verification, confirmation, experiment, demonstration.
(ANT.) fallacy, invalidity, failure.

propagate *(SYN.)* create, procreate, sire, beget, breed, father, originate, produce.
(ANT.) extinguish, kill, abort.

propel *(SYN.)* drive, push, transfer, actuate, induce.
(ANT.) stay, deter, halt, rest.

propensity *(SYN.)* leaning, proneness, trend, drift, aim, inclination, bias, proclivity.
(ANT.) disinclination, aversion.

proper *(SYN.)* correct, suitable, decent, peculiar, legitimate, right, conventional, decent, just.

prophet *(SYN.)* fortuneteller, oracle, seer, soothsayer.

propitious *(SYN.)* lucky, opportune, advantageous, favorable, fortunate.

proportion *(SYN.)* steadiness, poise, composure, relation, balance, equilibrium, comparison, section, part.
(ANT.) unsteadiness, imbalance, fall.

proposal *(SYN.)* plan, proposition, tender, scheme, program, offer, suggestion.
(ANT.) rejection, acceptance, denial.

propose *(SYN.)* offer, proffer, recommend, plan, mean, ex-

pect, move, design.
(ANT.) fulfill, perform, effect.
prosaic (SYN.) commonplace, common, everyday, ordinary, routine.
(ANT.) exciting, different, extraordinary.
prosper (SYN.) succeed, win, flourish, thrive.
(ANT.) miscarry, wane, miss.
prosperous (SYN.) rich, wealthy, affluent, well-to-do, sumptuous, well-off.
(ANT.) impoverished, indigent, beggarly, needy.
protect (SYN.) defend, preserve, save, keep, conserve.
(ANT.) impair, abandon, destroy, abolish, injure.
protuberance (SYN.) prominence, projection, bulge.
proud (SYN.) overbearing, arrogant, haughty, stately, vain, glorious, disdainful.
(ANT.) humble, meek, ashamed, lowly.
prove (SYN.) manifest, verify, confirm, demonstrate, establish, show, affirm.
(ANT.) contradict, refute, disprove.
proverb (SYN.) maxim, byword, saying, adage, saw, motto, apothegm.
provide (SYN.) supply, endow, afford, produce, yield, give.
(ANT.) strip, denude, divest, despoil.
provident (SYN.) saving, thrifty, economical, frugal.
(ANT.) wasteful, lavish, extravagant.
provoke (SYN.) excite, stimulate, agitate, arouse, incite, excite, irritate, annoy, anger.
(ANT.) quell, allay, pacify, calm, quiet.
proximate (SYN.) nigh, imminent, adjacent, neighboring, bordering, close, impending, approaching.
(ANT.) removed, distant, far.
prudence (SYN.) watchfulness, care, heed, vigilance, judgment, wisdom.
(ANT.) rashness, recklessness, abandon, foolishness.
prying (SYN.) inquisitive,

meddling, curious, inquiring, nosy, peering, searching, interrogative, snoopy.
(ANT.) unconcerned, incurious, indifferent.
psyche (SYN.) judgment, reason, understanding, brain, intellect, mentality, soul.
(ANT.) materiality, body.
psychosis (SYN.) derangement, insanity, madness, delirium, dementia, frenzy.
(ANT.) stability, rationality, sanity.
public (SYN.) common, civil, governmental, federal, unrestricted, people, society.
publish (SYN.) distribute, issue, declare, announce, reveal, proclaim, publicize.
pull (SYN.) attract, induce, prolong, draw, tow, drag, allure, entice, extract.
(ANT.) shorten, alienate, drive, propel.
pummel (SYN.) punish, correct, castigate, discipline, chastise, strike.
(ANT.) release, acquit, free, exonerate.
punctual (SYN.) timely, prompt, exact, ready, nice.
(ANT.) laggardly, tardy, dilatory, late.
punish (SYN.) correct, pummel, chasten, reprove, strike, castigate, chastise.
(ANT.) release, exonerate, reward, pardon, acquit, free.
puny (SYN.) feeble, impaired, exhausted, infirm, unimportant, weak, decrepit, trivial, forceless, delicate.
(ANT.) strong, forceful, lusty.
pupil (SYN.) student, undergraduate.
purchase (SYN.) get, procure, buy, shopping, acquire, obtain.
(ANT.) sell, dispose of, vend.
pure (SYN.) chaste, absolute, clean, immaculate, untainted, spotless, guiltless, modest, virgin, bare, unmixed, simple, undiluted, uncontaminated, innocent, chaste, undefiled, genuine, clear.

(ANT.) corrupt, mixed, defiled, foul, tainted, adulterated, polluted, tarnished.

purely *(SYN.)* entirely, completely.

purify *(SYN.)* cleanse, wash, clean, mop.
(ANT.) soil, dirty, sully, stain, pollute.

puritanical *(SYN.)* prim, stiff.
(ANT.) permissive.

purloin *(SYN.)* loot, plagiarize, steal, pilfer, burglarize, plunder, pillage, snitch, embezzle, swipe.
(ANT.) repay, return, refund, buy.

purport *(SYN.)* import, meaning, explanation, acceptation, drift, sense, significance, purpose, intent, gist.

purpose *(SYN.)* intention, end, goal, aim, objective.
(ANT.) hazard, accident, fate.

pursue *(SYN.)* persist, track, follow, hunt, hound, chase, trail.
(ANT.) evade, abandon, flee, elude.

pursuit *(SYN.)* hunt, chase.

push *(SYN.)* jostle, shove, urge, press, thrust, force, drive, crowd, hasten, shove, propel, promote.
(ANT.) ignore, falter, halt, drag, oppose.

pushy *(SYN.)* impudent, abrupt, prominent, insolent, forward, brazen, conspicuous, bold, striking.
(ANT.) retiring, timid, cowardly, bashful.

put *(SYN.)* set, place, state, express, say, assign, attach, establish.

putrefy *(SYN.)* disintegrate, decay, rot, waste, spoil.
(ANT.) grow, increase, luxuriate.

putrid *(SYN.)* decayed, rotten, moldy, decomposed.

puzzle *(SYN.)* mystery, mystify, confound, perplex, riddle, conundrum, confusion, question, bewilder, confuse.
(ANT.) key, solution, solve, explain, answer, resolution.

quack *(SYN.)* faker, fake, fraud, gaggle, clack, gabble, charlatan, impostor.

quackery *(SYN.)* charlatanism, deceit, sham.
(ANT.) integrity, probity, veracity, sincerity, honesty.

quaff *(SYN.)* swig, swill, swallow, sip, drink, ingurgitate.

quagmire *(SYN.)* swamp, bog, fen, ooze, morass, slough, dilemma, impasse, fix.

quail *(SYN.)* recoil, flinch, blench, falter, shrink, shake, hesitate, faint, droop.
(ANT.) brave, resist, defy.

quaint *(SYN.)* odd, uncommon, old-fashioned, antique, queer, charming.
(ANT.) usual, normal, novel, ordinary, current.

quake *(SYN.)* shake, tremble, stagger, shiver, temblor, throb, earthquake.

qualification *(SYN.)* efficiency, adaptation, restriction, aptness, skill, ability, aptitude, competence
(ANT.) incapacity, disability.

qualified *(SYN.)* clever, skillful, efficient, suitable, able, bounded, delimited, equipped, modified.
(ANT.) deficient, inept, impotent, categorical, unlimited, unfitted, unfit.

qualify *(SYN.)* fit, suit, befit, capacitate, condition, adapt, restrict, limit, change.
(ANT.) unfit, incapacitate, disable, disqualify, enlarge, reinforce, aggravate.

quality *(SYN.)* trait, feature, status, characteristic, kind, nature, constitution, mark.
(ANT.) nature, inferiority, mediocrity, triviality, indifference, inferior, shoddy.

qualm *(SYN.)* doubt, uneasiness, anxiety, suspicion.
(ANT.) security, comfort, confidence, easiness, invulnerability, firmness.

quandary *(SYN.)* predicament, perplexity, confusion, uncertainty, puzzle, plight.
(ANT.) ease, relief, certainty, assurance.

quantity *(SYN.)* sum, aggregate, bulk, mass, portion, amount, number, multitude.
(ANT.) zero, nothing.

quarrel *(SYN.)* contention, difference, disagree, bicker, tiff, argue, disagreement.
(ANT.) peace, friendliness, reconciliation, amity, agreement, sympathy, accord.

quarrelsome *(SYN.)* testy, contentious, edgy, peevish, irritable, snappish.
(ANT.) genial, friendly, peaceful, easygoing, peaceable.

quarter *(SYN.)* place, source, fount, well, origin, mainspring, spring, benevolence.
(ANT.) ruthlessness, brutality, cruelty, barbarity, harshness.

quarters *(SYN.)* residence, rooms, lodgings, dwelling, flat, billets, chambers.

quash *(SYN.)* void, annul, overthrow, nullify, suppress, cancel, quench, quell.
(ANT.) reinforce, sustain, authorize, sanction, validate.

quasi *(SYN.)* partial, synthetic, nominal, imitation, bogus.
(ANT.) certified, real, legitimate.

quaver *(SYN.)* tremble, shake, hesitate, trill, oscillate, quiver, falter, quake.

queasy *(SYN.)* sick, squeamish, uneasy, queer, restless, nauseous.
(ANT.) comfortable, easy, relaxed.

queer *(SYN.)* odd, quaint, curious, unusual, droll, strange, peculiar.
(ANT.) familiar, usual, normal, common, plain.

quell *(SYN.)* subdue, calm, pacify, quiet, cool, lull, mollify, reduce, crush, smother, suppress, stifle, extinguish.
(ANT.) encourage, foment, arouse, foster.

quench *(SYN.)* extinguish, stop, suppress, sate, allay, abate, stifle, slacken, put out, slake, satisfy.
(ANT.) set, light, begin, start.

querulous *(SYN.)* faultfinding, fretful, carping, critical, captious, petulant.
(ANT.) pleased, easygoing, contented, carefree.

query *(SYN.)* inquire, interrogate, demand, investigate, probe, examine, question, inquiry, ask.
(ANT.) answer.

quest *(SYN.)* investigation, interrogation, research, examination, search, question, exploration, seek, pursue.
(ANT.) negligence, inactivity, disregard.

question *(SYN.)* interrogate, quiz, doubt, ask, pump, challenge, inquiry, uncertainty, interview, suspect, examine, query.
(ANT.) accept, solution, reply, answer, result, response, attest, avow, confidence.

questionable *(SYN.)* uncertain, doubtful, dubious, implausible, debatable.
(ANT.) obvious, assured, indubitable, proper, unimpeachable, seemly.

queue *(SYN.)* file, row, line, series, chain, tier, sequence.

quibble *(SYN.)* cavil, shift, evasion, equivocation, dodge, sophism, prevaricate.

quick *(SYN.)* rapid, touchy, shrewd, active, hasty, testy, nimble, irascible, discerning, fast, swift, precipitate.
(ANT.) inattentive, dull, gradual, patient, slow, deliberate, sluggish.

quicken *(SYN.)* expedite, forward, rush, hurry, accelerate, push, hasten.
(ANT.) slow, impede, hinder, hamper, delay, kill, deaden.

quickly *(SYN.)* soon, rapidly, fast, at once, promptly, presently, swiftly, hastily.
(ANT.) deliberately, slowly, later, gradually.

quickness *(SYN.)* energy, vigor, intensity, action, movement, briskness.
(ANT.) sloth, idleness, inertia, dullness.

quick-witted *(SYN.)* astute, shrewd, alert, keen, penetrating, quick.

(ANT.) *slow, dull, unintelligent, plodding.*

quiescent (SYN.) latent, resting, silent, tranquil, undeveloped, still, quiet.
(ANT.) *visible, aroused, evident, active, patent, astir.*

quiet (SYN.) meek, passive, hushed, peaceful, calm, patient, quiescent, motionless, tranquil, gentle, undisturbed, mild, peace, silent.
(ANT.) *disturbed, agitation, excitement, loud, restless, noisy, boisterous, anxious.*

quietness (SYN.) tranquillity, repose, calm, silence, quietude, calmness.
(ANT.) *flurry, disturbance, fuss, turbulence, agitation.*

quirky (SYN.) odd, weird, whimsical, peculiar.
(ANT.) *normal, conventional.*

quisling (SYN.) collaborationist, traitor, subversive, betrayer.
(ANT.) *partisan, loyalist.*

quit (SYN.) leave, stop, desist, depart, abandon, resign, cease, vacate, end, halt.
(ANT.) *persevere, remain, stay, endure, persist, abide.*

quite (SYN.) somewhat, rather, completely, truly, absolutely, really, entirely.
(ANT.) *hardly, merely, barely.*

quitter (SYN.) shirker, dropout, defeatist, piker.

quiver (SYN.) quake, shake, shudder, tremble, vibrate.

quiz (SYN.) challenge, interrogate, inquire, pump, doubt, question, ask, dispute, test, query, examine.
(ANT.) *reply, say, inform, state.*

quota (SYN.) share, portion, apportionment, ratio, proportion, allotment.

quotation (SYN.) quote, selection, excerpt, repetition, cutting, reference.

quote (SYN.) refer to, recite, paraphrase, adduce, repeat, illustrate, cite, echo.
(ANT.) *retort, contradict, refute.*

rabble (SYN.) throng, mob, crowd.

race (SYN.) meet, run, clan, stock, lineage, strain, match.
(ANT.) *linger, dawdle, dwell.*

racket (SYN.) sound, cry, babel, noise, uproar, hubbub, clamor, fuss.
(ANT.) *stillness, hush, silence, quiet, tranquillity, peace.*

racy (SYN.) interesting, vigorous, lively, spirited, animated, entertaining.

radiance (SYN.) luster, brilliancy, brightness, splendor, effulgence, glowing.
(ANT.) *gloom, darkness, obscurity.*

radiate (SYN.) spread, emit, shine, gleam, illuminate.

ragamuffin (SYN.) tatterdemalion, wretch, beggar, vagabond, mendicant.

rage (SYN.) passion, ire, exasperation, fashion, fad, rant, storm, fume, overflow.
(ANT.) *peace, forbearance, conciliation, patience.*

raging (SYN.) raving, severe, passionate, boisterous, violent, fierce, wild, passionate.
(ANT.) *feeble, soft, calm, quiet.*

ragged (SYN.) tattered, torn, worn, shredded, seedy, threadbare, shabby.

rain (SYN.) shower, drizzle, rainstorm, sprinkle, deluge.

raise (SYN.) grow, muster, awake, rouse, excite, enlarge, increase, rise, breed.
(ANT.) *destroy, decrease, lessen, cut, depreciate, lower, abase, drop, demolish, level.*

rally (SYN.) muster, convoke, summon, convene, convention, assemblage.

ramble (SYN.) err, amble, walk, deviate, stroll, digress.
(ANT.) *stop, linger, stay, halt.*

rambunctious (SYN.) stubborn, defiant, unruly, aggressive, contrary.

rampage (SYN.) tumult, outbreak, uproar, rage, frenzy, ebullition, storm.

rampant (SYN.) excessive, flagrant, boisterous.

(ANT.) *bland, calm, mild.*

ramshackle (SYN.) rickety, decrepit, flimsy, dilapidated, shaky.

rancid (SYN.) spoiled, rank, tainted, sour, musty, putrid, rotten, putrescent.
(ANT.) *pure, fresh, wholesome, fragrant.*

rancor (SYN.) spite, grudge, malice, animosity, malevolence, hostility.
(ANT.) *kindness, toleration, affection.*

random (SYN.) haphazard, chance, unscheduled, unplanned, casual.
(ANT.) *intentional, specific, particular.*

range (SYN.) expanse, extent, limit, area, grassland, pasture, plain, change, wander.

ransack (SYN.) pillage, loot, ravish, search.

ransom (SYN.) release, deliverance, compensation.

rapacious (SYN.) greedy, wolfish, avaricious, ravenous, grasping, predatory.

rapid (SYN.) speedy, quick, swift, fast.
(ANT.) *deliberate, halting, sluggish, slow.*

rapine (SYN.) destruction, pillage, robbery, marauding.

rapport (SYN.) harmony, fellowship, agreement, mutuality, accord, empathy.

rapture (SYN.) joy, gladness, ecstasy, bliss, transport, exultation, delight, happiness, enchantment, ravishment.
(ANT.) *woe, misery, wretch, depression.*

rare (SYN.) unique, strange, precious, uncommon, infrequent, choice, singular.
(ANT.) *worthless, common, commonplace, usual, everyday, customary.*

rarely (SYN.) scarcely, hardly, infrequently, occasionally.
(ANT.) *usually, continually, often.*

rascal (SYN.) scoundrel, villain, trickster, rogue, scamp, swindler, imp, prankster.

rash (SYN.) quick, careless,

passionate, thoughtless, hotheaded, reckless, foolhardy, eruption.
(ANT.) *thoughtful, considered, prudent, reasoning, calculating, careful.*

raspy (SYN.) gruff, harsh, dissonant, grinding, hoarse.

ratify (SYN.) validate, certify, endorse, uphold.

rating (SYN.) assessment, position, status, classification.

ration (SYN.) portion, allowance, distribute, measure, allotment, share.

rationality (SYN.) cause, aim, understanding, ground, argument, mind, sense.

raucous (SYN.) raspy, harsh, grating, hoarse, discordant.
(ANT.) *dulcet, pleasant, sweet.*

ravage (SYN.) ruin, despoil, strip, waste, destroy, pillage, plunder, sack, havoc.
(ANT.) *conserve, save, accumulate.*

ravine (SYN.) chasm, gorge, crevasse, canyon, abyss.

raw (SYN.) harsh, rough, coarse, unrefined, undone, crude, unpolished, natural.
(ANT.) *finished, refined, processed.*

raze (SYN.) ravage, wreck, destroy, flatten, annihilate, obliterate, demolish.
(ANT.) *make, erect, construct, preserve, establish, save.*

reach (SYN.) overtake, extent, distance, scope, range, extend, attain, stretch.
(ANT.) *fail, miss.*

readable (SYN.) understandable, distinct, legible, plain, clear, comprehensible.
(ANT.) *obliterated, illegible.*

ready (SYN.) mature, ripe, arrange, prompt, prepared, completed, quick, mellow.
(ANT.) *undeveloped, immature, green.*

real (SYN.) true, actual, positive, authentic, genuine.
(ANT.) *counterfeit, unreal, fictitious, false, sham, supposed*

realize (SYN.) discern, learn, perfect, actualize, under-

stand, apprehend, know.
(ANT.) misunderstand, misapprehend.

really (SYN.) truly, actually, honestly, undoubtedly, positively, genuinely.
(ANT.) questionably, possibly, doubtfully.

realm (SYN.) land, domain, kingdom, sphere, department, estate, world.

reap (SYN.) gather, harvest, pick, acquire, garner.
(ANT.) plant, seed, sow, lose, squander.

rear (SYN.) posterior, raise, lift, train, nurture, rump, build, foster.

reason (SYN.) intelligence, objective, understanding, aim, judgment, common sense, sanity, gather, assume, sake.

reasonable (SYN.) prudent, rational, logical, sage, sound, moderate, intelligent, sensible, discreet.
(ANT.) unaware, imperceptible, insane, absurd, stupid, illogical, irrational.

rebel (SYN.) revolutionary, traitor, mutineer, mutiny, revolt, disobey.

rebellious (SYN.) unruly, forward, defiant, undutiful.
(ANT.) obedient, compliant, submissive.

rebuild (SYN.) restore, renew, refresh, reconstruct.

rebuke (SYN.) chide, scold, reproach, censure, upbraid, scolding, condemn.
(ANT.) praise, exonerate, absolve.

recall (SYN.) recollect, remembrance, withdraw, retract, remember, recollection, reminisce, mind, memory, remind.
(ANT.) forget, overlook, ignore.

receive (SYN.) entertain, acquire, admit, accept, shelter, greet, obtain, welcome.
(ANT.) reject, offer, give, bestow, discharge, impart.

recent (SYN.) novel, original, late, new, newfangled, fresh, modern, current.

(ANT.) old, antiquated, ancient.

recess (SYN.) hollow, opening, nook, cranny, dent, respite, rest, break, pause.
(ANT.) gather, convene.

recipe (SYN.) instructions, formula, prescriptions, procedure, method.

recital (SYN.) history, account, relation, chronicle, narrative, detail, narration.
(ANT.) distortion, confusion.

recite (SYN.) describe, narrate, declaim, rehearse, tell, mention, repeat, detail.

reckless (SYN.) thoughtless, inconsiderate, careless, imprudent, rash, indiscreet.
(ANT.) careful, nice, accurate.

reclaim (SYN.) reform, rescue, reinstate, regenerate.

recline (SYN.) stretch, sprawl, repose, rest, lounge, loll.

recluse (SYN.) hermit, eremite, loner, anchorite.

recognize (SYN.) remember, avow, own, know, admit, apprehend, recollect, recall.
(ANT.) disown, ignore, renounce.

recollection (SYN.) remembrance, retrospection, impression, recall.
(ANT.) forgetfulness, oblivion.

recommend (SYN.) hind, suggest, counsel, allude, praise, approve, intimate, advocate.
(ANT.) disapprove, declare, insist.

recommendation (SYN.) instruction, justice, trustworthiness, counsel, admonition, caution, integrity.
(ANT.) fraud, deceit, trickery, cheating.

reconcile (SYN.) meditate, unite, adapt, adjust, settle, reunite, appease.

reconsider (SYN.) ponder, reevaluate, mull over, reflect.

record (SYN.) enter, write, register, chronicle, history, account, document.

recount (SYN.) report, convey, narrate, tell, detail, recite, describe, repeat.

recover (SYN.) regain, re-

deem, recapture, retrieve, mend, heal.
(*ANT.*) *debilitate, succumb, worsen.*

recreation (*SYN.*) entertainment, amusement, enjoyment, diversion, fun.

recruit (*SYN.*) trainee, beginner, volunteer, draftee, select, enlist, novice.

recuperate (*SYN.*) regain, retrieve, cure, recapture, revive, recover, repossess.
(*ANT.*) *sicken, weaken, lose, forfeit.*

redeem (*SYN.*) claim, recover, repossess, regain, reclaim, cash in, retrieve.

reduce (*SYN.*) lessen, decrease, lower, downgrade, degrade, suppress, lower, abate, diminish.
(*ANT.*) *enlarge, swell, raise, elevate, revive, increase.*

reduction (*SYN.*) shortening, abridgment, abbreviation.
(*ANT.*) *amplification, extension.*

reek (*SYN.*) odor, stench, stink, smell.

refer (*SYN.*) recommend, direct, commend, regard, concern, mention.

referee (*SYN.*) judge, arbitrator, umpire, arbiter, moderator, mediator.

reference (*SYN.*) allusion, direction, mention, concern, respect, referral.

refine (*SYN.*) purify, clarify.
(*ANT.*) *pollute, debase, muddy, downgrade.*

refined (*SYN.*) purified, cultured, cultivated, courteous.
(*ANT.*) *rude, coarse, crude, vulgar.*

refinement (*SYN.*) culture, enlightenment, education.
(*ANT.*) *vulgarity, ignorance, boorishness.*

reflect (*SYN.*) muse, mirror, deliberate, cogitate, think, reproduce, ponder, consider, reason, meditate.

reflection (*SYN.*) warning, conception, intelligence, appearance, likeness, image, cogitation, notification.

reform (*SYN.*) right, improve, correction, change, amend.
(*ANT.*) *spoil, damage, aggravate, vitiate.*

refuge (*SYN.*) safety, retreat, shelter, asylum, sanctuary.
(*ANT.*) *peril, exposure, jeopardy, danger.*

refuse (*SYN.*) spurn, rebuff, decline, reject, trash, rubbish, withhold, disallow, waste, garbage, deny.
(*ANT.*) *allow, accept, welcome, grant.*

refute (*SYN.*) rebut, disprove, confute, falsify, controvert.
(*ANT.*) *prove, confirm, accept, establish.*

regain (*SYN.*) redeem, retrieve, recover, repossess.
(*ANT.*) *lose.*

regalement (*SYN.*) feast, dinner, celebration.

regard (*SYN.*) estimate, value, honor, affection, notice, care, consideration, consider, relation, respect, attend, thought, reference, care, concern, liking.
(*ANT.*) *neglect, disgust, antipathy.*

regenerate (*SYN.*) improve, reconstruct, remedy, reestablish, rebuild.

regimented (*SYN.*) ordered, directed controlled, orderly, rigid, disciplined.
(*ANT.*) *loose, free, unstructured.*

region (*SYN.*) belt, place, spot, territory, climate, area, zone, locality, station.

register (*SYN.*) catalog, record, book, list, roll, enter, roster, chronicle.

regret (*SYN.*) sorrow, qualm, lament, grief, compunction, misgiving, remorse.
(*ANT.*) *obduracy, complacency.*

regular (*SYN.*) steady, orderly, natural, normal, customary, methodical, symmetrical.
(*ANT.*) *odd, exceptional, unusual, irregular, abnormal.*

regulate (*SYN.*) control, manage, govern, direct, legislate, set, adjust, systematize.

rehabilitate *(SYN.)* renew, restore, rebuild, reestablish, repair, reconstruct.

rehearse *(SYN.)* repeat, practice, train, learn, coach, prepare, perfect, direct.

reimburse *(SYN.)* recompense, remunerate, compensate, remit.

reinforce *(SYN.)* brace, strengthen, fortify, intensify.

reiterate *(SYN.)* reproduce, recapitulate, duplicate, repeat, rephrase.

reject *(SYN.)* spurn, rebuff, decline, renounce, expel, discard, withhold.
(ANT.) endorse, grant, welcome, accept.

rejoice *(SYN.)* celebrate, delight, enjoy, revel, exhilarate, elate.

relapse *(SYN.)* worsen, deteriorate, regress, weaken, fade, worsen, sink, fail.
(ANT.) strengthen, progress, advance, get well.

relate *(SYN.)* refer, beat, report, describe, tell, correlate, narrate, recount, compare, connect.

relationship *(SYN.)* link, tie, bond, affinity, conjunction.
(ANT.) separation, disunion.

relative *(SYN.)* dependent, proportional, about, pertinent, regarding.

relax *(SYN.)* slacken, loosen, repose, rest, recline.
(ANT.) increase, tighten, intensify.

relaxation *(SYN.)* comfort, recess, breather, loafing.

release *(SYN.)* liberate, emancipate, relinquish, proclaim, publish, liberation, announce, deliver, free.
(ANT.) restrict, imprison, subjugate.

relegate *(SYN.)* entrust, authorize, remand, refer.

relent *(SYN.)* cede, yield, surrender, give, relax, abdicate.
(ANT.) strive, assert, struggle.

relentless *(SYN.)* eternal, dogged, ceaseless, incessant, persistent, determined.

relevant *(SYN.)* related,

material, apt, applicable, fit, relating, germane.
(ANT.) foreign, alien, unrelated.

reliable *(SYN.)* trusty, tried, certain, secure, trustworthy.
(ANT.) unreliable, eccentric, questionable, erratic.

reliance *(SYN.)* faith, confidence, trust.
(ANT.) mistrust, doubt, skepticism.

relic *(SYN.)* remains, fossil, throwback, heirloom, souvenir, keepsake.

relief *(SYN.)* help, aid, comfort, ease, backing, patronage, alms, support.
(ANT.) hostility, defiance, antagonism, resistance.

relieve *(SYN.)* diminish, soothe, calm, abate, pacify, lighten, comfort, alleviate.
(ANT.) disturb, irritate, agitate, trouble, aggravate.

religion *(SYN.)* tenet, belief, dogma, faith, creed.

religious *(SYN.)* godly, reverent, faithful, devout, zeal, pious, divine, holy, devoted, sacred, theological.
(ANT.) profane, irreligious, skeptical, impious, lax.

religiousness *(SYN.)* love, zeal, affection, devoutness, fidelity, ardor.
(ANT.) indifference, apathy.

relinquish *(SYN.)* capitulate, submit, yield, abandon, cede, sacrifice, disclaim.
(ANT.) overcome, conquer, rout, resist.

reluctance *(SYN.)* disgust, hatred, repulsion, abhorrence, distaste, repugnance.
(ANT.) enthusiasm, affection, devotion.

reluctant *(SYN.)* slow, averse, hesitant, unwilling, loath, disinclined, balky.
(ANT.) ready, eager, willing, disposed.

remain *(SYN.)* survive, rest, stay, abide, halt, endure, dwell, tarry, continue.
(ANT.) finish, leave, terminate, dissipate.

remainder *(SYN.)* leftover,

residue, rest, surplus, balance, excess.

remark (SYN.) comment, note, observe, observation, annotation, declaration.

remedy (SYN.) redress, help, cure, relief, medicine, restorative, rectify, alleviate, medication, correct.

remember (SYN.) recollect, reminisce, recall, memorize, mind, retain, remind.
(ANT.) *forget, overlook.*

remembrance (SYN.) monument, memory, recollection, souvenir, retrospection.

remiss (SYN.) delinquent, lax, careless, negligent, oblivious, forgetful, absent-minded, sloppy.

remit (SYN.) send, pay, forward, forgive, pardon, overlook, excuse, reimburse.

remnant (SYN.) remains, remainder, rest, residue, trace, relic.

remonstrate (SYN.) grouch, protest, complain, grumble, murmur, repine.
(ANT.) *rejoice, applaud, praise.*

remorse (SYN.) sorrow, compunction, repentance.
(ANT.) *obduracy, complacency.*

remote (SYN.) inconsiderable, removed, slight, far, unlikely, distant, inaccessible, unreachable, isolated.
(ANT.) *visible, nearby, current, close.*

remove (SYN.) transport, eject, move, vacate, withdraw, dislodge, transfer, murder, kill, oust, extract.
(ANT.) *insert, retain, leave, stay, keep.*

remuneration (SYN.) wages, payment, pay, salary, compensation, reimbursement.

render (SYN.) become, make, perform, do, offer, present, give, submit.

renegade (SYN.) defector, insurgent, dissenter, rebel, maverick, betrayer.

renew (SYN.) restore, renovate, overhaul, revise, mod-

ernize, reshape, redo.

renounce (SYN.) resign, disown, revoke, abandon, quit, retract, forgo, leave, forsake, abdicate, reject.
(ANT.) *assert, uphold, recognize.*

renovate (SYN.) restore, rehabilitate, rebuild, refresh, renew, overhaul.

renowned (SYN.) noted, famous, distinguished, well-known, celebrated.
(ANT.) *unknown, infamous, hidden, obscure.*

rent (SYN.) payment, rental, lease, hire.

repair (SYN.) rebuilding, mend, renew, tinker, correct, patch, restore, adjust, amend, rehabilitation.
(ANT.) *harm, break.*

repeal (SYN.) end, cancel, nullify, annul, quash, abolish, cancellation, rescind, abolition, abrogate.

repeat (SYN.) reiterate, restate, redo, rehearse, quote, reproduce.

repellent (SYN.) sickening, offensive, disgusting, nauseating, obnoxious.

repentance (SYN.) penitence, remorse, sorrow, compunction, qualm, grief.
(ANT.) *obduracy, complacency.*

repentant (SYN.) regretful, sorrowful, contrite, sorry.
(ANT.) *remorseless, obdurate.*

repetitious (SYN.) repeated, monotonous, boring.

repine (SYN.) protest, lament, complain, whine, regret, grouch, grumble.
(ANT.) *rejoice, applaud, praise.*

replacement (SYN.) understudy, proxy, alternate, substitute, replica, surrogate.

reply (SYN.) retort, rejoinder, answer, retaliate, respond, confirmation.
(ANT.) *summoning, inquiry.*

report (SYN.) declare, herald, publish, announce, summary, publish, advertise.
(ANT.) *suppress, conceal.*

represent (SYN.) picture, draw, delineate, portray, depict, denote.
(ANT.) misrepresent, caricature.

representative (SYN.) delegate, agent, substitute.

repress (SYN.) limit, stop, check, bridle, curb, restrain, constrain, suppress.
(ANT.) loosen, aid, incite, liberate.

reproach (SYN.) defamation, dishonor, insult, profanation, abuse, disparagement, misuse, reviling.
(ANT.) respect, laudation.

reproduction (SYN.) replica, copy, exemplar, transcript.

repugnance (SYN.) disgust, hatred, reluctance, abhorrence, aversion, loathing.
(ANT.) devotion, affection, enthusiasm, attachment.

repulsive (SYN.) repellent, ugly, homely, deformed, horrid, offensive, plain.
(ANT.) fair, pretty, attractive.

reputation (SYN.) class, nature, standing, name, fame, character, distinction.

repute (SYN.) class, nature, reputation, disposition.

require (SYN.) exact, need, lack, claim, demand, want.

requisite (SYN.) vital, necessary, basic, fundamental, indispensable, essential.
(ANT.) casual, nonessential, accidental.

rescind (SYN.) annul, quash, revoke, abolish, invalidate, abrogate, withdraw.

rescue (SYN.) liberate, ransom, release, deliver, deliverance, liberation.

research (SYN.) exploration, interrogation, query, examination, study.
(ANT.) inattention, disregard, negligence.

resemblance (SYN.) parity, similitude, analogy, likeness, correspondence.
(ANT.) distinction, difference.

resentment (SYN.) displeasure, bitterness, indignation, rancor, outrage, hostility.

(ANT.) complacency, understanding, good will.

reservation (SYN.) skepticism, restriction, objection, limitation, doubt.

reserve (SYN.) fund, hold, save, stock, maintain.
(ANT.) waste, squander.

residence (SYN.) home, dwelling, stay, seat, abode, quarters, domicile.

residue (SYN.) balance, remainder, rest, ashes, remnants, dregs, leftovers, ends.

resign (SYN.) vacate, withdraw, leave, surrender, quit.

resigned (SYN.) forbearing, accepting, composed, uncomplaining.
(ANT.) turbulent, chafing.

resist (SYN.) defy, attack, withstand, hinder, confront.
(ANT.) relent, allow, yield.

resolute (SYN.) firm, resolved, set, determined, decided.
(ANT.) irresolute, wavering, vacillating.

resolve (SYN.) determination, decide, persistence, determine, confirm, decision.
(ANT.) integrate, indecision, inconstancy.

resourceful (SYN.) inventive, imaginative, skillful.

respect (SYN.) honor, approval, revere, heed, value, admiration, reverence.
(ANT.) disrespect, neglect, abuse, scorn, disregard.

respectable (SYN.) becoming, tolerable, decent.
(ANT.) unsavory, vulgar, gross, disreputable.

response (SYN.) reply, acknowledgment, answer, retort, rejoinder.
(ANT.) summoning, inquiry.

responsibility (SYN.) duty, trustworthiness, trust, liability, commitment.

restitution (SYN.) recompense, satisfaction, refund, amends, retrieval.

restive (SYN.) balky, disobedient, fractious, impatient, unruly, fidgety.

restore (SYN.) repair, recover, rebuild, reestablish, renovate, return, renew, mend, reinstall, revive, rehabilitate.

restraint *(SYN.)* order, self-control, reserve, control, regulation, limitation.
(ANT.) freedom, liberty.

restrict *(SYN.)* fetter, restrain, confine, limit, engage, attach, connect, link, tie.
(ANT.) broaden, enlarge, loose, free.

result *(SYN.)* effect, issue, outcome, resolve, end, consequence, happen, determination, conclusion.
(ANT.) cause, beginning, origin.

resume *(SYN.)* restart, continue, recommence.

retain *(SYN.)* keep, hold, recall, remember, employ, hire, engage.

retard *(SYN.)* detain, slacken, defer, impede, hold back, delay, postpone.
(ANT.) accelerate, speed, hasten, rush.

retention *(SYN.)* reservation, acquisition, holding, tenacity, possession.

reticent *(SYN.)* reserved, subdued, quiet, shy, withdrawn, restrained, bashful.
(ANT.) outspoken, forward, opinionated.

retire *(SYN.)* resign, quit, abdicate, depart, vacate.

retiring *(SYN.)* timid, bashful, withdrawn, modest, quiet, reserved.
(ANT.) gregarious, assertive, bold.

retort *(SYN.)* reply, answer, response, respond, rejoin, rejoinder, retaliate.
(ANT.) summoning, inquiry.

retreat *(SYN.)* leave, depart, retire, withdraw, retirement, withdrawal, departure, shelter, refuge.
(ANT.) advanced.

retrench *(SYN.)* reduce, scrape, curtail.

retribution *(SYN.)* justice, vengeance, reprisal, punishment, comeuppance, vindictiveness, revenge, retaliation.

retrieve *(SYN.)* regain, recover, recapture, reclaim, salvage, recoup.

retrograde *(SYN.)* regressive, backward, declining, deteriorating, worsening.
(ANT.) onward, progression, advanced.

return *(SYN.)* restoration, replace, revert, recur, restore, retreat.
(ANT.) keep, take, retain.

reveal *(SYN.)* discover, publish, communicate, impart, uncover, tell, betray, divulge, disclose.
(ANT.) conceal, cover, obscure, hide.

revel *(SYN.)* rejoice, wallow, bask, enjoy, delight, savor, gloat, luxuriate, relish.

revelation *(SYN.)* hallucination, dream, phantoms, apparition, ghost, mirage, specter, daydream, suprise, shocker.
(ANT.) verity, reality.

revelry *(SYN.)* merriment, merry-making, carousal, feasting, gala, festival.

revenge *(SYN.)* vindictiveness, reprisal, requital, vengeance, repayment, repay, retribution, reparation.
(ANT.) reconcile, forgive, pity.

revenue *(SYN.)* take, proceeds, income, profit, return.

revere *(SYN.)* admire, honor, worship, respect, venerate, adore.
(ANT.) ignore, despise.

reverence *(SYN.)* glory, worship, homage, admiration, dignity, renown, respect, esteem, veneration, adoration, honor.
(ANT.) dishonor, derision, reproach.

reverent *(SYN.)* honoring, respectful, adoring, pious, devout, humble.
(ANT.) impious, disrespectful.

reverse *(SYN.)* overthrow, unmake rescind, opposite, invert, contrary, rear, back, misfortune, defeat, catastrophe, upset, counter-

mand, revoke.
(ANT.) vouch, stabilize, endorse, affirm.

revert (SYN.) revive, relapse, backslide, rebound, retreat, recur, go back.
(ANT.) keep, take, appropriate.

review (SYN.) reconsideration, examination, commentary, retrospection, restudy, journal, synopsis, study, reexamine, critique, inspection.

revile (SYN.) defame, malign, vilify, abuse, traduce, scandalize, smear.
(ANT.) honor, respect, cherish, protect.

revise (SYN.) change, alter, improve, correct, amend, update, rewrite, polish.

revision (SYN.) inspection, survey, retrospection, commentary, critique.

revival (SYN.) renaissance, exhumation, resurgence, renewal, revitalization.

revive (SYN.) refresh, lessen, decrease, renew, reduce, lower, abate, reanimate, diminish, rejuvenate, suppress.
(ANT.) increase, amplify, intensify.

revoke (SYN.) nullify, cancel, abolish, quash, rescind, abrogate.

revolt (SYN.) mutiny, rebel, disgust, revolution, uprising, rebellion, upheaval, takeover, insurgence, abolish.

revolting (SYN.) hateful, odious, abominable, foul, vile, detestable, loathsome, repugnant, sickening.
(ANT.) delightful, agreeable, pleasant.

revolution (SYN.) rebellion, mutiny, turn, coup, revolt, overthrow, cycle.

revolutionary (SYN.) insurgent, extremist, radical, subversive, mutinous.

revolve (SYN.) spin, wheel, rotate, circle, circle, turn, whirl, gyrate.

(ANT.) travel, proceed, wander.

revolver (SYN.) gun, pistol.

revulsion (SYN.) reversal, rebound, backlash, withdrawal, recoil.

reward (SYN.) bounty, premium, meed, award, compensation, prize, recompense, bonus, remuneration, wages.
(ANT.) charge, wages, punishment.

rewarding (SYN.) pleasing, productive, fruitful, profitable, favorable, satisfying, gratifying, fulfilling.

rhetoric (SYN.) style, verbosity, expressiveness, eloquence, flamboyance.

rhyme (SYN.) poem, verse, poetry, ballad, ditty, rhapsody, sonnet.

ribald (SYN.) suggestive, off-color, indecent, spicy, rude, vulgar.

rich (SYN.) ample, costly, wealthy, fruitful, prolific, abundant, well-off, affluent, plentiful, fertile, bountiful, luxuriant.
(ANT.) poor, unfruitful, beggarly, barren, impoverished, scarce, scanty, unproductive, destitute.

rickety (SYN.) unsound, unsteady, flimsy, unstable, shaky, decrepit, wobbly.
(ANT.) steady, solid, sturdy.

ricochet (SYN.) recoil, backfire, rebound, bounce, deviate, boomerang.

rid (SYN.) free, clear, shed, delivered, eliminate, disperse, unload, purge.

riddle (SYN.) puzzle, mystery, conundrum, problem, question, enigma.
(ANT.) key, solution, answer, resolution.

ride (SYN.) tour, journey, motor, manage, drive, control, guide.

ridge (SYN.) hillock, backbone, spine, crest, mound, hump.

ridicule (SYN.) gibe, banter, mock, jeering, deride, tease,

taunt, satire, mockery, derision.
(ANT.) *praise, respect.*
ridiculous (SYN.) silly, nonsensical, absurd, accurate, inconsistent, proper, laughable, apt, preposterous, foolish.
(ANT.) *sound, reasonable, consistent.*
rife (SYN.) widespread, abundant, innumerable, rampant, teeming.
rifle (SYN.) plunder, pillage, rummage, ransack, rob, steal.
rift (SYN.) crevice, fault, opening, crack, flaw, fissure, split, breach, opening.
right (SYN.) correct, appropriate, suitable, ethical, fit, real, legitimate, justice, factual, just, directly, virtue, true, definite, straight, honorably, seemly.
(ANT.) *immoral, unfair, wrong, bad, improper.*
righteous (SYN.) ethical, chaste, honorable, good, virtuous, good, noble.
(ANT.) *sinful, libertine, amoral, licentious.*
rigid (SYN.) strict, unyielding, stiff, stern, austere, rigorous, inflexible, stringent, unbendable, severe, harsh, unbending.
(ANT.) *supple, flexible, mild, compassionate, pliable, limp, relaxed.*
rigorous (SYN.) unfeeling, rough, strict, blunt, cruel, hard, severe, grating, coarse, jarring, stern, stringent.
(ANT.) *soft, mild, tender, gentle, smooth.*
rile (SYN.) irritate, nettle, hector, exasperate, provoke, gripe.
rim (SYN.) verge, frontier, boundary, fringe, brim.
(ANT.) *core, mainland, center.*
ring (SYN.) fillet, band, loop, circlet, circle, surround, encircle, peal, sound, resound.
rinse (SYN.) launder, cleanse, wash, soak, immerse, laundering, rinsing, immerse, bathe, clean.
riot (SYN.) disturbance, disorder, outburst, commotion, insurgence, uproar, confusion, tumult, revolt.
rip (SYN.) tear, rend, wound, lacerate, shred, scramble, dart, dash, split, disunite.
(ANT.) *unite, join, repair.*
ripe (SYN.) ready, finished, mature, complete, fullgrown, develop, mellow, avid, consummate.
(ANT.) *raw, crude, undeveloped, premature, unprepared, unripe, immature.*
riposte (SYN.) rejoinder, comeback, quip, retort, response, reply, wisecrack.
ripple (SYN.) wave, ruffle, gurgle, corrugation, rumple, crumple, dribble, bubble.
rise (SYN.) thrive, awaken, ascend, climb, mount, tower, prosper, advance, proceed.
(ANT.) *fall, drop, plunge, fade, slump, decline, sinking, setback, retrogression.*
risk (SYN.) hazard, peril, jeopardy, threat, vulnerability, contingency.
(ANT.) *protection, immunity, defense.*
risky (SYN.) menacing, chancy, threatening, critical, dicey, unsound, dangerous.
(ANT.) *guarded, safe, firm, secure.*
rite (SYN.) pomp, solemnity, ceremony, observance, ceremonial, formality.
ritual (SYN.) pomp, solemnity, ceremony, parade, rite, ritualism, prescription, routine, custom, tradition.
rival (SYN.) enemy, opponent, adversary, oppose, competitor, contest, antagonist.
(ANT.) *colleague, confederate, allay, collaborator, helpmate, teammate.*
rivalry (SYN.) contest, struggle, duel, race, vying, opposition, competition.
(ANT.) *alliance, collaboration, partnership, cooperation, teamwork, coalition.*

river (SYN.) brook, stream, tributary, creek.

road (SYN.) street, way, highway, pike, drive, highway, expressway, boulevard.

roam (SYN.) err, saunter, deviate, rove, range, wander, digress, ramble, stroll. (ANT.) stop, linger, stay, halt.

roar (SYN.) cry, bellow, yell, blare, scream, whoop, holler, yelp.

roast (SYN.) deride, ridicule, parody, burlesque.

rob (SYN.) fleece, steal, loot, plunder, burglarize, ransack, hold up, rip off, thieve.

robbery (SYN.) larceny, plundering, thievery, stealing, snatching, burglary.

robe (SYN.) housecoat, bathrobe, dressing gown, caftan, smock, cape.

robust (SYN.) well, hearty, hale, sound, healthy, strong. (ANT.) fragile, feeble, debilitated, reserved, refined, puny, frail, delicate.

rock (SYN.) pebble, boulder, stone, gravel, granite, roll, sway, limestone.

rod (SYN.) bar, pole, wand, stick, pike, staff, billy, baton.

rogue (SYN.) criminal, rascal, good-for-nothing.

roister (SYN.) bluster, swagger, swashbuckle, vaunt, bluff, flourish, rollick.

role (SYN.) task, part, function, characterization, portrayal, face, character.

roll (SYN.) revolve, rotate, reel, lumber, swagger, stagger, progress, proceed, turn.

rollicking (SYN.) spirited, frolicsome, exuberant, lighthearted, carefree.

romance (SYN.) affair, enchantment, novel, tale, adventure, enterprise, daring.

romantic (SYN.) poetic, mental, dreamy, fanciful, imaginative, extravagant, impractical, exaggerated, wild. (ANT.) homely, faint-hearted, familiar, unromantic, pessimistic, unemotional, cynical, literal, prosaic, factual.

room (SYN.) enclosure, cell, cubicle, reside.

roost (SYN.) coop, henhouse, hearth, lodgings.

rooted (SYN.) fixed, fast, firm, steadfast, immovable, stationary.

rope (SYN.) string, wire, cord, cable, line, strand, rigging, ropework, cordage.

roster (SYN.) list, census, muster, enrollment, listing.

rosy (SYN.) reddish, pink, healthy, fresh, cheerful, flushed, promising, favorable. (ANT.) pale, pallid, gray, wan, disheartening, ashen, unfavorable, gloomy.

rot (SYN.) putrefy, waste, dwindle, spoil, decline, decomposition, wane, rotting. (ANT.) increase, rise, grow, luxuriate.

rotary (SYN.) axial, rotating, rolling, rotational.

rotation (SYN.) turning, rolling, succession, gyration, swirling, spinning, whirling.

rote (SYN.) repetition, system, convention, routine, mechanization, habitude, habit, custom, perfunctoriness.

rotten (SYN.) decayed, decomposed, spoiled, putrid, contaminated, tainted. (ANT.) unspoiled, pure, sweet.

rough (SYN.) jagged, scratchy, craggy, stormy, rugged, unpolished, approximate, uneven, irregular, bumpy, coarse, unpolished, rude. (ANT.) calm, polished, civil, smooth, sleek, sophisticated.

round (SYN.) rotund, chubby, complete, spherical, circular, bowed. (ANT.) slender, trim, slim, thin, lean.

rouse (SYN.) waken, awaken, stimulate, excite, summon, arise, stir. (ANT.) rest, calm, sleep, restrain, sedate.

rout (SYN.) defeat, beat, quell, vanquish, conquer, humble, subdue, scatter. (ANT.) cede, retreat.

route (SYN.) street, course, thoroughfare, track, road.

routine (SYN.) way, habit, use, method, system, channel. (ANT.) unusual, rate, uncommon.

row (SYN.) file, order, series, rank, progression, sequence, arrangement.

royal (SYN.) lordly, regal, noble, courtly, ruling. (ANT.) servile, common, low, humble.

rubbish (SYN.) debris, garbage, trash, waste, junk.

rude (SYN.) gruff, impudent, blunt, impolite, boorish, insolent, saucy, rough, crude, unmannerly, coarse, impertinent. (ANT.) courtly, civil, stately, polished, courteous, cultivated, polite.

rudimentary (SYN.) essential, primary, fundamental, original, imperfect.

ruffle (SYN.) rumple, disarrange, disorder, disturb, trimming, frill.

rugged (SYN.) jagged, craggy, harsh, severe, tough. (ANT.) smooth, level, even.

ruin (SYN.) wreck, exterminate, devastate, annihilate, raze, demolish, spoil, wreck, destroy, destruction. (ANT.) save, establish, preserve.

ruination (SYN.) obliteration, annihilation, havoc, catastrophe.

rule (SYN.) law, guide, order, sovereignty, control.

ruler (SYN.) commander, chief, leader, governor.

ruling (SYN.) judgment, decision, decree.

ruminate (SYN.) brood, reflect, meditate, ponder, consider, speculate, mull.

rumple (SYN.) tousle, furrow, crease, wrinkle, dishevel.

run (SYN.) race, hurry, speed, hasten, sprint, dart.

rush (SYN.) dash, speed, hurry, hasten, run, scoot, hustle, scurry. (ANT.) tarry, linger.

sacrament (SYN.) communion, fellowship, association, participation, union. (ANT.) nonparticipation, alienation.

sacred (SYN.) consecrated, blessed, devout, divine, holy, spiritual, saintly. (ANT.) profane, evil, sacrilegious, worldly, secular.

sad (SYN.) dejected, cheerless, despondent, depressed, disconsolate, doleful. (ANT.) cheerful, glad, merry.

safe (SYN.) dependable, certain, harmless, secure, snug. (ANT.) hazardous, dangerous, unsafe, insecure, perilous.

sage (SYN.) intellectual, disciple, learner, savant, judicious, sagacious, rational. (ANT.) dunce, fool, dolt, idiot.

saintly (SYN.) virtuous, moral, holy, devout, righteous.

salary (SYN.) compensation, fee, payment, wages. (ANT.) gratuity, present, gift.

salubrious (SYN.) healthy, well, hygienic, wholesome. (ANT.) diseased, delicate, frail, injurious, infirm.

salutary (SYN.) beneficial, advantageous, profitable. (ANT.) destructive, deleterious, detrimental, injurious, harmful.

sample (SYN.) example, case, illustration, model, instance, pattern, prototype.

sanctuary (SYN.) harbor, haven, asylum, refuge, retreat, shelter. (ANT.) danger, hazard, exposure, peril.

sane (SYN.) balanced, rational, normal, sound. (ANT.) crazy, insane, irrational.

sarcastic (SYN.) biting, acrimonious, cutting, caustic. (ANT.) agreeable, pleasant.

satire (SYN.) cleverness, fun, banter, humor, irony, raillery, pleasantry. (ANT.) platitude, sobriety, stupidity.

satirical (SYN.) biting, caustic, derisive, sarcastic, sneering,

sardonic, taunting.
(ANT.) *affable, pleasant.*

satisfaction (SYN.) blessedness, beatitude, bliss, delight, contentment, felicity, pleasure, enjoyment.
(ANT.) *grief, misery, despair.*

satisfy (SYN.) compensate, appease, content, gratify, fulfill, suitable.
(ANT.) *displease, dissatisfy, annoy, frustrate, tantalize.*

savage (SYN.) brutal, cruel, barbarous, ferocious, inhuman, merciless, malignant.
(ANT.) *compassionate, forbearing, benevolent, gentle, tame, cultivated.*

save (SYN.) defend, conserve, keep, maintain, guard, preserve, protect, safeguard.
(ANT.) *abolish, destroy, abandon, impair, injure.*

say (SYN.) converse, articulate, declare, express, discourse, harangue, talk, state.
(ANT.) *hush, refrain, be silent.*

scale (SYN.) balance, proportion, ration, range, climb.

scandal (SYN.) chagrin, mortification, dishonor.
(ANT.) *glory, honor, dignity.*

scandalous (SYN.) disgraceful, discreditable, dishonorable, ignominious.
(ANT.) *honorable, renowned, esteemed.*

scant (SYN.) succinct, summary, concise, terse, inadequate, deficient.
(ANT.) *ample, big, abundant.*

scarce (SYN.) occasional, choice, infrequent, exceptional, incomparable.
(ANT.) *frequent, ordinary, usual, customary, abundant, numerous, worthless.*

scare (SYN.) alarm, papal, affright, astound, dismay, horrify, terrorize, shock.
(ANT.) *compose, reassure, soothe.*

scared (SYN.) apprehensive, afraid, fainthearted, frightened, fearful, timid.
(ANT.) *bold, assured, courageous, composed, sanguine.*

scheme (SYN.) conspiracy, cabal, design, machination, design, devise.

scope (SYN.) area, compass, expanse, amount, extent, reach, size, range.

scramble (SYN.) combine, mix, blend, hasten, clamber.

scrap (SYN.) fragment, rag, apportionment, part, portion, piece, section, share.
(ANT.) *whole, entirety.*

scrape (SYN.) difficulty, dilemma, condition, fix, predicament, plight, situation.
(ANT.) *comfort, calmness.*

script (SYN.) penmanship, hand, handwriting, text.

scrupulous (SYN.) conscientious, candid, honest, truthful, upright, painstaking.
(ANT.) *dishonest, fraudulent, lying deceitful, tricky.*

scurry (SYN.) scamper, scramble, hasten, hustle.

seal (SYN.) emblem, stamp, symbol, crest, signet.

search (SYN.) exploration, inquiry, pursuit, quest, explore, scrutinize, hunt.
(ANT.) *resignation, abandonment.*

season (SYN.) mature, perfect, ripen, develop, age.

seclusion (SYN.) insulation, isolation, loneliness, alienation, quarantine.
(ANT.) *fellowship, union, communion.*

secondary (SYN.) minor, poorer, inferior, lower.
(ANT.) *greater, superior.*

secret (SYN.) concealed, hidden, latent, covert, private, surreptitious, unknown.
(ANT.) *disclosed, exposed, known, obvious, conspicuous, open, public.*

section (SYN.) district, country, domain, dominion, division, land, place, province.

security (SYN.) bond, earnest, token, surety.

sedate (SYN.) controlled, serene, calm, composed.

seize (SYN.) check, detain, withhold, grab, grasp.
(ANT.) *free, liberate, release, activate, discharge, loosen.*

select *(SYN.)* cull, opt, pick, choose, elect, prefer.
(ANT.) reject, refuse.

self-important *(SYN.)* egotistical, proud, conceited, egocentric.

selfish *(SYN.)* illiberal, narrow, self-centered, self-seeking, mercenary, stingy, ungenerous, mean, miserly.
(ANT.) charitable.

sell *(SYN.)* market, retail, merchandise, vend, trade.

send *(SYN.)* discharge, emit, dispatch, cast, propel, impel, throw, transmit, forward, ship, convey, mail.
(ANT.) get, hold, retain, receive, bring.

senile *(SYN.)* antiquated, antique, aged, ancient, archaic, obsolete, old, elderly, old-fashioned, venerable.
(ANT.) new, youthful, young, modern.

sensation *(SYN.)* feeling, image, impression, apprehension, sense, sensibility, perception, sensitiveness.
(ANT.) insensibility, stupor, apathy.

sensational *(SYN.)* exciting, startling spectacular.

sense *(SYN.)* drift, connotation, acceptation, explanation, gist, implication, intent, import, interpretation, sensation, perception.

sensible *(SYN.)* apprehensible, perceptible, appreciable, alive, aware, awake, perceiving, conscious, sentient, intelligent, discreet, judicious, prudent, sagacious, reasonable.
(ANT.) impalpable, imperceptible, absurd, stupid, unaware, foolish.

sensual *(SYN.)* lascivious, earthy, lecherous, carnal, sensory, voluptuous, wanton, erotic, lustful, sexual.
(ANT.) chaste, ascetic, abstemious, virtuous.

sentiment *(SYN.)* affection, sensibility, passion, impression, opinion, attitude.
(ANT.) coldness, imperturb-

ability, anesthesia, insensibility, fact.

separate *(SYN.)* part sever, sunder, divide, allot, dispense, share, distribute, disconnect, split, isolate, segregate, different, distinct.
(ANT.) join, gather, combine.

separation *(SYN.)* insulation, isolation, loneliness, alienation, seclusion, retirement, solitude, segregation.
(ANT.) communion, fellowship, union, association.

sequence *(SYN.)* chain, graduation, order, progression, arrangement, series, succession, train, string.

serene *(SYN.)* composed, imperturbable, calm, dispassionate, pacific, placid.
(ANT.) frantic, turbulent, wild, excited, stormy, agitated, turbulent.

servant *(SYN.)* attendant, butler, domestic, valet, manservant, maid.

serve *(SYN.)* assist, attend, help, succor, advance, benefit, forward, answer, promote, content, satisfy, suffice, wait on, aid.
(ANT.) command, direct, dictate, rule.

servile *(SYN.)* base, contemptible, despicable, abject, groveling, dishonorable, ignominious, ignoble, lowly, low, menial, mean, sordid, vulgar, vile.
(ANT.) honored, exalted, lofty, esteemed, righteous, noble.

set *(SYN.)* deposit, dispose, position, pose, station, appoint, fix, assign, settle, establish.
(ANT.) mislay, misplace, disturb, remove, disarrange.

settle *(SYN.)* close, conclude, adjudicate, decide, end, resolve, agree upon, establish.
(ANT.) suspend, hesitate, doubt, vacillate, waver.

sever *(SYN.)* part, divide, sunder, split, cut, separate.
(ANT.) convene, connect, gather, join, unite, combine.

severe *(SYN.)* arduous, distressing, acute, exacting, hard, harsh, intense, relentless, rigorous, sharp, stern. (ANT.) genial, indulgent, lenient, yielding, merciful, considerate.

sew (SYN.) mend, patch, fix, stitch, refit, restore, repair. (ANT.) destroy, hurt, deface, injure.

shabby (SYN.) indigent, impecunious, needy, penniless, worn, ragged, destitute, poor, threadbare, deficient, inferior, scanty. (ANT.) rich, wealthy, ample, affluent, opulent, right, sufficient, good.

shack (SYN.) hovel, hut, shanty, shed.

shackle (SYN.) chain, fetter, handcuff.

shadowy (SYN.) dark, dim, gloomy, murky, black, obscure, dusky, unilluminated, dismal, evil, gloomy, sinister, indistinct, hidden, vague, undefined, wicked, mystic, secret, occult. (ANT.) bright, clear, light, pleasant, lucid.

shady (SYN.) shifty, shaded, questionable, doubtful, devious.

shaggy (SYN.) hairy, unkempt, uncombed, woolly.

shake (SYN.) flutter, jar, jolt, quake, agitate, quiver, shiver, shudder, rock, totter, sway, tremble, vibrate.

shaky (SYN.) questionable, uncertain, iffy, faltering. (ANT.) sure, positive, certain.

shallow (SYN.) exterior, cursory, flimsy, frivolous, slight, imperfect, superficial. (ANT.) complete, deep, abstruse, profound, thorough.

sham (SYN.) affect, act, feign, assume, pretend, simulate, profess. (ANT.) exhibit, display, reveal, expose.

shame (SYN.) chagrin, humiliation, abashment, disgrace, mortification, dishonor, ignominy, embarrassment, disrepute, odium mortify, humiliate, abash, humble, opprobrium, scandal. (ANT.) pride, glory, praise, honor.

shameful (SYN.) disgraceful, dishonorable, disreputable, discreditable, humiliating, ignominious, scandalous. (ANT.) honorable, renowned, respectable, esteemed.

shameless (SYN.) unembarrassed, unashamed, brazen, bold, impudent. (ANT.) demure, modest.

shape (SYN.) create, construct, forge, fashion, form, make, produce, mold, constitute, compose, arrange, combine, organize, frame, outline, figure, invent, appearance, pattern, cast, model, devise. (ANT.) disfigure, misshape, wreck.

shapeless (SYN.) rough, vague.

shapely (SYN.) attractive, well-formed, curvy, alluring. (ANT.) shapeless.

share (SYN.) parcel, bit, part, division, portion, ration, piece, fragment, allotment, partake, apportion, participate, divide, section. (ANT.) whole.

shared (SYN.) joint, common, reciprocal, correlative, mutual. (ANT.) unrequited, dissociated.

sharp (SYN.) biting, pointed, cunning, acute, keen, rough, fine, cutting, shrill, cutting, pungent, witty, acrid, blunt, steep, shrewd. (ANT.) gentle, bland, shallow, smooth, blunt.

sharpen (SYN.) whet, hone, strop.

shatter (SYN.) crack, rend, break, pound, smash, burst, demolish, shiver, infringe. (ANT.) renovate, join, repair, mend.

shattered (SYN.) fractured, destroyed, reduced, separated, broken, smashed,

flattened, rent, wrecked.
(ANT.) united, integral, whole.

shawl (SYN.) stole, scarf.

sheepish (SYN.) coy, embarrassed, shy, humble, abashed, diffident, timid, modest, timorous.
(ANT.) daring, outgoing, adventurous.

sheer (SYN.) thin, transparent, clear, simple, utter, absolute, abrupt, steep.

sheet (SYN.) leaf, layer, coating, film.

shelter (SYN.) retreat, safety, cover, asylum, protection, sanctuary, harbor, guard, haven, security.
(ANT.) unveil, expose, bare, reveal.

shield (SYN.) envelop, cover, clothe, curtain, protest, protection, cloak, guard, conceal, defense, shelter, hide, screen.
(ANT.) unveil, divulge, reveal, bare.

shift (SYN.) move, modify, transfer, substitute, vary, change, alter, spell, turn, transfigure.
(ANT.) settle, establish, stabilize.

shifting (SYN.) wavering, inconstant, changeable, fitful, variable, fickle.
(ANT.) uniform, stable, unchanging.

shiftless (SYN.) idle, lazy, slothful.
(ANT.) energetic.

shifty (SYN.) shrewd, crafty, tricky.

shilly-shally (SYN.) fluctuate, waver, hesitate, vacillate.

shimmer (SYN.) glimmer, shine, gleam.
(ANT.) dull.

shine (SYN.) flicker, glisten, glow, blaze, glare, flash, beam, shimmer, glimmer, radiate, brush, polish, twinkle, buff, luster, gloss, scintillate, radiance, gleam.

shining (SYN.) dazzling, illustrious, showy, superb, brilliant, effulgent, magnificent, splendid, bright.

(ANT.) ordinary, dull, unimpressive.

shiny (SYN.) bright, glossy, polished, glistening.
(ANT.) lusterless, dull.

shipshape (SYN.) clean, neat.
(ANT.) sloppy, messy.

shiver (SYN.) quiver, quake, quaver, tremble, shudder, shake, break, shatter.

shock (SYN.) disconcert, astonish, surprise, astound, amaze, clash, disturbance, bewilder, outrage, horrify, revolt, agitation, stagger, blow, impact, collision, surprise, startle, upset, stun.
(ANT.) prepare, caution, admonish.

shocking (SYN.) hideous, frightful, severe, appalling, horrible, awful, terrible, dire, fearful.
(ANT.) safe, happy, secure, joyous.

shore (SYN.) seaside, beach, coast.
(ANT.) inland.

short (SYN.) abrupt, squat, concise, brief, low, curtailed, dumpy, terse, inadequate, succinct, dwarfed, small, abbreviated, lacking, abridge, condensed, undersized, slight, little.
(ANT.) extended, ample, protracted.

shortage (SYN.) deficiency, deficit.
(ANT.) surplus, enough.

shortcoming (SYN.) error, vice, blemish, failure, flaw, omission, failing.
(ANT.) perfection, completeness.

shorten (SYN.) curtail, limit, cut, abbreviate, reduce, abridge, lessen, restrict.
(ANT.) lengthen, elongate.

shortening (SYN.) reduction, abridgment, abbreviation.
(ANT.) enlargement, amplification.

short-handed (SYN.) understaffed.

shortly (SYN.) soon, directly, presently.

shortsighted (SYN.) myopic,

shout (SYN.) ejaculate, cry, yell, roar, vociferate, bellow, exclaim.
(ANT.) whisper, intimate.

shove (SYN.) propel, drive, urge, crowd, jostle, force, push, promote.
(ANT.) retreat, falter, oppose, drag, halt.

shovel (SYN.) spade.

show (SYN.) flourish, parade, point, reveal, explain, movie, production, display, exhibit, spectacle, demonstrate, entertainment, tell, guide, prove, indicate, present, lead, demonstration.

showy (SYN.) ceremonious, stagy, affected, theatrical, artificial.
(ANT.) unaffected, modest, unemotional, subdued.

shred (SYN.) particle, speck, iota, mite, bit, smidgen, tear, slit, cleave, rip, disunite, wound, rend, mince, tatter.
(ANT.) bulk, unite, quantity, mend, aggregate, repair.

shrewd (SYN.) cunning, covert, artful, stealthy, foxy, astute, ingenious, guileful, crafty, sly, surreptitious, wily, tricky, clever, intelligent, clandestine.
(ANT.) frank, sincere, candid, open.

shriek (SYN.) screech, scream, howl, yell.

shrill (SYN.) keen, penetrating, sharp, acute, piercing, severe.
(ANT.) gentle, bland, shallow.

shrink (SYN.) diminish, shrivel, dwindle.

shrivel (SYN.) wizen, waste, droop, decline, sink, dry, languish, wither.
(ANT.) renew, refresh, revive, rejuvenate.

shun (SYN.) escape, avert, forestall, avoid, forbear, evade, ward, free.
(ANT.) encounter, confront, meet.

shut (SYN.) seal, finish, stop, close, terminate, conclude, clog, end, obstruct.
(ANT.) begin, open, start, unbar, inaugurate, unlock, commence.

shy (SYN.) reserved, fearful, bashful, retiring, cautious, demure, timid, shrinking, wary, chary.
(ANT.) brazen, bold, immodest, self-confident, audacious.

sick (SYN.) ill, morbid, ailing, unhealthy, diseased, unwell, infirm.
(ANT.) sound, well, robust, strong.

sickness (SYN.) illness, ailment, disease, complaint, disorder.
(ANT.) soundness, healthiness, vigor.

side (SYN.) surface, face, foe, opponent, rival, indirect, secondary, unimportant.

siege (SYN.) blockade.

sieve (SYN.) screen, strainer, colander.

sight (SYN.) eyesight, vision, scene, view, display, spectacle, eyesore.

sightless (SYN.) unmindful, oblivious, blind, unseeing, heedless, ignorant.
(ANT.) sensible, discerning, aware, perceiving.

sign (SYN.) omen, mark, emblem, token, suggestion, indication, clue, hint, approve, authorize, signal, gesture, symbol, portent.

signal (SYN.) beacon, sign, alarm.

significance (SYN.) connotation, drift, acceptation, explanation, implication, gist, importance, interpretation, intent, weight, meaning, purpose, purport, sense, signification.

significant (SYN.) grave, important, critical, material, indicative, meaningful, crucial, momentous, telling, weighty.
(ANT.) irrelevant, insignificant, meaningless, unimportant, negligible.

silent *(SYN.)* dumb, hushed, mute, calm, noiseless, quiet, speechless, tranquil, uncommunicative, taciturn.
(ANT.) communicative, loud, clamorous.

silly *(SYN.)* asinine, brainless, crazy, absurd, foolish, irrational, witless, nonsensical, simple, ridiculous, stupid.
(ANT.) sane, wise, judicious, prudent.

similarity *(SYN.)* likeness, parity, analogy, correspondence, resemblance.
(ANT.) distinction, variance, difference.

simple *(SYN.)* effortless, elementary, pure, easy, facile, mere, single, uncompounded, homely, humble.
(ANT.) artful, complex, intricate, adorned, wise.

simulate *(SYN.)* copy, counterfeit, duplicate, ape, imitate, impersonate, mock.
(ANT.) distort, diverge, alter, invent.

sin *(SYN.)* evil, crime, iniquity, transgress, guilt, offense, ungodliness, trespass, vice, transgression.
(ANT.) purity, goodness, virtue, righteousness.

sinful *(SYN.)* bad, corrupt, dissolute, antisocial, immoral, licentious, profligate, evil, indecent, unprincipled.
(ANT.) pure, noble, virtuous.

single *(SYN.)* individual, marked, particular, distinctive, separate, special, sole, unwed, unmarried, singular, unique.
(ANT.) ordinary, universal, general.

sink *(SYN.)* diminish, droop, extend, downward, drop, descend.
(ANT.) mount, climb, soar, steady, arise.

situation *(SYN.)* circumstance, plight, state, site, location, placement, locale, predicament, position, state, condition.

size *(SYN.)* bigness, bulk, dimensions, expanse, amplitude, measurement, area.

skeptic *(SYN.)* doubter, infidel, agnostic, deist, questioner, unbeliever.
(ANT.) believer, worshiper, adorer.

sketch *(SYN.)* draft, figure, form, outline, contour, delineation, drawing, picture.

skill *(SYN.)* cunning, deftness, cleverness, talent, readiness, skillfulness.
(ANT.) ineptitude, inability.

skin *(SYN.)* outside, covering, peel, rind, shell, pare.

skip *(SYN.)* drop, eliminate, ignore, exclude, cancel, delete, disregard, omit, overlook neglect, miss.
(ANT.) notice, introduce, include, insert.

slander *(SYN.)* libel, calumny, backbiting, aspersion, scandal, vilification.
(ANT.) praise, flattery, commendation, defense.

slant *(SYN.)* disposition, inclination, bias, bent, partiality, slope, tilt, pitch, penchant, prejudice, proneness, lean, tendency.
(ANT.) justice, fairness, impartiality, equity.

slaughter *(SYN.)* butcher, kill, massacre, slay, butchering.

sleep *(SYN.)* drowse, nap, nod, slumber, snooze.

slight *(SYN.)* lank, lean, meager, emaciated, gaunt, fine, tenuous, unimportant, slim.
(ANT.) regard, notice, enormous, large, major, huge.

slim *(SYN.)* thin, slender, lank, slight, weak.

slip *(SYN.)* error, fault, inaccuracy, shift, err, slide, mistake, glide, blunder.
(ANT.) precision, truth, accuracy.

slit *(SYN.)* slash, cut, tear, slot.

slothful *(SYN.)* indolent, idle, inactive, lazy, inert, supine, sluggish, torpid.
(ANT.) alert, diligent, active, assiduous.

slovenly *(SYN.)* sloppy, bedraggled, unkempt, messy.
(ANT.) meticulous, neat.

slow (SYN.) deliberate, dull, delaying, dawdling, gradual, leisurely, tired, sluggish, unhurried, late, behindhand.
(ANT.) rapid, quick, swift, speedy, fast.

sluggish (SYN.) dull, deliberate, dawdling, delaying, laggard, gradual, leisurely, tired, slow, lethargic.
(ANT.) quick, rapid, fast, speedy, swift, energetic, vivacious.

slumber (SYN.) drowse, catnap, nod, doze, repose, sleep, rest, snooze.

slump (SYN.) drop, decline, descent.

small (SYN.) little, minute, petty, diminutive, puny, wee, tiny, trivial, slight, miniature.
(ANT.) immense, enormous, large, huge.

smart (SYN.) dexterous, quick, skillful, adroit, apt, clever, bright, witty, ingenious, sharp, intelligent.
(ANT.) foolish, stupid, unskilled, awkward, clumsy, bungling, slow, dumb.

smell (SYN.) fragrance, fume, odor, perfume, incense, stink, scent, sniff, detect, bouquet.

smite (SYN.) knock, hit, dash, overpower, subdue, vanquish, rout.
(ANT.) surrender, fail, defend, shield.

smooth (SYN.) polished, sleek, slick, glib, diplomatic, flat, level, plain, suave, urbane, even, unwrinkled.
(ANT.) rugged, harsh, rough, blunt, bluff, uneven.

smother (SYN.) suffocate, asphyxiate, stifle.

smutty (SYN.) disgusting, filthy, impure, coarse, dirty, lewd, offensive, obscene, pornographic.
(ANT.) modest, refined, decent, pure.

snappish (SYN.) ill-natured, ill-tempered, fractious, irritable, fretful, peevish, testy, touchy, petulant.

(ANT.) good-tempered, pleasant, good-natured, affable, genial.

snare (SYN.) capture, catch, arrest, clutch, grasp, grip, lay, apprehend, seize, trap, net.
(ANT.) throw, release, lose, liberate.

sneer (SYN.) fleer, flout, jeer, mock, gibe, deride, taunt.
(ANT.) laud, flatter, praise, compliment.

sneering (SYN.) derision, gibe, banter, jeering, mockery, raillery, sarcasm, ridicule, satire.

sniveling (SYN.) whimpering, sniffling, weepy, whining, blubbering.

snug (SYN.) constricted, close, contracted, compact, firm, narrow, taut, tense, stretched, tight, cozy, comfortable, sheltered.
(ANT.) loose, lax, slack, relaxed, open.

soak (SYN.) saturate, drench, steep, wet.

soar (SYN.) flutter, fly, flit, float, glide, sail, hover, mount.
(ANT.) plummet, sink, fall, descend.

sober (SYN.) sedate, serious, staid, earnest, grave, solemn, moderate.
(ANT.) ordinary, joyful, informal, boisterous, drunk, fuddled, inebriated.

social (SYN.) friendly, civil, gregarious, affable, communicative, hospitable, sociable, group, common, genial, polite.
(ANT.) inhospitable, hermitic, antisocial, disagreeable.

society (SYN.) nation, community, civilization, organization, club, association, fraternity, circle, association, company.

soft (SYN.) gentle, lenient, flexible, compassionate, malleable, meek, mellow, subdued, mild, tender, supple, yielding, pliable, elastic, pliant.

(ANT.) *unyielding, rough, hard, rigid.*

soil *(SYN.)* defile, discolor, spot, befoul, blemish, blight, dirty.
(ANT.) *purify, honor, cleanse, bleach.*

solace *(SYN.)* contentment, ease, enjoyment, comfort, consolation, relief.
(ANT.) *torture, torment, misery, affliction, discomfort.*

sole *(SYN.)* isolated, desolate, deserted, secluded, unaided, lone, alone, only, single, solitary.
(ANT.) *surrounded, accompanied.*

solemn *(SYN.)* ceremonious, imposing, formal, impressive, reverential, ritualistic, grave, sedate, earnest, sober, staid, serious, dignified.
(ANT.) *ordinary, joyful, informal, boisterous, cheerful, gay, happy.*

solitary *(SYN.)* isolated, alone, lonely, deserted, unaided, sole.
(ANT.) *surrounded, attended, accompanied.*

somber *(SYN.)* dismal, dark, bleak, doleful, cheerless, natural, physical, serious, sober, gloomy, grave.
(ANT.) *lively, joyous, cheerful, happy.*

soon *(SYN.)* shortly, early, betimes, beforehand.
(ANT.) *tardy, late, overdue, belated.*

soothe *(SYN.)* encourage, console, solace, comfort, cheer, pacify.
(ANT.) *dishearten, depress, antagonize, aggravate, disquiet, upset, unnerve.*

soothing *(SYN.)* gentle, benign, docile, calm, mild, tame.
(ANT.) *violent, savage, fierce, harsh.*

sorcery *(SYN.)* enchantment, conjuring, art, charm, black, magic, voodoo, witchcraft, wizardry.

sorrow *(SYN.)* grief, distress, heartache, anguish, misery, tribulation, gloom, depression.
(ANT.) *consolation, solace, joy, happiness, comfort.*

sorrowful *(SYN.)* dismal, doleful, dejected, despondent, depressed, disconsolate, gloomy, melancholy, grave, aggrieved.
(ANT.) *merry, happy, cheerful, joyous.*

sorry *(SYN.)* hurt, pained, sorrowful, afflicted, grieved, mean, shabby, contemptible, worthless, vile, regretful, apologetic.
(ANT.) *delighted, impenitent, cheerful, unrepentant, splendid.*

sour *(SYN.)* glum, sullen, bitter, peevish, acid, rancid, tart, acrimonious, sharp, bad-tempered, unpleasant, cranky.
(ANT.) *wholesome, kindly, genial, benevolent, sweet.*

source *(SYN.)* birth, foundation, agent, determinant, reason, origin, cause, start, incentive, motive, spring, inducement, principle, beginning.
(ANT.) *product, harvest, outcome, issue, consequence, end.*

souvenir *(SYN.)* memento, monument, commemoration, remembrance.

sovereign *(SYN.)* monarch, king, emperor, queen, empress.

sovereignty *(SYN.)* command, influence, authority, predominance, control, sway.
(ANT.) *debility, incapacity, disablement, ineptitude, impotence.*

space *(SYN.)* room, area, location.

spacious *(SYN.)* capacious, large, vast, ample, extensive, wide, roomy, large.
(ANT.) *limited, confined, nar-*

row, small, cramped.
span (SYN.) spread, extent.
spare (SYN.) preserve, safeguard, uphold, conserve, protect, defend, rescue, reserve, additional, unoccupied.
(ANT.) impair, abolish, injure, abandon.
sparing (SYN.) economical, thrifty, frugal.
(ANT.) lavish.
sparkle (SYN.) gleam, glitter, twinkle, beam, glisten, radiate, shine, blaze.
spat (SYN.) quarrel, dispute, affray, wrangle, altercation.
(ANT.) peace, friendliness, agreement, reconciliation.
spawn (SYN.) yield, bear.
speak (SYN.) declare, express, say, articulate, harangue, converse, talk, utter.
(ANT.) refrain, hush, quiet.
special (SYN.) individual, uncommon, distinctive, peculiar, exceptional, unusual, extraordinary, different.
(ANT.) general, widespread, broad, prevailing, average, ordinary.
specialist (SYN.) authority, expert.
species (SYN.) variety, type, kind, class.
specific (SYN.) limited, characteristic, definite, peculiar, explicit, categorical, particular, distinct, precise.
(ANT.) generic, general, nonspecific.
specify (SYN.) name, call, mention, appoint, denominate, designate, define.
(ANT.) miscall, hint.
specimen (SYN.) prototype, example, sample, model, pattern, type.
speck (SYN.) scrap, jot, bit, mite, smidgen, crumb, iota, particle, spot.
(ANT.) quantity, bulk, aggregate.
spectacle (SYN.) demonstration, ostentation, movie, array, exhibition, show, display, performance, parade, splurge.

spectator (SYN.) viewer, observer.
speculate (SYN.) assume, deduce, surmise, apprehend, imagine, consider, view, think, guess, suppose, conjecture.
(ANT.) prove, demonstrate, conclude.
speech (SYN.) gossip, discourse, talk, chatter, lecture, conference, discussion, address, dialogue, articulation, accent.
(ANT.) silence, correspondence, writing.
speed (SYN.) forward, push, accelerate, hasten, rapidity, dispatch, swiftness.
(ANT.) impede, slow, block, retard.
spellbound (SYN.) fascinated, entranced, hypnotized, mesmerized, rapt.
spend (SYN.) pay, disburse, consume.
(ANT.) hoard, save.
spendthrift (SYN.) squanderer, profligate.
sphere (SYN.) globe, orb, ball, environment, area, domain.
spherical (SYN.) round, curved, globular.
spicy (SYN.) indecent, offcolor.
spin (SYN.) revolve, turn, rotate, whirl, twirl, tell, narrate, relate.
spine (SYN.) vertebrae, backbone.
spineless (SYN.) weak, limp, cowardly.
(ANT.) brave, strong, courageous.
spirit (SYN.) courage, phantom, verve, fortitude, apparition, mood, soul, ghost.
(ANT.) listlessness, substance, languor.
spirited (SYN.) excited, animated, lively, active, vigorous, energetic.
(ANT.) indolent, lazy, sleepy.
spiritless (SYN.) gone, lifeless, departed, dead, insensible, deceased, unconscious.
(ANT.) stirring, alive, living.
spiritual (SYN.) sacred, un-

earthly, holy, divine, immaterial, supernatural.
(ANT.) material, physical, corporeal.

spite *(SYN.)* grudge, rancor, malice, animosity, malevolence, malignity.
(ANT.) kindness, toleration, affection.

spiteful *(SYN.)* vicious, disagreeable, surly, ill-natured.
(ANT.) pretty, beautiful, attractive, fair.

splendid *(SYN.)* glorious, illustrious, radiant, brilliant, showy, superb, bright.
(ANT.) ordinary, mediocre, dull.

splendor *(SYN.)* effulgence, radiance, brightness, luster, magnificence, display.
(ANT.) darkness, obscurity, dullness.

splinter *(SYN.)* fragment, piece, sliver, chip, shiver.

split *(SYN.)* rend, shred, cleave, disunite, sever, break, divide, opening, lacerate.
(ANT.) repair, unite, join, sew.

spoil *(SYN.)* rot, disintegrate, waste, decay, ruin, damage, mold, destroy.
(ANT.) luxuriate, grow, flourish.

spoken *(SYN.)* verbal, pronounced, articulated, vocal, uttered, oral.
(ANT.) written, documentary.

spokesman *(SYN.)* agent, representative.

spontaneous *(SYN.)* impulsive, voluntary, automatic, instinctive, willing, extemporaneous, natural, unconscious.
(ANT.) planned, rehearsed, forced, studied, prepared.

sport *(SYN.)* match, play, amusement, fun, pastime, entertainment, athletics.

sporting *(SYN.)* considerate, fair, sportsmanlike.

spot *(SYN.)* blemish, mark, stain, flaw, blot, location, place, site, splatter.

spotty *(SYN.)* erratic, uneven, irregular.

(ANT.) regular, even.

spout *(SYN.)* spurt, squirt, tube, nozzle.

spray *(SYN.)* splash, spatter, sprinkle.

spread *(SYN.)* unfold, distribute, open, disperse, unroll, unfurl, scatter, jelly.
(ANT.) shut, close, hide, conceal.

sprightly *(SYN.)* blithe, hopeful, vivacious, buoyant, lively, light, nimble.
(ANT.) hopeless, depressed, sullen, dejected, despondent.

spring *(SYN.)* commencement, foundation, start, beginning, inception, jump, cradle, begin, birth, bound, originate.
(ANT.) issue, product, end.

sprinkle *(SYN.)* strew, scatter, rain.

spruce *(SYN.)* orderly, neat, trim, clear.
(ANT.) unkempt, sloppy, dirty.

spry *(SYN.)* brisk, quick, agile, nimble, energetic, supple, alert, active, lively.
(ANT.) heavy, sluggish, inert, clumsy.

spur *(SYN.)* inducement, purpose, cause, motive, impulse, reason, incitement.
(ANT.) effort, action, result, attempt.

squabble *(SYN.)* bicker, debate, altercate, contend, discuss, argue, quarrel.
(ANT.) concede, agree, assent.

squalid *(SYN.)* base, indecent, grimy, dirty, pitiful, filthy, muddy, nasty.
(ANT.) wholesome, clean, pure.

squander *(SYN.)* scatter, lavish, consume, dissipate, misuse.
(ANT.) preserve, conserve, save.

squeamish *(SYN.)* particular, careful.

stab *(SYN.)* stick, gore, pierce, knife, spear, bayonet.

stability *(SYN.)* steadiness, balance, proportion, composure, symmetry.
(ANT.) imbalance, fall, un-

steadiness.

stable *(SYN.)* firm, enduring, constant, fixed, unwavering, steadfast, steady.
(ANT.) irresolute, variable, changeable.

stagger *(SYN.)* totter, sway, reel, vary, falter, alternate.

stain *(SYN.)* blight, dye, tint, befoul, spot, defile, mark, color, tinge.
(ANT.) honor, bleach, decorate, purify.

stale *(SYN.)* tasteless, spoiled, old, inedible, trite, dry, uninteresting, flat, dull.
(ANT.) new, fresh, tasty.

stamp *(SYN.)* crush, trample, imprint, mark, brand, block.

stand *(SYN.)* tolerate, suffer, stay, remain, sustain, rest.
(ANT.) run, yield, advance.

standard *(SYN.)* law, proof, pennant, emblem, touchstone, measure, example.
(ANT.) guess, chance, irregular, unusual.

start *(SYN.)* opening, source, commence, onset, surprise, shock, beginning, origin, begin, initiate, jerk, jump.
(ANT.) completion, termination, close.

starved *(SYN.)* longing, voracious, hungry, craving, avid.
(ANT.) satisfied, sated, gorged.

state *(SYN.)* circumstance, predicament, case, situation, condition, affirm.
(ANT.) imply, conceal, retract.

stately *(SYN.)* lordly, elegant, regal, sovereign, impressive, magnificent, courtly, grand.
(ANT.) low, common, mean, servile, humble, vulgar.

statement *(SYN.)* announcement, mention, allegation, declaration, thesis.

station *(SYN.)* post, depot, terminal, position, place.

statuesque *(SYN.)* imposing, stately, regal, majestic.

status *(SYN.)* place, caste, standing, condition, state.

staunch *(SYN.)* faithful, true, constant, reliable, loyal.
(ANT.) treacherous, untrustworthy.

stay *(SYN.)* delay, continue, hinder, check, hold, hindrance, support, brace, line, rope, linger, sojourn, abide, halt, stand, rest, remain, tarry, arrest, wait.
(ANT.) hasten, progress, go, depart, advance, leave.

stead *(SYN.)* place.

steadfast *(SYN.)* solid, inflexible, constant, stable, unyielding, secure.
(ANT.) unstable, insecure, unsteady.

steadfastness *(SYN.)* persistence, industry, tenacity, constancy, persistency.
(ANT.) laziness, sloth, cessation.

steady *(SYN.)* regular, even, unremitting, stable, steadfast, firm, reliable, solid.

steal *(SYN.)* loot, rob, swipe, burglarize, pilfer, shoplift, embezzle, snitch.
(ANT.) restore, buy, return, refund.

stealthy *(SYN.)* sly, secret, furtive.
(ANT.) direct, open, obvious.

steep *(SYN.)* sharp, hilly, sheer, abrupt, perpendicular, precipitous.
(ANT.) gradual, level, flat.

steer *(SYN.)* manage, guide, conduct, lead, supervise, escort, navigate, drive, control, direct.

stem *(SYN.)* stalk, trunk, arise, check, stop, originate, hinder.

stench *(SYN.)* odor, fetor, fetidness, stink, aroma, smell, fume, scent.

step *(SYN.)* stride, pace, stage, move, action, measure, come, go, walk.

stern *(SYN.)* harsh, rigid, exacting, rigorous, sharp, severe, strict, hard, unyielding, unmitigated, stringent.
(ANT.) indulgent, forgiving, yielding, lenient, considerate.

stew *(SYN.)* ragout, goulash, boil, simmer.

stick *(SYN.)* stalk, twig, rod, staff, pole, pierce, spear, stab, puncture, gore, cling, adhere, hold, catch, abide, remain, persist.

stickler *(SYN.)* nitpicker, perfectionist, disciplinarian.

sticky *(SYN.)* tricky, delicate, awkward.

stiff *(SYN.)* severe, unbendable, unyielding, harsh, inflexible, unbending, rigid, firm, hard, solid, rigorous.
(ANT.) supple, yielding, compassionate, mild, lenient, resilient.

stifle *(SYN.)* choke, strangle, suffocate.

stigma *(SYN.)* trace, scar, blot, stain, mark, vestige.

still *(SYN.)* peaceful, undisturbed, but, mild, hushed, calm, patient, modest, nevertheless, motionless, meek, quiescent, stationary, besides, however, quiet, hush, tranquil, serene, placid.
(ANT.) agitated, perturbed, loud.

stimulate *(SYN.)* irritate, excite, arouse, disquiet, rouse, activate, urge, invigorate, animate, provoke.
(ANT.) quell, calm, quiet, allay.

stimulus *(SYN.)* motive, goad, arousal, provocation, encouragement.
(ANT.) discouragement, depressant.

stingy *(SYN.)* greedy, penurious, avaricious, mean, penny-pinching, cheap, selfish, miserly, tight, tightfisted.
(ANT.) munificent, generous, giving, extravagant, openhanded, bountiful.

stipend *(SYN.)* payment, earnings, salary, allowance, pay, compensation, wages.
(ANT.) gratuity, gift.

stipulate *(SYN.)* require, demand.

stir *(SYN.)* instigate, impel, push, agitate, induce, mix, rouse, move, propel.
(ANT.) halt, stop, deter.

stock *(SYN.)* hoard, store, strain, accumulation, supply, carry, keep, provision, fund, breed, sort.
(ANT.) sameness, likeness, homogeneity, uniformity.

stoical *(SYN.)* passive, forbearing, uncomplaining, composed, patient.
(ANT.) turbulent, chafing, hysterical.

stolid *(SYN.)* obtuse, unsharpened, dull, blunt, edgeless.
(ANT.) suave, tactful, polished, subtle.

stone *(SYN.)* pebble, gravel, rock.

stony *(SYN.)* insensitive, cold.

stoop *(SYN.)* bow, bend, lean, crouch.

stop *(SYN.)* terminate, check, abstain, hinder, arrest, close, bar, cork, halt, end, conclude, obstruct, finish, quit, pause, discontinue, stay, impede, cease.
(ANT.) start, proceed, speed, begin.

store *(SYN.)* amass, hoard, collect, market, shop, reserve, supply, deposit, bank, save, accrue, increase, stock.
(ANT.) dissipate, waste, disperse.

storm *(SYN.)* gale, tempest, tornado, thunderstorm, hurricane, rage, rant, assault, besiege.

stormy *(SYN.)* rough, inclement, windy, blustery, roaring, tempestuous.
(ANT.) quiet, calm, tranquil, peaceful.

story *(SYN.)* yarn, novel, history, tale, falsehood, account, fable, anecdote, narrative, fabrication, lie, level, floor, fiction, report.

stout *(SYN.)* plump, obese, chubby, fat, paunchy, overweight, portly, heavy, sturdy, strong, pudgy, thickset.
(ANT.) thin, slender, flimsy, gaunt, slim.

straight *(SYN.)* erect, honorable, square, just, direct, undeviating, unbent, right, upright, honest, uncurving, directly, moral, correct, orderly, vertical.

(ANT.) *dishonest, bent, circuitous, twisted, crooked.*

straightforward (SYN.) forthright, direct, open, candid, aboveboard.

(ANT.) *devious.*

strait (SYN.) fix, situation, passage, condition, dilemma, channel, trouble, predicament, difficulty, distress, crisis.

(ANT.) *ease, calmness, satisfaction, comfort.*

strange (SYN.) bizarre, peculiar, odd, abnormal, irregular, unusual, curious.

(ANT.) *regular, common, familiar, conventional.*

stranger (SYN.) foreigner, outsider, newcomer, alien, outlander, immigrant.

(ANT.) *friend, associate, acquaintance.*

strap (SYN.) strip, belt, thong, band.

stratagem (SYN.) design, ruse, cabal, plot, machination, subterfuge, trick, wile.

stream (SYN.) issue, proceed, flow, come, abound, spout, run, brook.

strength (SYN.) power, might, toughness, durability, lustiness, soundness, vigor.

(ANT.) *weakness, frailty, feebleness.*

stress (SYN.) urgency, press, emphasize, accentuate, accent, weight, strain, importance, compulsion.

(ANT.) *relaxation, lenience, ease.*

stretch (SYN.) strain, expand, elongate, extend, lengthen, spread, distend, protract.

(ANT.) *tighten, loosen, slacken, contract.*

strict (SYN.) rough, stiff, stringent, harsh, unbending.

(ANT.) *easygoing, lenient.*

strike (SYN.) pound, hit, smite, beat, assault, attack, affect, impress, overwhelm, sitdown, walkout, slowdown.

striking (SYN.) arresting, imposing, splendid, august, impressive, thrilling, stirring, awesome, aweinspiring.

(ANT.) *ordinary, unimpressive, commonplace, regular.*

stringent (SYN.) harsh, rugged, grating, severe, gruff.

strip (SYN.) disrobe, undress, remove, uncover, peel, ribbon, band, piece.

stripped (SYN.) open, simple, bare, nude, uncovered, exposed, bald, plain, naked, barren, defenseless.

(ANT.) *protected, dressed, concealed.*

strive (SYN.) aim, struggle, attempt, undertake, design, endeavor, try.

(ANT.) *omit, abandon, neglect, decline.*

stroke (SYN.) rap, blow, tap, knock, feat, achievement, accomplishment, caress.

stroll (SYN.) amble, walk, ramble.

strong (SYN.) potent, hale, athletic, mighty, sturdy, impregnable, resistant.

(ANT.) *feeble, insipid, brittle, weak, bland, fragile.*

structure (SYN.) construction, frame-work arrangement.

struggle (SYN.) fray, strive, fight, contest, battle, skirmish, oppose, clash.

(ANT.) *peace, agreement, truce.*

stubborn (SYN.) obstinate, firm, determined, inflexible, obdurate, uncompromising, pigheaded, contumacious, rigid, unbending, intractable.

(ANT.) *docile, yielding, amenable.*

student (SYN.) pupil, observer, disciple, scholar, learner.

studio (SYN.) workroom, workshop.

study (SYN.) weigh, muse, master, contemplate, reflect, examination, examine.

stuff (SYN.) thing, subject, material, theme, matter, substance, fill, ram, cram, pack, textile, cloth, topic.

(ANT.) *spirit, immateriality.*

stumble (SYN.) sink, collapse, tumble, drop, topple, lurch, trip, fall.
(ANT.) steady, climb, soar, arise.

stun (SYN.) shock, knock out, dumbfound, take, amaze, alarm.
(ANT.) forewarn, caution, prepare.

stunning (SYN.) brilliant, dazzling, exquisite, ravishing.
(ANT.) drab, ugly.

stunt (SYN.) check, restrict, hinder.

stupid (SYN.) dull, obtuse, half-witted, brainless, foolish, dumb, witless, idiotic.
(ANT.) smart, intelligent, clever, quick, bright, alert, discerning.

stupor (SYN.) lethargy, torpor, daze, languor, drowsiness, numbness.
(ANT.) wakefulness, liveliness, activity.

sturdy (SYN.) hale, strong, rugged, stout, mighty, enduring, hardy, well-built.
(ANT.) fragile, brittle, insipid, delicate.

style (SYN.) sort, type, kind, chic, smartness, elegance.

subdue (SYN.) crush, overcome, rout, beat, reduce, lower, defeat, vanquish.
(ANT.) retreat, cede, surrender.

subject (SYN.) subordinate, theme, case, topic, dependent, citizen, matter.

sublime (SYN.) lofty, raised, elevated, supreme, exalted, splendid, grand.
(ANT.) ordinary, vase, low, ridiculous.

submerge (SYN.) submerse, dunk, sink, dip, immerse, engage, douse, engross.
(ANT.) surface, rise, uplift, elevate.

submissive (SYN.) deferential, yielding, dutiful, compliant.
(ANT.) rebellious, intractable.

submit (SYN.) quit, resign, waive, yield, tender, offer, abdicate, cede, surrender.
(ANT.) fight, oppose, resist,

struggle, deny, refuse.

subordinate (SYN.) demean, reduce, inferior, assistant, citizen, liegeman.
(ANT.) superior.

subsequent (SYN.) later, following.
(ANT.) preceding, previous.

subside (SYN.) decrease, lower, sink, droop, hang, collapse, downward.
(ANT.) mount, steady, arise, climb.

subsidy (SYN.) support, aid, grant.

substance (SYN.) stuff, essence, importance, material, moment, matter.
(ANT.) spirit, immaterial.

substantial (SYN.) large, considerable, sizable, actual, real, tangible, influential.
(ANT.) unimportant, trivial.

substantiate (SYN.) strengthen, corroborate, confirm.

substitute (SYN.) proxy, expedient, deputy, makeshift, replacement, alternate, lieutenant, representative, surrogate, displace, exchange.
(ANT.) sovereign, master.

substitution (SYN.) change, mutation, vicissitude, alteration, modification.
(ANT.) uniformity, monotony.

subterfuge (SYN.) pretext, excuse, cloak, simulation, disguise, garb, pretension.
(ANT.) reality, truth, actuality, sincerity.

subtle (SYN.) suggestive, indirect.
(ANT.) overt, obvious.

subtract (SYN.) decrease, reduce, curtail, deduct, diminish, remove, lessen.
(ANT.) expand, increase, add, enlarge, grow.

succeed (SYN.) thrive, follow, replace, achieve, win, flourish, prevail, inherit.
(ANT.) miscarry, anticipate, fail, precede.

successful (SYN.) fortunate, favorable, triumphant.

succor (SYN.) ease, solace, comfort, consolation.
(ANT.) suffering, discomfort,

torture, affliction, torment.

sudden *(SYN.)* rapid, swift, immediate, abrupt, unexpected, unforeseen, hasty.
(ANT.) slowly, anticipated.

suffer *(SYN.)* stand, experience, endure, bear, feel, allow, let, permit, sustain.
(ANT.) exclude, banish, overcome.

suggest *(SYN.)* propose, offer, recommend, allude.
(ANT.) dictate, declare, insist.

suggestion *(SYN.)* exhortation, recommendation, intelligence, caution, admonition, warning, advice.

suitable *(SYN.)* welcome, agreeable, acceptable, gratifying.
(ANT.) offensive, disagreeable.

sullen *(SYN.)* moody, fretful, surly, crabbed, morose.
(ANT.) merry, gay, pleasant, amiable.

sum *(SYN.)* amount, total, aggregate, whole, increase, append, add.
(ANT.) sample, fraction, reduce, deduct.

summit *(SYN.)* peak, top, crown, pinnacle.
(ANT.) bottom, foundation, base, foot.

sunny *(SYN.)* cheery, cheerful, fair, joyful, happy.
(ANT.) overcast, cloudy.

superficial *(SYN.)* flimsy, shallow, cursory, slight, exterior.
(ANT.) thorough, deep, abstruse, profound.

superior *(SYN.)* greater, finer, better, employer, boss.
(ANT.) inferior.

superiority *(SYN.)* profit, mastery, advantage, good, service, edge, utility.
(ANT.) obstruction, harm, detriment, impediment.

supernatural *(SYN.)* unearthly, marvelous, miraculous.
(ANT.) plain, human, physical, common.

supervise *(SYN.)* rule, oversee, govern, command, direct, superintend, control.
(ANT.) submit, forsake,

abandon.

supervision *(SYN.)* oversight, charge, management.

supervisor *(SYN.)* manager, boss, foreman, director.

supple *(SYN.)* lithe, pliant, flexible, limber, elastic.
(ANT.) stiff, brittle, rigid, unbending.

supplication *(SYN.)* invocation, plea, appeal, request.

supply *(SYN.)* provide, inventory, hoard, reserve, store, accumulation, stock, furnish, endow, give.

support *(SYN.)* groundwork, aid, favor, base, prop, assistance, comfort, basis, succor, living, subsistence, encouragement, backing.
(ANT.) discourage, abandon, oppose, opposition, attack.

suppose *(SYN.)* believe, presume, deduce, apprehend, speculate, guess, conjecture.
(ANT.) prove, demonstrate, ascertain.

suppress *(SYN.)* diminish, reduce, overpower, abate, lessen, decrease, subdue.
(ANT.) revive, amplify, intensify, enlarge.

sure *(SYN.)* confident, fixed, trustworthy, reliable, unquestionable, convinced, stable, firm, safe, solid, destined, fated, inevitable.
(ANT.) probable, uncertain, doubtful.

surface *(SYN.)* outside, exterior, cover, covering.

surly *(SYN.)* disagreeable, hostile, ugly, antagonistic.

surname *(SYN.)* denomination, epithet, title, name, appellation, designation.

surpass *(SYN.)* pass, exceed, excel, outstrip, outdo.

surplus *(SYN.)* extravagance, intemperance, superabundance, excess, immoderation, remainder, extra, profusion, superfluity.
(ANT.) want, lack, dearth, paucity.

surprise *(SYN.)* miracle, prodigy, wonder, awe, marvel.
(ANT.) expectation, triviality,

indifference, familiarity.

surrender *(SYN.)* relinquish, resign, yield, abandon, sacrifice, submit, cede.
(ANT.) overcome, conquer.

surround *(SYN.)* confine, encompass, circle, encircle, girdle, fence, circumscribe.
(ANT.) open, distend, expose.

suspect *(SYN.)* waver, disbelieve, presume, suppose, suspected, assume, doubt.
(ANT.) decide, believe, trust.

suspend *(SYN.)* delay, hang, withhold, interrupt, postpone, dangle, adjourn, poise.
(ANT.) proceed, maintain.

suspicious *(SYN.)* suspecting, distrustful, doubtful, doubting, questioning, suspect.

sustain *(SYN.)* bear, carry, help, advocate, back, encourage, maintain, assist.
(ANT.) discourage, betray, oppose, destroy.

sway *(SYN.)* control, affect, stir, actuate, impel, impress, bend, wave, swing, persuade, influence.

swear *(SYN.)* declare, state, affirm, vouchsafe, curse.
(ANT.) demur, oppose, deny.

sweeping *(SYN.)* extensive, wide, general, broad, tolerant, comprehensive, vast.
(ANT.) restricted, confined.

swift *(SYN.)* quick, fast, fleet, speedy, rapid, expeditious.

swindle *(SYN.)* bilk, defraud, con, deceive, cheat, guile, imposture, deception, artifice, deceit, trick.
(ANT.) sincerity, honesty.

sympathetic *(SYN.)* considerate, compassionate, gentle, affable, merciful.
(ANT.) unkind, merciless, unsympathetic, indifferent, intolerant, cruel.

sympathy *(SYN.)* compassion, commiseration, pity.
(ANT.) indifference, unconcern, antipathy, malevolence.

system *(SYN.)* organization, procedure, regularity, arrangement, mode, order.
(ANT.) confusion, chance, disorder.

table *(SYN.)* catalog, list, schedule, postpone, chart, index, shelve, delay, put off.

taboo *(SYN.)* banned, prohibited, forbidden.
(ANT.) accepted, allowed, sanctioned.

tack *(SYN.)* add, join, attach, clasp, fasten.

tackle *(SYN.)* rigging, gear, apparatus, equipment, grab.

tact *(SYN.)* dexterity, poise, diplomacy, judgment, savoirfaire, skill, finesse.
(ANT.) incompetence, vulgarity, blunder, rudeness, awkwardness, insensitivity.

tactful *(SYN.)* discreet, considerate, judicious, adroit, sensitive, diplomatic.
(ANT.) coarse, gruff, tactless, boorish, unfeeling, rude.

tactical *(SYN.)* foxy, cunning, proficient, deft, adroit.
(ANT.) blundering, gauche, clumsy, inept.

tail *(SYN.)* rear, back, follow, end, shadow, pursue, trail.

tailor *(SYN.)* modiste, couturier, modify, redo, shape.

tainted *(SYN.)* crooked, impure, vitiated, profligate, debased, spoiled, corrupted.

take *(SYN.)* accept, grasp, catch, confiscate, clutch, adopt, assume, receive.

tale *(SYN.)* falsehood, history, yarn, chronicle, account, fable, fiction.

talent *(SYN.)* capability, knack, skill, endowment, ability, cleverness, genius.
(ANT.) ineptitude, incompetence, stupidity.

talk *(SYN.)* conversation, gossip, report, speech, communicate, discuss, confer, chatter, preach, argue, converse, chat, mutter, speak, discussion.
(ANT.) silence, correspondence, meditation, writing.

tall *(SYN.)* elevated, high, towering, big, lofty, imposing.
(ANT.) tiny, low, short, small, stunted.

tame *(SYN.)* domesticated, uninteresting, gentle, sub-

dued, insipid, flat, unexciting, submissive.
(ANT.) spirited, savage, wild, exciting, animated, undomesticated.

tamper (SYN.) mix in, interrupt, interfere, meddle.

tangle (SYN.) confuse, knot, snarl, twist, ensnare, embroil, implicate.

tantalize (SYN.) tease, tempt, entice, titillate, stimulate.

tantrum (SYN.) outburst, fit, fury, flare-up, conniption.

tardy (SYN.) slow, delayed, overdue, late, belated.
(ANT.) prompt, timely, punctual, early.

tarnish (SYN.) discolor, blight, defile, sully, spot, befoul, disgrace, stain.
(ANT.) honor, purify, cleanse, gleam, sparkle.

tarry (SYN.) dawdle, loiter, linger, dally, remain, delay.

tart (SYN.) sour, acrid, pungent, acid, sharp, distasteful, bitter.
(ANT.) mellow, sweet, delicious, pleasant.

task (SYN.) work, job, undertaking, labor, chore, duty.

taste (SYN.) tang, inclination, liking, sensibility, flavor, savor, try, sip, sample, zest.
(ANT.) indelicacy, disinclination, antipathy, insipidity.

tasteful (SYN.) elegant, choice, refined, suitable, artistic.
(ANT.) offensive, unbecoming.

tasteless (SYN.) flavorless, insipid, unpalatable, rude, unrefined, uncultivated.

tattered (SYN.) ragged, torn, frayed, tacky, seedy.

taunt (SYN.) tease, deride, annoy, pester, bother, ridicule, jeer.
(ANT.) praise, compliment, laud, flatter.

taut (SYN.) tight, constricted, firm, stretched, snug, tense.
(ANT.) slack, loose, relaxed, open, lax.

tax (SYN.) duty, assessment, strain, tribute, tariff, assess, encumber, overload, im-

post, custom, exaction, ra muneration, wages.
(ANT.) reward, gift, re muneration, wages.

teach (SYN.) inform, school, educate, train, inculcate, instruct, instill, tutor.
(ANT.) misinform, misguide.

teacher (SYN.) tutor, instructor, professor, lecturer.

team (SYN.) company, band, party, crew, gang, group.

tear (SYN.) rend, shred, sunder, cleave, rip, lacerate, divide, drop, wound, split.
(ANT.) mend, repair, join, unite, sew.

tease (SYN.) badger, harry, taunt, vex, annoy, disturb, plague, aggravate, provoke.
(ANT.) please, delight, soothe, comfort, gratify.

technical (SYN.) industrial, technological, specialized.

technique (SYN.) system, method, routine, approach.

tedious (SYN.) boring, dilatory, humdrum, sluggish, dreary, dull, tiring, burdensome, tiresome, wearisome.
(ANT.) interesting, entertaining, engaging, exciting, amusing, quick.

teeter (SYN.) sway, hesitate, hem and haw, waver.

tell (SYN.) report, mention, state, betray, announce, recount, relate, narrate, rehearse, mention, utter, confess, disclose, direct.

temerity (SYN.) rashness, foolhardiness, audacity, boldness, recklessness.
(ANT.) prudence, wariness, caution, hesitation, timidity.

temper (SYN.) fury, choler, exasperation, anger, passion, petulance, disposition, nature, rage, soothe, soften.
(ANT.) peace, self-control, forbearance, conciliation.

temperance (SYN.) abstinence, sobriety, self-denial, forbearance, abstention.
(ANT.) intoxication, excess, self-indulgence, gluttony, wantonness.

tempest (SYN.) draft, squall, hurricane, commotion, tu-

...ault, zephyr.
(ANT.) *calm, tranquillity, peace.*

temporal (SYN.) mundane, earthly, lay, profane, worldly, terrestrial, laic.
(ANT.) *spiritual, ecclesiastical, unworldly, heavenly.*

temporary (SYN.) brief, momentary, shortlived, fleeting, ephemeral, passing, short, transient.
(ANT.) *lasting, permanent, immortal, everlasting, timeless, abiding.*

tenable (SYN.) correct, practical, rational, reasonable, sensible, defensible.

tenacity (SYN.) perseverance, steadfastness, industry, constancy, persistence.
(ANT.) *laziness, rest, cessation, idleness, sloth.*

tenant (SYN.) renter, lessee, lodger, lease-holder, dweller, resident.

tend (SYN.) follow, care for, lackey, watch, protect, take care of, attend.

tendency (SYN.) drift, inclination, proneness, leaning, bias, aim, leaning, disposition, predisposition, propensity, trend, impulse.
(ANT.) *disinclination, aversion, deviation.*

tender (SYN.) sympathetic, sore, sensitive, painful, gentle, meek, delicate, fragile, proffer, bland, mild, loving.
(ANT.) *rough, severe, fierce, chewy, tough, cruel, unfeeling, harsh.*

tenet (SYN.) dogma, belief.

tense (SYN.) strained, stretched, excited, tight.
(ANT.) *loose, placid, lax, relaxed.*

tension (SYN.) stress, strain, pressure, anxiety, apprehension, distress.

tenure (SYN.) administration, time, regime, term.

term (SYN.) period, limit, time, boundary, duration, name, phrase, interval, session, semester, expression.

terminal (SYN.) eventual,

final, concluding, decisive, ending, fatal, latest, last, ultimate, conclusive.
(ANT.) *original, first, rudimentary, incipient, inaugural.*

terminate (SYN.) close, end, finish, abolish, complete, cease, stop, conclude, expire, culminate.
(ANT.) *establish, begin, initiate, start, commence.*

terminology (SYN.) vocabulary, nomenclature, terms, phraseology.

terms (SYN.) stipulations, agreement, conditions, provisions.

terrible (SYN.) frightful, dire, awful, gruesome, horrible, shocking, horrifying, terrifying, horrid, hideous, appalling.
(ANT.) *secure, happy, joyous, pleasing, safe.*

terrific (SYN.) superb, wonderful, glorious, great, magnificent, divine, colossal, sensational, marvelous.

terrify (SYN.) dismay, intimidate, startle, terrorize, appall, frighten, petrify, astound, alarm, affright, horrify, scare.
(ANT.) *soothe, allay, reassure, compose, embolden.*

territory (SYN.) dominion, province, quarter, section, country, division, region, domain, area, place, district.

terror (SYN.) fear, alarm, dismay, horror, dread, consternation, fright, panic.
(ANT.) *calm, security, assurance, peace.*

terse (SYN.) concise, incisive, succinct, summary, condensed, compact, neat, pithy, summary.
(ANT.) *verbose, wordy, lengthy, prolix.*

test (SYN.) exam, examination, trial, quiz, analyze, verify, validate.

testify (SYN.) depose, warrant, witness, state, attest, swear.

testimony (SYN.) evidence, attestation, declaration, witness, confirmation.

(ANT.) refutation, argument, disproof, contradiction.

testy *(SYN.)* ill-natured, irritable, snappish, waspish, fractious, fretful, touchy, ill-tempered, peevish, petulant.

(ANT.) pleasant, affable, good-tempered, genial, good-natured.

tether *(SYN.)* tie, hamper, restraint, bridle.

text *(SYN.)* textbook, book, manual.

textile *(SYN.)* material, cloth, goods, fabric.

texture *(SYN.)* construction, structure, make-up, composition, grain, finish.

thankful *(SYN.)* obliged, grateful, appreciative.

(ANT.) thankless, ungrateful, resenting.

thaw *(SYN.)* liquefy, melt, dissolve.

(ANT.) solidify, freeze.

theater *(SYN.)* arena, playhouse, battlefield, stadium, hall.

theatrical *(SYN.)* ceremonious, melodramatic, stagy, artificial, affected, dramatic, showy, dramatic, compelling.

(ANT.) unemotional, subdued, modest, unaffected.

theft *(SYN.)* larceny, robbery, stealing, plunder, burglary, pillage, thievery, depredation.

theme *(SYN.)* motive, topic, argument, subject, thesis, text, point, paper, essay, composition.

theoretical *(SYN.)* bookish, learned, scholarly, pedantic, academic, formal, erudite, scholastic.

(ANT.) practical, ignorant, commonsense, simple.

theory *(SYN.)* doctrine, guess, presupposition, postulate, assumption, hypothesis, speculation.

(ANT.) practice, verity, fact, proof.

therefore *(SYN.)* consequently, thence so, accordingly,

hence, then.

thick *(SYN.)* compressed, heavy, compact, viscous, close, concentrated, crowded, syrupy, dense.

(ANT.) watery, slim, thin, sparse, dispersed, dissipated.

thief *(SYN.)* burglar, robber, criminal.

thin *(SYN.)* diluted, flimsy, lean, narrow, slender, spare, emaciated, diaphanous, gauzy, meager, slender, tenuous, slim, rare, sparse, scanty, lank, gossamer, slight.

(ANT.) fat, wide, broad, thick, bulky.

think *(SYN.)* picture, contemplate, ponder, esteem, intend, mean, imagine, deliberate, contemplate, recall, speculate, recollect, deem, apprehend, consider, devise, plan, judge, purpose, reflect, suppose, assume, meditate, muse.

(ANT.) forget, conjecture, guess.

thirst *(SYN.)* appetite, desire, craving, longing.

thirsty *(SYN.)* arid, dry, dehydrated, parched, craving, desirous.

(ANT.) satisfied.

thorn *(SYN.)* spine, barb, prickle, nettle, bramble.

thorough *(SYN.)* entire, complete, perfect, total, finished, unbroken, perfect, careful, thoroughgoing, consummate, undivided.

(ANT.) unfinished, careless, slapdash, imperfect, haphazard, lacking.

thoroughfare *(SYN.)* avenue, street, parkway, highway, boulevard.

(ANT.) byway.

though *(SYN.)* in any case, notwithstanding, however, nevertheless.

thought *(SYN.)* consideration, pensive, attentive, heedful, prudent, dreamy, reflective, introspective, meditation, notion, view, deliberation, sentiment, fancy, idea, im-

pression, reasoning, contemplation, judgment, regard.
(ANT.) thoughtlessness.

thoughtful (SYN.) considerate, attentive, dreamy, pensive, provident, introspective, meditative, cautious, heedful, kind, courteous, friendly, pensive.
(ANT.) thoughtless, heedless, inconsiderate, rash, precipitous, selfish.

thoughtless (SYN.) inattentive, unconcerned, negligent, lax, desultory, inconsiderate, careless, imprudent, inaccurate, neglectful, indiscreet, remiss.
(ANT.) meticulous, accurate, nice, careful.

thrash (SYN.) whip, beat, defeat, flog, punish, flog, strap, thresh.

thread (SYN.) yarn, strand, filament, fiber, string, cord.

threadbare (SYN.) shabby, tacky, worn, ragged, frayed.

threat (SYN.) menace, warning, danger, hazard, jeopardy, omen.

threaten (SYN.) caution, warning, forewarn, menace, intimidate, loom.

threatening (SYN.) imminent, nigh, approaching, impending, overhanging, sinister, foreboding.
(ANT.) improbable, retreating, afar, distant, remote.

threshold (SYN.) edge, verge, start, beginning, doorsill, commencement.

thrift (SYN.) prudence, conservation, saving, economy.

thrifty (SYN.) saving, economical, sparing, frugal, provident, stingy, saving, parsimonious.
(ANT.) wasteful, spendthrift, intemperate, self-indulgent, extravagant.

thrill (SYN.) arouse, rouse, excite, stimulation, excitement, tingle.
(ANT.) bore.

thrive (SYN.) succeed, flourish, grow, prosper.

(ANT.) expire, fade, shrivel, die, fail, languish.

throb (SYN.) pound, pulsate, palpitate, beat, pulse.

throe (SYN.) pang, twinge, distress, suffering, pain, ache, grief, agony.
(ANT.) pleasure, relief, ease, solace, comfort.

throng (SYN.) masses, press, crowd, bevy, populace, swarm, rabble, horde, host, mass, teem, mob, multitude.

throttle (SYN.) smother, choke, strangle.

through (SYN.) completed, done, finished, over.

throughout (SYN.) all over, everywhere, during.

throw (SYN.) propel, cast, pitch, toss, hurl, send, thrust, fling.
(ANT.) retain, pull, draw, haul, hold.

thrust (SYN.) jostle, push, promote, crowd, force, drive, hasten, push, press, shove, urge.
(ANT.) ignore, falter, retreat, drag, oppose, halt.

thug (SYN.) mobster, hoodlum, mugger, gangster, assassin, gunman.

thump (SYN.) blow, strike, knock, jab, poke, pound, beat, clout, bat, rap, bang.

thunderstruck (SYN.) amazed, astounded, astonished, awed, flabbergasted, surprised, dumbfounded, bewildered, spellbound.

thus (SYN.) hence, therefore, accordingly, so, consequently.

thwart (SYN.) defeat, frustrate, prevent, foil, stop, baffle, circumvent hinder, obstruct, disappoint, balk, outwit.
(ANT.) promote, accomplish, fulfill, help, further.

ticket (SYN.) stamp, label, tag, seal, token, pass, summons, certificate, ballot, sticker, slate, citation.

tickle (SYN.) delight, entertain, thrill, amuse, titillate, excite.

ticklish *(SYN.)* fragile, delicate, tough, difficult.

tidings *(SYN.)* message, report, information, word, intelligence, news.

tidy *(SYN.)* trim, clear, neat, precise, spruce, orderly, shipshape.
(ANT.) disheveled, unkempt, sloppy, dirty, slovenly.

tie *(SYN.)* bond, join, relationship, bind, restrict, fetter, connect, conjunction, association, alliance, union, fasten, engage, attach, restrain, oblige, link, affinity.
(ANT.) separation, disunion, unfasten, open, loose, untie, free, isolation.

tier *(SYN.)* line, row, level, deck, layer.

tiff *(SYN.)* bicker, squabble, argue, row, clash, dispute, altercation.

tight *(SYN.)* firm, taut, penny-pinching, constricted, snug, taut, parsimonious, secure, fast, strong, sealed, fastened, watertight, locked, close, compact, stingy.
(ANT.) slack, lax, open, relaxed, loose.

till *(SYN.)* plow, work, money-box, depository, cultivate, vault.

tilt *(SYN.)* slant, slope, incline, tip, lean.

timber *(SYN.)* lumber, wood, logs.

time *(SYN.)* epoch, span, term, age, duration, interim, period, tempo, interval, space, spell, season.

timeless *(SYN.)* unending, lasting, perpetual, endless, immemorial.
(ANT.) temporary, mortal, temporal.

timely *(SYN.)* prompt, exact, punctual, ready, precise.
(ANT.) slow, dilatory, tardy, late.

timepiece *(SYN.)* clock, watch.

timetable *(SYN.)* list, schedule.

timid *(SYN.)* coy, humble, sheepish, abashed, embar-

rassed, modest, bashful, confident, shamefaced, retir, fearful, faint-hearted, s, timorous.
(ANT.) gregarious, bold, daring, adventurous, fearless, outgoing.

tinge *(SYN.)* color, tint, dye, stain, flavor, imbue, season, impregnate.

tingle *(SYN.)* shiver, chime, prickle.

tinker *(SYN.)* potter, putter, fiddle with, dawdle, dally, dabble.

tinkle *(SYN.)* sound, peal, ring, jingle, chime, toll.

tint *(SYN.)* color, tinge, dye, stain, hue, tone, shade.

tiny *(SYN.)* minute, little, petty, wee, slight, diminutive, miniature, small, insignificant, trivial, puny.
(ANT.) huge, large, immense, big, enormous.

tip *(SYN.)* point, end, top, peak, upset, tilt, reward, gift, gratuity, clue, hint, suggestion, inkling.

tirade *(SYN.)* outburst, harangue, scolding.

tire *(SYN.)* jade, tucker, bore, weary, exhaust, weaken, wear out, fatigue.
(ANT.) restore, revive, exhilarate, amuse, invigorate, refresh.

tired *(SYN.)* weary, exhausted, fatigued, run-down, sleepy, faint, spent, wearied, worn, jaded.
(ANT.) rested, fresh, hearty, invigorated, energetic, tireless, eager.

tireless *(SYN.)* active, enthusiastic, energetic, strenuous.
(ANT.) exhausted, wearied, fatigued.

tiresome *(SYN.)* dull, boring, monotonous, tedious.
(ANT.) interesting.

titan *(SYN.)* colossus, powerhouse, mammoth.

title *(SYN.)* epithet, privilege, name, appellation, claim, denomination, due.

toil *(SYN.)* labor, drudgery,

...rk, travail, performance, ...siness, achievement, employment, occupation, slave. ANT.) recreation, ease, vacation, relax, loll, play, repose.

...oken (SYN.) mark, sign, sample, indication, evidence, symbol.

tolerate (SYN.) endure, allow, bear, authorize, permit, brook, stand, abide. (ANT.) forbid, protest, prohibit, discriminating, unreasonable.

tone (SYN.) noise, sound, mood, manner, expression.

tongue (SYN.) diction, lingo, cant, jargon, vernacular, phraseology. (ANT.) nonsense, drivel, babble, gibberish.

tool (SYN.) devise, medium, apparatus, agent, implement, utensil, agent, vehicle. (ANT.) preventive, hindrance, impediment, obstruction.

top (SYN.) crown, pinnacle, peak, tip, cover, cap, zenith, apex, crest, chief, head. (ANT.) bottom, foundation, base, foot.

topic (SYN.) subject, thesis, issue, argument, matter.

torpid (SYN.) sluggish, idle, slothful, indolent, motionless, lethargic. (ANT.) alert, assiduous, diligent, active.

torrid (SYN.) scorching, ardent, impetuous, passionate, scalding, warm, fiery, hot-blooded, sultry, tropical, intense, sweltering. (ANT.) passionless, impassive, cold, frigid, apathetic, freezing, indifferent, temperate.

torture (SYN.) anguish, badger, plague, distress, ache, throe, afflict, misery. (ANT.) aid, relief, comfort, ease, encourage, mitigation.

toss (SYN.) throw, cast, hurl, pitch, tumble, thrust, fling. (ANT.) retain, pull, draw, haul, hold.

total (SYN.) entire, complete, concluded, finished, thorough, whole, entirely, collection, aggregate, perfect. (ANT.) part, element, imperfect, unfinished, ingredient, particular, lacking.

touch (SYN.) finger, feel, handle, move, affect, concern, mention, hint, trace, ability, talent.

touchy (SYN.) snappish, irritable, fiery, choleric, testy, hot, irascible, nervous, excitable, petulant, sensitive. (ANT.) composed, agreeable, tranquil, calm, serene, cool.

tough (SYN.) sturdy, difficult, trying, vicious, incorrigible, troublesome, hard, stout, leathery, strong, laborious. (ANT.) vulnerable, submissive, easy, tender, frail.

tour (SYN.) rove, travel, go, visit, excursion, ramble. (ANT.) stop, stay.

tournament (SYN.) tourney, match, contest, competition.

tow (SYN.) tug, take out, unsheathe, haul, draw, remove, extract, pull, drag. (ANT.) propel, drive.

town (SYN.) hamlet, village, community, municipality.

toxic (SYN.) deadly, poisonous, fatal, lethal, harmful. (ANT.) beneficial.

toy (SYN.) play, romp, frolic, gamble, stake, caper, plaything, wager, revel.

trace (SYN.) stigma, feature, scar, sign, trial, trace, suggestion, characteristic, vestige, symptoms.

track (SYN.) persist, pursue, trace, path, route, road, carry, hunt, chase. (ANT.) escape, evade, abandon, flee, elude.

tractable (SYN.) yielding, deferential, submissive, dutiful, compliant, obedient. (ANT.) rebellious, intractable, insubordinate, obstinate.

trade (SYN.) business, traffic, occupation, profession, livelihood, barter, exchange.

tradition (SYN.) custom, legend, folklore, belief, rite

traduce (SYN.) defame,

malign, vilify, revile, abuse.
(ANT.) protect, honor, cherish, respect, support, extol.

tragedy (SYN.) unhappiness, misfortune, misery, adversity, catastrophe.

trail (SYN.) persist, pursue, chase, follow, drag, draw, hunt, track.
(ANT.) evade, flee, abandon, elude, escape.

train (SYN.) direct, prepare, tutor, bid, instruct, order.
(ANT.) distract, deceive, misguide, misdirect.

trait (SYN.) characteristic, feature, attribute, peculiarity, mark, quality, property.

traitor (SYN.) turncoat, betrayer, spy, double-dealer, conspirator.

tranquil (SYN.) composed, calm, dispassionate, imperturbable, peaceful, pacific, undisturbed, unruffled.
(ANT.) frantic, stormy, excited, disturbed, upset, turbulent, wild.

transcend (SYN.) overstep, overshadow, exceed.

transfer (SYN.) dispatch, send, transmit, remove, transport, transplant, consign, move, shift, reassign.

transform (SYN.) change, convert, alter, modify, transfigure, shift, vary, veer.
(ANT.) establish, continue, settle, preserve, stabilize.

transient (SYN.) ephemeral, evanescent, brief, fleeting, momentary, temporary.
(ANT.) immortal, abiding, permanent, lasting, timeless.

transmit (SYN.) confer, convey, communicate, divulge, disclose, impart, send, inform, relate, notify, reveal, dispatch, tell.
(ANT.) withhold, hide, conceal.

transparent (SYN.) crystalline, clear, limpid, lucid, manifest, plain, evident, explicit, obvious, open.
(ANT.) opaque, muddy, turbid, thick, ambiguous.

transpire (SYN.) befall, be-

chance, betide, happen.

transport (SYN.) carry, bear, enrapture, transfer, lift, entrance, ravish, stimulate.

trap (SYN.) artifice, bait, ambush, intrigue, net, lure, pitfall, ensnare, deadfall, ruse, entrap, bag, trick, stratagem.

trash (SYN.) refuse, garbage, rubbish, waste.

trauma (SYN.) ordeal, upheaval, shock, disturbance.

travail (SYN.) suffering, torment, anxiety, distress, anguish, misery, ordeal.

travel (SYN.) journey, go, touring, ramble, rove, voyage, cruise, tour, roam.
(ANT.) stop, stay, remain, hibernate.

treasure (SYN.) cherish, hold dear, abundance, guard, prize, appreciate, value.
(ANT.) disregard, neglect, dislike, abandon, reject.

treat (SYN.) employ, avail, manipulate, exploit, operate, utilize, exert, act, exercise, practice, handle.
(ANT.) neglect, overlook, ignore, waste.

tremendous (SYN.) enormous, huge, colossal, gigantic, great, large.

trenchant (SYN.) clear, emphatic, forceful, impressive.

trend (SYN.) inclination, tendency, drift, course, tendency, direction.

trial (SYN.) experiment, ordeal, proof, test, examination, attempt, effort, endeavor, essay, affliction, misery.
(ANT.) consolation, alleviation.

tribulation (SYN.) anguish, distress, agony, grief, misery, sorrow, torment, suffering, woe, disaster, calamity, evil, trouble, misfortune.
(ANT.) elation, delight, joy, fun, pleasure.

trick (SYN.) artifice, antic, fraud, hoax, guile, imposture, ruse, ploy, stratagem, trickery, deceit, jest, joke.
(ANT.) exposure, candor, openness, honesty, sincerity.

icky (SYN.) artifice, antic, furtive, guileful, insidious, sly, shrews, stealthy, surreptitious, subtle, underhand.
(ANT.) frank, candid, ingenuous, sincere, open.

trigger (SYN.) generate, provoke, prompt, motivate, activate.

trim (SYN.) nice, clear, orderly, precise, tidy, spruce, adorn, bedeck, clip, shave, prune, cut, shear, compact, neat, decorate, embellish, garnish.
(ANT.) deface, deform, spoil, mar, important, serious, momentous, weighty.

trimmings (SYN.) accessories, adornments, decorations, garnish, ornaments.

trinket (SYN.) bead, token, memento, bauble, charm, knick-knack.

trio (SYN.) threesome, triad, triple.

trip (SYN.) expedition, cruise, stumble, err, journey, jaunt, passage, blunder, bungle, slip, excursion, tour, pilgrimage, voyage, travel.

trite (SYN.) common, banal, hackneyed, ordinary, stereotyped, stale.
(ANT.) modern, fresh, momentous, stimulating, new.

triumph (SYN.) conquest, achievement, success, prevail, win, jubilation, victory, ovation.
(ANT.) succumb, failure, defeat.

triumphant (SYN.) celebrating, exultant, joyful, exhilarated, smug.

trivial (SYN.) insignificant, frivolous, paltry, petty, trifling, small, unimportant.
(ANT.) momentous, important weighty, serious.

troops (SYN.) militia, troopers, recruits, soldiers, enlisted men.

trophy (SYN.) award, memento, honor, testimonial, prize.

tropical (SYN.) sultry, sweltering, humid, torrid.

trouble (SYN.) anxiety, affliction, calamity, distress, hardship, grief, pain, misery, sorrow, woe, bother, annoyance, care, embarrassment, irritation, torment, pains, worry, disorder, problem, disturbance, care, effort, exertion, toil, inconvenience, misfortune, labor.
(ANT.) console, accommodate, gratify, soothe, joy, peace.

troublemaker (SYN.) rebel, scamp, agitator, demon.

troublesome (SYN.) bothersome, annoying, distressing, irksome, disturbing, trying, arduous, vexatious, difficult.
(ANT.) amusing, accommodating, easy, pleasant.

trounce (SYN.) lash, flog, switch, whack, punish, whip.

truant (SYN.) delinquent, absentee, vagrant, malingerer.

truce (SYN.) armistice, ceasefire, interval, break, intermission, respite.

trudge (SYN.) march, trek, lumber, hike.

true (SYN.) actual, authentic, accurate, correct, exact, genuine, real, veracious, veritable, constant, honest, faithful, loyal, reliable, valid, legitimate, steadfast, sincere, trustworthy.
(ANT.) erroneous, counterfeit, false, spurious, fictitious, faithless, inconstant, fickle.

truly (SYN.) indeed, actually, precisely, literally, really, factually.

truncate (SYN.) prune, clip, pare, shorten.

truss (SYN.) girder, brace, framework, shoring.

trust (SYN.) credence, confidence, dependence, reliance, faith, trust, depend on, rely on, reckon on, believe, hope, credit, commit, entrust, confide.
(ANT.) incredulity, doubt, skepticism, mistrust.

trusted (SYN.) trustworthy, reliable, true, loyal, staunch, devoted.

trustworthy 179

trustworthy (SYN.) dependable, certain, reliable, secure, safe, sure, tried, trust.
(ANT.) fallible, dubious, questionable, unreliable, uncertain.

truth (SYN.) actuality, authenticity, accuracy, correctness, exactness, honesty, fact, rightness, truthfulness.
(ANT.) falsity, falsehood, fiction, lie, untruth.

truthful (SYN.) frank, candid, honest, sincere, open, veracious, accurate, correct.
(ANT.) misleading, sly, deceitful.

try (SYN.) endeavor, attempt, strive, struggle, undertake, afflict, test, prove, torment, trouble, essay, examine.
(ANT.) decline, ignore, abandon, omit, neglect, comfort, console.

trying (SYN.) bothersome, annoying, distressing, irksome, disturbing, troublesome, arduous, vexatious, burdensome, difficult, tedious.
(ANT.) amusing, easy, accommodating, pleasant, gratifying.

tryst (SYN.) rendezvous, meeting, appointment.

tube (SYN.) hose, pipe, reed.

tubular (SYN.) hollow, cylindrical.

tuck (SYN.) crease, fold, gather, bend.

tuft (SYN.) bunch, group, cluster.

tug (SYN.) pull, wrench, tow, haul, draw, yank, jerk.

tuition (SYN.) instruction, schooling, teaching, education.

tumble (SYN.) toss, trip, fall, sprawl, wallow, lurch, flounder, plunge, topple, stumble.

tumble-down (SYN.) ramshackle, decrepit, brokendown, dilapidated, rickety.

tumult (SYN.) chaos, agitation, commotion, confusion, disarray, disarrangement, disorder, noise, hubbub, ferment, stir, to-do, ado, jumble, disturbance, uproar, turmoil.
(ANT.) peacefulness, order, peace, certainty, tranquillity.

tune (SYN.) song, concord, harmony, air, melody.
(ANT.) aversion, discord, antipathy.

tunnel (SYN.) passage, grotto, cave.

turbid (SYN.) dark, cloudy, thick, muddy, murky.

turbulent (SYN.) gusty, blustery, inclement, rough, roaring, stormy, tempestuous, disorderly, violent, tumultuous, unruly, windy.
(ANT.) clear, calm, quiet, peaceful, tranquil.

turf (SYN.) lawn, grassland, sod, grass.

turmoil (SYN.) chaos, agitation, commotion, confusion, disarray, disarrangement, disorder, jumble, uproar, ferment, stir, pandemonium, tumult.
(ANT.) order, peace, certainty, quiet, tranquillity.

turn (SYN.) circulate, circle, invert, rotate, revolve, spin, twist, twirl, whirl, wheel, avert, reverse, become, sour, spoil, ferment, deviate, deflect, divert, swerve, change, alter, transmute.
(ANT.) fix, stand, arrest, stop, continue, endure, proceed, perpetuate.

turncoat (SYN.) renegade, defector, deserter, rat, betrayer, traitor.
(ANT.) loyalist.

turret (SYN.) watchtower, belfry, steeple, tower, cupola, lookout.

tussle (SYN.) wrestle, struggle, contend, battle, fight, scuffle.

tutor (SYN.) instruct, prime, school, teach, train, prepare, drill.

tweak (SYN.) squeeze, pinch, nip.

twig (SYN.) sprig, branch, shoot, stem.

light *(SYN.)* sunset, sundown, nightfall, eventide, dusk.

.win *(SYN.)* lookalike, imitation, copy, double, replica, duplicate, match, likeness.

twine *(SYN.)* string, cordage, rope, cord.

twinge *(SYN.)* smart, pang, pain.

twinkle *(SYN.)* shine, gleam, glisten, sparkle, glitter, shimmer, scintillate.

twirl *(SYN.)* rotate, spin, wind, turn, pivot, wheel, swivel, whirl.

twist *(SYN.)* bow, bend, crook, intertwine, curve, incline, deflect, lean, braid, distort, contort, warp, interweave, stoop, turn.
(ANT.) resist, break, straighten, stiffen.

twitch *(SYN.)* fidget, shudder, jerk.

two-faced *(SYN.)* deceitful, insincere, hypocritical, false, untrustworthy.
(ANT.) straightforward, honest.

tycoon *(SYN.)* millionaire, industrialist, businessman.

tyke *(SYN.)* rascal, urchin, brat, ragamuffin, imp.

typhoon *(SYN.)* hurricane, cyclone, storm, tornado, whirlwind, twister.

typical *(SYN.)* common, accustomed, conventional, familiar, customary, habitual ordinary, characteristic, normal, plain, representative, regular, symbolic, usual, vulgar.
(ANT.) marvelous, extraordinary, remarkable, odd, atypical, uncommon, strange.

typify *(SYN.)* symbolize, illustrate, signify, represent, incarnate, indicate.

tyrannous *(SYN.)* arbitrary, absolute, authoritative.
(ANT.) conditional, accountable, contingent, qualified, dependent.

tyrant *(SYN.)* dictator, autocrat, despot, oppressor, slave driver, martinet.

ugly *(SYN.)* hideous, homely, plain, deformed, repellent, unpleasant, wicked.
(ANT.) beautiful, fair, pretty, attractive, handsome.

ultimate *(SYN.)* extreme, latest, final, concluding, decisive, hindmost, last.
(ANT.) foremost, opening, first, beginning, initial.

unadulterated *(SYN.)* genuine, clear, clean, immaculate, spotless, pure.
(ANT.) foul, sullied, corrupt, tainted, polluted, tarnished.

unalterable *(SYN.)* fixed, unchangeable, steadfast.

unassuming *(SYN.)* humble, lowly, compliant, modest, plain, meek, simple.
(ANT.) haughty, showy, pompous, proud, vain, arrogant.

unattached *(SYN.)* apart, separate, unmarried, single, free, independent.
(ANT.) committed, involved.

unavoidable *(SYN.)* inescapable, certain, inevitable.

unbalanced *(SYN.)* crazy, mad, insane, deranged.

unbearable *(SYN.)* insufferable, intolerable.
(ANT.) tolerable, acceptable.

unbeliever *(SYN.)* dissenter, apostate, heretic, schismatic, nonconformist, sectary.

unbending *(SYN.)* firm, inflexible, decided, determined.
(ANT.) flexible.

unbiased *(SYN.)* honest, equitable, fair, impartial, reasonable, unprejudiced, just.
(ANT.) partial, fraudulent, dishonorable.

unbroken *(SYN.)* complete, uninterrupted, continuous.

unburden *(SYN.)* clear, disentangle, divest, free.

uncertain *(SYN.)* dim, hazy, indefinite, obscure, indistinct, undetermined.
(ANT.) explicit, lucid, specific, certain, unmistakable.

uncertainty *(SYN.)* distrust, doubt, hesitation, incredulity, scruple, ambiguity.
(ANT.) faith, belief, certainty, conviction, determination.

uncivil (SYN.) impolite, rude, discourteous.
(ANT.) polite.
unclad (SYN.) exposed, nude, naked, bare, stripped, defenseless, uncovered, open.
(ANT.) concealed, protected, clothed, covered, dressed.
uncommon (SYN.) unusual, rare, odd, scarce, strange, peculiar, queer, exceptional.
(ANT.) ordinary, usual.
unconcern (SYN.) disinterestedness, impartiality, indifference, apathy.
(ANT.) affection, fervor, passion, ardor.
unconditional (SYN.) unqualified, unrestricted, arbitrary, absolute, pure, complete, actual, authoritative.
(ANT.) conditional, contingent, accountable, dependent, qualified.
unconscious (SYN.) lethargic, numb, comatose.
uncouth (SYN.) green, harsh, crude, coarse, ill-prepared, rough, raw, unfinished.
(ANT.) well-prepared, cultivated, refined, civilized.
uncover (SYN.) disclose, discover, betray, divulge, expose, reveal, impart, show.
(ANT.) conceal, hide, cover, obscure, cloak.
under (SYN.) beneath, underneath, following, below, lower, downward.
(ANT.) over, above, up, higher.
undergo (SYN.) endure, feel, sustain, experience, let, allow, permit, feel, tolerate.
(ANT.) overcome, discard, exclude, banish.
underhand (SYN.) sly, secret, sneaky, secretive, stealthy.
(ANT.) honest, open, direct.
undermine (SYN.) demoralize, thwart, erode, weaken, subvert, sabotage.
understand (SYN.) apprehend, comprehend, appreciate, conceive, discern, realize, see, perceive.
(ANT.) misunderstand, mistake, misapprehend, ignore.

understanding (SYN.) agreement, coincidence, concord, harmony, unison, compact.
(ANT.) variance, difference, discord, dissension.
understudy (SYN.) deputy, agent, proxy, representative, alternate, lieutenant.
(ANT.) head, principal, sovereign, master.
undertaking (SYN.) effort, endeavor, attempt, experiment, trial, essay.
(ANT.) laziness, neglect.
undersigned (SYN.) casual, chance, contingent, accidental, fortuitous, incidental.
(ANT.) decreed, planned, willed, calculated.
undesirable (SYN.) obnoxious, distasteful, objectionable, repugnant.
(ANT.) appealing, inviting, attractive.
undivided (SYN.) complete, intact, entire, integral, total, perfect, unimpaired, whole.
(ANT.) partial, incomplete.
undying (SYN.) endless, deathless, eternal, everlasting, ceaseless, immortal.
(ANT.) transient, mortal, temporal, ephemeral, finite.
unearthly (SYN.) metaphysical, ghostly, miraculous, marvelous, preternatural.
(ANT.) physical, plain, human, natural, common.
uneducated (SYN.) uncultured, ignorant, illiterate, uninformed, unlearned.
(ANT.) erudite, cultured, educated, literate, formed.
unemployed (SYN.) inert, inactive, idle, jobless.
(ANT.) working, occupied, active, industrious, employed.
uneven (SYN.) remaining, single, odd, unmatched, rugged, gnarled, irregular.
(ANT.) matched, even, flat, smooth.
unfaithful (SYN.) treacherous, disloyal, deceitful.
(ANT.) true, loyal, steadfast, faithful.
unfasten (SYN.) open, expand, spread, exhibit, un-

ar, unlock, unfold, unseal.
(*ANT.*) shut, hide, conceal.

favorable (*SYN.*) antagonistic, contrary, adverse, opposed, opposite, disastrous, counteractive, unlucky.
(*ANT.*) benign, fortunate, lucky, propitious.

unfeeling (*SYN.*) hard, rigorous, cruel, stern, callous, numb, hard, strict.
(*ANT.*) tender, gentle, lenient.

unfold (*SYN.*) develop, create, elaborate, amplify, evolve, mature, expand.
(*ANT.*) wither, restrict, contract, stunt, compress.

unfurnished (*SYN.*) naked, mere, bare, exposed.
(*ANT.*) concealed, protected, covered.

unhappy (*SYN.*) sad, miserable, wretched, melancholy, distressed, depressed, wretched.
(*ANT.*) joyful, happy, joyous, cheerful.

unhealthy (*SYN.*) infirm, sick, diseased, sickly.
(*ANT.*) vigorous, well, healthy.

uniform (*SYN.*) methodical, natural, customary, orderly, normal, consistent.
(*ANT.*) rare, unusual, erratic, abnormal, exceptional.

unimportant (*SYN.*) petty, trivial, paltry, trifling, insignificant, indifferent, minor.

uninhibited (*SYN.*) loose, open, liberated, free.
(*ANT.*) constrained, tense, suppressed.

unintelligible (*SYN.*) ambiguous, cryptic, dark, cloudy, indistinct, obscure, vague.
(*ANT.*) lucid, distinct, bright, clear.

uninteresting (*SYN.*) burdensome, dilatory, dreary, dull, monotonous, sluggish, tedious, tardy, wearisome.
(*ANT.*) entertaining, exciting, quick, amusing.

union (*SYN.*) fusion, incorporation, combination, joining, concurrence, solidarity, agreement.
(*ANT.*) schism, disagreement,

separation, discord.

unique (*SYN.*) exceptional, matchless, distinctive, choice, peculiar, singular, rare, sole, single.
(*ANT.*) typical, ordinary, commonplace, frequent.

unison (*SYN.*) harmony, concurrence, understanding.
(*ANT.*) disagreement, difference, discord, variance.

unite (*SYN.*) attach, blend, amalgamate, combine, conjoin, associate, connect.
(*ANT.*) sever, divide, separate, sever, disrupt, disconnect.

universal (*SYN.*) frequent, general, popular, common, familiar, prevailing.
(*ANT.*) scarce, odd, regional, local, extraordinary.

unkempt (*SYN.*) sloppy, rumpled, untidy, messy.
(*ANT.*) presentable, well-groomed, tidy, neat.

unkind (*SYN.*) unfeeling, unsympathetic, unpleasant.
(*ANT.*) considerate, sympathetic, amiable, kind.

unlawful (*SYN.*) illegitimate, illicit, illegal, outlawed, criminal, prohibited.
(*ANT.*) permitted, law, honest, legal, legitimate, authorized.

unlike (*SYN.*) dissimilar, different, distinct, contrary, diverse, divergent, opposite.
(*ANT.*) conditional, accountable, contingent, qualified.

unmistakable (*SYN.*) clear, patent, plain, visible, obvious.

unnecessary (*SYN.*) pointless, needless, superfluous.

unoccupied (*SYN.*) empty, vacant, uninhabited.

unparalleled (*SYN.*) peerless, unequaled, rare, unique.

unpleasant (*SYN.*) offensive, disagreeable, repulsive, obnoxious, unpleasing.

unqualified (*SYN.*) inept, unfit, incapable, incompetent, unquestioned, absolute.

unreasonable (*SYN.*) foolish, absurd, irrational, inconsistent, nonsensical, ridiculous, silly.
(*ANT.*) reasonable, sensible,

sound, consistent, rational.

unsafe *(SYN.)* hazardous, insecure, critical, dangerous, precarious, threatening.

(ANT.) protected, secure, firm, safe.

unselfish *(SYN.)* bountiful, beneficent, magnanimous, openhanded, munificent.

(ANT.) miserly, stingy, greedy, selfish, covetous.

unsightly *(SYN.)* ugly, unattractive, hideous.

unsophisticated *(SYN.)* frank, candid, artless, ingenuous, naive, open, simple, natural.

(ANT.) sophisticated, worldly, cunning, crafty.

unsound *(SYN.)* feeble, flimsy, weak, fragile, sick, unhealthy, diseased, invalid, faulty, false.

unstable *(SYN.)* fickle, fitful, inconstant, capricious, changeable, variable.

(ANT.) steady, stable, trustworthy, constant.

unswerving *(SYN.)* fast, firm, inflexible, constant, secure, stable, solid, steady, steadfast, unyielding.

(ANT.) sluggish, insecure, unsteady, unstable, loose, slow.

untainted *(SYN.)* genuine, pure, spotless, clean, clear, unadulterated, guiltless, innocent, chaste, modest, undefiled, sincere, virgin.

(ANT.) polluted, tainted, sullied, tarnished, defiled, corrupt, foul.

untamed *(SYN.)* fierce, savage, uncivilized, barbarous, outlandish, rude, undomesticated, desert, wild, frenzied, mad, turbulent, impetuous, wanton, boisterous, wayward, stormy, extravagant, tempestuous, foolish, rash, giddy, reckless.

(ANT.) quiet, gentle, calm, civilized, placid.

untidy *(SYN.)* messy, sloppy, disorderly, slovenly.

untoward *(SYN.)* disobedient, contrary, peevish, fractious, forward, petulant, obstinate,

intractable, stubborn, ~~p~~ verse, ungovernable.

(ANT.) docile, tractable, obl~~i~~ ing, agreeable.

unusual *(SYN.)* capricious, abnormal, devious, eccentric, aberrant, irregular, variable, remarkable, extraordinary, odd, peculiar, uncommon, strange, exceptional, unnatural.

(ANT.) methodical, regular, usual, fixed, ordinary.

unyielding *(SYN.)* fast, firm, inflexible, constant, solid, secure, stable, steadfast, unswerving, steady.

(ANT.) sluggish, slow, insecure, loose, unsteady, unstable.

upbraid *(SYN.)* blame, censure, berate, admonish, rate, lecture, rebuke, reprimand, reprehend, scold, vituperate.

(ANT.) praise, commend, approve.

uphold *(SYN.)* justify, espouse, assert, defend, maintain, vindicate.

(ANT.) oppose, submit, assault, deny, attack.

upright *(SYN.)* undeviating, right, unswerving, direct, erect, unbent, straight, fair, vertical.

(ANT.) bent, dishonest, crooked, circuitous, winding.

uprising *(SYN.)* revolution, mutiny, revolt, rebellion.

uproar *(SYN.)* noise, disorder, commotion, tumult, disturbance.

upset *(SYN.)* disturb, harass, bother, annoy, haunt, molest, inconvenience, perplex, pester, tease, plague, trouble, worry, overturned, toppled, upend, capsize, fluster, agitate.

(ANT.) soothe, relieve, please, gratify.

upshot *(SYN.)* conclusion, result, outcome.

urbane *(SYN.)* civil, considerate, cultivated, courteous, genteel, polite, accomplished, refined, well-

...annered.
(ANT.) rude, uncouth, boorish, uncivil.

...rge (SYN.) craving, desire,
longing, lust, appetite, aspiration, yearning, incite,
prod, press, plead, per-
suade, implore, beg.
(ANT.) loathing, hate, distaste,
aversion, coerce, deter, restrain, compel, dissuade.

urgency (SYN.) emergency, ex-
igency, pass, pinch, strait.

urgent (SYN.) critical, crucial,
exigent, imperative, impelling, insistent, necessary.
(ANT.) trivial, unimportant,
petty, insignificant.

use (SYN.) custom, practice,
habit, training, usage, manner, apply, avail employ,
operate, utilize, exert.
(ANT.) disuse, neglect, waste,
ignore, overlook, idleness.

useful (SYN.) beneficial, helpful, good, serviceable,
wholesome, advantageous.
(ANT.) harmful, injurious,
deleterious, destructive.

usefulness (SYN.) price, merit,
utility, value, excellence,
virtue, worth, worthiness.
(ANT.) useless, cheapness,
valuelessness, uselessness.

useless (SYN.) bootless, empty, idle, pointless, vain,
valueless, worthless.
(ANT.) profitable, potent, effective.

usual (SYN.) customary, common, familiar, general, normal, habitual, regular.
(ANT.) irregular, exceptional,
rare, extraordinary.

utensil (SYN.) instrument,
tool, vehicle, apparatus, device, implement.
(ANT.) preventive, hindrance,
obstruction.

utilize (SYN.) use, apply, devote, busy, employ, occupy.
(ANT.) reject, banish, discharge, discard.

utter (SYN.) full, perfect,
speak, say, complete, superlative, supreme, total.
(ANT.) imperfect, deficient,
lacking, faulty, incomplete.

vacancy (SYN.) void, emptiness, vacuum, hollowness.
(ANT.) plenitude, fullness,
profusion, completeness.

vacant (SYN.) barren, empty,
blank, bare, unoccupied.
(ANT.) filled, packed, employed, full, replete, busy.

vacate (SYN.) abjure, relinquish, abdicate, renounce,
abandon, resign, surrender.
(ANT.) stay, support, uphold.

vacillate (SYN.) hesitate, oscillate, undulate, change.
(ANT.) adhere, persist, stick.

vacillating (SYN.) contrary, illogical, contradictory, contrary, inconsistent.
(ANT.) correspondent, congruous, consistent.

vacuity (SYN.) space, emptiness, vacuum, void, blank.
(ANT.) matter, fullness, content, substance, knowledge.

vacuous (SYN.) dull, blank, un-
comprehending, imbecillic,
foolish, thoughtless.
(ANT.) responsive, alert, attentive, bright, intelligent.

vacuum (SYN.) void, gap, emptiness, hole, chasm.

vagabond (SYN.) pauper, ragamuffin, scrub, beggar, mendicant, starveling, wretch.
(ANT.) responsible, established, rooted, installed.

vagary (SYN.) notion, whim,
fantasy, fancy, daydream.

vague (SYN.) indefinite, hazy,
obscure, undetermined, unclear, unsure, unsettled.
(ANT.) certain, spelled out,
specific, lucid, clear, definite,
distinct, explicit, precise.

vain (SYN.) fruitless, empty,
bootless, futile, idle, abortive, ineffectual, unavailing,
vapid, pointless, valueless.
(ANT.) meek, modest, potent,
rewarding, self-effacing, diffident, profitable, effective.

vainglory (SYN.) conceit,
pride, self-esteem, ar-
rogance, self-respect.
(ANT.) shame, modesty, meekness, humility, lowliness.

valid (SYN.) cogent, conclusive, effective, convincing,

weighty, well-founded, real.
(ANT.) *weak, unconvincing, void, unproved, null, spurious, counterfeit.*

valley (SYN.) dale, dell, lowland, basin, gully, vale.
(ANT.) *highland, hill, upland, headland.*

valor (SYN.) courage, heroism, bravery, boldness, intrepidity, fearlessness.

value (SYN.) price, merit, usefulness, value, virtue, utility, appreciate, prize, hold dear.
(ANT.) *valuelessness, uselessness, cheapness.*

vanity (SYN.) complacency, conception, notion, haughtiness, self-respect, whim, smugness, vainglory.
(ANT.) *meekness, humility, diffidence.*

vanquish (SYN.) defeat, crush, rout, quell, subjugate.
(ANT.) *surrender, cede, lose, retreat, capitulate.*

vapid (SYN.) hackneyed, inane, insipid, trite, banal.
(ANT.) *striking, novel, fresh, original, stimulating.*

variable (SYN.) fickle, fitful, inconstant, unstable, shifting, changeable, unsteady.
(ANT.) *unchanging, uniform, stable, unwavering, steady.*

variant (SYN.) dissimilar, different, distinct, contrary, sundry, various.
(ANT.) *similar, same, congruous, identical, alike.*

variety (SYN.) dissimilarity, diversity, heterogeneity, medley, mixture, miscellany, variousness, form.
(ANT.) *likeness, monotony, uniformity, sameness.*

various (SYN.) miscellaneous, sundry, divers, several, contrary, distinct, dissimilar.
(ANT.) *identical, similar, same, alike, congruous.*

vast (SYN.) big, capacious, extensive, huge, great, ample, enormous, measureless.
(ANT.) *tiny, small, short, little.*

vault (SYN.) caper, jerk, jump, leap, bound, crypt, sepulcher, hop, spring, safe, start.

vehement (SYN.) exc.., fiery, glowing, impett.., hot, irascible, passionat..
(ANT.) *calm, quiet, co.. apathetic, deliberate.*

veil (SYN.) clothe, concea.. cover, cloak, web, hide, curtain, disguise, gauze, film.
(ANT.) *reveal, unveil, bare.*

velocity (SYN.) quickness, rapidity, speed, swiftness.

venerable (SYN.) antiquated, aged, antique, ancient.
(ANT.) *young, new, youthful.*

venerate (SYN.) approve, esteem, admire, appreciate, wonder, respect.
(ANT.) *dislike, despise.*

vengeance (SYN.) requital, reprisal, reparation, retribution, revenge.
(ANT.) *forgiveness, remission, pardon, mercy.*

verbal (SYN.) oral, spoken, literal, unwritten, vocal.
(ANT.) *printed, written, recorded.*

verbose (SYN.) communicative, glib, chattering, chatty, garrulous, loquacious.
(ANT.) *uncommunicative.*

verdict (SYN.) judgment, finding, opinion, decision.

verge (SYN.) lip, rim, edge, margin, brink, brim.

verification (SYN.) confirmation, demonstration, evidence, proof, test.
(ANT.) *terseness, laconic, conciseness.*

verify (SYN.) confirm, substantiate, acknowledge, determine, assure, establish, approve, fix, settle, ratify.

veritable (SYN.) authentic, correct, genuine, real, true, accurate, actual.
(ANT.) *false, fictitious, spurious, erroneous, counterfeit.*

very (SYN.) exceedingly, extremely, greatly.

vestige (SYN.) stain, scar, mark, brand, stigma, characteristic, trace, feature, trait, suggestion, indication.

veto (SYN.) refusal, denial, refuse, deny, negate, forbid.

...T.) approve, approval.

...ation (SYN.) chagrin, irritation, annoyance, mortification, irritation, pique. (ANT.) comfort, pleasure, appeasement, gratification.

vibrate (SYN.) flutter, jar, ungodliness, tremble, wrong.

vice (SYN.) iniquity, crime, offense, evil, guilt, sin, ungodliness, wickedness, depravity, corruption, wrong. (ANT.) righteousness, virtue, goodness, innocence, purity.

vicinity (SYN.) district, area, locality, neighborhood, environs, proximity, nearness, adjacency. (ANT.) remoteness, distance.

vicious (SYN.) bad, evil, wicked, sinful, corrupt, cruel, savage, dangerous.

victimize (SYN.) cheat, dupe, swindle, deceive, take advantage of.

victor (SYN.) champion, winner. (ANT.) loser.

victory (SYN.) conquest, jubilation, triumph, success, achievement, ovation. (ANT.) defeat, failure.

view (SYN.) discern, gaze, glance, behold, eye, discern, stare, watch, examine, witness, prospect, vision, vista, sight, look, panorama, opinion, judgment, belief, impression, perspective, range, regard, thought, observation, survey, scene, conception, outlook, inspect, observe. (ANT.) miss, overlook, avert, hide.

viewpoint (SYN.) attitude, standpoint, aspect, pose, disposition, position, stand, posture.

vigilant (SYN.) anxious, attentive, careful, alert, circumspect, cautious, observant, wary, watchful, wakeful. (ANT.) inattentive, neglectful, careless.

vigor (SYN.) spirit, verve, energy, zeal, fortitude,

vitality, strength, liveliness. (ANT.) listlessness.

vigorous (SYN.) brisk, energetic, active, blithe, animated, frolicsome, strong, spirited, lively, forceful, sprightly, vivacious, powerful, supple. (ANT.) vapid, dull, listless, insipid.

vile (SYN.) foul, loathsome, base, depraved, debased, sordid, vulgar, wicked, abject, ignoble, mean, worthless, sinful, bad, low, wretched, evil, offensive, objectionable, disgusting. (ANT.) honorable, upright, decent, laudable, attractive.

vilify (SYN.) asperse, defame, disparage, abuse, malign, revile, scandalize. (ANT.) protect, honor, praise, cherish.

village (SYN.) hamlet, town. (ANT.) metropolis, city.

villain (SYN.) rascal, rogue, cad, brute, scoundrel, devil, scamp.

villainous (SYN.) deleterious, evil, bad, base, iniquitous, unsound, sinful, unwholesome, wicked. (ANT.) honorable, reputable, moral, good, excellent.

violate (SYN.) infringe, break.

violent (SYN.) strong, forcible, forceful. (ANT.) gentle.

vindicate clear, assert, defend, absolve, excuse, acquit, uphold, support. (ANT.) accuse, convict, abandon.

violate (SYN.) disobey, invade, defile, break, desecrate, pollute, dishonor, debauch, profane, deflower, ravish.

violence (SYN.) constraint, force, compulsion, coercion. (ANT.) weakness, persuasion, feebleness, impotence, frailty.

violent (SYN.) strong, forceful, powerful, forcible, angry, fierce, savage, passionate, furious. (ANT.) gentle.

virgin *(SYN.)* immaculate, genuine, spotless, clean, clear, unadulterated, chaste, untainted, innocent, guiltless, pure, untouched, modest, maid, maiden, sincere, unused, undefiled, pure.
(ANT.) foul, tainted, defiled, sullied, polluted, corrupt.

virile *(SYN.)* hardy, male, mannish, lusty, bold, masculine, strong, vigorous.
(ANT.) feminine, unmanly, weak, effeminate, womanish, emasculated.

virtue *(SYN.)* integrity, probity, purity, chastity, goodness, rectitude, effectiveness, force, honor, power, efficacy, quality, strength, merit, righteousness, advantage, excellence, advantage.
(ANT.) fault, vice, lewdness, corruption.

virtuous *(SYN.)* good, ethical, chaste, honorable, moral, just, pure, righteous, upstanding, upright, scrupulous.
(ANT.) licentious, unethical, amoral, sinful, libertine, immoral.

virulent *(SYN.)* hostile, malevolent, malignant, bitter, spiteful, wicked.
(ANT.) kind, affectionate, benevolent.

vision *(SYN.)* dream, hallucination, mirage, eyesight, sight, fantasy, illusion, specter, revelation, phantom, spook, ghost, imagination, far-sightedness, keenness, foresight, apparition.
(ANT.) verity, reality.

visionary *(SYN.)* faultless, ideal, perfect, unreal, supreme.
(ANT.) real, actual, imperfect, faulty.

visit *(SYN.)* attend, see, call on, appointment.

visitor *(SYN.)* caller, guest.

vista *(SYN.)* view, scene, aspect.

vital *(SYN.)* cardinal, living, paramount, alive, essential, critical, basic, indispensable, urgent, life-and-death.
(ANT.) lifeless, unimportant, inanimate, nonessential.

vitality *(SYN.)* buoyancy, being, life, liveliness, existence, spirit, vigor.
(ANT.) death, lethargy, dullness, demise.

vitiate *(SYN.)* allay, abase, corrupt, adulterate, debase, defile, depress, deprave, pervert, improve, restore.

vivid *(SYN.)* brilliant, striking, strong, graphic.
(ANT.) dim, dusky, vague, dull, dreary.

vocal *(SYN.)* said, uttered, oral, spoken, definite, outspoken, specific.

void *(SYN.)* barren, emptiness, bare, unoccupied, meaningless, invalid, useless.
(ANT.) employed, full, replete.

volatile *(SYN.)* effervescent, resilient, buoyant, animated, vivacious.
(ANT.) depressed, sullen, hopeless, dejected.

volition *(SYN.)* desire, intention, pleasure, preference, choice, decision, resolution.
(ANT.) disinterest, compulsion, indifference.

voluble *(SYN.)* glib, communicative, verbose, loquacious, chatty, chattering.
(ANT.) uncommunicative, laconic, taciturn, silent.

volume *(SYN.)* capacity, skill, power, talent, faculty, magnitude, mass, book, dimensions, quantity, size.
(ANT.) stupidity, inability, impotence, incapacity.

voluntary *(SYN.)* extemporaneous, free, automatic, spontaneous, offhand.
(ANT.) forced, planned, required, rehearsed, compulsory, prepared.

volunteer *(SYN.)* extend, offer, present, advance, propose.
(ANT.) receive, spurn, reject, accept, retain.

voyage *(SYN.)* tour, journey, excursion.

vulnerable *(SYN.)* unguard, defenseless, unprotected.

wafer *(SYN.)* cracker, lozenge.

waft *(SYN.)* convey, glide, sail, float.

wage *(SYN.)* conduct, pursue.

wager *(SYN.)* stake, bet, play, gamble, speculate, risk.

wagon *(SYN.)* carriage, buggy, cart, surrey, stagecoach.

waif *(SYN.)* guttersnipe, ragamuffin, tramp, vagrant.

wail *(SYN.)* mourn, moan, cry, bewail, lament, bemoan.

wait *(SYN.)* linger, tarry, attend, bide, watch, delay, await, abide, stay, serve.
(ANT.) hasten, act leave, expedite.

waive *(SYN.)* renounce, abandon, surrender, relinquish.
(ANT.) uphold, maintain.

wake *(SYN.)* awaken, rouse, waken, arouse, stimulate.
(ANT.) doze, sleep.

walk *(SYN.)* step, stroll, march, amble, saunter, hike, lane, path, passage.

wall *(SYN.)* barricade, divider, partition, panel, stockade.

wan *(SYN.)* colorless, haggard, gaunt, pale, pallid, pasty.

wander *(SYN.)* rove, stroll, deviate, ramble, digress, roam, traipse, range, err.
(ANT.) linger, stop, settle.

wane *(SYN.)* abate, weaken, fade, ebb, decrease, wither.

want *(SYN.)* penury, destitution, crave, desire, requirement, poverty, wish.
(ANT.) wealth, plenty, abundance.

warble *(SYN.)* sing, trill, chirp.

ward *(SYN.)* annex, wing.

warden *(SYN.)* custodian, guard, guardian, keeper, turnkey, jailer, curator.

wardrobe *(SYN.)* chiffonier, bureau, closet, armoire.

wares *(SYN.)* merchandise, staples, inventory, commodities, goods.

wariness *(SYN.)* heed, care, watchfulness, caution.
(ANT.) carelessness, abandon.

warlike *(SYN.)* hostile, unfriendly, combative, belligerent, antagonistic.
(ANT.) cordial, peaceful, amicable.

warm *(SYN.)* sincere, cordial, hearty, earnest, sympathetic, ardent, heated, gracious, enthusiastic.
(ANT.) cool, aloof, taciturn, brisk, indifferent.

warmhearted *(SYN.)* loving, kind, kindhearted, friendly.

warmth *(SYN.)* friendliness, cordiality, geniality, understanding, compassion.

warn *(SYN.)* apprise, notify, admonish, caution, advise.

warning *(SYN.)* advice, information, caution, portent, admonition, indication.

warp *(SYN.)* turn, bend, twist, distort, deprave.

warrant *(SYN.)* pledge, assurance, warranty, guarantee, authorize, approve.

warrior *(SYN.)* combatant, fighter, soldier, mercenary.

wary *(SYN.)* careful, awake, watchful, heedful, attentive, alive, mindful, cautious.
(ANT.) unaware, indifferent, careless, apathetic.

wash *(SYN.)* launder, cleanse, rub, touch, reach, border, wet, clean, scrub, bathe.
(ANT.) soil, dirty, stain.

waste *(SYN.)* forlorn, bleak, wild, solitary, dissipate, abandoned, spend, bare, consume, dwindle, decay.
(ANT.) cultivated, attended.

wasteful *(SYN.)* wanton, costly, lavish, extravagant.

watch *(SYN.)* inspect, descry, behold, distinguish, guard, attend, observe.

watchful *(SYN.)* alert, careful, attentive, vigilant, wary, cautious.

watertight *(SYN.)* impregnable, firm, solid.

wave *(SYN.)* ripple, whitecap, undulation, breaker, surf, swell, sea, surge, tide, flow.

waver *(SYN.)* question, suspect, flicker, deliberate, doubt, distrust, hesitate, falter.
(ANT.) confide, trust, believe, decide.

wavering *(SYN.)* fickle, shift-

ing, variable, changeable, vacillating, fitful.
(ANT.) unchanging, constant, uniform.

wavy (SYN.) rippling, serpentine, curly.

wax (SYN.) raise, heighten, expand, accrue, enhance, extend, multiply, enlarge, augment.
(ANT.) contract, reduce, atrophy, diminish.

way (SYN.) habit, road, course, avenue, route, mode, system, channel, track, fashion, method, walk, approach, manner, technique, means.

wayward (SYN.) stubborn, headstrong, contrary, obstinate, naughty, disobedient, rebellious, refractory.

weak (SYN.) frail, debilitated, delicate, poor, wavering, infirm, bending, lame, defenseless, vulnerable, fragile, pliant, feeble, watery, diluted.
(ANT.) strong, potent, sturdy, powerful.

weakness (SYN.) incompetence, inability, impotence, handicap, fondness, liking, affection, disability, incapacity.
(ANT.) strength, ability, dislike, power.

wealth (SYN.) fortune, money, riches, possessions, means, abundance, opulence, affluence, property, quantity, profession, luxury.
(ANT.) want, need.

wealthy (SYN.) rich, exorbitant, prosperous, affluent.
(ANT.) poverty-stricken, poor, indigent, impoverished, beggarly, destitute, needy.

wear (SYN.) erode, fray, grind, apparel, clothes, garb, attire.

weary (SYN.) faint, spent, worn, tired, fatigued, exhausted, tiresome, bored, wearied, tedious, jaded.
(ANT.) rested, hearty, fresh.

weave (SYN.) lace, interlace, plait, intertwine, braid, knit.

web (SYN.) netting, network,

net, cobweb, trap, entanglement.

wedlock (SYN.) marriage, union, espousal, wedding.

wee (SYN.) small, tiny, miniature, petite, microscopic.

weep (SYN.) mourn, sob, bemoan, cry, lament, whimper.

weigh (SYN.) heed, deliberate, consider, study, reflect, evaluate.
(ANT.) neglect, ignore.

weight (SYN.) importance, emphasis, load, burden, import, stress, influence, gravity, significance.
(ANT.) triviality, levity, insignificance, lightness.

weird (SYN.) odd, eerie, strange, unnatural, peculiar.

welcome (SYN.) take, entertain, greet, accept, receive, reception, gain, greeting.
(ANT.) reject, bestow, impart.

welfare (SYN.) good, wellbeing, prosperity.

well (SYN.) hearty, happy, sound, hale, beneficial, good, convenient, expedient, healthy, favorably, fully, thoroughly, surely, competently, certainly, undoubtedly, fit, profitable.
(ANT.) infirm, depressed.

well-bred (SYN.) cultured, polite, genteel, courtly.
(ANT.) crude, vulgar, boorish.

well-known (SYN.) famous, illustrious, celebrated, noted, eminent, renowned.
(ANT.) unknown, ignominious, obscure, hidden.

wet (SYN.) moist, dank, soaked, damp, drenched, dampen, moisten.
(ANT.) arid, dry, parched.

whimsical (SYN.) quaint, strange, curious, odd, unusual, droll, queer.
(ANT.) normal, common, usual, familiar.

whole (SYN.) total, sound, all, intact, complete, well, hale, healed, entire, uncut, undivided, unbroken, undamaged, intact.
(ANT.) partial, defective, im-

perfect, deficient.

wholesome *(SYN.)* robust, well, hale, healthy, sound, salutary, nourishing.
(ANT.) frail, noxious, infirm, delicate, injurious, diseased.

wicked *(SYN.)* deleterious, iniquitous, immoral, bad, evil, base, ungodly, unsound, sinful, bitter, blasphemous.
(ANT.) moral, good, reputable, honorable.

wide *(SYN.)* large, broad, sweeping, extensive, vast.
(ANT.) restricted, narrow.

wild *(SYN.)* outlandish, uncivilized, untamed, irregular, wanton, foolish, mad, barbarous, rough, waste, desert, uncultivated.
(ANT.) quiet, gentle, placid, tame, restrained, civilized.

will *(SYN.)* intention, desire, volition, decision, resolution, wish, resoluteness.
(ANT.) disinterest, coercion, indifference.

win *(SYN.)* gain, succeed, prevail, achieve, thrive, obtain, get, acquire, earn, flourish.
(ANT.) lose, miss, forfeit, fail.

winsome *(SYN.)* winning, charming, agreeable.

wisdom *(SYN.)* insight, judgment, learning, sense, discretion, reason, prudence, erudition, foresight.
(ANT.) nonsense, foolishness, stupidity, ignorance.

wise *(SYN.)* informed, sagacious, learned, penetrating, enlightened, advisable, prudent, profound, deep, erudite, scholarly, knowing, sound, intelligent, expedient.
(ANT.) simple, shallow, foolish.

wish *(SYN.)* crave, hanker, long, hunger, yearning, lust, craving, yearn, want.
(ANT.) hate, aversion, loathing, distaste.

wit *(SYN.)* sense, humor, pleasantry, satire, intelligence, comprehension, banter, mind, wisdom, intellect, wittiness, fun, drollery,

humorist, wag, comedian, raillery, irony, witticism.
(ANT.) solemnity, commonplace, sobriety.

witch *(SYN.)* magician, sorcerer, enchanter, sorceress, enchantress, warlock.

witchcraft *(SYN.)* enchantment, magic, wizardry, conjuring, voodoo.

withdraw *(SYN.)* renounce, leave, abandon, recall, retreat, go, quit, retire, depart, retract, remove, forsake.
(ANT.) enter, tarry, abide, place, stay.

wither *(SYN.)* wilt, languish, dry, shrivel, decline, fade, decay, sear, shrink.
(ANT.) renew, refresh, revive.

withhold *(SYN.)* forbear, abstain, repress, check, refrain.
(ANT.) persist, continue.

withstand *(SYN.)* defy, contradict, bar, thwart, oppose, hinder, combat, resist.
(ANT.) succumb, cooperate, support.

witness *(SYN.)* perceive, proof, spectator, confirmation, see, attestation, watch, observe, eyewitness, declaration, notice.
(ANT.) refutation, contradiction, argument.

wizardry *(SYN.)* voodoo, legerdemain, conjuring, witchcraft, charm.

woe *(SYN.)* sorrow, disaster, trouble, evil, agony, suffering, distress, misery.
(ANT.) pleasure, delight, fun.

womanly *(SYN.)* girlish, womanish, female, ladylike.
(ANT.) mannish, virile, male, masculine.

wonder *(SYN.)* awe, curiosity, surprise, wonderment, marvel, conjecture, amazement.
(ANT.) expectation, familiarity, indifference, apathy.

wonderful *(SYN.)* extraordinary, marvelous.

wont *(SYN.)* practice, use, custom, training, habit, usage.
(ANT.) inexperience, disuse.

word (SYN.) phrase, term, utterance, expression.

work (SYN.) opus, employment, achievement, performance, toil, business, exertion, travail, effort.
(ANT.) recreation, leisure, vacation, ease.

worldly (SYN.) bodily, fleshy, gross, voluptuous, base.
(ANT.) refined, temperate, exalted, spiritual.

worship (SYN.) honor, revere, adore, idolize, reverence.
(ANT.) curse, scorn, blaspheme, despise.

worth (SYN.) value, price, deserving, excellence, usefulness, utility, worthiness.
(ANT.) uselessness, valuelessness, cheapness.

worthless (SYN.) empty, idle, abortive, ineffectual, bootless, pointless, vain.
(ANT.) meek, effective, modest, potent.

wound (SYN.) mar, harm, damage, hurt, dishonor, injure, injury, spoil, wrong.
(ANT.) compliment, benefit, preserve, help.

wrangle (SYN.) spat, bickering, affray, argument, dispute, quarrel, altercation.
(ANT.) peace, friendliness, reconciliation, harmony.

wrap (SYN.) cover, protect, shield, cloak, mask, clothe, curtain, guard, conceal.
(ANT.) reveal, bare, unveil.

wreck (SYN.) ravage, devastation, extinguish, destroy, demolish, destruction, ruin.
(ANT.) make, construct, preserve, establish.

wretched (SYN.) forlorn, miserable, comfortless.
(ANT.) noble, contented, happy, significant.

writer (SYN.) creator, maker, inventor, author, father, composer.

wrong (SYN.) awry, incorrect, improper, amiss, naughty, faulty, inaccurate, askew, sin, incorrectness, false.
(ANT.) proper, true, correct, suitable.

yacht (SYN.) sailboat, boat, cruiser.

yank (SYN.) pull, wrest, draw, haul, tug, jerk, wrench, heave, extract.

yap (SYN.) howl, bark.

yard (SYN.) pen, confine, court, enclosure, compound, garden.

yardstick (SYN.) measure, criterion, gauge.

yarn (SYN.) wool, tale, narrative, thread, story, fiber, anecdote, spiel.

yaw (SYN.) tack, change course, pitch, toss, roll.

yawn (SYN.) open, gape.

yearly (SYN.) annually.

yearn (SYN.) pine, long for, want, desire, crave, wish.

yearning (SYN.) hungering, craving, desire, longing, appetite, lust, urge, aspiration, wish.
(ANT.) distaste, loathing, abomination, hate.

yell (SYN.) call, scream, shout, whoop, howl, roar, holler, wail, bawl.

yellow (SYN.) fearful, cowardly, chicken.
(ANT.) bold, brave.

yelp (SYN.) screech, squeal, howl, bark.

yen (SYN.) longing, craving, fancy, appetite, desire, lust, hunger.

yet (SYN.) moreover, also, additionally, besides.

yield (SYN.) produce, afford, breed, grant, accord, cede, relent, succumb, bestow, allow, permit, give way, submit, bear, surrender, supply, fruits, give up, abdicate, return, impart, harvest, permit, accede, acquiesce, crop, capitulate, pay, concede, generate, relinquish.
(ANT.) assert, deny, refuse, resist, struggle, oppose, strive.

yielding (SYN.) dutiful, submissive, compliant, obedient, tractable.
(ANT.) rebellious, intractable, insubordinate.

yoke (SYN.) tether, leash, bridle, harness.

yokel (SYN.) hick, peasant, hayseed, innocent.

young (SYN.) immature, undeveloped, youthful, underdeveloped, juvenile, junior, underage.
(ANT.) old, mature, elderly.

youngster (SYN.) kid, lad, stripling, minor, youth, child, fledgling.
(ANT.) adult, elder.

youthful (SYN.) childish, immature, young, boyish, childlike, callow, girlish, puerile.
(ANT.) old, elderly, senile, aged, mature.

yowl (SYN.) yell, shriek, cry, wail, whoop, howl, scream.

zany (SYN.) clownish, comical, foolish, silly, scatterbrained.

zap (SYN.) drive, vim, pep, determination.

zeal (SYN.) fervor, eagerness, passion, feverency, vehemence, devotion, intensity, excitement, earnestness, inspiration, warmth, ardor, fanaticism, enthusiasm.
(ANT.) unconcern, ennui, apathy, indifference.

zealot (SYN.) champion, crank, fanatic, bigot.

zealous (SYN.) enthusiastic, fiery, keen, eager, fervid, ardent, intense, vehement, fervent, glowing, hot, impassioned, passionate.
(ANT.) cool, nonchalant, apathetic.

zenith (SYN.) culmination, apex, height, acme, consummation, top, summit, pinnacle, climax, peak.
(ANT.) floor, nadir, depth, base, anticlimax.

zero (SYN.) nonexistent, nil, nothing, none.

zest (SYN.) enjoyment, savor, eagerness, relish, satisfaction, gusto, spice, tang, pleasure, exhilaration.

zestful (SYN.) delightful, thrilling, exciting, stimulating, enjoyable.

zip (SYN.) vigor, vim, energy, vitality, spirited, animation, provocative.

zone (SYN.) region, climate, tract, belt, sector, section, district, locality, precinct, territory.

zoo (SYN.) menagerie.

zoom (SYN.) zip, fly, speed, whiz, roar, race.

ing, variable, changeable, vacillating, fitful.
(ANT.) unchanging, constant, uniform.

wavy (SYN.) rippling, serpentine, curly.

wax (SYN.) raise, heighten, expand, accrue, enhance, extend, multiply, enlarge, augment.
(ANT.) contract, reduce, atrophy, diminish.

way (SYN.) habit, road, course, avenue, route, mode, system, channel, track, fashion, method, walk, approach, manner, technique, means.

wayward (SYN.) stubborn, headstrong, contrary, obstinate, naughty, disobedient, rebellious, refractory.

weak (SYN.) frail, debilitated, delicate, poor, wavering, infirm, bending, lame, defenseless, vulnerable, fragile, pliant, feeble, watery, diluted.
(ANT.) strong, potent, sturdy, powerful.

weakness (SYN.) incompetence, inability, impotence, handicap, fondness, liking, affection, disability, incapacity.
(ANT.) strength, ability, dislike, power.

wealth (SYN.) fortune, money, riches, possessions, means, abundance, opulence, affluence, property, quantity, profession, luxury.
(ANT.) want, need.

wealthy (SYN.) rich, exorbitant, prosperous, affluent.
(ANT.) poverty-stricken, poor, indigent, impoverished, beggarly, destitute, needy.

wear (SYN.) erode, fray, grind, apparel, clothes, garb, attire.

weary (SYN.) faint, spent, worn, tired, fatigued, exhausted, tiresome, bored, wearied, tedious, jaded.
(ANT.) rested, hearty, fresh.

weave (SYN.) lace, interlace, plait, intertwine, braid, knit.

web (SYN.) netting, network, net, cobweb, trap, entanglement.

wedlock (SYN.) marriage, union, espousal, wedding.

wee (SYN.) small, tiny, miniature, petite, microscopic.

weep (SYN.) mourn, sob, bemoan, cry, lament, whimper.

weigh (SYN.) heed, deliberate, consider, study, reflect, evaluate.
(ANT.) neglect, ignore.

weight (SYN.) importance, emphasis, load, burden, import, stress, influence, gravity, significance.
(ANT.) triviality, levity, insignificance, lightness.

weird (SYN.) odd, eerie, strange, unnatural, peculiar.

welcome (SYN.) take, entertain, greet, accept, receive, reception, gain, greeting.
(ANT.) reject, bestow, impart.

welfare (SYN.) good, well-being, prosperity.

well (SYN.) hearty, happy, sound, hale, beneficial, good, convenient, expedient, healthy, favorably, fully, thoroughly, surely, competently, certainly, undoubtedly, fit, profitable.
(ANT.) infirm, depressed.

well-bred (SYN.) cultured, polite, genteel, courtly.
(ANT.) crude, vulgar, boorish.

well-known (SYN.) famous, illustrious, celebrated, noted, eminent, renowned.
(ANT.) unknown, ignominious, obscure, hidden.

wet (SYN.) moist, dank, soaked, damp, drenched, dampen, moisten.
(ANT.) arid, dry, parched.

whimsical (SYN.) quaint, strange, curious, odd, unusual, droll, queer.
(ANT.) normal, common, usual, familiar.

whole (SYN.) total, sound, all, intact, complete, well, hale, healed, entire, uncut, undivided, unbroken, undamaged, intact.
(ANT.) partial, defective, im-

perfect, deficient.

wholesome *(SYN.)* robust, well, hale, healthy, sound, salutary, nourishing.
(ANT.) frail, noxious, infirm, delicate, injurious, diseased.

wicked *(SYN.)* deleterious, iniquitous, immoral, bad, evil, base, ungodly, unsound, sinful, bitter, blasphemous.
(ANT.) moral, good, reputable, honorable.

wide *(SYN.)* large, broad, sweeping, extensive, vast.
(ANT.) restricted, narrow.

wild *(SYN.)* outlandish, uncivilized, untamed, irregular, wanton, foolish, mad, barbarous, rough, waste, desert, uncultivated.
(ANT.) quiet, gentle, placid, tame, restrained, civilized.

will *(SYN.)* intention, desire, volition, decision, resolution, wish, resoluteness.
(ANT.) disinterest, coercion, indifference.

win *(SYN.)* gain, succeed, prevail, achieve, thrive, obtain, get, acquire, earn, flourish.
(ANT.) lose, miss, forfeit, fail.

winsome *(SYN.)* winning, charming agreeable.

wisdom *(SYN.)* insight, judgment, learning, sense, discretion, reason, prudence, erudition, foresight.
(ANT.) nonsense, foolishness, stupidity, ignorance.

wise *(SYN.)* informed, sagacious, learned, penetrating, enlightened, advisable, prudent, profound, deep, erudite, scholarly, knowing, sound, intelligent, expedient.
(ANT.) simple, shallow, foolish.

wish *(SYN.)* crave, hanker, long, hunger, yearning, lust, craving, yearn, want.
(ANT.) hate, aversion, loathing, distaste.

wit *(SYN.)* sense, humor, pleasantry, satire, intelligence, comprehension, banter, mind, wisdom, intellect, wittiness, fun, drollery,

humorist, wag, comedian, raillery, irony, witticism.
(ANT.) solemnity, commonplace, sobriety.

witch *(SYN.)* magician, sorcerer, enchanter, sorceress, enchantress, warlock.

witchcraft *(SYN.)* enchantment, magic, wizardry, conjuring, voodoo.

withdraw *(SYN.)* renounce, leave, abandon, recall, retreat, go, quit, retire, depart, retract, remove, forsake.
(ANT.) enter, tarry, abide, place, stay.

wither *(SYN.)* wilt, languish, dry, shrivel, decline, fade, decay, sear, shrink.
(ANT.) renew, refresh, revive.

withhold *(SYN.)* forbear, abstain, repress, check, refrain.
(ANT.) persist, continue.

withstand *(SYN.)* defy, contradict, bar, thwart, oppose, hinder, combat, resist.
(ANT.) succumb, cooperate, support.

witness *(SYN.)* perceive, proof, spectator, confirmation, see, attestation, watch, observe, eyewitness, declaration, notice.
(ANT.) refutation, contradiction, argument.

wizardry *(SYN.)* voodoo, legerdemain, conjuring, witchcraft, charm.

woe *(SYN.)* sorrow, disaster, trouble, evil, agony, suffering, distress, misery.
(ANT.) pleasure, delight, fun.

womanly *(SYN.)* girlish, womanish, female, ladylike.
(ANT.) mannish, virile, male, masculine.

wonder *(SYN.)* awe, curiosity, surprise, wonderment, marvel, conjecture, amazement.
(ANT.) expectation, familiarity, indifference, apathy.

wonderful *(SYN.)* extraordinary, marvelous.

wont *(SYN.)* practice, use, custom, training, habit, usage.
(ANT.) inexperience, disuse.